Wings for Our Courage

FLASHPOINTS

The series solicits books that consider literature beyond strictly national and disciplinary frameworks, distinguished both by their historical grounding and their theoretical and conceptual strength. We seek studies that engage theory without losing touch with history and work historically without falling into uncritical positivism. FlashPoints aims for a broad audience within the humanities and the social sciences concerned with moments of cultural emergence and transformation. In a Benjaminian mode, FlashPoints is interested in how literature contributes to forming new constellations of culture and history and in how such formations function critically and politically in the present. Available online at http://repositories.cdlib.org/ucpress.

Series Editors: Ali Behdad (Comparative Literature and English, UCLA); Judith Butler (Rhetoric and Comparative Literature, UC Berkeley), Founding Editor; Edward Dimendberg (Film & Media Studies, UC Irvine), Coordinator; Catherine Gallagher (English, UC Berkeley), Founding Editor; Jody Greene (Literature, UC Santa Cruz); Susan Gillman (Literature, UC Santa Cruz); Richard Terdiman (Literature, UC Santa Cruz)

1. *On Pain of Speech: Fantasies of the First Order and the Literary Rant,* by Dina Al-Kassim

2. *Moses and Multiculturalism,* by Barbara Johnson, with a foreword by Barbara Rietveld

3. *The Cosmic Time of Empire: Modern Britain and World Literature,* by Adam Barrows

4. *Poetry in Pieces: César Vallejo and Lyric Modernity,* by Michelle Clayton

5. *Disarming Words: Empire and the Seductions of Translation in Egypt,* by Shaden M. Tageldin

6. *Wings for Our Courage: Gender, Erudition, and Republican Thought,* by Stephanie H. Jed

Wings for Our Courage

*Gender, Eruditon, and
Republican Thought*

Stephanie H. Jed

UNIVERSITY OF CALIFORNIA PRESS
Berkeley · Los Angeles · London

University of California Press, one of the most distinguished
university presses in the United States, enriches lives around
the world by advancing scholarship in the humanities, social
sciences, and natural sciences. Its activities are supported by
the UC Press Foundation and by philanthropic contributions
from individuals and institutions. For more information, visit
www.ucpress.edu.

University of California Press
Berkeley and Los Angeles, California

University of California Press, Ltd.
London, England

© 2011 by The Regents of the University of California

Library of Congress Cataloging-in-Publication Data

Jed, Stephanie H, 1953–
    Wings for our courage : gender, erudition, and republican thought / Stephanie H. Jed.
        p. cm.—(FlashPoints ; 6)
    Includes bibliographical references.
    ISBN 978-0-520-26769-5 (pbk. : alk. paper)
    1. Italian literature—16th century—History and criticism.
2. Politics and literature—Italy—History—16th century.
3. Republicanism in literature. 4. Republicanism—Italy—
Florence—History—16th century. 5. Republicanism—History.
I. Title.
    PQ4080.J43 2011
    850.9'004—dc22
                                                        2011005498

Manufactured in the United States of America
20 19 18 17 16 15 14 13 12 11
10 9 8 7 6 5 4 3 2 1

In keeping with a commitment to support environmentally
responsible and sustainable printing practices, UC Press
has printed this book on Rolland Enviro100, a 100% post-
consumer fiber paper that is FSC certified, deinked, processed
chlorine-free, and manufactured with renewable biogas energy.
It is acid-free and EcoLogo certified.

*for Eduardo, Bruno, and Lucas
with love and gratitude*

Contents

List of Illustrations	xi
Acknowledgments	xiii
Introduction	1
Section One: Slaying the Tyrant, 1536–2011	23
Folder 1. *The Republic of Letters: Its Fascist Legacy*	30
Folder 2. *Humanistic and Imperial Ambition*	41
Folder 3. *The Republic of Letters and Its Imperial Context*	45
Folder 4. *The Tyrant in the Field: Intelligence Gathering, Economy, and the Maintenance of Empire*	50
Folder 5. *The Politics and Economy of Grain*	64
Folder 6. *Sexual Politics and Imperial Documentation Projects*	66
Folder 7. *The (Com)passionate Hand*	73
SOCIAL INTERSECTION: 1565–1995, between Mexico City, the Mountains of Chiapas, Bologna, Friuli, and Los Angeles	79
Section Two: Wings for My Courage	84
Shelf List 1. Cataloguers, Compilers, and the State	87
Frapporsi 1. Claiming Space on the Shelf	90

Shelf List 2. Noses/Political Gnosis	91
Frapporsi 2. The Father's Nose (and Bowels): The Education of Sons and Daughters	93
Shelf List 3. Gender in the Public Library	94
Frapporsi 3. The Importance of Social Relations in Libraries to Investigations of Gender and History	95
Shelf List 4. Catalog, Capitalism, Spatial Arrangements	96
Frapporsi 4. Spatial and Temporal Location	100
Shelf List 5. Work Habits, Movements, Transcription	103
Frapporsi 5. Against Academic Arguments: Tarabotti and Mozzoni	106
Shelf List 6. Hands, Instruments of Writing	108
Frapporsi 6. Hands That Take Up the Pen in Specious Reasoning	110
Shelf List 7. Debauchery, Erudition	112
Frapporsi 7. The Bestiality and Deceit of Political Erudition	115
Shelf List 8. Daughters in the Order of Political Knowledge	116
Frapporsi 8. Tyranny (and Freedom) from the Daughter's Perspective	117
Shelf List 9. Bibliographic Categories and Armies of Nuns	119
Frapporsi 9. A Bibliographic Army of Nuns	123
Shelf List 10. The Librarian as Political Actor	123
Frapporsi 10. Women, Liberty, the State	126
Gender and the Library as Fictions of Research	129
SOCIAL INTERSECTION: 1536–2011, between San Diego, Milan, Rome, Venice, Florence, and Paris	136
Section Three: Gender, Erudition, and the Italian Nation	140
Enter Allart	142
Lexicon	145
Allargare (and restringere)	145
Amazon	147
Archives	147
Body parts and intellect	149
Carraresi	152
Chinese	153
Coquetteries	153
Dominate	154
Dreams of the nation	156
Erudite relations	156
Fear	158

Filial relations	159
Florence	160
French lessons	160
Insults and compliments	161
Italy and Italian	163
Making scenes	163
Mixing	164
Organization/classification	165
Past and present	165
Placing copies of the *Histoire de la république de Florence* in Florence	168
Political relations with books	172
Preface	176
Process	176
Protection	176
Rules	176
Study as consolation	177
Translation	178
Tyranny	179
Vanity	180
What we share	180
Withholding	182
Women of Italy	182
Conclusion	183
Afterword	187
Appendix	191
Notes	201
Bibliography	261
Index	277

Illustrations

1. *The Scene of Tyranny*. Photograph by Larry Stein.   18
2. *Myopic Politics*. Photograph by Larry Stein.   18
3. *Categories of Knowledge*. Photograph by Larry Stein.   19
4. *Wings for My Courage*. Photograph by Larry Stein.   20
5. *The Nose Knows*. Photograph by Larry Stein.   21
6. Facsimile of Giovanni Antonio's letter to Marino Caracciolo, January 9, 1537. Courtesy of the Archivio di Stato of Milan.   24

Acknowledgments

This book has taken way too long to complete, but at a certain point it took on a life of its own, and I couldn't find a way to hurry the pace. Finally, at project's end, I have the opportunity to thank and appreciate my teacher Paolo Valesio. From the first, he encouraged me to take intellectual risks. When he wisely advised me many years ago *not* to mix my research on Lorenzino with my newer projects, I didn't follow his advice. Now, however, I am satisfied that this book is a better tribute to all that I learned from Valesio . . . a stylistic expansiveness, a sense of critique, an interest in theorizing practice and practicing theory, and an ability to connect with my sources through writing. Thank you, Paolo, for giving me the tools I would need on this journey.

I have been blessed with many more teachers, colleagues, friends, and family members who have generously supported and encouraged my work along the way and to whom I am deeply grateful: Leonard and Florence Jed, Erica Jed, John Freccero, Hayden White, Margaret Brose, Mary-Kay Gamel, Harry Berger, the Galassi Beria family, the Majnoni family, Luciana Siddivò and family, Maurizio Sabini, the Calitri/Bagatella family, Teresa de Lauretis, William Tay, Margit Frenk, Jaime Concha, Page duBois, Roy Harvey Pearce, Cecilia Ubilla, Armando Petrucci, Franca Nardelli, Grazia Peduzzi, Alberto Rollo, Vittoria Salierno, Carlos Blanco Aguinaga, Marta Sanchez, Rosaura Sanchez, Andrew Wright, Susan Kirkpatrick, Lori Chamberlain, Julie Hemker, Lisa Lowe, Bett Miller, Jennifer Robertson,

Maria Teresa Koreck, Michael Meranze, Robert Westman, Randolph Starn, Carlo Ginzburg, Paula Findlen, Luce Giard, Susan Larsen, Nicole Tonkovich, Kathryn Shevelow, Pasquale Verdicchio, Adriana De Marchi Gherini, Michael Davidson, Winnie Woodhull, Jorge Mariscal, Roddey Reid, Todd Kontje, Don Wayne, Louis Montrose, Oumelbanine Zhiri, Seth Lerer, John Marino, Janet Smarr, Lisa Lampert-Weissig, Marguerite Waller, Richard Terdiman, Albert Ascoli, Barbara Spackman, Carla Freccero, Natalie Zemon Davis, Jane Newman, Jane Tylus, Dianella Gagliani, Luciano Casali, Lorna Hutson, Deanna Shemek, Michael Wyatt, Gianni Celati, Watson Branch, Heather Fowler, Michelle Stuckey, Lisa Vernoy, and Mary Eyring.

I am grateful to the following institutions and people who provided financial, institutional, and editorial support for my work: the Fulbright Program, for supporting the beginnings of this research; the Academic Senate of the University of California–San Diego, for numerous travel grants and research support; the National Endowment for the Humanities, for supporting my participation in 1983 in the very important and influential paleography seminar taught at the Newberry Library by professors Petrucci and Nardelli; my colleagues at the Newberry Library, for their hospitality and support of my work in 1983 and beyond, especially John Tedeschi, Mary Beth Rose, and Paul Gehl; the archivists and staff at the Archivio di Stato in Milan, especially Maria Pia Bortolotti, who warmly welcomed and generously supported me as a novice archival researcher, and the director of the Archive, Dr. Maria Barbara Bertini, for granting permission to publish the letter of Giovanni Antonio, "il sarto"; the archivists and librarians at the Biblioteca Trivulziana in Milan and the Archivio Storico Capitolino and the Cineteca Nazionale in Rome, for the special courtesies they extended to me; Marilyn Migiel and Juliana Schiesari for inviting me to participate in the 1988 conference they organized and the volume they edited, *Refiguring Woman: Perspectives on Gender and the Italian Renaissance* (Cornell University Press, 1991); Nancy Armstrong and Leonard Tennenhouse, for inviting me to contribute to their volume *The Violence of Rhetoric* (Routledge, 1989); Kirstie McClure, for inviting me to participate in the Pembroke Center Roundtable on Resistance and Revolution in 1989 and for posing important questions that informed the conceptualization of this book; Jonathan Crewe, for inviting me to participate in a 1990 NEH-sponsored symposium and in a volume he edited, *Reconfiguring the Renaissance: Essays in Critical Materialism* (Bucknell University Press, 1992); the editors of the *Lies of Our Times*, for inviting me to write a column of media criticism entitled "The Other Coast" that helped me critique the sixteenth-century "media" I had found in Milan; Lorna Hutson, for the invitation to participate in the London Renaissance Seminar of 1990; Albert Ascoli, for the invitation to participate in a 1993 NEH summer institute at Northwestern University; Marta Sutton Weeks and my colleagues and friends at the Stanford Humanities Center, especially Mary Jane Parrine, Patricia Parker, Clifton Crais, Hillary Schor, Wanda Corn, Michael Wyatt, Gwen Lorraine, Sue Dambrau, and Susan Sebbard, for their generosity that gave me the time to read widely for a year and to start working on the project of this book; Patricia Parker and Margo Hendricks, for inviting me to contribute to their volume *Women, "Race," and Writing in the Early Modern Period* (Routledge, 1994); Roland Greene and Elizabeth Fowler, for inviting me to contribute to their volume *The Project of Prose in the Early Modern West* (Cambridge University Press, 1997); Elissa Weaver, for inviting me to speak at the 1997 international conference she organized with Meredith Ray and Lynn Westwater on Arcangela Tarabotti and for inviting me to contribute to the volume she edited, *Arcangela Tarabotti: A Literary Nun in Baroque Venice* (Longo, 2006); Patricia Fumerton, for inviting me to contribute to the volume she edited with Simon Hunt, *Renaissance Culture and the Everyday* (University of Pennsylvania Press, 1999); Jane Tylus and Mary Layoun, for inviting me to participate in a 1999 conference on Transnational and Comparative Literature at the University of Wisconsin, Madison; Kathleen Biddick and Graham Hammill, for inviting me to speak to their students at Notre Dame in 2000; Dianella Gagliani and Luciano Casali, for inviting me to speak in 2000 to the History Department at the University of Bologna; Marguerite Waller, for inviting me to speak about my book in 2006 at University of California–Riverside; Deanna Shemek and Michael Wyatt (and the Olschki publishing house), for organizing and publishing a volume of essays in honor of professors Petrucci and Nardelli, *Writing Relations: American Scholars in Italian Archives* (Olschki, 2008), and for inviting me to contribute to this volume a shorter version of the materials I offer here in Section Three; Dr. Isabelle de Conihout, head curator of the Fonds anciens in the Mazarine Library, who generously shared information about the dates of acquisition of Tarabotti's works and attached copies of the shelf lists in which her works appear; and Richard Terdiman, Ed Dimendberg, Eric Schmidt, Lynne Withey, Tim Roberts, Elisabeth Magnus, the University of California Press readers, and the Flashpoints editorial board members, for the generous, careful, and critical attention they all paid to my book.

Two wonderful teachers, Sybil Rubottom and Sarah Voorhies, and two dear friends, Teresa McGee and Lynn Susholtz, supported the production of my art pieces in this book. Teresa McGee's support for a number of months as my book coach was also invaluable to the completion of this project. Many thanks and appreciation to Larry Stein, who photographed the art.

I am deeply grateful to other important teachers/friends in my life: Jack and Sydney Ramey, Kenneth Greif (who generously read and helped to edit large portions of the book), Amy Macht (and family), Susan Blaustein (and family), Christy Walker, Holly McMillan, Sharon Plaché, Susan Thompson, Rusty Bresser, Peter Larson, Mel Freilicher, Joseph Keenan, Teresa Odendahl, Melanie Ross, Patty Cohen, Connie Hall, Ellen Schmeding, and Franzi Spiegelberg. I want to sing a special note of gratitude to my aikido sensei, Martin Katz, and all of my aikido partners who always believe in me and give so energetically of themselves at all times. My apologies and gratitude to anyone I may have omitted here.

I dedicate this work to my biggest teachers—my husband, Eduardo, and our sons, Bruno and Lucas—who inspire the greatest creativity in all aspects of life and a strong sense of what is important.

Introduction

In the summer of 1983, I experienced a kind of intellectual conversion at the Newberry Library in a seminar on paleography taught by professors Armando Petrucci and Franca Nardelli. As we studied and analyzed, each day, different exempla of "Italian" handwriting from the thirteenth to the seventeenth centuries, I learned to shift my interpretive focus from linguistic signs and their relation to "things" out in the world to graphic signs and their signification of social relations on the page. We learned that the various physical clothing in which language appears—including different types of handwriting, varying degrees of handwriting proficiency, and different kinds of margins or corrections to the text—could tell *us* something important about the social context of writing.[1] It was as if, in the course of our observations, we ourselves began to participate in a narrative about the physical production of writing.

The irregular margins and lack of spacing in a letter by Vittoria Colonna, for example, told us about the contrast between her cultural refinement and the qualities of her handwriting that showed she was self-educated. The inconsistent application of ink in a letter by Diomede Caraffa told us that he didn't always draw enough ink from the inkwell. A letter by Boccaccio in mercantile handwriting reminded us of his story as a cultural figure who participated in several graphic cultures of his time. A manuscript page of Giovanni Villani's *Cronica* written in mercantile hand told us a story of how his text was disseminated not only among humanistic readers but also among merchants and artisans. The physical appearance of a sixteenth-century diplomatic letter told us something about the literacy of its writer, the amount of time he had to compose his letter, and the relations of power in which he was working. These pages of writing were telling us stories about their own production, the relation of writing to society, the social position of writers, and dissonant registers and spaces that were opened up in the dissemination of the text. But how did "we" participate in these stories? And who were we, the participants? Were we a sum of scholarly egos trained to suppress our own stories (marked by gender, sexuality, race, and class) in the interest of knowing the past? Or did we (and our personal stories) change by virtue of our participation in these stories from the past? Did we change the stories by virtue of our participation in them? I became very interested in answering such questions, as I looked for ways to theorize and narrate my participation in stories from the past.

In that seminar of 1983, Petrucci and Nardelli seemed to sketch possible epistemological connections between researchers and the writing they examine. We learned, for example, that the key to deciphering what might seem, at first, to be illegible script was to "become" the scribe, to practice forming the letters in any given style until comprehension became more habitual. By the same token, we learned that our research questions and interests did not emerge as disinterested ones, disconnected from the ways knowledge was actually organized in libraries and archives: "If you have become interested in a topic," Petrucci commented, "it is because a trace of that history has reached you. There will be other traces to find and follow, a detective investigation, sometimes an obsessive one that will lead you to study documents that matter to no one but you." Coming from a different kind of scholar, this talk about traces might have sounded phenomenological or metaphysical. But coming, as it did, from a historian of graphic culture, the term *traces* referred to the physical aspects of writing; I was especially interested to know what story might emerge if I followed the traces uncovered in my own detective investigations and made myself an active subject of the research materials I was collecting about Lorenzino de' Medici.

I became interested in Lorenzino de' Medici's assassination, in 1537, of his cousin Alessandro de' Medici, Duke of Florence, many years ago when I was writing a dissertation on the representation of tyrannicide in classic texts of historiography and philosophy from

Thucydides, Herodotus, and Aristotle to Livy, Suetonius, and Tacitus and the sixteenth-century historiographers Machiavelli, Giovio, Varchi, Nardi, Nerli, and Ammirato. Later I became curious to know if archival documentation might have represented this event differently, with less attention to classical models of tyrannicide. In the seminar on paleography I learned that if I had become interested in Lorenzino's assassination of his cousin it was because I was already enmeshed in some aspect of how knowledge of that story was assembled, organized, and conserved. This book is an investigation of that enmeshment.

It was not just the themes of the historiographic narratives that attracted me. At a conscious, symbolic level, I uncomfortably aspired to "become" Lorenzino, the self-styled tyrant-slayer and vindicator of a dishonored woman, a scholar of the classics who had emerged from the isolation of his study to perform his knowledge on the public stage of politics. Indeed, at different moments, I identified with all of the characters—tyrants, tyrant-slayers, violated sisters and mothers— but this identification was partial at best. The women represented in the historiographic narratives had no voice, and the classical learning and aspirations of the tyrant-slayers in no way resembled my aspirations or relation to classical learning. On the other hand, I knew that "I," the researcher, was very active and involved in the materials I was collecting on Lorenzino, scholarly relations, archivists and librarians, and Italian nation building. If I was collecting these materials, at some level, these materials were also addressing me, making me a part of their history. I was not just a free-floating researcher with my own particular intellectual autobiography but a social subject who was being constructed, in part, by my experiences of research.

I was, after all, doing research in libraries and archives, requesting materials, photocopies, speaking with archivists and librarians. Not wanting to naturalize these research experiences or remove them from historical investigation, I began to think about how I might draw attention to the historicity of these experiences. In the paleography seminar, we learned how details about the formation of libraries and archives of state often help us historicize the dissonant registers of literacy involved in relations between producers and users of culture. Vespasiano de' Bisticci, for example, had a Latin nickname—*princeps librariorum*, or the prince of libraries. But he was semiliterate and came from an artisanal background. He wrote in a mercantile hand and managed a sort of fifteenth-century copy shop in which his copyists produced "humanistic" libraries that served as political-ideological symbols of display for the likes of Cosimo de' Medici, Duke of Florence; Mattía Corvino, king of Hungary; and Federico da Montefeltro, Duke of Urbino. Although Vespasiano closed his shop in 1479 because of competition from the printing press, his model of the humanistic library as a physical manifestation of the complex relation between geopolitical sites, rulers, and books is still operative today.

We also learned that the study of historical details about the formation of libraries and state archives would help us locate materials that interested us. In other words, at some point in our research we would need to represent the historicity of the research institutions in which we collected our materials. Who collected and organized the materials, under what categories, under whose direction, with what political and economic pressures—all of these questions required some narration, as it was this historicity that was producing the quality of my research experiences and the details of what I might know.

The stories of libraries and books can be unsettling. How, for example, do we evaluate the veracity of Thucydides' story of the first tyrant-slayers, Harmodius and Aristogiton, when we learn, from at least one source, that Thucydides' history went up in flames in the library of Athens? Only because Demosthenes "remembered the work from beginning to end . . . , allowing a new copy to be made of the precious text," are we able today to appreciate this important work of western historiography.[2] Or how do we consider Aristotle's canonical text of political theory when we read of the vicissitudes to which this text was subjected? In the words of Luciano Canfora, "Some owners of the Aristotelian scrolls wanted to hide them, to keep them safe from the hands of the royal librarians. A deep hole was dug underneath their house, and there the precious scrolls were left. Their owners gave no further thought to them. They were valuables to be hoarded, not books to be studied. It never occurred to them that damp and moths might spoil their buried treasure."[3]

The stories of all manuscript collections are replete with such incidents of destruction, loss, and political passions. Imagine, for example, that you are sitting quietly in the Vatican Library waiting for a custodian to deliver to your desk a manuscript copy of Virgil's *Eclogues* from the Palatine collection. You are quietly excited about your research skills—you were able to locate the text you needed and now you have successfully requested it. You have never asked yourself how the text actually got to the Vatican in the first place. What compelled you to come looking for it? What might your walking into the library, stooping down to lift up the heavy Palatine catalogs, and pouring over the entries have to do with your research questions? These are questions that might endow your movements with a history, a history that would reflect your own interests, connections, and dramas.

Indeed, the transport of the Palatine manuscripts from Heidelberg to Rome in 1623 was a rescue operation that amounted to the sacking of a library ("Salvataggi del sapere, che erano insieme saccheggi"). Leone Allacci, the Vatican scriptor of Greek, organized this transport, ensuring that the books were loaded onto forty-eight carriages and accompanied by troops like "a marching army" ("un esercito che marciasse"). Allacci lamented that he was "not able to set a fire in God's honor" ("non haver possuto esser istromento di questo incendio in honor d'Iddio") to destroy all the heretical books in the collection, as Rome had evidently recommended. But he also wanted to steer clear of future retaliation. Still, "by his hand, the ax of the Counter-Reformation fell, all the same, upon the library" ("per sua mano la scure della Controriforma si abbatterà ugualmente sulla biblioteca"). Bound books were "thrown about" ("strapazzati") and "the unbound ones were all mixed up" ("posti in confusione li sciolti"), so that "the library no longer seemed a library but a ruin" ("non pare più libreria, ma ruina"). Allacci, in the freezing nights in Heidelberg, fed the stove with books by heretical authors. Other pages ended up, as Allacci assured the authorities of the Roman Curia, stoking the muskets of the soldiers. We might ask ourselves: Was the formation of this collection part of a military campaign? Accompanied by fire, devastation, destruction, freezing nights? The will to destruction and the will to deliverance—it was business as usual in the bellicose climate of the Counter-Reformation ("Volontà di distruzione e volontà di salvezza, com'era consueto nel clima pugnace della Controriforma").[4] Now, as you await the delivery of your Palatine Virgil, you are participating in this bellicose climate; the library has remade you as a custodian of these stories and a part of its history of devastation.

The same unsettling sense of devastation pervades the manuscripts of the Vatican's Urbinate collection. When Francesco Maria II della Rovere, the last duke of Urbino, died in 1631, the Duchy of Urbino passed to the Holy See. Although the duke had specifically willed his library to the city of Urbino, the new Chigi pope, Alessandro VII, an avid bibliophile, claimed it belonged to his inheritance of the duchy. As a part of his politics of subordinating the provinces to the central power of the Holy See, Alessandro usurped the ownership of the library despite the protests of the intellectuals of Urbino because Urbino was indebted to the pope. So the rich manuscript collection of Urbino also traveled across the Appennines to Rome on the backs of mules, again in the dead of winter, this time the winter of 1657. Debt and rumor were two of the recurring motifs in the secret negotiations prior to the expedition that transported the books. Recurring phrases like "a rumor is circulating" ("corre voce") and "it has come to our ears" ("ci è giunta all'orecchia") helped to construct the conditions of distrust, avarice, desperation, and intrigue under which the books were eventually transported.[5] On November 22, Flaminio Catellani, the official chaperone of the expedition, wrote to Monsignor Fani, informing him about the terrible roads, the dangerous passes, and the inclement weather. One of the thirty-five mules, laden with two crates full of books (weighing approximately 180 kilos), slipped from a precipice and fell into a river.[6] These were unavoidable misfortunes, but Catellani saw to it that the crates were opened and, with the help of the mayor of Cantiano, his hometown, removed the books to let them dry. The wet books were of little value, but in any case they were not damaged, as would become evident in Rome. Catellani could have neglected to mention the whole incident, but he preferred to inform Monsignor Fani directly so that he would not learn of it from others.[7]

In his letter of November 24 to Homodei, Catellani complained that he was no longer a "doctor" but the "head mule-driver" ("se però la Mulatinaria ha il Capo si piccolo"). He then apologized for his joke with the excuse that he needed to cheer himself up and to find respite from the discomforts of the journey and the continuous pain of an abscessed tooth.[8] The library arrived in Rome on December 4 after a difficult forty-one-day journey.

The stories in this book, then, when taken together, foreground relations of research in archives, libraries, and scholarly societies that produce and conserve representations of politics and history. My premise is that stories about scholarly relations form part of the landscape and meaning of the questions, problems, events, and texts we research. I have "piled side by side" such stories of research relations and experiences—usually relegated to a footnote, found in disconnected sources, or forever lost—with the intent of reorganizing those narratives, categories, and "relations of writing" that have traditionally contributed to our understandings of tyranny and freedom.[9] In particular, I aim to represent those relations of research, which have metaphorically crowded

Introduction | 7

the margins of my studies and literally haunted my places of research, as central to the ways in which I have come to know about Lorenzino's assassination of Alessandro de' Medici.[10]

Over the years, this book has changed shape numerous times to approximate the changes in my thinking about reorganizing knowledge of the republican tradition, tyranny, and freedom. In 2005, a dear friend, also a professional life coach, suggested that I might benefit from seeing my book in three dimensions. Maybe, she suggested, I could construct some mobiles to keep a sculptural presence of my book around the house, a physical presence that would also help me organize my materials. At the same time, another generous friend offered me a corner of her studio to work in and moral and artistic support. These relations of research (not just the scholarly and affective ones) are important to appreciate as dimensions (not explicitly represented by Virginia Woolf) of the "room of one's own" I was fortunate enough to inhabit as I struggled with the organization of my research.

Although I have no formal training as an artist, I found that thinking about my work in three dimensions helped me create an experimental structure for this book that encompassed the social relations I had developed in the course of my research on Lorenzino. In this process, I connected both with scholars, archivists, and librarians who are the present-day custodians of libraries and archives in which I have worked and with historical figures whose scholarly trajectories influenced my approach to republican thought. In particular, as I affixed particular texts to each of the "objects" I made, I realized that I was assembling historical materials that usually did not belong together.

Through my arrangements of historical materials in the three sections of this book, I aspire to make vivid for the reader three different social relations of writing: (1) the relation between humanistic and imperial writers who represented Alessandro's assassination or other tyrannicides; (2) the relation, via political theory and the history of state libraries, between a seventeenth-century Venetian nun, Arcangela Tarabotti, and the French erudite and librarian of state Gabriel Naudé; and finally, (3) the relation between a practically forgotten (though extensively studied) nineteenth-century historian of Florence, Hortense Allart, and Florentine nationalist scholars, particularly Gino Capponi.

In each of the three sections of this book, I am interested in challenging traditional approaches to republican thinking with materials that would complicate such approaches, and in recording the reconfigured knowledge I have obtained as a result of such complications. I am also interested in complicating our ideas of hetero- and homosociality with a focus on the agency of books and documents in the construction of gender and sexual politics. More specifically, to place Tarabotti and Allart in relation to Naudé and Capponi is not to construct or make visible heretofore impossible or unacknowledged heterosexual couplings but to explore, among other things, those aspects of sexualities that are inherent in our relations with books and writing and intrinsic and inseparable parts of our relations of research. I am inspired by Joan Scott and Natalie Zemon Davis, among others, in thinking that such relations, irreducible to such ahistorical categories as hetero- or homo-, must also include me as an active producer of knowledge.[11]

In any case, while endeavoring to balance scholarly integrity and loyalty to historical records with attention to this different epistemological picture that emerged in each area of my research, I found that the three-dimensional art pieces I had made helped me consider that perhaps I was actively meditating on and experimenting with the very epistemological instruments—archival inventories, library shelf lists, and lexicons—that organized the texts I was studying. These epistemological instruments became, therefore, the experimental structures for presenting my research. In particular, an inventory of my own research files about Lorenzino, a series of imaginary shelf lists in the Mazarine Library that included the work of Tarabotti, and a lexicon that illustrated a scholarly connection between Hortense Allart and Gino Capponi became my experimental templates for understanding the production of republican thought and the Italian nation as relations of research.

SECTION ONE: SLAYING THE TYRANT, 1536–2011

Humanist tyrant-slayers have always modeled their thoughts and deeds after those of the ancient Greek and Roman *auctores*, often drawing the criticism that their lives were too "literary" and separate from political "reality." We can still see this separation today in so many aspects of our profession, from the construction of literature and politics as binary opposites to jokes about the absent-minded professor.[12] My aim in Section One is to make visible the ideological elements of this separation between "literature" and political "reality" by making the obvious claim that literature is not fundamentally at odds with such political activities as writing, gathering intelligence, and procuring food.

Instead of commencing with "the story" of how Lorenzino de'

Medici, on the evening of January 6, 1537, slew his cousin Alessandro de' Medici, Duke of Florence, Section One begins with my own scholarly encounter in December 1983 at the State Archive of Milan with a letter of an imperial postal bureaucrat in Bologna who writes to Marino Caracciolo, the imperial governor in Milan, that he has seen Lorenzino de' Medici passing by. The purpose of this beginning is to move away from traditional representations that narrate the assassination in a humanistic frame (without acknowledging the historicity of the frame). Here, in the State Archive of Milan, it becomes clear that Lorenzino's assassination of the duke was significant not just in the context of Florentine history or as a legacy of the classical tyrannicides, but also in the broader context of Charles V's imperial network. Here we can examine and touch documents that inhabit a social intersection between humanistic accounts of the assassination written for a literary audience and political reports written for Charles V's governor in Milan; we can historicize one locale in which archivists have, over the centuries through foreign occupations, Italian state formation, and postunification laws, organized, reorganized, and conserved knowledge about this event until the present day; and we can mark how the history of Lorenzino has not yet definitively passed—it was still passing in those days when I was requesting documents from the Milanese state chancery and transcribing the details of his deed from those pages.

Indeed, to start with an archival experience is to acknowledge my enmeshment as a scholar in a particular organization of knowledge determined by the archival inventory, a "finding" tool that is subject to historical vicissitudes generation after generation. Starting with this personal encounter, I am interested less in history as a personal experience than in understanding history as a social process that occurs in relation to writers, scholars, and archivists from the past. Finally, starting with one particular moment in a history of organizing and conserving knowledge about Lorenzino allows me to take account of the ways I organize and conserve knowledge from my vantage point as a late twentieth-/early twenty-first-century scholar. To illustrate how scholarly activities, categories, and relations of knowledge are crucial components of any historicizing and interpretive enterprise, I arrange and organize, in Section One, my own experimental archive, presenting my materials in subsections or archival "folders" that represent different dimensions and categories of my research.

Arranging and creating an inventory of my own archive helped me make sense of existing frameworks and categories for research on

Lorenzino and the ways in which the various stages of my research diverged from those existing frameworks.[13] What emerged in my research, for example, were the legacies of humanistic frameworks; the socially constructed nature of the everyday commerce of information, ideas, commodities, and geopolitical inequalities; the interests represented by imperial documentation projects in the Milanese chancery, dismembered and reorganized by successive generations of archivists; and representations of the hand in sexual politics, in sixteenth-century documents, and in my own activities as a researcher transcribing, compiling, and organizing historical materials. Arranging my research in archival files that reflected these various stages of research enabled me to interrupt the tacit reproduction of a model we have for seeing literature as removed from politics and for seeing the researcher as separate from her materials of research.

Indeed, my archival inventory of knowledge about Lorenzino shows considerable overlap between humanistic historiography and imperial politics. It shows, moreover, that the commonplace perception about the shortsightedness of tyrant-slayers who, because they read "too much," were never successful in the realm of political action is just as shortsighted, blinding us to the ways in which literary and political modes of knowing overlap and depend upon each other. But most important, it makes social relations of writing and my own social construction as a researcher central to the construction of historical knowledge. My account of one particular social relation between the historian Carlo Ginzburg, a sixteenth-century miller, Menocchio, a political scientist in Mexico City (Adolfo Gilly), and the Zapatista subcomandante Marcos shows the conditions of tension and overlap between writers situated in the "republic of letters" and writers situated in resistance to neoimperial capitalism. I present this account as a transitional "social intersection," since it enables me to further articulate and theorize my scholarly endeavors of Section One and to anticipate the research of Sections Two and Three.

SECTION TWO: "WINGS FOR MY COURAGE"

While Section One presents many complex social relations in the context of Charles V's empire and its aftermath, Sections Two and Three each focus on one particular social relation of research. Section Two takes up the relationship that a seventeenth-century Venetian nun and political theorist, Arcangela Tarabotti, established with Gabriel

Naudé, librarian of state and the father of library science. Responding to Naudé's (hypothetical) invitation to send her works for inclusion in the Mazarine Library, Tarabotti imagined her books "intervening" ("frapporsi"), or taking up physical shelf space, "among the most eminent writers" ("tra i più celebri Scrittori") of the Mazarine.[14] I take my cue from Tarabotti's term *frapporsi* (to intervene, to come between) to imagine Tarabotti's political ideas physically coming between particular books on library shelves. In this section, I use the epistemological instrument of the shelf list, or the list of books in the order in which they appear on the shelf, to reflect on the arrangement of the "library shelves" I construct. Here, fulfilling Tarabotti's desire to take up space on the shelves of the Mazarine, I include (at least) one of her works on each shelf and organize and present my materials as discussions of the titles I collect for each "shelf," with insertions or interventions by Tarabotti (entitled "Frapporsi") on these discussions.

The term *catalog*, which derives from the Greek word meaning "to enumerate" (καταλεγειν) and represents a concept as old as Homeric epic, may be defined as an ordered list of names or objects. The first modern catalogs, born in the same decades of Lorenzino's murder of the duke (the early decades of the sixteenth century), responded to a need to guide scholars among the labyrinthine paths of new objects and facts with new instruments and new conceptual systems for organizing such knowledge. Even as they reflected such traditional medieval categories as theology, law, medicine, and philosophy, the new catalogs went beyond previous inventories in their aspiration to configure new categories, to publicize the fame of libraries, and, in some cases, to enhance the authority of the state.[15]

My shelf lists differ from sixteenth- and seventeenth-century library catalogs in several aspects. First, my categories aim to create an order of political knowledge that centers on the texts of a significant seventeenth-century political thinker who aspired to have her works take up physical and intellectual space among the most important writers of the Mazarine. My selection of this relational and intellectual aspiration as the principal classificatory criterion brings together subjects that would ordinarily inhabit very different parts of a library. My connection to Tarabotti's aspiration also draws attention to my active, historical role as an organizer of political knowledge and consequently to the historicity of catalogs (and shelf lists), organized according to systems that developed from particular epistemological interests and relations among scholars.[16]

Second, my shelf lists collect and organize pieces of information and understanding about Tarabotti, Naudé, and seventeenth-century learning in such a way as to locate Tarabotti, a learned daughter, at the center of republican history and political thought, as "integral to and indissoluble from state-making itself,"[17] giving priority to her perspectives over the misogynistic attitudes of most learned men of her time. In my shelf lists, the request by librarian of state Gabriel Naudé for the works of a seventeenth-century feminist theorist marks a watershed moment in the history of European culture whose effects persist still today. Tarabotti's self-inscription in the worlds of bibliography and politics, I suggest, helps us today to make political sense of our modes of research and our physical movements in public libraries. Moreover, the convergence of Tarabotti's figure of the daughter as central to the processes of state making with Naudé's figuration of the library as "daughter" enables us to complicate and interrupt Lorenzino's republican aspiration to vindicate the honor of a violated noblewoman with a focus on the contributions of intellectual daughters to the history of learned culture.

Tarabotti conceived the very possibility of republican thought and politics to depend upon the suffering of daughters. In particular, her political reflections on the centrality of daughters in the republican state of Venice and her general challenges to the politics of knowledge give rise to new categories for thinking about republican politics in relation to the collocation of her works in the Mazarine. These categories, including daughters, gender, library, space, work habits, instruments of writing, hands, fiction, and deceit, are not objectifying but relational categories that situate people in places, relations, and activities of knowing.[18] As a creator of shelf lists, I use these categories to reorganize republican thought in such a way as to feature the centrality of learned women in processes of state making.

Third, my shelf lists highlight the particular hypothetical ways in which Tarabotti might have intervened in the history of republican thought, if and when her neighbors on the shelf had modified their own views in relation to the presence of her theorizing in the library. Tarabotti used the term *frapporsi* (literally, "to place between," "to insert") to imagine her works taking up their place among the most famous writers of the Mazarine Library, claiming a public significance for herself in a library of state. Who were these most famous writers? Xenophon, Aristotle, Thomas Aquinas, Machiavelli, Botero, Montaigne, Charron? Whoever they were,

Tarabotti wanted her works to intervene or come between them in the library, come between them on the shelf, and interrupt their intimate conversations and relations that rarely permitted the presence of an alien, feminist voice. Was she just naive to think that she could survive intact on the shelves of the Mazarine Library? Indeed, if the most famous writers were to take seriously Tarabotti's ways of thinking and knowing about the state, they would have to modify their own political theories to include the oppression of daughters. Just as Tarabotti imagined her works taking up space among the most important writers of the Mazarine, it is important to insert ("frapporsi") and mark particular spaces on the shelves for Tarabotti's interventions, to promote a historic and spatial sense of the wedges she created in republican thinking.

Finally, my shelf lists draw attention to the constructed or fictitious character of all categories and orderings of knowledge. For Tarabotti, traditional thinking about tyranny in terms of Roman history was nothing more than a "deceit"—a fictional construct that served the interests of fathers in denial about the tyranny they exercised over their own daughters. One way to remediate or defend against such deceits is to create new fictions or categories that situate intellectual daughters within processes of state formation. As Chartier has taught us, reading is "rebellious and vagabond," creating constant change in the order of books.[19] The shelf lists presented here form a Bibliothèque that, "more than an accumulation of outcomes, . . . encompasses the imaginable etched within." A mere reordering of the books on a shelf can easily deliver us from "the inevitability of history" to its "potentials" and "possibilities." As Silverblatt, citing Lukacs, reminds us: "By restoring possibilities to our foremothers and fathers, . . . we also restore possibilities to ourselves."[20]

My construction of imaginary shelf lists and interventions from the works of Tarabotti foregrounds my own agency in the production of historical knowledge once again. At the end of this section, I tell the story of one fictional scholar, Sasha Harvey, who aspired to dissolve the dualism of subject and object in relations of research but instead found herself isolated and confined in her study much as Tarabotti had been isolated in the convent. Only after her death did Harvey's research files come to occupy a socially enmeshed position in the special collections of a library where other scholars could now examine her research activities. I present this account as a second transitional "social intersection" that enables me to further articulate and theorize my scholarly experiences of Section Two and to ponder my own position in the research of Section Three.

SECTION THREE: GENDER, ERUDITION, AND THE ITALIAN NATION

Section Three focuses on a relation of research between the French feminist historian, novelist, and Italophile Hortense Allart and her erudite friend in Florence, the historian, philosopher, and protagonist of Risorgimento politics Gino Capponi. In the preface to his *Storia della Repubblica di Firenze*, published in 1875 and considered to be the first modern history of Florence, Capponi gave credit to another previously published Florentine history, written by his French friend Allart.[21] Writing words that "he would have been sorry to silence" ("voglio pur dire . . . alcune cose che poi mi dispiacerebbe avere taciute"), Capponi described the magnitude of his debt: "A kind French lady, Ortensia Allart . . . published in 1843 a compendium of the History of the Florentine Republic, which in many respects is the best of all that have been attempted so far. Alessandro Carraresi translated it, but some things were too much for us Italians, others weren't enough. So I started to make some mental notes, then to cut some passages of the French text and lengthen others. In this way, little by little, I found myself with all of the thought inside my History of Florence . . . In [my history] I even find certain intonations that early on came to me from the French writer, for which I thank the kind lady." ("Una gentile francese, madama, Ortensia Allart . . . mandò alle stampe nel 1843 un ristretto della Storia della Repubblica Fiorentina, che per molti rispetti è il migliore di quanti se ne abbiano tentati fin qui. Di questo Libro il signore Alessandro Carraresi negli anni seguenti aveva compito una traduzione: ma in esso alcune cose erano di troppo per noi Italiani, altre non bastavano. Mi posi a farvi così a mente alcune note, poi a ristringere alcuni brani del testo francese, altri ad allargare: così a poco a poco mi trovai con tutto il pensiero dentro alla Storia di Firenze. . . . In essa ritrovo perfino certe intonazioni che nei primi tempi a me venivano dallo Scrittore francese; di che io ringrazio la Donna gentile.")[22]

By today's standards, we might judge Capponi's takeover of Allart's work to be dishonest. But such a moral judgment might prevent us from analyzing the specific conditions for the production of Capponi's work. Ernesto Sestan writes that Capponi's *Storia* was "born" as he scribbled observations in the margins of a Florentine history published in Paris in 1843 by "an amiable, bizarre, and somewhat crazy French lady, who had, with her daring spirit, stirred up, if not the feelings (but the feelings, too), definitely the fantasy and dialectical inspiration of Capponi" ("Nato, occasionalmente, da osservazioni marginali a una storia fiorentina scritta da una amabile, bizzarra e un po' anche mattarella madama francese, la quale col suo spirito indiavolato, aveva acceso, se non i sensi [ma un po' anche questi], certo la fantasia e l'estro dialettico del Capponi").[23] Capponi appropriated many aspects of the organization of Allart's history and in many places translated her words into Italian or, as he said, "reduced some passages," while "lengthening" others. He called her *Histoire de la République florentine* "un ristretto"—a condensation or compendium of Florentine history, implying that his own work was more voluminous, ponderous, and definitive than hers. Actually, the 1843 edition of Allart's *Histoire* cited by Capponi numbered 556 pages and the print was small—hardly a *ristretto*. But this was a moot point for Capponi's readers, who never had the opportunity to become familiar with Allart's work.

Although this story of intellectual trespass would be a fascinating one to pursue, the story I narrate in this section is rather about the scholarly relations between the Italian Capponi and the French Allart and about their passionate co-production of the history of Florence. Capponi and Allart shared an intellectual passion for Florentine history. Capponi sent books to Allart and was a source and resource for her questions and research. As we have seen, he acknowledged her in his preface as a writer worthy of being described in the male gender as a "Scrittore francese" (with an uppercase "S").[24] On her end, Allart, for thirty years, regularly encouraged Capponi to bring his *History* to completion. This encouragement, together with her own publication of *Histoire de la République florentine* in 1843, was instrumental in the production and completion of Capponi's *Storia*.[25]

During the thirty years in which Capponi worked on his *Storia*, his intellectual work was closely related to his politics. He became a senator in the Tuscan Parliament, a political minister, a city council member, and a senator in the new Kingdom of Italy,[26] and he was involved in numerous editorial projects, including the founding of the *Archivio storico italiano*. These positions and projects represented an intense nationalist engagement in the writing of Tuscan, and especially Florentine, history. In this section, I ask: How does our interpretation of Capponi's *Storia* and his political investments change if we see them in the context of his more than thirty-year intellectual relationship with a French historian, feminist, novelist, and political theorist, Hortense Allart?

To respond to this question, I investigate the production of Capponi's *Storia della Repubblica di Firenze* as a "relation of writing." Armando Petrucci coined this inventive expression ("rapporto di scrittura") to refer to the relational space between an author and the physical production of his or her writing.[27] Here, I extend the pertinence of this expression to refer to the complex gender dynamics represented in Capponi's *Storia*. Taking the view that writing and ideas emerge from social relations, I suggest that correspondence between Allart, Capponi, and other Florentine erudites from the 1820s onward engendered part of the "ideological vision of writing" ("visione ideologica dello scrivere") that conditioned the production of Capponi's Florentine history and also played a role in the conception of nationalist thought among erudites in this period.[28] Examining especially Allart's letters to Capponi, we no longer see the production of Capponi's history as his exclusive work that "he imposed upon himself as a civic duty of a son toward his mother, a monument of nobility and rectitude" ("che si impose . . . come un dovere civico di figlio verso la madre, . . . un monumento di nobiltà e di rettitudine").[29] Rather, we begin to see Capponi's *Storia della Repubblica di Firenze* as a relation of writing, a relation whose lexicon is rich with terms that open up projects and perspectives on the intellectual co-production of the Italian nation.[30]

Because Capponi and Allart shared a love for the history of Florence and because their relationship involved an intense labor of cultural translation that went far beyond the French and Italian languages that they both knew so well, I organize my research in this section as a lexicon representing the collaborative dimension of archive and nation building. Dictionaries and lexicons are fundamental to any scholarly enterprise. Allart, for example, indirectly acknowledged her extensive work with dictionaries in her historiographic writing, writing that "even though the [Italian] chronicles were tedious to read and especially to translate," she continued "to enjoy" and never "grew tired" of her activities of translation ("bien que les chroniques fussent souvent sèches à lire, et surtout à traduire, je m'amuse infiniment de mon entreprise sans m'en lasser jamais").[31]

I organize the materials of research in this section as a lexicon both to acknowledge the excessive amounts of (enjoyable) time I have also spent with dictionaries in the work of preparing this book and to acknowledge the lexicon as a repertoire of specialized terms that—with a seemingly neutral intent—can stipulate requirements for membership in a group.³² In her brilliant book *Il lessico filologico degli umanisti*, Silvia Rizzo showed how the philological lexicon of the humanists also represented their scholarly affect, activities, and relations, the definition of their social group, and the terms of their belonging. My intent in this section is to create a lexicon that, instead of lamenting the marginalization of Allart from the work of the Florentine erudites associated with the Gabinetto Vieusseux, represents the lexical terms shared between Allart and Capponi and the ways in which their common constructions complicate the project of the Italian nation. Rather than argue the transnational and gendered dynamics of nation building (or represent Capponi and Allart's relationship in unequal terms of domination and invisibility), my experimental lexicon arranges the terms of Allart and Capponi's relation in such a way as to show Allart collaborating and intervening in the history of republican thought at a crucial time in the history of Italy, the period in which ideas of the future Italian nation were formed in discussions about Florentine and Tuscan history.³³ Throughout the three sections of this book, I intervene in organizations of historical knowledge with the purpose of reorganizing knowledge about Lorenzino and republican thought. In this final section, my lexicon of Capponi and Allart's relations of research enables me to make room for the complex transnational and gendered stories that emerge when we begin to "imagine beyond the boundaries of received categorizations."³⁴

THE ARTWORKS

Three artworks that I made characterize the theoretical questions that pertain to Section One and are sustained throughout the book: *The Scene of Tyranny, Myopic Politics,* and *Categories of Knowledge*.

In *The Scene of Tyranny,* the physical staging in one "theater" of various "hands" that write, that handle a dagger, or that register to use a state archive enabled me to bring together my research in the historiographic tradition about tyrannicide and my archival research about Lorenzino in the State Archive of Milan with my hand actively transcribing and compiling historical materials.³⁵

Myopic Politics focuses on the topos of the shortsightedness of tyrant-slayers who, because they read "too much," were never successful in the realm of political action. I am fascinated by this topos, so often present in contests between "literature" and "politics," from Shakespeare's Cassius, who used his eyes too much in reading, to Gino

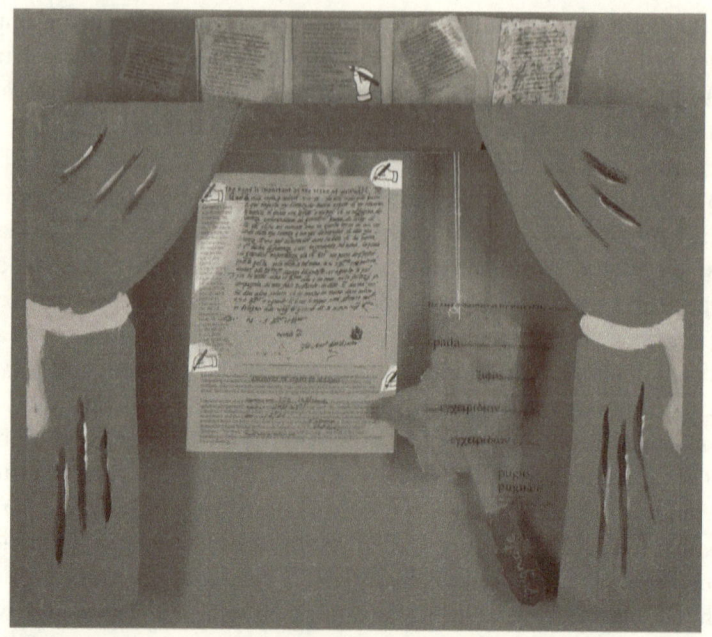

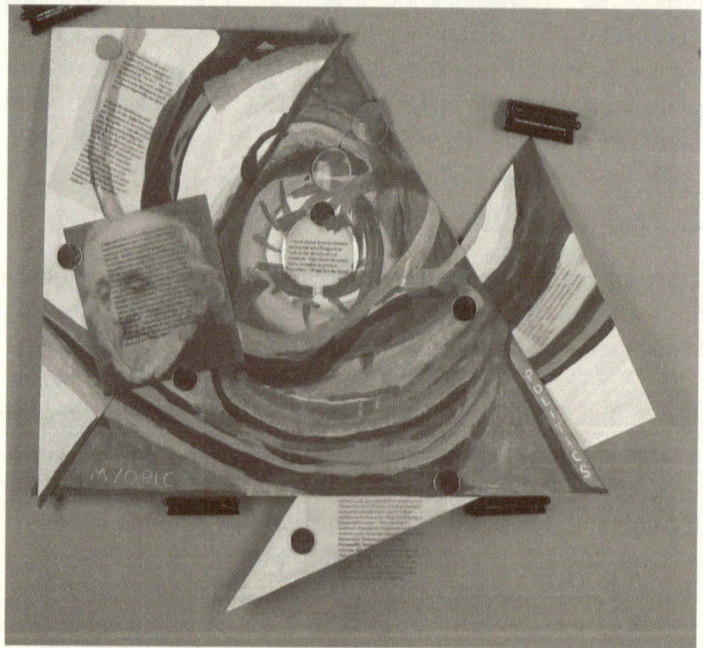

FIGURE 1. *The Scene of Tyranny*. Photograph by Larry Stein.
FIGURE 2. *Myopic Politics*. Photograph by Larry Stein.

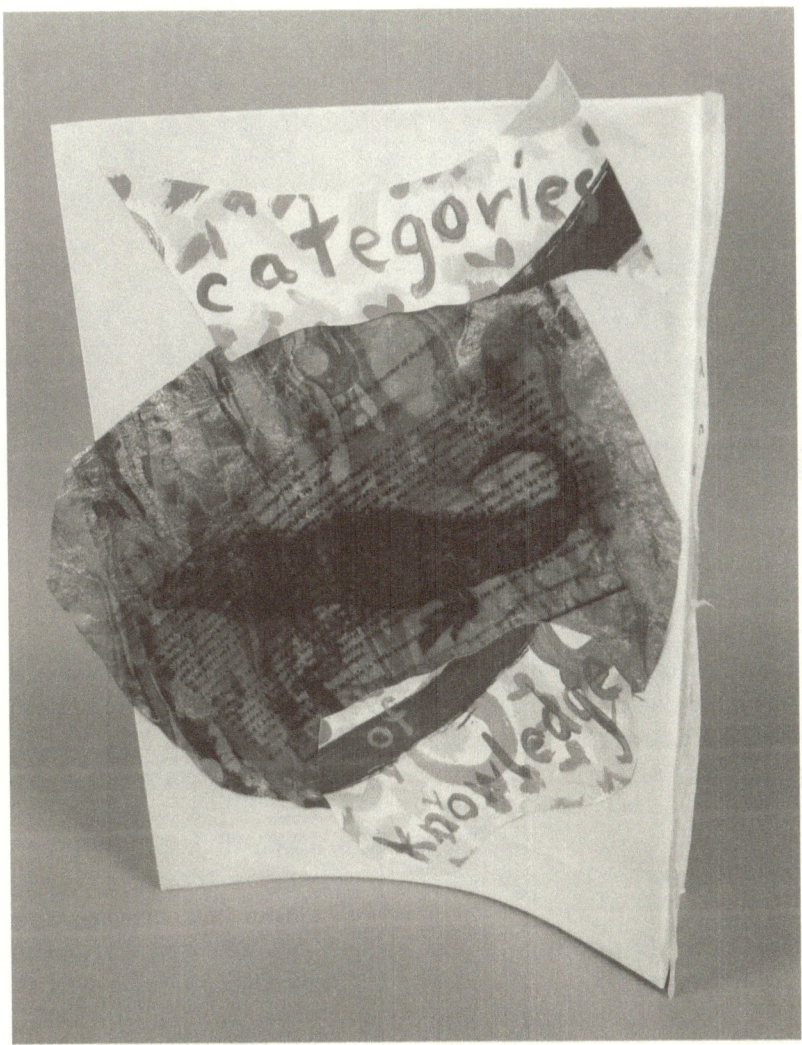

FIGURE 3. *Categories of Knowledge*. Photograph by Larry Stein.

Capponi, who progressively lost his eyesight. Bringing together these different cases of shortsightedness enabled me to consider how the excessive close-up work of scholars can limit our interpretive and epistemological vision.

Categories of Knowledge helped me bring to the fore the economic underpinnings of what we construct as "natural" and "normal" in our

FIGURE 4. *Wings for My Courage*. Photograph by Larry Stein.

everyday commerce of information, ideas, commodities in a context of geopolitical inequalities.

Two more artworks took up the theoretical questions that were especially pertinent to Sections Two and Three: *Wings for My Courage* and *The Nose Knows*.

Wings for My Courage helped me understand that what I really wanted to do in Section Two was to construct the physical conditions in which a seventeenth-century political theorist and nun, Arcangela Tarabotti, could fulfill her aspirations to take up physical space on the shelves of the Mazarine Library.

Finally, *The Nose Knows* helped me focus, in all three sections, on the ways in which different body parts—the hands, the eyes, the nose, the heart—contribute to the construction of historical knowledge. This piece especially helped me to play, in Section Three, with the ways in which the "nose" (and other senses) might be related to knowing (and other forms of gnosis) and sexual politics.

FIGURE 5. *The Nose Knows*. Photograph by Larry Stein.

SECTION ONE

Slaying the Tyrant, 1536–2011

This letter is only to inform Your Most Reverend Lordship how today at seven Messer Lorenzo de Medici, the nephew of Messer Ottaviano de Medici, passed by here in the mail coach. He was wounded, and it seems that he was fleeing from Florence and he left with the greatest fear, because yesterday at eight someone came to this city looking for said Messer Lorenzo, and I think I heard that said Messer Lorenzo, and I think I heard, as I said, that he has killed the Lord Duke of Florence, and so hearing this news that is of greatest importance to His Imperial Majesty, I thought of sending this letter to Your Most Reverend Lordship only for this news, so that you will be able to inform the Most Illustrious Lord Marquis of Guasto if you like.

And then I heard that the Most Reverend Cibo had entered the fortress in the company of a bastard son of the said lord duke, so I will say no more except that as news comes in [di mano in mano] I will inform Your Most Reverend Lordship, and I kiss your hands and I offer and commit myself to you in Bologna on the 9th day of January 1537.

The humble servant of Your Most Reverend and Illustrious Lordship Giovanni Antonio, known as "the Tailor"

[Questa mia esola per avisare vostra signoria Reverendissima cum alli 7 del presente passo per qui imposta messer Lorenzo de Medici nepotte di messer ottaviano de medici il quale era ferite e mi pare che se ne fugiva da fiorenza esene andava cum grandissima paura di sortte che alli otti che fu eri evenute uno in questa terra che va cercando ditto messer Lorenzo e me pare de intendere che ditto messer Lorenzo, E me pare de intendere como ho ditte che ha morto il signor ducha di fiorenza e cosi intendende tal nova, la quale e di grandissima importanza ala maesta Cesarea me parse de espedire questa posta solamente per tal nova a vostra signoria Reverendissima ne poterá avisare allo Illustrissimo signor Marges dil guasto, si a quela li pare.

E piu ho inteso como el Reverendissimo cibo e intrato ne la fortezza in compagnia di uno fiolo Bastardo di ditto signor ducha cosí non diro altro solum che di mano in mano daro aviso a vostra signoria Reverendissima e a quelo li basso le mane e mi offero et raccomando in bologna a di viiij di Gienaro MDxxxvij

Di Vostra Signoria Reverendissima et Illlustrissima umile servitore Giovanni Antonio ditto il sarto][1]

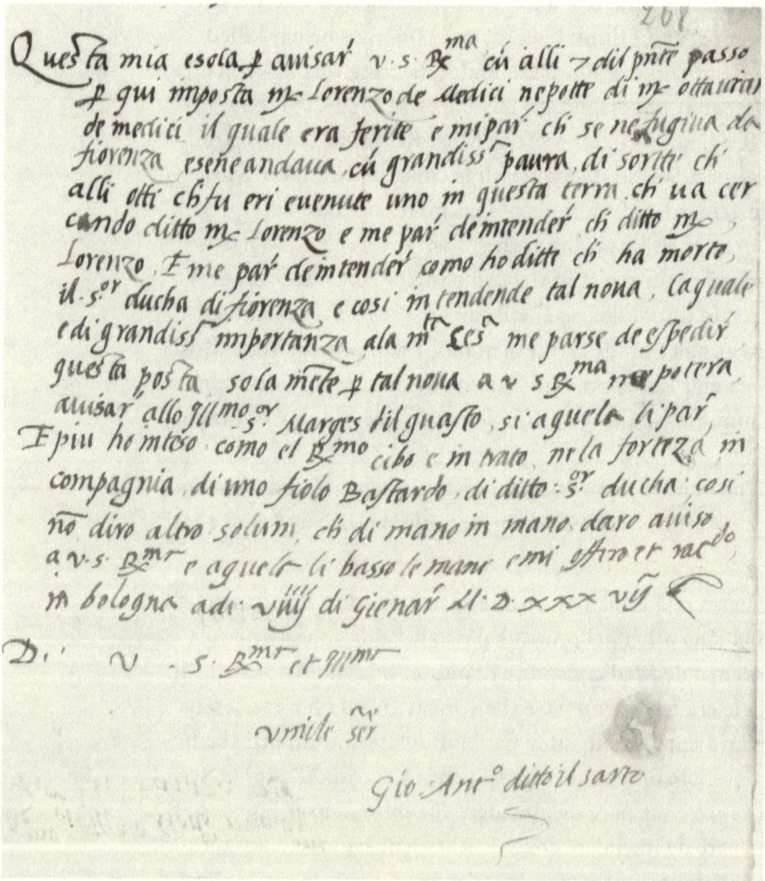
Questa mia esola ꝑ auisar v. s. Rma chi alli 7 dil pnte passo
ꝑ qui imposta m. lorenzo de medici nepotte di m. ottauiano
de medici il quale era ferite e mi par chi se ne fugiua da
fiorenza e se ne andaua cũ grandiss paura, di sortte chi
alli otti chi fu eri euenute uno in questa terra chi ua cer
cando ditto m. lorenzo e me par de intender chi ditto m.
lorenzo. E me par de intender como ho ditti chi ha morto
il s.or ducha di fiorenza e cosi intendende tal noua, laquale
e di grandiss importanza ala mta Cesa me parse de espedir
questa posta sola mente ꝑ tal noua a v. s. Rma ne potera
auisar allo Illmo s.or Marges dil guasto, si a quela li par.
E piu ho inteso como el Rmo cibo e intrato ne la fortezza in
compagnia di uno fiolo Bastardo di ditto s.or ducha cosi
no diro altro solum chi di mano in mano daro auiso
a v. s. Rma e a quelo li basso le mane e mi offero et racdo
in bologna adi viiij di Gienaro M.D.xxxvij

Di V. S. Rma et Illma

umile ser.r

Gio. Anto ditto il sarto

FIGURE 6. Facsimile of Giovanni Antonio's letter to Marino Caracciolo, January 9, 1537. Courtesy of the Archivo di Stato of Milan.

Instead of beginning with a published account of Lorenzino's murder of Alessandro de' Medici, the Duke of Florence, I begin with a letter written three days after the murder (on January 9, 1537) by Giovanni Antonio, nicknamed "the Tailor," a low-level bureaucrat in Charles V's imperial machinery. He was employed by Charles V's governor of Milan, Marino Caracciolo, to supervise the postal station of Bologna and to send any news of importance to imperial politics.[2] His letters are conserved in the State Archive of Milan under the classifications "Chancery of the State of Milan" (Cancelleria dello Stato di Milano) and "The Postal Service" (Poste). When I arrived in Milan in 1983, the archivist Maria Pia Bortolotti had just finished reordering this correspondence chronologically. Earlier archivists, including such significant nineteenth-century cultural figures as Peroni, Osio, and Cantù, had also dismembered and reordered this correspondence according to topical and chronological criteria.[3] Although sixteenth-century hands had produced these letters, many later hands had intervened to give these documents their twentieth-century configuration. As I examined and transcribed Giovanni Antonio's letter, I became a part of this archival story whose protagonists were imperial diplomats, military captains, and functionaries who generated and sent letters to Caracciolo and then secretaries in the Milanese chancery and archivists who conserved and organized this correspondence. This archival story differed from the historiographic narrative of how Lorenzino had assassinated the duke.

. . .

Historiographic accounts record that on the evening of January 6, 1537, Lorenzino de' Medici murdered his cousin Alessandro de' Medici, the Duke of Florence.[4] Lorenzino had carefully devised the plot, following the examples of tyrannicide in ancient historiography. He knew, for example, from his reading of the classics, that there had to be a chaste noblewoman in the picture and that Alessandro, as proof of his tyranny, had to have designs on her, because the first tyrant-slayers, Harmodius and Aristogiton, were glorified for their slaying of Hipparchus after he had dishonored Harmodius's sister.[5] And Lucius Junius Brutus was celebrated as the founder of Roman liberty because he expelled the Tarquin tyrants after Sextus Tarquinius had raped Lucretia. Some accounts even tell us that part of Marcus Brutus's motivation for murdering Caesar was his desire to vindicate his sister's and mother's honor, which had been stained by their adulterous affairs with Caesar. So Lorenzino followed suit: by promising to procure for Alessandro the sexual favors of a chaste noblewoman, he lured Alessandro into coming to his place without bodyguards. So blinded by his lust was Alessandro that he even removed his sword and dagger and let Lorenzino place these out of reach. Lorenzino went out, leaving Alessandro in bed unarmed and convinced that his lust would soon be satisfied. Lorenzino returned, not with the girl but with his point man Scoronconcolo, and together they attacked the duke. They finally slew him, but not without considerable struggle, during which the duke clamped his teeth down on Lorenzino's hand, causing him significant bleeding and pain. Because of this injury, Lorenzino was unable to apprise the Florentine people of the news and of their narrative obligation, according to the classical model, to rise up and take the government in their own hands. Instead, he fled to Venice, where he was, according to some reports, hailed as the "new Brutus"—a great Althusserian moment in history, a moment in which the force of interpellation persuaded many that Lorenzino was indeed a great champion of liberty and an authentic tyrant-slayer in the tradition of Brutus.[6] This was the confirmation Lorenzino required to complete his historiographic fiction. Once represented as the "new Brutus," Lorenzino could justify his act of murder by citing each citizen's legal right and duty to slay a tyrant.

Several aspects of Lorenzino's assassination of the duke and its representation in humanist historiography are problematic for the modern reader interested in issues of social and political change. First is the monolithic fiction of "the people," who, undifferentiated by gender, "race," or class, should always be organized and waiting to rise up and concretize humanistic ideals of freedom that they had no hand in devising and from which they will receive no benefits. Second is the fiction that the narrative paradigm of tyrannicide is a universal and comprehensive one capable of representing every political struggle and every political subject in every age and place. This second fiction obscures, in particular, the social specificity of the narrative, made for and by humanists or scholars of the western classics in different historical moments and to serve different interests. Each example of tyrannicide appeals to an audience of humanists, who are always on the side of liberty and truth but who, in their obsequiousness to tradition, have never questioned the variety of invisible oppressions on which such liberty and truth are founded.[7]

The final and most obvious problem of the humanistic tyrannicide narrative is its incorporation of the subjugation of women into its formula for freedom. Though women are absent from the actual physical struggle between tyrant and tyrant-slayer, the violated body of a woman is the foundation of this struggle, the ground upon which this struggle comes into being. Moreover, the very act of telling this story in its humanistic version reinforces and reproduces a transhistorical paradigm for the violation and subjugation of women in politics. Where are we in historical space and time when we reproduce this traditional humanistic paradigm? And how does this "location" relate to the concrete locations in which we conduct our research? Can the narrative paradigm of tyrannicide, transmitted by the humanistic tradition, provide any opportunities for reorganizing political theory and practice around issues of gender?[8] One way to reorganize knowledge about Lorenzino is to tell the story differently.

. . .

The story of Giovanni Antonio is that he wrote a letter in great haste and excitement to Caracciolo in Milan, telling him that Lorenzino had just passed through Bologna. Giovanni's hand was large, hurried, and scrawling, and the informal margins were unjustified—all of this pointing to his informal graphic education as much as to the anxiety and fear he felt in response to his sighting of Lorenzino. Giovanni applied sand to the ink to help the ink dry, but he sent the news to Caracciolo in such a hurry that the sand remained embedded in the ink. Quick—write it, seal it, send it. No time to mention either a dishonored woman or the Brutus myth. The grains of sparkling sixteenth-century sand, embedded in the ink—the vehicle that conveyed Giovanni's haste—became, as well, a conveyor of memories that connected the historical, social dimensions of my research to my subjectivity as a scholar. For the sand was still there sparkling on the paper in December 1983 when I read this document for the first time.

It was the last day of my visit to the State Archive in Milan in 1983. Fixing intently on the sand sparkling in ink on that day, I became aware of Giovanni's Antonio's hand in relation to my own hand scribbling away on my note paper. As I wrote, my hand participated in a representation of the reported murder and in an assembly of knowledge about Lorenzino. The letter of Giovanni Antonio powerfully illustrated how, in our acts of requesting and finding historical materials, a fiction of our hands and our selves emerges as part of the historical record. The hand was important at the scene of the assault. The hand was and is still important at the scene of writing. Lorenzino's fear, his wounded hand, his flight, Giovanni's hasty and anxious hand, and my own transcribing hand all became part of the historicity of the archive in which

I was doing research.⁹ In this letter of Giovanni Antonio (and my transcription of it), it was clear that the past was still passing.

...

As I transcribed this letter with the sparkling sand, my own hand became somewhat shaky. I had already been studying this episode of political violence for some time and was concerned about my fascination with Lorenzino's humanist self-fashioning as a classical tyrant-slayer. Lorenzino compared himself to the ancient tyrant-slayers who were willing to sacrifice themselves for liberty and eternal fame. And he cited those ancient tyrants who had raped noblewomen, murdered their own mothers, and cut down noble citizens.¹⁰ He read these stories from antiquity to create a blueprint for constructing his own murder plan. I always understood that I was a new reader in this chain. But now, for the first time, my reading eyes and transcribing hand were directly related to the thoughts, feelings, eyes, and hands of Giovanni Antonio, who wrote that he had seen Lorenzino pass through Bologna.

With my reading eyes and transcribing hand, I understood that Giovanni Antonio's letter provided evidence of a bureaucratic relation, of a relationship of power in Charles V's empire.¹¹ It, along with hundreds of other letters documenting Lorenzino's murder of Alessandro from an imperial perspective, provided evidence that Florence was no longer an autonomous political entity but was dependent on imperial power managed from Milan. This evidence lifted the story of Lorenzino outside the bounds of Florentine (and ancient) history and into the field of "real" imperial politics. Although his humanistic aspirations to restore republican politics to Florence failed—the murdered duke Alessandro was immediately replaced by Cosimo de' Medici—Lorenzino's classical learning nonetheless had a significant impact on imperial politics and writing.

...

I begin with Giovanni Antonio's letter because it was historically situated in quotidian relations of writing and power. The collocation of this letter in a particular rhetorical and relational frame (which included me the reader) enabled me to put together the various stages of my research on Lorenzino. First, taking a linguistic-rhetorical approach, I had studied the sixteenth-century historiographic accounts of Lorenzino's murder of the duke in relation to ancient historiographic representations of tyrants and tyrant-slayers. I had been interested in how the transmission, translation, and exportation of elements from ancient historiographic texts to sixteenth-century historiography worked to construct a literary tradition or republic of letters that was perceived to be detached from politics. Letters like that of Giovanni Antonio, exhibiting the direct impact of literary motifs on imperial politics, provided a perspective for critiquing this perception, still common today, of a rupture between literature and politics. Moreover, Giovanni Antonio's letter showed that news of Lorenzino emanating both from the republic of letters and from the imperial network was passing "from hand to hand" ("di mano in mano") in two seemingly distinct circuits and converging in my archival notes. Indeed, Giovanni Antonio's letter pointed to an overlap between those two circuits that a scholar in her study was not positioned to see.

Second, letters like that of Giovanni Antonio enabled me to examine Lorenzino's murder of the duke in the context of an emerging world system of which Florence was a part. Archival representations of this event conserved in Charles V's chancery in Milan pointed both to the immediate contingencies made necessary by political disturbance in Florence and to imperial relations of ruling in sixteenth-century Europe. Those "facts" that were collected to represent Lorenzino's act of murder tell us much about the writing and power relations of those who collected them. And institutions of collecting and recording that took form around this event (and others) made their impact on practices of empire and state formation for centuries to come.

Finally, beginning with Giovanni Antonio's letter has allowed me to mark a space for myself as a (feminist) scholar in the western male transmission and tradition of understanding tyranny and liberty. The fact that "I" was "there," too, situated among the chancery documents, receiving the news that Lorenzino had passed by the post of Bologna (and making the connection between Giovanni Antonio's hand and my transcribing hand) enabled me to situate myself "here" as well, in my study, in particular relations of a humanistic past and imperial present, of an imperial past and humanistic present, reorganizing political knowledge and research around feminist subjectivity.[12] As long as I had limited myself to telling the historiographic narrative of how Lorenzino had murdered the duke, I remained in the transhistorical time and space of the humanistic tradition that was implied and reinforced by the story. I was able neither to disassemble the components of this narrative nor to loosen the grip they had on me. Now, with this archival letter of Giovanni Antonio, I was able to reorganize this narrative, assembling knowledge around relations of research that included my own. What follows, then, is a sort of inventory that endeavors to theorize, construct, document, and inhabit a social intersection between a republic of letters, imperial knowledge (past and present), and my own active construction of knowledge about liberty and tyranny.[13] Here, in this intersection, we become aware of the interdependence of classical learning and imperial knowledge[14]—of the scholar in her study and the scholar in the "field" (of libraries, archives, everyday life), opening up new possibilities for political subjectivity and knowing.

. . .

Folder 1

THE REPUBLIC OF LETTERS: ITS FASCIST LEGACY

My study of Lorenzino began and ended with the study of fascist appropriations of Renaissance topics. I first became interested in the humanistic rhetoric of conspiracy when I read two fascinating and important essays by the historian Delio Cantimori: "Il caso di Boscoli e la vita del Rinascimento," published in 1927 in the fascist journal *Giornale critico della filosofia,* and "Rhetoric and Politics in Italian Humanism," published in 1937 in the second issue of the *Journal of the Warburg Institute*, a journal founded, at least in part, in response to the threat that fascism posed to European humanistic ideals.[15] I concluded my research on Lorenzino with the study of two fascist films: Guido Brignone's *Lorenzino de' Medici* (1935) and Luis Trenker's *Condottieri* (1937). Although the study of fascist culture in relation to Renaissance and humanistic topics is an area that falls well outside my areas of competence, I will cautiously offer a reading of how this historical relation may have framed my studies of Lorenzino.

To explore the relation of fascism to our practices as scholars of humanism and the Renaissance is a complex endeavor.[16] We have, on the one hand, the model of those scholars who, in their opposition, fled the politics and culture of fascism and Nazism and were fortunately able, as refugees, to pursue their studies in safer havens. I am thinking of such figures as Paul Oskar Kristeller, Hans Baron, and Gaetano Salvemini and of all the ways in which their ideas, their scholarship, and their resistance to fascism continue to inspire and enliven our scholarship today. We have, on the other hand, those scholars, filmmakers, and writers who actively supported or were supported by fascist politics and culture as they pursued their studies and representations of the Renaissance. In his construction of the Renaissance roots of fascism, the historian Delio Cantimori traced a historical process in which Renaissance figures gradually emerged from the republic of letters to influence the field of history. In the area of fascist cinema, I will focus on two of the numerous fascist filmmakers who took up Renaissance topics, Guido Brignone and Luis Trenker.[17]

Delio Cantimori, a monumental historian of the Renaissance, researched a wide range of topics, from Italian heretical movements to humanism, Machiavelli, Luther, historiography, and much more. Born in 1901, he joined the Fascist Party in 1926 and was an active contributor to fascist culture at least until 1936. He was a student and follower of Giovanni Gentile, and as a professor at the Scuola Normale Superiore in Pisa he had a strong influence on a whole generation of eminent (leftist) Italian historians, including such figures as Renzo De Felice, Carlo Ginzburg, and Adriano Prosperi. Scholars still debate the chronology of Cantimori's conversion to communism. But, in any case, after the war and until his death in 1966, Cantimori was a member of the Italian Communist Party.[18]

To separate Cantimori's Renaissance scholarship from his political writing, as Michele Ciliberto has noted, would be to blind ourselves to the ways in which his analyses of contemporary politics informed the development of his historiographic perspectives.[19] Indeed, at the same time as he was conducting his research on heretical movements in both Italy and Germany, Cantimori contributed regularly to the major fascist cultural journals, including *Vita nova*, *Leonardo*, *L'archivio di studi corporativi*, *Studi germanici*, and *Civiltà fascista*;[20] he translated *The Principles of National Socialism* of Carl Schmitt and commented on the *Scritti e discorsi* of Mussolini; and in his reviews of books on Renaissance topics he would easily slip into citations of fascist writers. These kinds of intersecting preoccupations and reflections were in perfect keeping with the place held by the Renaissance in fascism's representations of its historical roots.

In an article published in 1929 in *Vita nova*, in which he announced his program of research on heretical movements, Cantimori wrote that Italy needed to affirm its own unique contribution to the construction of the United States of Europe. This unique contribution consisted in Italy's status as the birthplace of the Renaissance. "We Italians," he wrote, "feel ourselves to be spiritual children of that last truly European movement, the Renaissance" ("Noi italiani ci sentiamo figli spirituali dell'ultimo grande movimento veramente europeo, del Rinascimento").[21] Renaissance humanism was also represented in Cantimori's writings as a marker of Italian fascism's particular significance, inasmuch as it "represent[ed] the universality of Italian thought, because precisely in that period, we, who were lacking a political nationality, were exercising a real spiritual imperialism" ("rappresenta l'universalità del pensiero italiano, perché proprio in quel periodo, noi che mancavamo di una nazionalità politica, esercitavamo un vero e proprio imperialismo spirituale").[22] We will see later how fascism urged the movie industry to capitalize on this "imperialismo spirituale" in its search for actors who embodied the Italian people's "intense spiritual wealth" ("l'intensa ricchezza spirituale di cui è forte il popolo [italiano]").[23] What I would like to suggest here is that Cantimori's creation of a spiritual genealogy enabled him to bring the Renaissance into the present, to make the Renaissance receptive to fascist ideological superimpositions.

In 1931, Giuseppe Saitta, the editor of *Vita nova*, called to the attention of the fascist press an important article in which Cantimori returned to this theme of the political importance of Renaissance culture to fascism. In Cantimori's words, "The Risorgimento was indebted to the revolutionary movement of the [medieval] city-states that culminated in Renaissance culture, the initiator of modern European civilization: fascism is the continuation and renewal of this *action* and is, for this reason, revolutionary" ("Il Risorgimento ... si riallacciò al movimento rivoluzionario dei comuni, culminato nella cultura del Rinascimento, iniziatrice della moderna civiltà europea: il Fascismo è il proseguimento ed il rinnovamento di questa azione, ed è per questo rivoluzionario").[24] With this understanding of Renaissance culture as "action" Cantimori was, in fact, representing a fascist cultural goal to critique and transform the traditional intellectual from an abstract, autonomous thinker to a protagonist of history whose objective was to *practice* culture and knowledge as *action*. This superimposition of fascist ideology was especially important in Cantimori's writings of the 1930s in which he fashioned a Renaissance clothed in the fascist ideology of revolutionary action.

Like many other fascist intellectuals of his time, Cantimori adhered to a distinction, reinforced frequently in the journal *Critica fascista*, between "intelligence as 'consciousness' of an action and intellectualism, understood as separateness, as a splitting off from reality" ("intelligenza come 'coscienza' di un'azione e intellettualismo, inteso come separatezza, come scissione rispetto alla realtà").²⁵ Fascist culture, of course, intensely promoted a politics of "cultura-azione" against the image of the scholar removed from contemporary politics.²⁶ These were the years in which the philosopher Ugo Spirito was elaborating a conception of "life as research" ("vita come ricerca") in which classical education was a barrier to action and the researcher's goal was to "terminate his research in order to truly reach reality" ("terminare la ricerca per raggiungere davvero la realtà").²⁷ These links between culture and action, the Renaissance and action, and the classics as "instruction and encouragement for action itself" ("insegnamento e conforto all'operare stesso") became the criteria Cantimori used to analyze Renaissance historical figures.²⁸ It was almost as if he wanted to see how certain figures would stand up to standards of fascist political culture, straddling the fence between the republic of letters and the stage of politics.

In his 1927 essay "Il caso di Boscoli e la vita del Rinascimento," Cantimori remade two humanist figures to exemplify the fascist preoccupation with "that type of literary man who is disengaged from life and the world that surrounds him" ("quel tipo di letterato astratto dalla vita e dal mondo che lo circonda").²⁹ On the one hand, Girolamo Olgiati, a student of Latin and co-conspirator in the 1476 assassination of Galeazzo Sforza, lived and died in the republic of letters, believing that it made sense to reenact the Roman figure of Brutus in the political situation of Milan in 1476 and to recite words in Latin as he waited execution: "Mors acerba, fama perpetua, stabit vetus memoria facti."³⁰ Although the republic of letters was enough to sustain Olgiati through death, his practice of "culture as action" was too removed from his own political world to be effective. On the other hand, Pier Paolo Boscoli, awaiting execution after his 1512 plot to assassinate Giovanni dei Medici, begged his friend Luca della Robbia: "Get Brutus out of my head, so that I can take this last step entirely a Christian" ("Cavatemi della testa Bruto, acciò ch'io faccia questo passo interamente da cristiano").³¹ Boscoli also shared the abstract republican ideals that characterized "the moral life of the Renaissance" ("la vita morale del Rinascimento"),³² but unlike Olgiati, Boscoli was able to glimpse the dissonance between ancient Rome and sixteenth-century Florence, between his learned culture and the act of murder he had committed.

Cantimori observes, with Gentile, that humanism had infused both Olgiati and Boscoli with a kind of "detachment from life" ("si comincia in Italia a staccar l'uomo dalla vita") and "indifference, characteristic of the aesthetic spirit" ("quella indifferenza che è propria dello spirito estetico") of the Renaissance.[33] But the case of Boscoli was much more poignant for Cantimori because even the "confusion and uncertainty" ("confusione e incertezza mentale") that Boscoli expressed with respect to Brutus and Christianity did not enable him to enter the "concrete life of the present" ("l'attualità della vita concreta").[34] At the end of his life, Boscoli's "enthusiasms and desires" ("entusiasmi e desideri") were, according to Cantimori, still "purely intellectual" ("puramente intellettuali") and "cut off" ("come tutto fosse scisso") from political reality.[35]

Cantimori's studies of heretical movements focused precisely on those historical figures whose "concept of Renaissance man placed in the center of the life of the universe" ("il concetto dell'uomo dal Rinascimento riposto al centro della vita universale") enabled them to surpass the aesthetic constraints of Olgiati and Boscoli, to enter "the concrete life of the present," and to "found the modern world" ("entrando nella attualità della vita concreta, fondano il mondo moderno").[36] It is difficult not to read in this essay and especially in his evaluation of Boscoli's "confusion and uncertainty" Cantimori's own preoccupations about whether his own research would truly reach "the actuality" of fascist life that he so fervently supported at the time. If Boscoli's confusion and uncertainty as a humanist and Christian remained purely intellectual and cut off from political reality, how would Cantimori's own intellectual confusions manage to blur the boundary between "culture" and "action"? Indeed, "confusion and uncertainty" was almost a leitmotiv of Cantimori's reflections on the relation of culture or the republic of letters to political action.[37]

While Boscoli's ideological confusion never left the intellectual realm of "literary construction" ("costruzione letteraria"), Cantimori endeavored, in his writings, to transform this confusion almost into a prerequisite for entering "the actuality of concrete life."[38] In his 1928 essay "Observations on Concepts of Culture and the History of Culture," he defined "culture" as a *confused* stirring of desires, intentions, ideas, intuitions, and cognitions that move and take on different aspects and forms but are all unified by the effort to emerge and reach a more concrete, a more real unity" ("un muoversi confuso di desiderî, propositi, idee, intuizioni, cognizioni, che si muovono e prendono varî aspetti e forme, ma son tutti unificati dallo sforzo di uscire e di raggiungere una più concreta, una reale unità").[39] It is still difficult today to evaluate whether Cantimori's confusion was culturally productive: Did it enable him to effectively blur the boundaries between his "research" and "life," between the republic of letters, or "culture," and fascist political "action"? Or was it, more probably, a rhetorical resource to accompany the political transformation produced by fascism?[40]

. . .

The fascist intellectual journals (and the antifascist *Journal of the Warburg Institute*) were not the only stage on which fascist preoccupations about and projections on the Renaissance were played out. Indeed, such preoccupations found an even more receptive space for projection on the cinematic screen, with approximately twenty fascist films set in the Renaissance. In his study of historical films produced under fascism, Jean Gili considered the reasons why fascism favored this period as a cinematic subject. On the one hand, the Renaissance represented in Italian history "a period of wealth, power, intellectual splendor and artistic supremacy for the Italian states" ("un periodo di ricchezza, di potenza, di splendore intellettuale, di supremazia artistica per gli stati italiani").[41] At the same time, the Renaissance could be more easily "exploited" than other periods, "since its distance in time offer[ed] contemporaneously the possibility of rewriting the facts . . . and of exalting a period presented as a stage in the process of Italian state formation" ("si tratta di una materia 'raffreddata,' che si presta ad essere sfruttata senza rischio, poiché la sua lontananza nel tempo offre contemporaneamente la possibilità di riscrivere i fatti . . . e di esaltare un periodo presentato come una tappa dell'unità italiana in processo di formarsi").[42] Although scholars in the republic of letters rarely would admit to "rewriting the facts," film directors, of course, were not constrained by such rules, and certainly, two films made in the 1930s and set in the sixteenth century—Guido Brignone's *Lorenzino de' Medici* (1935) and Luis Trenker's *Condottieri* (1937)—took ample liberties with historical sources.

On December 5, 1934, the film magazine *Cinema Illustrazione* reported that while visiting the set of *Lorenzino de' Medici* Luigi Freddi, the fascist official in charge of cinema (the direttore generale della cinematografia), was "absorbed for a long time" in the costumes and the set design for the film ("si è intrattenuto lungamente interessandosi molto alla preparazione dei costumi, dell'ammobiliamento e dell'allestimento scenico del film *Lorenzino de' Medici*").[43] It was not unusual for fascist officials to frequent the studios of Cines (and later Cinecittà). Galeazzo Ciano, the undersecretary of state for the press and propaganda, also regularly visited the film studios and closely followed the various phases of film production.⁴⁴ Especially interested in the production of historical films, Ciano issued generic directives to film producers, such as "Draw your inspiration from the glories of history" ("[Ispiratevi] alle glorie della storia").⁴⁵ And Mussolini himself, at the inauguration of the Centro Sperimentale di Cinema, emphasized the importance of the historical film: "We Italians must insist especially on historical films; for us, history is alive, indeed, it is our very life. We must draw inspiration from it, we must make use of it." ("E' proprio sul film storico che noi italiani dobbiamo battere; per noi la storia è cosa viva, è anzi la nostra stessa vita. Ad essa dobbiamo ispirarci, di essa dobbiamo servirci.")⁴⁶

Guido Brignone's film *Lorenzino de' Medici*, released in 1935, presents an interesting version of this historical inspiration. It represents the odd heroics of a courtier, Lorenzino de' Medici, who in 1536 assassinated his cousin Alessandro de' Medici, the Duke of Florence. Alessandro Moissi, a famous stage actor who had just finished playing *Hamlet* at Teatro Argentina, plays Lorenzino as an avid reader of Machiavelli with a sumptuous library. Applying Machiavelli's justification of the *colpo di stato*—"We can say we have made good use of those cruelties that are exercised only once and transformed to the benefit of citizens" ("Bene usate si possono chiamare quelle crudeltà che si fanno una volta sola e si convertiscono in vantaggio per i sudditi")⁴⁷—Lorenzino creates a plan to slay the duke. Unlike the Florentine exiles, who are collectively organizing an insurrection against the duke, Lorenzino plans his assassination as a single actor. When the exiles want to know what part he is playing, Lorenzino responds: "You will know at the right time, when the man will emerge from the actor" ("Lo saprete al suo tempo, quando dall'istrione uscirà l'uomo").

Lorenzino sees the exiles as too removed from concrete politics to enact their culture as action. Indeed, his is a Machiavellian plan, always changing to fit the exigencies of the moment. When the exiles ask Lorenzino to join them in their plans for an insurrection, he responds: "I leave you to your pipe dreams" ("Vi lascio alle vostre chimere"). Lorenzino's political thinking is like that of Mussolini himself—too dynamic to fit within the scheme of any fixed ideology.⁴⁸ But it is unwavering in one respect; he consistently targets the duke's vulnerability in matters of sex. Brignone is here faithful, in part, to the historiographic tales of Alessandro's sexual exploits, embellishing those exploits historiographically recorded with two extra love stories of his own creation. For Brignone, it was not enough to portray a Renaissance man who could successfully convert his culture into effective political action. Brignone had also to pay attention to the bottom line—he had to dress up Renaissance figures for success at the box office. The subjugation of women in "culture as action" was still an easy sell.

. . .

The film *Condottieri* (released in 1937) was a collaborative German-Italian production directed by and starring Luis Trenker as Giovanni dalle Bande Nere (1498–1526), the famous condottiere and infantry captain, son of Caterina Sforza and Giovanni de' Medici. Participation of the Forze Armate Italiane is noted at the beginning of the film, along with a rolling caption that explains how the *condottieri* "for the first time led the civil militias of the people who rose up against mercenary troops and soldiers of fortune with the goal of unifying the Italian fatherland" ("guidarono per la prima volta le civili milizie del popolo che risorgeva contro truppe mercenarie e di ventura, avendo a meta l'unità della patria italiana").[49] The first scene, showing the defeat of Caterina Sforza and her very young child at the hands of the Borgias in 1500, is closely followed by a scene portraying Giovanni, Caterina's son from her subsequent marriage to Giovanni de' Medici. The son Giovanni is a young man who is recruiting volunteers for his militia. He speaks to a crowd of onlookers, saying: "Italy. A single state [stretching] from the Alps to the sea . . . Give me your trust. With your help, we will make Italy." ("L'Italia. Un unico stato dalle Alpi al mare . . . Datemi la vostra fiducia. Con il vostro aiuto, noi faremo l'Italia.") At first, his words are met with laughter. They make no sense, at first, in the 1520s. Soon after, though, we see a group of men rushing to join, and we hear a marching song sung by Tito Gobbi: "With our great captain we will know how to liberate and unify our fatherland. Whoever of you has an Italian heart will hasten to the flag." ("Col nostro grande capitan noi sapremo la patria liberar e unificar. Chi di voi ha il cuore italiano alla bandiera sua accorrerà.")

The newly recruited soldiers give a German salute and take a very fascist-sounding oath to "believe," "obey," and "fight": "I swear to believe in the supreme goal of a great and unified Italy; to obey the orders of my commander; to serve with all of my strength until the last drop of blood" ("Giuro di *credere* al fine supremo di un'Italia grande e unita, *ubbidire* gli ordini del mio capo, *servire con tutte le mie forze fino all'ultima goccia di sangue*" [emphasis mine]). These soldiers and their captain lead a simple, virtuous, Spartan existence, unlike their mercenary counterparts, who are portrayed as excessively indulging in food and women. Even Giovanni's death at the end of the film is portrayed as an apotheosis of his ideals of strength, virtue, and unity. Indeed, Trenker was explicitly concerned, in his portrayal of Giovanni's death, to create a mythic hero. In an article he published in *Cinema* in 1937, he wrote that "symbolic content" ("il contenuto simbolico") was, above all, important in a historical film: "In my new film *Condottieri*, for example, the figure of the dead hero is set free from its marble mask to illuminate the entire sarcophagus. In this way, I wanted to express, in poetic synthesis, how time is transformed into eternity and man into a myth." ("Nel mio nuovo film CONDOTTIERI, per esempio, si sprigiona dalla maschera marmorea la visione della figura dell'eroe morto che illumina l'intero sarcofago. Ho voluto esprimere così, in poetica sintesi, come il tempo si tramuti in eternità e l'uomo in mito.")[50]

In a transparent allusion to Mussolini, Trenker has Giovanni delle Bande Nere wear a black shirt and thereby encourages us to see fascism as a historical outgrowth of Renaissance roots.[51] It is interesting to reflect on this "dressing" of Giovanni in fascist garb in light of some of the preoccupations held in the film studios about how actors were supposed to look. In October 1938, the film magazine *Cinema Illustrazione* published an unsigned article entitled "The Italian Type in Cinema." The article urges Italian film-makers to find and recruit "Italian types" for their films. This "type," according to the writer, was one that embraced both "the physical ideal of our race" ("l'ideale fisico della nostra razza") and its "spiritual serenity" ("serenità spirituale").[52] Where were filmmakers supposed to look for this "type"? "If we travel all over Italy, we will meet this 'type' in the fields, on assembly lines, in laboratories, in businesses wherever work is in full swing. It is the 'type' that reveals in his features and lineaments the Italian people's gift of intense spiritual wealth." ("Se noi percorriamo l'Italia noi lo incontriamo questo 'tipo' nei campi, nelle officine, nei laboratori, nelle aziende ovunque ferve il lavoro. E' il 'tipo' che rivela, nelle sue fattezze, nei suoi lineamenti, l'intensa ricchezza spirituale di cui è forte il popolo.")[53] Luis Trenker would seem to embody this type to perfection. What, then, did it mean for Giovanni de' Medici to be dressed up as a German actor in a black shirt?

. . .

One critic who tried to interview Brignone on the subject of his historical films found him "too busy to answer questions" ("troppo indaffarato per rispondere alle domande"). Still, this writer (who signed his note M.A.)

concluded, it was Brignone's "temperament as a commercial director" ("temperamento di regista commerciale") that led him to dress up Renaissance figures on the fascist screen.[54] It is interesting to speculate what it might have meant commercially and politically to enact Renaissance culture in scholarship and cinema dressing up Renaissance figures in fascist clothing.

In a brief article of 1953 entitled "The Third Cines Puts on the Black Shirt," Libero Solaroli suggests that two factors in particular may have influenced the production of so many historical films during fascism: the country's disastrous economy and the regime's financial management of cinema. In the years 1935–36 a state monopoly was created for the acquisition of foreign films, and the Banca Nazionale del Lavoro created a separate division specifically for lending to the movie industry. Lenders rewarded films that could be made inexpensively because they made bigger profits at the box office. And they especially liked historical films for their avoidance of current economic problems, an evasion that ultimately served the regime.[55] But as we all know, culture never produces a seamless fabric of ideology. We need to know more about the daily decision making of directors as they dressed up Renaissance figures in fascist film studios. In particular, who and what influenced them in their creation of analogies between Renaissance and fascist cultures, in their temporal slippages and confusions, in their choices of subjects? Or what influence did these films have on the scholarly imagination of fascist militants who studied the Renaissance? Indeed, the clever title of Solaroli's article, "La Terza Cines indossa la camicia nera," encourages us to look at the seams and montage of our own scholarship. In what ways do we continue to avoid and address current economic ills as we dress up the Renaissance in the clothing of our own times?

To me, it is important to acknowledge that somehow the efforts of fascist scholars and filmmakers to work through humanistic subjects and to complicate them with parallels to contemporary situations still influence the ways in which we scholars approach the Renaissance today. First, I would like to return for a moment to Cantimori's 1929 essay that pointed to the Renaissance as a model for the fascist idea of a United States of Europe. To what extent are our own reconstructions of the Renaissance as a European movement still influenced by this fascist frame? And, parenthetically, to what extent is the current project of European unity the conclusion of a fascist aspiration? Second, I think it may be important to acknowledge that the critique of the traditional intellectual, so crucial to work in cultural studies today, is not only a

Gramscian legacy but a discourse that emerged from both sides of the political spectrum of Italy in the 1930s. In particular, the fascist ambivalence and confusion about those Renaissance figures who translated their culture and learning into political action may have an enduring effect on our own evaluations: for example, the fact that we are still absorbed and confused by the problem of evaluating Lorenzino's or Boscoli's grasp on political "reality" may be a direct fascist legacy.

Finally, I would like to allude briefly to two other themes of fascist discourse that require our critical perspectives today. The first is the issue of "race." In his 1928 essay "Observations on Concepts of Culture and the History of Culture," Cantimori writes of the importance of making concrete, rather than ignoring, "pseudoconcepts" like "race" ("i concetti (o pseudoconcetti) di razza"). In the past, he writes, the concept of race, understood as a "spiritual value" ("valor[e] spiritual[e]"), has only been damaging to culture and society; now (in 1928), it is important to bring the concept of race "back to earth" ("ricondurre in terra") and to consider it as a concrete element of cultural history.[56] In the wake of the ensuing racial politics of fascism and Nazism it is troubling but important to analyze, from an antifascist and antiracist perspective, the fascist scholarly attention to race and nationalism in cultural history for any possible methodological or disciplinary legacies.

The second and last fascist cultural theme I will mention is the debate, among fascist scholars, about humanism. This debate was a lively one in discussions about fascist scholastic reform. For Ugo Spirito, the problem with humanism was that it was "exclusively 'historical and literary' and not alive and modern" ("un umanismo esclusivamento 'storico e letterario' e non vivo e moderno").[57] Humanism in the schools performed the "terrible, inhuman work" of "alienating thousands and thousands of young people from reality, forcing them to live for years among works of Greek and Latin literature, . . . consuming and dulling their souls . . . and closing them off from the life of which they would otherwise be capable" ("la terribile e disumana opera che si compie in nome dell'umanismo estraniando dalla realtà migliaia e migliaia di giovani, costringendoli a vivere per anni tra opere greche e latine, che scivolano sulle loro anime, le logorano, le ottundono, senza mai entrarvi, e le chiudono alla vita di cui pure sarebbero state capaci").[58] Although Cantimori acknowledged with Spirito that an education based in books could indeed become an obstacle to action, he himself believed that the job of a humanistic education was to guide students from books to action: "A book is a book, a dead letter, a gray and monotonous manual, rhetoric, repetition; but the classic is a man, a living man, a great man; and contact with him is contact with true and great action; it is the very teaching and encouragement of action." ("Il libro è il libro, lettera morta, manuale grigio e monotono, retorica, ripetizione; ma il classico è un uomo, un uomo vivo, grande; e il contatto con esso è contatto con il vero e il grande operare, insegnamento e conforto all'operare stesso.")[59] The importance of addressing the legacy of this debate in contemporary discourse and scholarship about humanism, humanist tyrant-slayers, and the republic of letters needs little comment. For this reason, I put this fascist legacy up front—to prevent a kind of historical thinking that deletes from our frames of knowing all the thinking that has had an impact on our own between "then" and "now."

...

Folder 2

HUMANISTIC AND IMPERIAL AMBITION

Cola Montano was an "ambitious scholar" ("litterato ambizioso") who taught Latin and rhetoric in Milan to the noble youth of the city.[60] He became particularly intimate with three young students, Giovanandrea Lampognano, Carlo Visconti, and Girolamo Olgiati, teaching them to believe that the Duke of Milan, Galeazzo Maria Sforza, was a tyrant in the tradition of classical tyrants.[61] Galeazzo "was lascivious and cruel.... Not only did he rape noble women [including women associated with Visconti and Olgiati]; he received even more pleasure in publicizing their dishonor. He wasn't satisfied to kill men unless he had killed them by some cruel means. He lived with the infamy of having killed his own mother." ("Era Galeazzo libidinoso e crudele . . . perché non solo non gli bastava corrompere le donne nobili, che prendeva ancora piacere di publicarle; né era contento fare morire gli uomini, se con qualche modo crudele non gli ammazzava. Non viveva ancora sanza infamia di avere morta la madre.")[62] These details, purportedly describing the "facts" of a tyrant's rule, circulated as a type of currency that was shared and enjoyed by successive generations of citizens in the republic of letters.

Cola Montano's ambition was to convey the tools of humanistic literacy to the noble youth of the city, to make the stories of ancient tyrannicide come alive in their actions, and to ground their politics in the republic of letters. As a measure of his success, his students, Olgiati,

Lampognano, and Visconti, constructed a classical tyrant in the person of the duke and worked to assimilate the political "reality" of Milan in 1476 to the story of Brutus, who liberated the Romans from the Tarquin tyranny. Although this "work of resemblance" failed—the liberation of Milan did not follow the slaying of the duke—Cola Montano's ambition was nonetheless realized.[63] Even today, when we humanists talk about "tyranny" and "freedom," we tacitly refer to the republic of letters promoted by Cola Montano.

Humanists mostly believed—and still do—in republican ideals of liberty. We are lovers of books, of Latin, of Roman liberty. But this love affair has an edge—many of us are ambitious. Tyrants are despised in the republic of letters; yet the tyrannical crime of ambition also taints a humanist's love for books and liberty.[64] The ambition to make our views prevail also makes us close ranks around our activities and ideas, blind to the overlaps between our literary republic and the empire in which our ideas take shape.

. . .

In the aftermath of the murder of Alessandro de' Medici, imperial correspondents were also ambitious, aspiring to help contain the political crisis in Florence and thereby rise in the estimation of Charles V and his governor, Caracciolo, in Milan. One way to measure this ambition is in the envoys' reports of their own diligence or the diligence of others in serving imperial interests. One ambitious correspondent, Bernardo Sanctio, wrote to Caracciolo immediately upon being awakened in the middle of the night by the news of the murder of Alessandro de' Medici. Sanctio seemed disoriented, as if he had begun to write before fully waking up: "In this hour whose date is two a.m." ("In questa hora che somo adi ij di nocte").[65] He confused the names and details of what he had been told, revealing that he was too sleepy to understand the news. But still, he proved his diligence by jumping to his job in the middle of the night.

Another correspondent, Captain Speciano, the imperial envoy in Piedmont, reported to Caracciolo that the Marchese del Vasto was using the imperial writing network quite efficiently on behalf of the emperor. As soon as the death of the duke was confirmed, the marchese ambitiously sent an envoy to Florence with diplomatic credentials, but also with blank sheets bearing his official signature "so that he could write to whomever necessary" ("con lettere credentiali . . . et tre bianchi sottoscritti per potere scrivere a cui serà il bisogno").[66] Filling up blank pages with authorized writing was tantamount to affirming imperial power, and agents demonstrated their ambition by their eagerness to show full support. Phrases like "you probably already heard [this] from another source" ("Penso Vostra Signoria Reverendissima haverà per altri avisi meglio di me") abound in the letters.[67] Or we find extra details and extra gory details that likewise demonstrate an eagerness among envoys to fill up pages and promote their own positions in a network of imperial writers: "[Alessandro] had twenty-four stab wounds—it seems they wanted to surpass the murderers of Julius Caesar, who received only twenty-three—and they cut off the end of his nose and an ear and took it away, it was never found" ("havea xxiiij pugnalate, parmi volessero superare gli occisori di Julio Cesare che non ne diedero se non xxiij, et gli havea levata la ponta del naso, et una orecchia, et portata via che non s'è trovata").[68]

Imperial correspondents consistently emphasized their sense of obligation to the network, especially the obligation to write everything of importance for the maintenance of imperial power, to write reliably and without omissions. As one ambitious correspondent put it, he was writing because he didn't want to "leave anything in his pen" ("non mi pare tenire in la pena alcuna cossa").[69] And his sentiment was registered in the letters of many correspondents, for whom omission was like defaulting on an imperial loan. Just as Cola Montano was ambitious in his efforts to make humanistic ideals of liberty prevail in the city of Milan, so imperial agents were ambitious in their efforts to make the imperial network prevail over any challenges to imperial order.

. . .

Not all imperial agents, however, had the ambition or the vision to see their way to a secure position of political influence in the imperial network. Cardinal Salviati, for example, was excluded from the imperial network because he did not see the Florentine crisis as easily contained.[70] He reported "great confusion and anguish" in Florence ("in Firenze, trovamo le cose in gran confusione et travaglio") and large-scale troop movements of the exile armies.[71] He expressed anger that the imperial troops were not observing the terms of the peace accord: the Florentines had stopped fighting, as the agreement stipulated, but the imperial troops continued to advance and grow, destroying the city and committing atrocities against its citizens ("[le imperiali] sono venute avanti, ingrossano tutto il giorno et destrugono quel povero paese . . . non li bastando di molte ingiurie particolari che ci hanno fatto").⁷² Although many other correspondents also wrote about the troop movements of the exile army, they did so in reports on the 2,500 Spanish reinforcements about to arrive or in the context of affirming Florentine loyalty to Charles V. "News keeps coming in," writes one ambitious correspondent from Parma, "that there has been no change in Florence and the people of that city appear to be on our side [imperiali] and all of the fortresses are loyal to his Majesty" ("Qui si ha nuova anchora come in Fiorenza non è successo per hora nuovità alcuna e che li populari di quella città si monstrano Imperiali e che le forteze tutte stano a devotione di Sua Maesta").⁷³ In the midst of this rosy media coverage, Salviati's more critical report of anguish and war crimes was unlikely to get a hearing.

. . .

Many classical tyrant-slayers lacked the vision to realize their political ambitions, and it was precisely this lack of vision that worried the men in political power. Plutarch quoted Julius Caesar as saying, in reference to Brutus and Cassius, that "he was not troubled by those fat men with good eyesight, but by the pallid and thin" ("egli non era molestato da quegli huomini grassi, e di buona vista, ma da pallidi, e magri").⁷⁴ The term ωχρους, meaning "pallid" or "yellow," may have implied a certain albino aspect. Perhaps following Plutarch, Shakespeare's Julius Caesar was suspicious of Cassius, who also weakened his eyes with too much reading.⁷⁵ Brutus, too, "a man of letters" ("huomo di lettere") and "a scholar of philosophy" ("studioso di filosofia") in Plutarch's *Life of Brutus,* impresses us in Shakespeare for his excessive concern, after hearing of the death of his wife, Portia, to find the book he was reading and to take up reading where he left off.⁷⁶ Although we are ambitious in the republic of letters, we can also be quite shortsighted about how we might make our perspectives prevail.

Pier Paolo Boscoli was a leader of a 1512 conspiracy against Giuliano, Giulio, and Giovanni de' Medici. "He was devoted to literature, although his excessive blondness made it almost impossible for him to see" ("attendea alle lettere come che per la molta biondezza gli fusse quasi impedito il vedere").⁷⁷ Was Boscoli afflicted by albinism, or was it his devotion to literature that made him nearsighted? Luca della Robbia sat with Boscoli on the night before he was decapitated, recording his last thoughts: "And because I knew he was of exceptional intelligence and culture . . . I diligently noted down all of his words . . . so that his example of willpower and strength of character would not be lost after the loss of such a good, noble and generous citizen, a young man of about thirty-two years. He was blond and beautiful and he had an air of kindness, but he was shortsighted." ("E perchè sapevo era di singolare ingegno e di buone lettere . . . notai diligentemente tutte le sue parole . . . e acciò che non si perdesse un tanto e sì fatto esempio di fortezza e gagliardia d'animo, dopo il danno d'uno tanto buono, nobile e generoso cittadino, giovane circa d'anni 32, biondo e bello e di gentile aspetto, ma di vista corta.")[78]

Did Lorenzino also experience visual deterioration? The historian Rudolf von Albertini claimed that Lorenzino's erudition caused Lorenzino and an entire generation of humanistic opponents of Medicean rule to see through a literary filter: "The years of exile, that most of them had spent in literary work" prevented and protected them from looking at the details of the Italian and Florentine political situation. Their vision became fuzzy, and "memories and hopes, little by little removed from reality, had assumed a literary hue."[79]

Often, in the republic of letters, we have the impulse to protect ourselves through the limited vision of close-up literary work, all the while desiring to see the histories we study converge with the histories we live. We are ambitious to fill up these expansive spaces between past and present with a far-reaching vision, but too much close work in the confines of our studies limits these ambitions. Is it possible that the willingness to examine the concrete details and conditions of our scholarship—physical, emotional, intellectual—might facilitate a more expansive vision? Stories of the "myopic politics" of such figures as Boscoli and Lorenzino help us to reflect on the ambitious ways we assemble political knowledge to promote an ideology of a republic of letters that might prevail over "real" politics.[80]

. . .

Folder 3

THE REPUBLIC OF LETTERS AND ITS IMPERIAL CONTEXT

Lorenzino's (wounded) hand was important at the scene of the assault, and the writing hands that represented the murder provided evidence of participation in the social relations of sixteenth-century writing and its transmission (or manumission—"di mano in mano") to the present. In particular, the writing hands of scholars (from then until now) provide evidence of citizenship in a republic of letters, a citizenship that scholars share with Lorenzino, while the writing hands of imperial envoys, military captains, spies, and bureaucrats, conserved under the category "Cancelleria dello Stato di Milano," provide evidence of a particular historical/political context for the republic of letters in 1537. Just as fascist scholarship made this republic of letters problematic for its understanding of "culture" as a conduit to fascist action, so Lorenzino's citizenship in this transhistorical republic was, already in 1537, problematic in its own right; he claimed that when he murdered the duke he had been enacting on the public stage of history the republican ideals he had studied privately as a scholar. His murderous act might encourage us to examine republican politics in the world of letters in relation to its imperial context, a context that also frames, sustains, and permeates our research and ways of knowing.

Scholars have noted that the republic of letters, without any physical support on the political map of Europe, nonetheless became a powerful political fiction that came to govern (and still governs), by means of particular ideologies, the sociabililty of scholars. Ideologies of work in common, progress, commerce, freedom of thought, war, and the body emerged at the outset from the social relations of men of letters to generate social forms, rules, customs, methods, and taboos of research that sustained and perpetuated those relations. As early as 1417 we can see how these ideologies evolved in Francesco Barbaro's 1417 letter to Poggio Bracciolini. Responding to Poggio's missive that listed the manuscripts he had found on an expedition to Germany, the Venetian humanist Barbaro wrote to thank him for working "for the profit of all" and for joining the society of those "who have brought so much support and distinction to this republic of letters" ("pro communi utilitate; qui huic literariae Reip. plurima adjumenta atque ornamenta contulerunt").[81] Their exchange implicitly set a standard of service as a primary requirement for belonging to the literary state.

The republic of letters, a literary state that promoted tolerant, freethinking scholars without masters or monarchs and reined in the tyranny of orthodox opinion, generally discouraged its citizens from acknowledging the service, and sometimes servitude, that was the primary condition of their citizenship. Citizenship in the republic of letters, that is, required scholars to serve "letters" in a particular system of exchange. Citizens were required to engage in the business of letters, exchanging manuscripts, books, catalogs, and information. Aspiring to deposit knowledge as currency in a "general Banck" of ideas or to trade knowledge as commodity in a "free-port" of intellectual exchange, citizens of this republic were "merchants of Letters" who imagined themselves opening up avenues of scholarly "commerce" in the name of profit (and domination).[82]

In the course of their commerce, scholars were sometimes explicit about how their intellectual exchanges differentiated them from the citizens of the political states in which they actually lived. From the fourteenth century, scholar-citizens understood that the Roman ideal of *otium* was a source of rich productivity for them, while for the ordinary citizen the same leisure time might signify lack of business, disgrace, exile, or old age. Indeed, literary *otium*, seen as a virtuous occupation for a man of action who was temporarily removed from the stage of politics, could also provide a model for participating in political life through study and writing.[83] And the proliferation of the genre of "lives" provided citizens of the republic of letters with plentiful models for how to organize the space and time of lettered activity.[84]

Scholars operated with the idea, born from the ideal of monastic life and religious community, that they, too, from the solitude of libraries, archives, and studies, could create communities across time and space with other scholars who were remote and/or dead.[85] With respect to this transhistorical time, Bacon imagined (much later), in the *New Atlantis*, scholars who, across generations, would "pass through the vast seas of time, and make ages so distant to participate of the wisdom, illuminations and inventions, the one to the other."[86] And with respect to transhistorical space, the Royal Society foresaw the need for and provided the common space of a register in which fellows around the world could assemble and unite their individual research experiences.[87] These ideologies of progress and collaborative advances in knowledge that depended on a particular organization of scholarly time and space were cornerstones of statecraft in the republic of letters.[88]

Indeed, this organization of scholarly time and space had the effect of constructing a social border or wall differentiating scholars from those who, for whatever reason, did not participate in the solitary/collaborative activities of literary *otium*. In the *Antibarbarorum Liber*, Erasmus designated this border as *antiquae letterae* and denounced all those who opposed the new literary movement as threats to the republic of letters.[89] It is interesting to note that these enemies of the literary state were, for a number of reasons, incapable of posing a physical threat to its scholar-citizens or even disrupting their commerce. First, the republic of letters presented a united front to its external adversaries, as if it were one body ("comme s'ils faisoient un corps") that served as a shield to the physical-social body of its citizens.⁹⁰ But even in the event of wars and suffering, this "body of letters" could transcend its misery because (1) the republic's treaties with the Muses were stronger than the laws of war ("même les lois de la guerre étaient impuissantes à interrompre les 'commerces' des savants, à briser les pactes conclus avec les muses"), (2) the Muses had effective "remedies for every affliction" ("Il s'en faut sauver du mieux que l'on peut dans le sein des Muses qui ont des remèdes pour toutes afflictions, et qui adoucissent toutes les douleurs si elles ne les guérissent"), and (3) any pain ("malheur") that could not be cured would be, in any case, alleviated by the consolation of study ("A ceux qui comme nous sommes outre cela citoyens de la République des Lettres, il y a une autre sorte de consolation à prendre, ou si ce n'est une consolation, au moins une diversion en un si grand mal").⁹¹ Later, in Section Two, we shall see just how influential the republic's treaties with the Muses would be in seventeenth-century politics of knowledge and state formation. For now, it is important to place the republic of letters in its sixteenth-century context of imperial politics.

. . .

Although the assassination of Alessandro de' Medici by his cousin Lorenzino is represented in historiography as a significant episode in the humanistic republic of letters and in Florentine history, marking the last gasp of Florentine republican aspirations, in fact Florence, in 1536, was no longer an autonomous city-state that could determine its own political destiny. Having married the emperor's daughter, Margherita d'Austria, in 1536, Duke Alessandro had become a client of the Emperor Charles V.⁹² The murder of Alessandro thus created a political crisis not only in Florence but in Milan, as well, dramatically destabilizing the balance of power in the empire for several months. Lorenzino may have intended to emulate the tyrant-slayers he had studied in ancient historiography, and Florentine exiles like Filippo Strozzi may have exalted Lorenzino's act of murder as tyrannicide; nonetheless, the murder had many unintended effects outside the republic of letters in the world of imperial politics. Soon after the assassination, imperial agents from all over Italy wrote to Caracciolo to report to him whatever they knew of the Florentine crisis and to help him with the task of managing it. Many reporters appropriated humanistic motifs conceptualized in the republic of letters in their representation of political events. Precisely against the background of this official imperial record, we can understand how the Florentine crisis was so rapidly contained. Alessandro's successor, Cosimo de' Medici, proved friendly to imperial interests, and imperial forces definitively crushed an army of anti-Medici exiles at the battle of Montemurlo in August of that year.

It is clear from a quick perusal of documents conserved under the category "Chancery of the State of Milan" that imperial domination of Italy and the world was sustained, in part, from the Milanese writing offices. Italy was an important site of the contest between Charles V and the French king François I for the domination of Europe and the world. And this claim to dominion was, in part, produced in the reports to Caracciolo that constructed a dependency of local Italian needs upon imperial management.[93] Complaints of commanders about overdue salaries to soldiers, complaints about the financial burden and offensive behavior of the occupying troops, reports of mutinies, and military budget requests all helped support the authority of imperial administrators by representing the administration of Italy as dependent on the resources of imperial domination.[94] Lorenzino's act of murder meant that still more and unexpected expenditures, especially military, would be required to command continued loyalty to the emperor in the wake of this disruption. Illustrating the extent of this economic dependence of Milan on imperial finances, the imperial ambassador to Genova wrote to Caracciolo in November of 1537: "Milan's necessities are so great that [the gold and silver of] seven Peru's wouldn't be enough to take care of them" ("Son tan grandes las necessidades, que no bastarían siete Peru para remediadarlas").[95] Thus the Milanese chancery was constructed as a center for the circulation of imperial ideology and a kind of settlement office administering Italy as an internal European colony.

A state archive is a "'private' and 'practical' affair" ("Fatto 'privato' e 'pratico'"). The state archive's taxonomy "conserves the internal memory of that institution," the particular interests of those who categorized and inventoried, "their specific historical vicissitudes" ("[l'archivio] conservava sì una memoria, ma era la memoria stessa dell'istituzione, delle sue vicende e dei suoi interessi peculiari"). This private and practical memory, conserved in the history of categories and classifications, "permeates" the environment of the archive and produces the historicity of our research ("E' perciò comprensibile che tale concezione permeasse la realtà dell'archivio").[96] For the year in which Lorenzino murdered the duke, the State Archive of Milan conserves an internal memory of Charles V's Italian administration; although the documents have been rearranged by successive generations of archivists, letters received in the Cancelleria dello Stato di Milano in the year 1537 constitute an important repository for understanding how humanistic thinking, formed in the republic of letters, intersected with imperial politics.

. . .

As we have seen, the construction of a transhistorical republic of letters depended on a protocapitalist rhetoric that represented scholarly practice as a type of commerce, whereby knowledge acquired in the name of profit could be invested in a "general Banck" of ideas or traded in a "free-port" for intellectual exchange. In the case of Lorenzino, many ancient stories of tyrants and tyrant-slayers had been invested in such a "Banck" of political historiography for the "profit" of scholars of republican thought. Because our scholarly practices are formed within this republic of letters, we tend not to ask if there might be some relation between Lorenzino as a literary actor and Charles V as an author of domination; or between a "Banck" or "port" of humanistic ideas about liberty and tyranny and the actual banks and ports that sustained the profits of Charles V's empire. When Lorenzino used his scholarly knowledge of ancient tyrant-slayers to murder the duke and thereby destabilize imperial domination of Italy, he also provided an opportunity for subsequent scholars to challenge the rupture between letters, politics, and the economy and, instead, to question and explore the relation among them. We can see that this relation has been prominent since ancient times, once we look for the economic factors that might efface and mediate the borders between scholars and politics.

. . .

Folder 4

THE TYRANT IN THE FIELD: INTELLIGENCE
GATHERING, ECONOMY, AND THE
MAINTENANCE OF EMPIRE

One prominent story invested in the humanistic "Banck" of ideas that encourages us to explore the relation between empire and the intelligence gathering of scholars and intellectuals is the story of Periander, the tyrant of Corinth, who sent a messenger to Thrasybulus, the tyrant of Miletus, asking how he might best govern his state. In response to this query, Thrasybulus led the messenger to a field and cut off the tallest standing ears of grain, all the while questioning the messenger about his arrival from Corinth. The messenger then returned to Corinth and reported to Periander how he received no response from Thrasybulus and how Thrasybulus seemed crazy to him for the way in which he had destroyed his grain. Upon hearing the messenger's report, Periander knew he had been advised to murder his most powerful subjects: the cutting of the tallest standing grain in Miletus was understood in Corinth as a sign to decapitate the most prominent citizens.[97] The messenger had unwittingly gathered intelligence and transmitted it to the tyrant without understanding its meaning in the realm of politics.

This tale of tyranny was transmitted and codified by a tradition of thinkers, writers, and scholars who found metaphorical stories about political violence central to their own concerns. Aristotle, for example, reminded his readers of Periander and Thrasybulus in his discussion of ostracism as a means of maintaining equality in the state.[98] And Antonio Brucioli translated Aristotle's *Politics* during his exile from Florence after the anti-Medici conspiracy of 1522. Believing that Florence had "fallen into the hands of a most wicked, tyrannical Dionysius" ("la nostra misera patria ... caduta hora nelle mani di questo sceleratissimo Dionisio"), he translated the Greek participle αφαιρουντα ("taking away") as "reaping" the most eminent ears ("mietando le sopraeminenti spighe").[99]

In Livy's retelling of the story, Sextus Tarquinius, the son of the cruel tyrant of Rome Tarquinius Superbus, deceived the citizens of Gabii into thinking that he had fled his father's cruelty and that he wanted to lead them in a war against Rome. At a certain point, Sextus, without arousing suspicion, sent a messenger to ask his father how he might maintain this deceit. The tyrant Tarquin, taking the messenger to a garden near the house, did not respond with words to the queries of the messenger because the messenger seemed unworthy of his trust. Instead, he responded by "beating off the heads of the tallest poppies with a stick" ("summa papaverum capita dicitur baculo decussisse"). Sextus, like Periander, understood that the tallest poppies meant the "principal" or most prominent citizens of Gabii ("i principali cittadini della terra").[100] The "principal citizens," of course, were a threat to the *principe*.[101]

By the end of the fifteenth century, it was common for learned writers, when pondering the relation of rulers to prominent citizens, to remember—explicitly or implicitly—the stories of Thrasybulus and Tarquin. In his *Trattato circa el reggimento e governo della città di Firenze* (commissioned in 1496), the anti-Medici preacher Savonarola implicitly likened the typical tyrant to Thrasybulus and Periander, describing him as one who, "always looking to strike down the most prominent citizens" ("cerca sempre di abbassare *li potenti*, per assicurarsi; e però amazza o fa male capitare *li uomini eccellenti*" [emphasis mine]), would speak in "lopped off" or truncated words ("parole mozze"), advising other princes without really saying what they were to do ("Ha secrete intelligenzie con li altri principi, e poi, non dicendo el secreto che ha, fa consiglio di quello che s'ha a fare").[102] The political historian and diplomat Filippo Cavriani (1535–1606) was more explicit in his use of historical examples in Tacitus to determine that "the best way to suppress rebellions is the one demonstrated first by Thrasybulus and then imitated by Tarquin, the father of Sextus Tarquinius, who struck to the ground the heads of the tallest and most beautiful poppies in the garden" ("la vera strada d'opprimere le ribellioni sia quella mostrataci primieramente da Aristobolo: et imitata poi da Tarquinio di Sesto Tarquinio padre, col gettare a terra i capi dei più belli, et de i più grossi papaveri dell'horto, nel quale venia passeggiando").[103] Finally, in his *Considérations politiques sur le coup d'état* (first published in 1639), the librarian/statesman Gabriel Naudé (1600–1653) advised the tyrant to follow the models of Tarquin and Thrasybulus by "knock[ing] down those minds which appeared above the others" ("il se contentera peut-être d'abattre comme Tarquin les têtes des pavots plus élevés, ou comme Thrasibule et Périandre les esprits qui paraissent par dessus les autres").[104]

Although the transmission of this narrative of the tyrant in the field was actualized by distinct agents operating in different historical moments, the accumulation of these instances produced an overall rhetorical effect. The entire series of tyrants in the field was transmitted (and continues to be handed down) to the scholar of western tradition in one package, as if it were one text punctuated by the recurrence of this tyrannical motif.[105] Or, to put it another way, the entire series of tyrants in the field also produced a field of study. What began in Herodotus as the establishment of an analogic relation between the tallest standing grain and the most prominent citizens became, by virtue of the acquired familiarity of the story, a *topos* (a place or field) of humanistic discourse about tyrants. Francesco Maria Molza was surely deploying this commonplace to taint Lorenzino with tyrannical characteristics when he wrote that Lorenzino, in an escapade in Rome in 1534, had "removed the heads of the tallest statues" ("le teste delle statue, le quali erano più eminenti, levò via").[106]

Shakespeare would also draw on this topos in *Richard II*, placing political advice in the mouth of a gardener:

> Go thou and, like an executioner,
> Cut off the heads of too fast growing sprays
> That look too lofty in our commonwealth,
> All must be even in our government. (3.4.39–42)[107]

The creation of this topos, of course, does not occur in a social or political vacuum but results from the narrative's codification by a particular class of readers in whose interests it is to codify the tyrant's "decapitation" of ears of grain as a referent of its own conceptualizations of power and violence.[108] Every allusion to the tyrant's message of violence refers not only to Herodotus's text but also to the history of reading and writing practices by means of which Herodotus's text is transmitted and codified. But somehow the scholar, even as she is aware of the centrality of this story, seems to overlook how her own gathering of intelligence may also have political consequences, and violent ones at that. Is there a more affirmative possibility here for the scholar, becoming aware of her complicity, to somehow change the story?

Evidence of this relation between the tyrant in the field and the scholar in her field of study emerges only if we consider the scholar's own gathering of intelligence as an active reproduction of Thrasybulus's coded message of violence. The scholar may unwittingly configure herself as a tyrant, understanding from Thrasybulus's message that if she is to maintain her field of study as an inviolate space over which she rules, she must cut down those who would grow up around her. Or, configuring herself more as a citizen in the republic of letters, a scholar will conceive herself more as the messenger, who must exercise a constant vigilance against the encroachment of politics, or, more concretely, will deny any political meaning in her scholarly methods or relations of research. Scholars today often rebel against the ways our intelligence gathering may unwittingly serve the aims of tyranny or imperial domination; we fervently look for scholarly pathways out of this conundrum.

Yet humanism, the ancestor of our modern-day humanities, discourages us from scrutinizing the specificity of humanistic topoi to a particular kind of literacy, a particular political-cultural class, and particular scholarly practices in a political "field" often referred to as the republic of letters.[109] In the transmission of the tyrant in the field from humanist to humanist, the sender and the addressee are also interpretants (or semiotic effects of this transmission), stimulated by their study of the classics to make these texts a part of their daily activity.[110] Just as Thrasybulus transmitted a message of metaphorical decapitation so that Periander would enact the metaphor on the heads of citizens, humanists, in their codification of classical learning, transmit figural messages to other humanists in the hope that they will enact these figures in their own lives. For the most part, this enactment takes the form of discussions, editions, reproductions, interpretations, and citations of the classical texts, all within the confines of the republic of letters. But in cases of narratives of tyranny and freedom, classical texts have been enacted in real political propaganda, real political opposition, and even in real violence, real murders. The tyrant and the scholar, at the end of the day, are both active in their fields. The interpretive activities of each affect the world of the other.

. . .

Perhaps we humanists might find our way out of the dialectic of unwitting service to tyranny by documenting this relation of the intelligence-gathering scholar (understood as messenger) to the practices of ruling, or by juxtaposing this humanistic typology of the tyrant in the field with the practices of ruling of Charles V, who also sent his messengers out into the field to glean intelligence about potential threats to imperial power. Although the particular element of the tallest standing ears of grain was no longer meaningful in the imperial context, Charles V's envoys learned to transmit other kinds of code.

Five months after Lorenzino assassinated Alessandro (on May 30, 1537), Alfonso Piccolomini wrote to Caracciolo from Siena without much news to report but to satisfy his habit of reproducing the imperial point of view for the governor: "From here, I have no news to report that isn't old to you. Still, to fill up the page, I will say that I have understood from the last dispatches from Florence that the count is carrying forward the peace negotiations. . . . The Turkish threat seems to be reviving." ("Di qua non ho cosa da render in cambio a quello di nuovo, ch'io non pensi essergli vecchia, pur per empir il foglio, dirò che per li ultimi avvisi ho di Firenze intendo che 'l signor Conte continovi tuttavia la practica di comporre quelle cose a commune quiete. . . . Le cose del Turco pare che vadino rinfrescando.")[111]

Whether or not there were matters of urgency to report, the job of the imperial reporter was to fill up the page with a standard repertoire of intelligence that had been gathered about Florence and the Turks. On January 5, 1537, a day before Lorenzino murdered the duke, the imperial ambassador to Venice, Lope de Soria, enclosed in his letter a report written in cipher including the intelligence he had gathered that the Turkish ambassador Janus Bey was expected to show up at any time in Venice on his way to scheme with the king of France against the imperial interests of Charles V. To facilitate recognition and capture, Lope described Janus Bey as "a tall man with a somewhat dark complexion and a beard that is white, thick and round, cut like a soldier's. He wears a turban like a Turk, but it is believed that he will take it off along the way and will have his hair cut in the Italian, Greek, and Latin style" when he gets to Italy. ("El Janus bey es hombre alto de cuerpo y la cara algo bruno y barba blanca y espessa y rredonda corta ala stradiota. Trae turnante como Turco perho es de creer que se lo quitara por camino y tendra la cabesa rrasa a la Italiana griego y latino.")[112]

Days after the murder, Lope wrote a longer letter in cipher, underscoring the impression that Janus Bey, in his Italian clothes, might be inconspicuous and difficult to recognize and apprehend.[113] This report also warned Caracciolo of the intentions of the Turks to create an antiimperial alliance with Venice and France: "This Signoria has promised not to get involved in the affairs of Florence, I mean in favoring or helping the exiles in any way that would be of disservice to Your Majesty. [But I know for certain that the death of Duke Alexander pleased them and that they would be happy for Florence to return to freedom.]" ("Esta signoria me ha prometido que no se empachara en las cosas de Florencia digo en dar favor ni ayuda a los foraxidos para cosa que sea contra el servicio de su Maestad. [Perho yo se cierto que les ha plazido la muerte del Duque Alexandro y que holgarian que volviese Florencia en libertad.]")[114] From this moment on, the routine gathering and juxtaposition of intelligence about Florence and the Turks became a standard for naturalizing the image of Florentine dissidents as Other with respect to the aims of empire.

Lope's reports representing Turkish difference and sameness showed how "knowledge" of the "infidel" and its racial subtext were, at least in part, a product of intelligence gathering practices in the Milanese chancery. For the Turkish threat, according to these practices, consisted not so much in any intrinsic difference of Janus Bey as in his ability to blend into a Christian background merely by removing his turban and cutting his hair. To counter this threat of sameness, imperial agents developed habits of gathering intelligence about appearance, clothing, and hairstyles that would maintain a strict differentiation between "self" and "other." Concepts and categories, such as "Turkish" or "Italian, Greek, and Latin," emerged as much from the everyday relations of administrative intelligence gathering as from any stylistic feature of dress and appearance. In this way, the daily gathering of such intelligence in the Milanese chancery became an important force behind Charles V's imperialist goals.

Even in the area of language, it was the sameness, not difference, of the Turkish ambassador that constituted a threat to Christian empire. As Lope noted in his letter of January 8, there was not only the problem that Janus Bey was capable of physically blending in; the fact that he was also fluent in Italian and Latin ("parla Italiano et latino") would create an even greater obstacle to his being identified as an enemy.[115] In the absence of definitive linguistic markers of difference, the duty of recognizing and securing the captivity of Janus Bey was left, by default, to the tireless work of spies, messengers, and other imperial agents in Venice who gathered coded messages about Janus Bey that would lie beyond their grasp as long as the ambassador's whereabouts remained unknown. "When we have this Janus Bey in our hands," remarked Lope, "we will know many things, and this will be of great service to his Imperial Majesty" ("Quando si havesse nelle manj questo Zanusbej . . . si sapria assaj cose, et serria molto servitio alla Cesarea Maesta").[116] Such intelligence efforts generated particular social relations that, in some sense, expressed imperial fantasies to decipher secret codes of political rule.

Lope camouflaged his own intelligence efforts with a report of the more humdrum activity of shopping for the governor. The description of Janus Bey, written in cipher—or secret code—and deciphered upon receipt in the Milanese chancery, was physically enclosed within a letter of January 5 largely about the rugs Lope had bought for the governor to be sent in a separate package. It is clear from this letter that, to glean intelligence about Janus Bey, Lope had to be out and about Venice doing other errands for Caracciolo.[117] And the physical embeddedness of the report in secret code within the pages of the more mundane letter further attests to the crucial relation between everyday activities of intelligence gathering and the production of difference.

In the case of these rugs, Lope's letter points to an extensive familiarity with the marketing of non-European products and particularities in taste among Christian elites: "I send with today's mail three rugs from Cairo, two small ones that cost thirteen ducats each and the medium one, which is square, costs twenty-four ducats, and I'm not sure if Your Most Reverend Lordship will like it. I send it because the medium-sized rectangular one you asked for is not to be found." ("Mando con l'ordinario d'hoggi tappeti tre cairinj duoj piccioli che costano l'uno ducati tredeci, et il meggiano che e quadro costa ducati vintiquatro, non so se piacera a Vostra Reverendissima Signoria, lo mando perche non se ne trova di quelli meggianj da tavola ch'ella mi scrisse.")[118] More important, however, the insistence throughout the letter upon the details of size and price of these rugs and two others from Constantinople shows how the intelligence gathering about the "infidel" emerges, at least in part, from a complex setting of East-West commercial relations and the daily negotiations of such relations in writing.

Finally, Lope's reports represent a microcosm of the relations of hierarchy, power, and service around which imperial intelligence gathering was organized. For example, the five different hands and three languages (Spanish, Italian, and secret code) employed in the single packet that makes up Lope's report of January 5 on the Turks and the rugs point to varying degrees of dominion over writing and written language. It is important to note, in the context of this hierarchy of literacy and power, that Lope's hurried and sprawling hand (represented at the end of his letter) reveals that he received less formal graphic training than his secretary, who penned the body of the letter in a regular italic hand; that his note at the end of the letter, apprising the governor, in brief, of the imminent arrival of the Turkish ambassador, suggests that Lope, who had read the report in cipher, did not want his secretary to know its contents; that Lope's skills in Italian and the Spanish language of the report in cipher point to the everyday ramifications of Spain's presence in "Italy" and the bilingual basis of imperial exchange;[119] and that the deciphering of the coded report points to a cadre of specialists working in the Milanese chancery.

The conceptual construction of Janus Bey as an enemy "Other" loomed so large in the scene of imperial dominion that we tend to lose sight of how the writing relations and intelligence-gathering practices of diplomats, secretaries, spies, and code specialists were organized around the production and maintenance of this concept. Sent out in the field, the imperial agents of Charles V apprehended the relations of hierarchy, power, service, and "Otherness" in which they were enmeshed. The actual movements of Janus Bey, the shopping for rugs, the description of Janus Bey in cipher, and so on became expressions of these relations and messages to the emperor of how to maintain his dominion. As Charles V and all of his agents recorded their movements and intelligence-gathering activities in prose, they became themselves the *cavalieri erranti*, marching out to defend Christendom against the encroachments of the "infidel." We scholars today might investigate and transform the ways in which our own social practices of intelligence gathering produce "Otherness" and enmity and thereby evolve beyond the story of the tyrant in the field.

. . .

In his *Historia verdadera de la conquista de la Nueva España (True History of the Conquest of New Spain)* (1550–84), Bernal Díaz del Castillo tells of the amazement he and his soldiers felt along the way to Mexico City as they came upon cities, towers, and buildings resembling the marvels described in "the best" of all romances of chivalry, the *Amadís de Gaula* (1508): "When we saw so many cities and villages built in the waters [of the lake] and other large towns on dry land, and that straight and level causeway leading into Mexico City, we were amazed, and we said that it was like the enchanted things related in the book of Amadis" ("Desde que vimos tantas ciudades y villas pobladas en el agua, y en tierra firme otras grandes poblazones, y aquella calzada tan derecha y por nivel cómo iba a México, nos quedamos admirados, y decíamos que parecía a las cosas de encantamiento que cuentan en el libro de Amadís").[120]

Many scholars have cited this and other passages in the literature of the conquest of New Spain as evidence of the extent to which romances of chivalry filled the imaginations of soldiers, explorers, and conquerors and motivated them to perform military feats, convert "heathen" souls to Christianity, and enrich the Christian empire with lucrative trade ventures.[121] According to Leonard, "The more literate . . . adventurers were likely to be addicted" to the romances of chivalry, from Charles V—who was known to treasure the romance *Belianis de Grecia* and to take with him at least two chivalric novels into retirement—to the lowly soldier, who gathered courage in battle from the tales of valorous knights, believing them to be true.[122]

We, modern Renaissance scholars, may deplore the deleterious effects produced by knights errant as they inspired deeds of conquest, genocide, and economic exploitation. But we tend not to analyze the particular sixteenth-century diplomatic, economic, and military settings in which this imperial ideology became a social possibility. Although each of these settings was characterized by the daily intelligence-gathering practices and relations of particular secretaries, diplomats, administrators, entrepreneurs, and military commentators, it is difficult to discern the local practices and relations made in prose that shaped the imperial ideology of, say, Charles V, historiographers, culture brokers, or the canonical epic poet Ludovico Ariosto.

. . .

One important scholar/agent who gathered intelligence in the service of imperial domination was Gonzalo Fernández de Oviedo, author of the *Historia general y natural de las Indias* (1535). Official historiographer of the Indies, military governor of the fortress of Santo Domingo, and author also of a chivalric romance, Oviedo was particularly well qualified to gather intelligence about New World plants and animals from a "European" imperial perspective. In book 12, chapter 7 of his *Historia general*, Oviedo described the iguana, representing this creature in the context of the European trade in exotic specimens and facts. For European readers, part of the monstrosity (and marvel) of the iguana was the taxonomic confusion this creature produced—Oviedo related that it was difficult to know if the iguana belonged to the category of animal or fish.

But the most marvelous aspect of Oviedo's account was the mystery of the iguana's eating habits:

> It is such a quiet animal, that it neither screams nor moans nor makes any sound, and it will stay tied up wherever you put it, without doing any damage or making any noise, for ten or twenty days and more without eating or drinking anything. Some say, on the contrary, that if you give the iguana a little cassava or grass or something similar, it will eat it. But I have had some of these animals sometimes tied up in my house, and I never saw them eat, and I had them watched day and night, and in the end, I never knew nor was able to understand what they were eating in the house, and everything that you give them to eat remains whole.

> [Es tan callado animal, que ni grita, ni gime, ni suena, y está atado a do quier que le pongan, sin hacer mal alguno ni ruido, diez o veinte días e más, sin comer ni beber cosa alguna. Mas, si se lo dan, también como un poco de cazabi o hierba, o cosa semejante, segund dicen algunos. Pero yo he tenido algunos destos animales atados en mi casa algunas veces, e nunca los vi comer, e los he fecho aguardar e velar, e en fin, no he sabido ni podido entender qué comían, estando en casa, e todo lo que les dan para que coman, se está entero.][123]

With the inclusion of these marvelous facts about the iguana, Oviedo affirmed the importance of the trade in exotic specimens and facts to the organization of Europe's dominion over newly encountered civilizations and to the marketing of his own *Historia general*. Just as Lorenzino effaced the borders between the republic of letters and imperial relations of ruling when he murdered the duke, Oviedo showed how organizations of knowledge about the New World were directly intertwined with relations of capital developed in the context of imperial rule.

Oviedo produced his New World knowledge of the exotic, not only in relation to what he actually observed in the field, but in the context of everyday social and economic relations with other imperial agents, diplomats, writers, and culture brokers. One such important relation embedded in Oviedo's descriptions was his relation to Giovanni Battista Ramusio, secretary of Venice's Council of Ten, Italian publisher of Oviedo's *Historia*, and Oviedo's partner in an international trade venture. Oviedo's representation of the iguana's nourishment was, in fact, an address to his Italian publisher and business partner Ramusio:

> Having written the above, two of the bigger iguanas were brought to me, and we ate part of one in my house, and the other I had put away, tied up, to send to Venice to the Magnificent Mr. Joan Baptista [Ramusio], chancellor of the Signoria, and it was tied to a post on the patio of this fortress of Santo Domingo for more than forty days, during which time, it never ate any of the many things it was given; and I was told that these animals ate only earth, and I had a hundred pounds of dirt put in a barrel as the iguana's provisions, so that there would be no lack of it at sea. And I hope that while I am correcting these treatises, ships will arrive to let us know if the iguana arrived alive in Spain and with what nourishment. When I arrived in Spain in 1546, however, I found out from the one who took the animal that it had died at sea.
>
> [Teniendo escripto lo que es dicho, me trujeron dos animales déstos de los mayores, y del uno comimos en mi casa, y el otro hice guardar, atado, para lo enviar a Venecia al magnífico Micer Joan Baptista, secretario de la Señoría, e estuvo en el patio desta fortaleza de Sancto Domingo atado a un poste más de cuarenta días, que nunca comió de cosa de cuantas se le dieron; y dijéronme que no comían estos animales sino tierra, y yo hice que para su matalotaje le metiesen un quintal della en un barril, porque en la mar no le faltase. Y espero, en tanto que estoy corrigiendo estos tractados, que vernán naos para saber si llegó vivo a España, e con qué mantenimiento. Pero llegado en España el año de mill e quinientos e cuarenta e seis, supe, del que trujo aquel animal, que se le murió en la mar.][124]

Statements about the iguana's exotic eating habits thus ultimately refer to this ill-fated expedition and to Oviedo's relation with Ramusio, showing how the exotic was constructed in the context of imperial social relations.

Only in the context of colonial trade companies and the relations of inequality and domination required to sustain such ventures could it have made sense to send an iguana to Venice in a barrel of dirt. Statements like "I never saw them eat" or "Everything that you give them to eat remains whole" were selected and organized not only to rationalize the iguana's expedition in a barrel of dirt but to promote a market of readers and investors in New World exotica and fantastic quests.[125] To such readers and investors it made no difference if the iguana lived or died or what kinds of exploitation would be required to extract profit from the New World. The shipment of the iguana made perfect sense because it satisfied a need to justify economic exploitation with new knowledge and profits. It thus becomes imperative to investigate this concept of sense or reason (and the intelligence gathering on which it was based), as it characterized the production of the exotic in sixteenth-century Europe.

In some ways, Oviedo's relation with the Venetian Ramusio was emblematic of the intercultural relations that sustained the profit-making dynamics of empire.[126] Oviedo informs us that when he sent off a live iguana to Venice in 1540, Ramusio was the secretary or chancellor of Venice's Council of Ten. He had come into contact with Oviedo through the official imperial network: Andrea Navagero, the official historiographer of the Venetian Republic, had established relations with Pietro Martire and with various members of the Council of the Indies in Seville and probably met Oviedo there in 1525 when Oviedo was preparing the abridged version of his *Historia general*. Navagero not only put Oviedo and Ramusio in contact with each other but saw to it that Oviedo's *Sumario* or abridged version of his *Historia* would be published in Venice in Italian in 1534.[127] In terms of editorial activities, then, Venice had become a capital of cultural speculation on narratives of the Spanish conquest: the publishing of these accounts always guaranteed good profits.[128]

The epistolary relation between Oviedo and Ramusio, who never met in person, was essentially one between an informant from the periphery and a metropolitan broker of knowledge. Because of his powerful position as knowledge broker and important administrator of the Venetian state, Ramusio was sometimes better informed about New World developments than his informants and at times even shaped the construction of Oviedo's "reality" by providing accounts from other correspondents. It is important to see Oviedo's collection of facts and intelligence about Hispaniola in relation to the interests of publishers like Ramusio, who would market these facts in a particular ideological frame. And it is in this context of Oviedo's relation with his Venetian knowledge broker that the rationale for producing the exotic emerges.

Ramusio had constructed and cornered a market of consumers of news about the New World that included traditional intellectuals, merchants, bankers, and a general reading public that somehow identified itself in the drama of New World encounters. To attract this general reading public, Ramusio organized his collection of New World accounts around the cultural paradigm of chivalry and conquest whose traditional function in European literature was to idealize and disguise the waging of war in the garb of epic poetry.[129] Oviedo's literary talents as an author of a chivalric romance and his military role as governor of the fortress of Santo Domingo made him a perfect fit for this paradigm;[130] his collection of intelligence about New World animals and plants and his expedition of the exotic iguana to Venice served to romanticize, in the guise of natural history, his economic partnership with Ramusio, a relation that entailed intense exploitation of New World resources and people.[131]

On January 1, 1538, two years before Oviedo packed up the iguana, Oviedo and Ramusio invested four hundred gold ducats in an economic partnership to which they committed themselves for six years. According to their agreement, this money would be used to buy Italian and Venetian goods to send to Santo Domingo, where Oviedo would sell them at a profit and use the money to buy liquors and sugars to sell in Cadiz, again, obviously, at a profit: "And on behalf of the company there shall be a person in Cadiz, designated by the said secretary and procurator of St. Mark, who shall receive the merchandise to be forwarded to the said commandant in Santo Domingo . . . and who shall sell syrups and sugars [licuori et zucchari]."[132] The contract they signed formed a written relationship that not only promoted the exploitation of new markets but made it profitable to construct exotic facts to attract more investors.

This partnership, tracing the route of the infamous rum triangle, was among the first of its kind and provided a model for subsequent, larger-scale enterprises. In 1548, another group of Venetians founded an even more intercultural trading company, including partners from Milan and Antwerp and tracing a trade route that included Venice,

Seville, Mexico, Peru, and Constantinople. This time, the investment was much more significant—thirty thousand ducats to be invested in mirrors, other glass objects, and books. Although this venture was unsuccessful, it was replicated by the heirs of Tommaso Giunti, the publishers of Ramusio's collection *Navigazioni e viaggi*. In 1560, these editorial magnates invested a part of their publishing profits in a trading company that would take earnings from the selling of books and glass products and turn them into sugar and pepper for European markets.[133] If the trade in exotic facts and the trade in exotic commodities had once served separate functions in the construction of imperial domination, now these two functions were completely intertwined.

Oviedo's gathering of exotic facts about the iguana was necessary to the construction of his economic and cultural relationship with Ramusio. Indeed, the description of the iguana's eating habits and its expedition to Venice in a barrel of dirt were two important building blocks in the construction of future trading relations. The business contract between Oviedo and Ramusio provides an especially important key to understanding the production and marketing of the exotic in Oviedo's *Historia general* and Ramusio's *Navigazioni e viaggi*. Economic relations and profits opened up channels for the trade in exotic specimens and facts, just as cultural exchange participated in the promotion of more business and profit. The appeal of the exotic to readers and investors thus became the frame in which intelligence about the New World was gathered and a key element for understanding how intelligence gathered in the republic of letters and intelligence gathered in imperial settings mutually reinforced one another. Making visible this frame, do we have the opportunity to understand and transform the way we scholars make our profits?

...

As a postscript to this account, it is important to add that about fifty years after Alessandro's death, the assassination was reconstructed, printed, illustrated, and reprinted in verse. Lorenzino was represented, in these later reconstructions, as a traitor so dangerous that the devil refused to welcome him to hell for fear that he would betray Pluto and try to usurp his domain.[134] When the devil told Lorenzino (in 1584) that he was "hated by every person in the world" ("Tu sei in odio al mondo à tutta gente"), he meant the Christian imperial world that extended by this time from Europe to the Americas and Asia. Lorenzino's alienation from this Christian world was explicitly constructed in terms of his allegiance to Islamic peoples and places.[135] "Since I don't think God will ever forgive my sin," Lorenzino confessed, "I think I will go to Turkey to renounce the faith. . . . I don't believe that in pagan parts of the world there is one Tartar, Moor, Turk, or Catalan who has been crueler than I." ("Tanto che mai non penso che da Dio / questo peccato mi sia perdonato / . . . Mi penso . . . ire in Turchia à rinegar la fede / . . . Non credo nella parte de pagani / un piu di me sia stato si crudele / Tartari, neri, Turchi, o Catelani.")[136] Lorenzino, in these verses, was transformed from the humanist who enacted his learning on the stage of politics to the epitome of an imperial traitor. As an emblematic type, he joined the heroes and villains of empire whose stories were mass-produced, collected, and added to the already established intelligence-gathering machinery of imperial dominion. Today, we scholars, as we gather intelligence in our fields, might instead explore our potential to focus on all that our "heroes" and "villains" (past and present) hold in common.

. . .

Folder 5

THE POLITICS AND ECONOMY OF GRAIN

Thrasybulus cut the tallest standing ears of grain, and in the ancient world this act, establishing an analogic relation between grain and humans, had political implications that extended well beyond agriculture.[137] In ancient historiography, Ceres, the goddess of grain, often gave her blessing to those who rid their cities of the scourge of tyranny.[138] And in the *Discourses*, Machiavelli cited the following verses by Juvenal to acknowledge the role of Ceres in the violent downfall of tyrants: "Most tyrants go down to the son-in-law of Ceres by slaughter and injury, a bloody death" ("Ad generum Cereris sine caede et vulnere pauci/descendunt reges et sicca morte tiranni").[139] Domizio Calderino and Giorgio Valla commented on these verses: "To the son-in-law of Ceres. To Pluto who raped Persephone, the daughter of Ceres."[140] Calderino and Valla remind us that Ceres was not just the goddess of grain; her name also conjured up stories of tyranny, sexual violence, and loss. Perhaps Machiavelli understood Ceres' loss of Persephone in relation to his own political end. Exile at Sant'Andrea in Percussina, bodily torture in the Bargello, the vivid memory of being arrested for his complicity in a republican plot against the Medici

(1512), grief and rage against the Medici: Could these verses of Juvenal have offered him a vision of regaining his lost "daughter," the Florentine republic?

Aside from these associations between politics and Ceres, the story of the tyrant in the field also drew attention, even within the republic of letters, to the politics of grain and those citizens made hungry by a tyrant's greed for money. In ancient times, this greed was represented in the association between the first coins minted in Lydia and the tyranny of Gyges. As Marc Shell noted, just as "coinage was associated with the Lydians, so too was political tyranny. . . . [Gyges] was the archetypal tyrant as he was the archetypal minter."[141] And Alessandro de' Medici was both a minter, when he commissioned from Benvenuto Cellini a coin or medal ("medaglia") to portray him, and a ruler who earned the accusation of tyranny, in part for his levy of a "dishonest, harsh and unjust" tax on grain ("un'aspra gravezza . . . sulla macina . . . disonesta, acerba ed ingiusta").[142]

Perhaps the most prominent (tallest-standing) opponent of Alessandro's tyranny was Filippo Strozzi, a large-scale investor in and supplier of grain who signed contracts to supply and distribute Sicilian grain in Rome in the first years of Alessandro's rule (1531–33). For several periods during the year 1532, Strozzi held the exclusive rights to sell grain to Roman bakers, and during a critical shortage of grain in 1533 he received a commission to supply Sicilian grain that testified to the Romans' hunger.[143] But imperial politics soon intervened to the detriment of this lucrative business relation.

Almost as soon as Strozzi had purchased the grain from Sicilian suppliers, Charles V's viceroy in Sicily placed an imperial embargo on grain exports to Rome.[144] An additional investment was therefore required. This time, Strozzi purchased French grain from Brittany and Picardy. The shipping and overhead expenses considerably diminished the margin of profit, but, as if such bad fortunes weren't enough, some of the grain was lost en route, and some arrived damaged. By the end of the summer of 1534, Strozzi's agents were gouging the Romans, doubling the price of grain to make up for losses.[145] Roman consumers made violent assaults against these middlemen, and when Pope Clement died in September 1534, the people of Rome brought a lawsuit against Strozzi, demanding seven hundred thousand scudi in damages for his failure to provide grain at a fair price.[146] Did Strozzi's involvement in the politics of grain, along with his active support of the anti-Medici exile army, make him a "too fast growing spray" in the imperial "commonwealth"? It would seem so. Like Perillus, who devised a bronze bull for the torture of prisoners under the tyranny of Phalaris and died as a prisoner of that same structure, Strozzi died in the Fortezza da Basso, whose construction he had helped to finance.[147]

Strozzi's economic involvement in grain commerce no doubt had to do with economic motives of investments, profits, and supplying basic needs. But Strozzi was also a humanist, a translator of Polybius, and a leader among the anti-Medici exiles. Here, in the relation between the tyrant in the field (as a historiographic topos) and Strozzi the scholar and grain magnate, the humanistic tradition that associated Ceres with republican politics intersected with the economic domain of grain commerce.[148] People needed bread to survive, but inscribed in this economic necessity were stories of the rape of Persephone connected to the seasons and the harvest. The financial setback suffered by Strozzi as a result of the imperial embargo had to do with grain from Sicily, sacred to Ceres because it was here that Pluto raped Persephone. Like Ceres, Strozzi mourned the loss of his daughter, Luisa, whose death was related to a sexual insult she received from Duke Alessandro. This intersection between culture and economics was busy with sexual politics as well.

. . .

Folder 6

SEXUAL POLITICS AND IMPERIAL
DOCUMENTATION PROJECTS

In the humanistic tradition, sexual politics has always played an important role in the downfall of tyrannical regimes. Machiavelli's assertion that "the rape of Lucretia deprived the Tarquins of their rule" ("lo eccesso fatto a Lucrezia tolse lo stato ai Tarquinii") is axiomatic.[149] But "erotic offenses" (ερωτικη ξυντυχια) have always been important in maintaining and disrupting relations of rule, ever since the first story of tyrannicide told by Thucydides.[150] This was a story of the bonds of love between two men, Harmodius and Aristogiton, and of the unsuccessful attempts of the tyrant Hipparchus to seduce Harmodius by abusing his position. Since Harmodius did not respond and Hipparchus had no intention of using force, the tyrant decided that Harmodius's sister would bear the burden of his unrequited love. Hipparchus first invited and then forbade Harmodius's sister to take part in a procession of basket carriers. His hope was that Harmodius would feel that he was complicit in this insult to his sister and feel great shame as a result. But this last offense against Harmodius's sister, too great for Harmodius and Aristogiton to bear, incited them to devise a reckless plot against the life of Hipparchus. As Aristotle, Justinus, and others transmitted the story, the "erotic offenses" against Harmodius and the love between Harmodius and Aristogiton slowly disappeared from the account.[151] Eventually, it was told that Hipparchus had raped Harmodius's sister and that Harmodius and Aristogiton had murdered Hipparchus to avenge this act of heterosexual violence. A story of a homosexual triangle was made straight, and every subsequent story of tyrannicide was predicated upon an act of heterosexual violence.[152] As historiographers and diplomats wrote to and for each other, they insisted on the replication of heterosexual rape in the representation of their political relations.

. . .

In the aftermath of Alessandro's assassination, imperial officials in Milan privileged a particular coverage of events that blamed anti-imperial views for provoking this political crisis. The case of Cardinal Salviati, opponent of imperial domination, shows how the Milanese chancery required critics of empire to change their critical tone if they wanted to become part of the official record. On January 14, Caracciolo wrote to Salviati and other opponents of empire, offering them material rewards for imperial service: "I wanted to remind you that now is the time to perform great service, . . . repressing every insurrection . . . and making everyone straight on the straight path to universal gain. And you can be sure that His Imperial Majesty . . . will keep good accounts of the services performed for the personal and universal gain of the state. Your honor and profit will accrue from those services." ("Ho voluto recordarli che hora il tempo è che la gli può fare servitio grande . . . reprimendo ogni sedizione . . . et driciando ognuno al camino dritto . . . al benefitio universale et Vostra Signoria Reverendissima può essere sicura che la Cesarea Maestà . . . tenerà bono conto delli offitii si farano in benefitio particulare et universale di quello stato et ne seguirà honore et utile a Vostra Signoria Reverendissima.")[153]

Using the terms *drizzare* (to straighten) and *dritto* (straight), Caracciolo made clear that "making everyone straight" entailed not only repressing anti-imperial sentiments and activities but forging a written link with the chancery of Milan. Although, of course, these terms have no lexical connection to our contemporary use of the term *straight* for "heterosexual," readers will certainly not miss the import of his injunction to "make everyone straight," keeping everyone within the bounds of a tradition of tyrannicide that required an instance of heterosexual assault by the tyrant and the rapid succession of a new ruler. This is one of many moments in which imperial writing about Lorenzino acknowledged, with the purpose of containing, the disturbing potential of Lorenzino's act.

...

Four years after Harmodius and Aristogiton murdered Hipparchus (510 B.C.), Lucius Junius Brutus was celebrated as the founder of Roman liberty because he expelled the Tarquin tyrants to avenge the rape of Lucretia. Lucius Junius Brutus, the one who feigned stupidity, then evolved into Marcus Brutus, the melancholy scholar who murdered Caesar (and Lorenzino, the duke's confused and ambivalent cousin, who brooded over books). Some accounts tell us that part of Marcus Brutus's motivation for murdering Caesar was his desire to vindicate his sister's and mother's honor, which had been stained by their adulterous affairs with Caesar.[154] This tradition was still very much alive in Florence in 1400, when Coluccio Salutati, following Suetonius, wrote: "Everyone knows that Brutus was the son of Caesar. . . . We can read in the story of Caesar's assassination that when the dictator saw Brutus rushing towards him with a drawn sword, he said in Greek: 'And you, my son?'"[155]

Aristotle and Machiavelli explicitly theorized the relation of sexual violence to the downfall of tyrants.[156] And Lorenzino de' Medici followed in this formulaic tradition when, on the evening of January 6, according to historiographic accounts, he persuaded Alessandro to come to his place without bodyguards by promising him the sexual favors of a chaste noblewoman. Alessandro was infamous for insulting noblewomen, climbing convent walls, and every other activity typically associated with a tyrant's lust.[157] Lorenzino, as we have seen, wanted to figure himself as a "new Brutus" also in this detail of vindicating the honor of offended chaste noblewomen.

...

On January 11, four days after the murder of the duke, a writer in the Milanese chancery expressed annoyance that no reliable information was coming in from Lope de Soria in Venice. He drafted a message to Lope: "Here we have heard by way of Bologna that the Duke of Florence has been murdered. And because the letters are of the 8th and 9th from Bologna and today it is the night of the 11th and we haven't heard anything else, it is thought that the news is not true." The writer then crossed out these lines and substituted with a different pen: "Here, we have heard that some disaster has befallen the Duke of Florence but it is not believed." ("~~Qui se e inteso per via di bologna chel Duca di fiorenza sia stato amazato. Et perche le lettere sono de viij et viiij da bologna et Hogi siamo a li xj ala nocte et non se e inteso altro se existima che la nova non sia vera . . .~~ Qui se inteso che sia occorso qualche sinistro al Signor Duca de fiorenza perho non se li presta fede.")[158] Implicit in this message was the Milanese writer's censure of Lope for leaving Caracciolo in the dark. He had fallen short of his obligations to keep the governor informed about everything of importance to the interests of empire.

Lope, of course, had not been remiss. His letter, dated January 10 and penned by a secretary, was on the way. He explained that after he had sent his last letter Lorenzino had arrived in Venice, reporting that he had murdered the duke, and then had left for some undisclosed place. After signing off and dating the letter, Lope continued dictating to his secretary: "I subsequently heard that the aforesaid Lorenzo went with Filippo Strozzi in the direction of Florence and that he murdered the duke in his house where the aforesaid duke used to frequently meet a woman" ("Ho doppo inteso che il detto Lorenzo e andato con Philippo Strozzi alla volta di Fiorenza, et che amazzo il Duca in casa sua dove soleva andare spesso con una donna il detto duca").[159] This news must have been too important for Lope to leave it to his secretary to write. He took the pen from his secretary and continued in his own, less professional and more interested hand: "This matter is of great importance for the affairs of his family. No one knows this better than Your Most Reverend Sanctity, for this reason, it is so important for me to notify you so quickly. . . . I believe that all these [Venetian] signori are pleased about the death of the aforementioned duke and would be pleased for Florence to return to her former liberty." ("Questa cosa e di molta importanza per le cose di sua casata. So che vostra Reverendissima signoria el sa meglio che altro, percio importa asai che sua Maesta sia presto avisata. . . . Non mi par che despiaza a tuti questi signori la morte del detto duca ne che ritorne Fiorenza in la antica liberta, etc.")[160]

What especially interests me in this letter from Lope is the direct link made between the duke's heterosexual exploits, the murder, and the importance of informing Caracciolo. Contrary to what we might expect, the motif of Alessandro's violation of the honor of a noblewoman that led to his ambush is not unique to the more "literary" historiographic texts, seemingly related to ancient historiography and penned and published by men of letters, but is commonly presented also in these unedited reports to Caracciolo. It is in this common ground between humanistic historiography and archival records that we may investigate the overlapping interests between literary or humanistic and imperial writing projects. Letters to the Milanese state demonstrated the importance of representing heterosexuality as an aid to containing the disruptiveness of Alessandro's assassination.

. . .

In the winter of 1534, many festivities were organized in Florence with the purpose of surrounding the duke with beautiful noblewomen. Luisa, the daughter of Filippo Strozzi, was invited to all of these gatherings. Married to Luigi Capponi, she was renowned in her city for her good qualities and morals, for her noble origin and wealth. She was "just as honest and virtuous, as she was beautiful, fine and charming" ("non meno onesta e virtuosa, che bella, nobile e di leggiadre maniere").[161]

Luisa was present when Alessandro came to dinner dressed as a monk and accompanied by Giuliano Salviati, an evil and reprehensible man ("uomo di cattiva vita e di biasimevole stato").[162] In keeping with his character, Salviati found the occasion to offend Luisa Strozzi with his gestures and words and told her that he "wanted to have sex with her at any price" ("voleva giacer con seco a ogni modo"). He even went so far as to boast in public of his offense to Luisa's honor, an offense from which she never recovered.[163]

On March 13, 1534, Salviati was assaulted on the street as he was returning late at night from Palazzo Medici. Piero Strozzi was arrested and imprisoned as a suspect in the injury of Salviati and proved to be a very uncooperative defendant. After mocking and deriding his examiners, Piero wrote a sonnet to the judges asking to be released because he was of noble birth and only the dregs of society deserved to be so mistreated. Trying to deflect blame from himself to the real offender, Duke Alessandro, he ended his sonnet with this line: "I am not the one who is watching over the gardens" ("Ch'io non son pero quel, ch'ha in guardia gli orti").[164] The case of Salviati's injuries was never solved, and Piero was set free.

. . .

Writing to Caracciolo in Milan, reporters took care to qualify the reliability of the news they were transmitting in relation to Lorenzino's "horrendous" betrayal of the duke. One message of these collected records seems to be that a report on Lorenzino's betrayal was proof of the reporter's own loyalty to empire. On January 11, Alessandro Landriano, the imperial envoy to Parma, wrote to Caracciolo, taking care to assure the governor that the truth of the story had been confirmed by various sources: "I think you have received some other letters in which I communicated the horrendous death of his most illustrious Duke Alessandro de' Medici, and although I wrote that it was of dubious truth, now it is coming to be confirmed that last Saturday at eight o'clock in the evening, while His Excellency was coming from pleasure, he was disemboweled by Lorenzo de' Medici" ("Penso . . . ne habbi recevutto de le altre ne le quali li ho significato la morte horenda dello illustrissimo Signor duca Alexandro de Medici e anchora chio lhabi scritta dubiosa pure si va accertando come Sabato passato alle octo hore de nocte, venendo sua Excellenza da Piacere fu sventrato da Laurentio de Medici").[165]

. . .

On December 4, 1534, Luisa Strozzi, dining at the home of her sister Maria Ridolfi, was seized by violent stomach pains and died two hours later. The doctors verified that she had been poisoned, and many theories were advanced to explain why. Some said the duke had had her poisoned because she had rudely denied him the honor of her presence at a party.[166] Others thought her own relatives had poisoned her as a preventive remedy against the duke's violence.[167] The Strozzi family, considering Alessandro to be an enemy, suspected "he would want to stain Luisa's virtue or their family's distinction with deception or fraud" ("volesse nella persona della Luisa con qualche inganno, o con qualche fraude imporre alcuna macchia all'onestà, e alla chiarezza del sangue loro").[168] In any case, there was a consensus that Luisa had become a victim of wicked times and men. With no social support for her virtue and innocence, she slipped easily into her final misery ("L'onestà e l'innocenza, la quale non ha altro aiuto, che se stessa, cade agevolmente in ultima miseria").[169]

∴

Bernardo Sanctio, providing the fullest account of Alessandro's sexual activity the evening of his murder, took great pains to qualify his report by referring, as did Landriano, to conflicting opinions. He wrote on January 13: "Having arrived in Bologna, I have found true information about the Florentine event and so [I write] to your lordship. *They say* that because the duke was the cousin and very close friend of Lorenzo . . . , a very melancholy young man, and because he had total trust in Lorenzo, Alessandro used Lorenzo as a pimp to obtain a certain noblewoman. *Others say* it was a nun. *Others say* it was a widowed sister of Lorenzo. *All concur* that one Saturday night Alessandro arranged to go to Lorenzo's house to have there a woman." ("Essendo arrivato in Bologna ho trovato vera Informatione del caso de Fiorenza et cosi ad Vostra Signoria. Dicono che essendo el Signor Duca cugino et molto amici strecto de Lorenzo . . . giovene molto malinconico et fidandose estremamente in dicto Lorenzo, lo uso per mezano per otenere una certa gentildonna. Altri dicono una Monicha. Altri una sorella vidua de dicto Lorenzo. Tutti concorreno che uno sabbato ad sera conpose de ire a sua casa per havere li una donna.")[170]

Sanctio never abandoned this balanced style of reporting on Alessandro's lust, even bringing in the humanistic perspective that perceived Lorenzino as a melancholy Brutus figure who thought too much: "Lorenzo says the only motive of his action was to liberate his city. *Others say* it was the honor of his sister. *Many say* that it was the melancholy humor of this young man, whom they say was very oppressed by his constant pensiveness and resemblance to Brutus. Whatever was the cause, the poor duke carelessly let himself get caught in the trap, and because of his lack of caution he lost his life and moved the affairs of Florence once again on the chessboard." ("La causa che habia mosso dicto Lorenzo de Medici ad tale effecto da lui e narrato essere stato solo per liberare la patria. Altri dicono per honore della sorella, molti che e stato uno humore malencolico de questo giovene del qual dicono essere molto oppresso per stare sempre cogitabondo et de effigie simile al Bruto, quaecumque fuerit causa, il povero Duca se e lassato pigliare alla trappola et per sua advertentia ce ha posta la vita et ha anchor mosse le cose de fiorenza in su el tavoleri.")[171] And indeed, whatever was the truth of the incident, it was clear in these reports that all of the correspondents strove to provide reliable information to the Milanese chancery about Alessandro's sexual desires as a part of their job of upholding imperial authority.

These reports in the Milanese state chancery encourage us to reflect on the procedures through which imperial correspondents, in their foregrounding of Alessandro's heterosexual desires, may have been normalizing such representations as appropriate knowledge for governing. But such images of masculinity were represented in these reports also as the passion, expressed by many correspondents, for creating homosocial writing networks among the loyal supporters of empire. This construction of homosocial loyalty among these correspondents also depended on Lorenzino's betrayal of the duke. The collection of reports affirming this betrayal had the double effect of, first, reinforcing the loyalty among male supporters of empire, and second, naturalizing male heterosexual lust as a part of that bond among men. In this way, the heterosexual motive (or history made straight) and its homosocial subtext became linked to the documentation project of the Milanese chancery. If the assassination of the duke had a real potential, as many thought, of disrupting imperial rule, this disruption was effectively contained by all the reporters who made Alessandro's heterosexual politics part of the official record.

. . .

Folder 7

THE (COM)PASSIONATE HAND

spada (sword) passione παθειν patior (I suffer)[172]

As we have seen, the sword, an instrument useful for lopping off heads, is also an instrument of "passion." With a sword, the tyrant threatens to assault noble women. In one tradition of verbal intuitions, sword (*spatha*) and passion (*passio*) share a common ground in the words for suffering and compassion (*patior*, παθειν).[173] In another typology of lexical formation, the sword is related to the hand (or fist) that holds it. The hand was important at the scene of the assault. The hand was and is still important at the scene of writing.

ξιφος (sword) spada
    ξιφος εγχειριδιον spada **pugnale**
        εγχειριδιον χειρ (hand)

pugio **pugnale** pugna (fist) pux (with a clenched fist)

Plutarch's Brutus made his way toward the Senate on the Ides of March, hiding an εγχειριδιον/pugnale under his clothes. But when he drew his weapon on Caesar, it had been mysteriously transformed into a ξιφος/spada. When the conspirators suspected that Popilius Laenas had uncovered their plot to assassinate Caesar, they took hold of their εγχειριδια/spade in preparation for a premature attack. Finally, having bathed their hands in the blood of Caesar, Brutus and his companions went to the Campidoglio to show their ξιφη γυμνα/*spade ignude* and to call the people to liberty.[174] Just as the term εγχειριδιον contains the Greek word for "hand," χειρ, so *pugnale* in Italian contains the term for "fist," *pugna*. What speaks out from this text, both strange and familiar, is a marked emphasis on the nudity of the sword and on the hand from which its violence flows.

. . .

In Suetonius (as in the Vulgate telling of Judith and Holofernes), the instrument of assassination was the **pugio**: the conspirators came upon Caesar with **pugio**nibus/**pugna**li. There was no neutralization of the force of the hand, as the etymon *pux*, meaning with a clenched fist, rippled through the story of Caesar's assassination.

Caesar stashed away in his left hand ("sinistra manu"), among other petitions to be read later, the warning of his imminent death. He reached with his hand ("messo mano") for a writing stylus to stab Casca and force his way from the hands ("fatto forza d'uscir loro delle mani") of the conspirators. They were coming at him from every side with their daggers drawn ("strictis pugionibus"). Caesar wrapped his clothing around his head, and with his left hand ("sinistra manu") he stretched his hem down to his heels. Covering the lower parts of his body, at least he would fall to the ground with less shame.[175]

The hand is important at the scene of the assault. Caesar's hand, the wounded hand of Brutus, the hands of the conspirators bathed in blood and the sexual aspect of their assault as they grab at Caesar's hands and kiss his head and breast.

. . .

In the history of early Rome it was the son of the tyrant, Sextus Tarquinius, who carried the sword. Unlike Caesar's assassins, who used their weapons in a sexual assault upon the head of state, Sextus Tarquinius, with his *stricto gladio* ("pugnale ignudo"), raped a noblewoman, his relative Lucretia. In Livy's text, the act of sexual aggression with a sword preceded the overturning of the state, and its violence was directed against a woman. While Caesar was assaulted by the many hands of the conspirators, in Livy's text Lucretia was touched only once: in order to awaken her, Tarquin pressed her breast with his left hand. The term *gladius* reinforced this sense of distance: unlike the *pugnale*, whose name is generated from a part of the body, the term *gladius* derives from the striking and cutting activity of a sword, independent of its contact with bodies. Sextus Tarquinius, by means of his sexual aggression, became the agent of his own downfall—the outrage committed against Lucretia deprived the Tarquins of their rule.[176] And the instrument, or agency, that he used in this self-sabotage was the *stricto gladio/pugnale ignudo*.

. . .

A bronze statue of Lucius Junius Brutus in the act of drawing his sword ("εσπασμενον ξιφos/che traheva fuori la spada") displaced and replaced Lucretia's rape as the agent of the founding of Republican Rome.[177] The sword became part of Brutus's image and external shape, but even his inward nature was made of the stuff of swords. If you extinguish a burning sword in cold water, it becomes very hard. Brutus was like that—"Just as a burning sword becomes hard in cold water, so Brutus became hard and stubborn, with such a tremendous courage to oppose the tyrants" ("Egli a guisa di spada affocata, che essendo spenta in acqua fredda viene perciò a farsi molto dura, havendo havuto da natura uno ingegno duro, et ostinato, fu d'animo tanto terribile contra i Tiranni").[178] Imprinted in the image of Brutus's sword—first hot, then cold, first soft, then hard—was the image of Tarquin's encounter with Lucretia and the relation of that meeting to the changing of the state.

. . .

After slaying the duke, Lorenzino wrote: "The blood that was flowing in an extraordinary quantity from my hand that had been bitten made me afraid that when I went around Florence what I had done would become clear. It was necessary to keep the deed secret for a while to ensure a more positive outcome." ("Il sangue, che mi usciva in quantità straordinaria di una mano che mi era stata morsa, mi fece temere che nell'andare attorno non si manifestasse quello che bisognava tener segreto un pezzo, volendo far cosa buona.")[179]

...

Handing down, from the Latin *tradere* (*tradit*—it is handed down), is the work of tradition (and betrayal or deceit).[180] In the humanistic tradition, this activity of handing down is generally visualized as a solitary, perhaps not totally innocent (but certainly not deceitful), occupation of the scholar in his study. Still, even the solitary activity of handing down invokes a crowd of deceivers: to hand over the stories of antiquity about tyranny and tyrant-slayers—stories of political betrayal—is to betray them to collectors, compilers, classifiers, translators, and sometimes actors (like Lorenzino), who, by the work of their hands, inflict upon them strained, anachronistic, and potentially deceptive interpretations.[181] Betrayal or deceit, then, is a motif in the story of Lorenzino and also in the history of the story's transmission. Lorenzino betrayed the duke, but he was also betrayed. Those who betrayed him were scholars who, transmitting stories of betrayal, created a false promise of their potential efficacy on the stage of history. My work, then—a work of translation, a collection of historiographic bits of research handed down to 2011—attempts to span the distance between the hand that betrays in murder and the hand that betrays in handing down the stories.

In the company of all these historical hands, I take up company with those contemporary feminist writers who have reflected on the agency of hands in historical narration. We would do well to pay attention to the hands that make history and to read history books, as Levins Morales does, "with the skepticism of an incest survivor at a family gathering. I watch everyone's hands." What is the purpose of the stories being told? Whose interests are sacrificed in their telling?[182] In Daphne Marlatt's novel *Ana Historic*, the protagonist Annie pieces together the history of Ana Richards, an Englishwoman who came to British Columbia to work as a schoolteacher. She comes across a letter Mrs. Richards wrote to her father in England describing the people she had encountered in Canada. They are a "Rough Lot" and not the appropriate company for a "Gentlewoman." "Still," she writes, "I would rather be here than cooped up there as your handmaiden." Annie, the researcher, muses on Mrs. Richards's use of the term *handmaiden,* "that Biblical word. with what shade of emotion did she choose it? 'a female personal attendant or servant.' personal? the object of whose hands?"[183]

. . .

In his essay "Latin Paleography and Manuscript Studies in North America," Richard H. Rouse paints a fascinating picture of the conditions under which we New World scholars carry out our research quests in European libraries and archives. To use primary resources in our work, we are obliged to traverse not only physical but conceptual distances.[184] If in theory, according to Rouse, this distance might promote in us a "broader," more "comparative approach" to resources of European libraries and archives, in fact we tend not to take advantage of this difference from our European counterparts. During vacations and sabbatical leaves, we "make a hasty run" to work on European manuscripts, paying little attention to the social, political, and cultural organizations of these textual materials. And since we "have to run a little farther" than our European colleagues, our long-distance sprint leaves little time to reflect upon our relation to such organizations of knowledge.[185]

The distance, the "hasty run," the excitement of writing a request for a particular manuscript that you read about in the States and that you expect to yield incredible treasures and insights about how early modern writers and thinkers viewed themselves; the heady first moments of handling the materials, coming into contact with sixteenth-century hands and what you realize is sixteenth-century sand; the disappointment upon finding that the manuscript you traveled to see contains a series of mostly published letters that yield none of the long-awaited secrets (at least not to you); the desperation upon finding a series of illegible or irrelevant documents in place of the ones you imagined would fit neatly into your next essay; the pleasure of making the acquaintance of an especially capable archivist who has just finished writing an inventory of some materials you are very interested in, or of getting to know a protective librarian who lets you read an incunable piece by piece, who compliments you every day on your Italian, and whom you are surprised to see chain-smoking in the courtyard of the library housed in fifteenth-century military fortifications that you enter each day to do your research; the awkwardness of running into a colleague you didn't necessarily want to see in Europe—these are some standard elements of one type of research narrative. This narrative tells a story of heightened affect, moments in which the researcher and her hands are drawn into the network of relations between early modern writers and contemporary custodians of their prose.

The researcher, however, rarely represents these moments of affect in her scholarly prose. She returns home to the "responsibilities and distractions" of "teaching and university committees and the like" and writes up the contents of her findings.[186] She tends to reduce the experience of social relations abroad to a brief note of acknowledgment outside the body of her essay or book; the exciting encounters with materials that made lights go off and bells ring, the often intense relations with librarians and archivists and pages, the feelings of disappointment at experiences that will not produce publishable thoughts, and those relations at home that motivated the journey in the first place are rarely included as part of the "text" to be analyzed. Although these experiences of service, profit, and affect form the social basis for her scholarly ideas, she has no time to think of the relations between these ideas and her experiences; she must begin thinking about the next dash to Europe and the prospects of more finds and disappointments.

Unless, that is, the scholar feels drawn into the network of social relations she studies. And that happens when the researcher includes her self among the addressees of sixteenth-century writers, relating her transcribing hand to the hands that produced, conserved, and transmitted ("di mano in mano") the histories she studies. In the course of my transcriptions of texts and documents, starting with the letter of Giovanni Antonio and ending with the "hands" of Morales and Marlatt, I have included myself and my hand as an addressee, transcriber, and collector of communications about political violence produced by hands from the sixteenth century until the present day. No longer an individual traveler, "I" have become a socially constructed scholar who, disassembling and reorganizing the narrative of Lorenzino, can now connect the republic of letters to its imperial context and see those geopolitical contingencies in which Lorenzino's—and my—story have participated.

SOCIAL INTERSECTION

1565–1995, between Mexico City, the Mountains of Chiapas, Bologna, Friuli, and Los Angeles

In September 1994, the political scientist Adolfo Gilly sent a copy of Carlo Ginzburg's essay "Clues: Roots of an Evidential Paradigm" to the Zapatista subcomandante Marcos in Chiapas with the following handwritten dedication: "This theorizing of the thought of old Antonio (and of Heriberto) (and sometimes yours . . .) goes with all my affection" ("Con todo cariño, va esta teorización sobre el pensamiento del viejo Antonio [y de Heriberto] [y el tuyo, a veces . . .]").[1] On October 22, Marcos responded to Gilly with a critique of the essay. On April 16, 1995, Gilly wrote again, explaining at length the reasons he found Ginzburg's work so important and showing the convergences he saw (and sees) between the work of subaltern historians like Ginzburg and the work of revolutionaries like Marcos. Both, he explained, work within the paradigm of informal knowledges theorized by Ginzburg in his essay—that is, from the "art of knowing human beings. Like so many other true forms of knowledge, this one has to do with the senses and experience" ("[el arte] de conocer a los seres humanos. Como tantos otros saberes verdaderos, éste tiene mucho que ver con los sentidos y la experiencia").[2] In October 1995, in Mexico City, this exchange between Gilly and Marcos was published in a volume, together with Ginzburg's essay and an interview with Marcos; the title of the volume is *Discusión sobre la historia*.

What makes this volume so intellectually exciting is the way Gilly constructs an "imagined community" around Ginzburg's work, a community that, spanning several nationalities (Italy—Ginzburg; England—E. P. Thompson; France—Marc Bloch; the United States—James C. Scott; Mexico, Argentina, Bolivia, Chile, Peru, Cuba, and Guatemala—locales of Gilly's political and intellectual work), also spans centuries, constructing a relation of similarity between the experiences of Marcos in Chiapas and those of the sixteenth-century miller Menocchio (as they have come down to us through the studies of Ginzburg). What emerges from this heterogeneous array is not only a diversity of positions and methods for thinking about history but a very concrete sense of how we actually come to know about history—through a diversity of filters, experiences and displacements, all of which need to be negotiated in the telling of our stories. In my reading of this volume, I longed to find my own place, research, and intellectual aspirations represented in the community imagined by Gilly.

Gilly sent Ginzburg's essay to Marcos in the hopes that they might share a revolutionary interest in Ginzburg's argument, which distinguishes two paradigms of knowledge: an informal one based on quotidian, sensual experience and a formal one based on abstract thought. According to Ginzburg's scheme, historians depend on the first, an experiential type of knowledge in which conjectures are formed from "clues," or the apprehension of material traces or tracks. Gilly adds that revolutionaries, too, work within this experiential paradigm of knowledge so richly historicized by Ginzburg.

Gilly himself had learned, in his own political experiences, to follow the experiential knowledge of Argentinian workers, Bolivian miners, Chilean steelworkers, Peruvian textile workers, Cuban workers, Guatemalan peasants and armed rebels, and Mexican political prisoners, electricians, and students.[3] Now it would seem that, via Ginzburg's essay, Gilly would like to see the work habits of his revolutionary life converge with the work habits of his life as an activist historian and political scientist, inasmuch as both historians and revolutionaries pay attention to the concrete particulars of individuals and their combinations of formal and subaltern ways of knowing. He hopes that Marcos, upon reading Ginzburg's essay, will see himself engaged in a concrete and intuitive art of political knowing, that he will see the "problematic of Ginzburg's essay" as pertaining to the experience of all the Zapatistas and, in particular, his own ("la problemática del ensayo... tiene mucho que ver con la experiencia de ustedes allá arriba, y en particular con la tuya").[4] He even goes so far as to see Marcos's ways of knowing reflected in the sixteenth-century conceptual practices of Menocchio, whose subaltern cosmology, derived in part from printed books and learned environments, ultimately grew, according to Ginzburg, out of "an obscure, almost unfathomable, layer of remote peasant traditions."[5] "Does this Italian reflection of 1976 touch some part of your experience?" Gilly asked. "I would say yes." ("Toca esta reflexión italiana de 1976 alguna parte de tu experiencia? Diría que sí.")[6]

Unhappily for Gilly, Marcos would (and did) say no. After reading Ginzburg's essay, Marcos concluded that the conjectural paradigm Ginzburg had outlined was an idealistic "tautology" ("tautologia"). Ginzburg showed how, in the nineteenth-century methods of art history, criminology, and psychoanalysis, clues were collected from the "trivial details"—the "earlobes, fingernails, footprints, cigarette ashes, discarded information"—of paintings, scenes of crime, and patients' self-presentations in order to prove authenticity, guilt, and neurosis.[7] But for Marcos this method of collecting clues produced "truth" because it served the ideological goal of identifying the originality of a painting and the individuality of the artist or the author of a crime. What was true (or unexamined) about the ideology was therefore true (or unexamined) about the method ("Su supuesto es tomado como verdadero [el marco de referencia con el que se contrastan los 'indicios'] y, ergo, es verdadera la conclusión [el método de 'recolección' de 'indicios']").[8] At the end of his essay, Ginzburg contextualized the development of this conjectural paradigm in the frame of "new capitalist modes of production" and "a new bourgeois concept of property" in the late nineteenth century.[9] Perhaps for this reason, Marcos was especially impatient: Why, in today's neoliberal context, would Gilly propose this paradigm as a tool for understanding ways of knowing in Chiapas?

Still, I imagine that Gilly, as a revolutionary and academic, was pleased to represent the terms of Marcos's impatience. Gilly may have been unhappy that Marcos distanced himself from Ginzburg's conjectural paradigm and its early exemplar Menocchio, but he nonetheless seemed to learn something from this critique. For example, Gilly begins his response to Marcos's critique by bringing to the fore the frame of reference that separates their positions: he laments the fact that Marcos's contemplative space, in which he has written "seven single-spaced pages" about the history of the Zapatistas ("siete páginas a renglón cerrado"), was interrupted by a federal reconaissance flight requiring his immediate attention. Although Gilly would have liked for Marcos to continue his reflections on Ginzburg and to make, via Ginzburg, a bridge between the life of a revolutionary and the life of a politically interested and active academic, he nonetheless underscores the line that prevents their communion (though not their community):

> And how would your historical explanation have continued if the airplane hadn't come? We will never know: as so often happens, here history (life, experience, the struggle, however you want to call it), in the shape of an airplane came to interrupt your history (your discourse on the history of the EZLN). . . . And here again, as so many other times, the airplane—that is to say, the history of them—was unable to interrupt this other history that is our dialogue, the dialogue of those on this side of the famous, often invisible but never vanished line between classes.
>
> [Y cómo habría seguido tu explicación histórica si el avión no hubiera venido? Nunca lo sabremos: como tantas veces, aquí la historia [la vida, la experiencia, la lucha, como quiera llamarle] bajo la forma de un avión vino a interrumpir tu historia [tu discurso sobre la historia del EZLN]. . . . Y aquí, también como tantas otras veces, el avión—es decir, la historia de ellos—no pudo cortar esta otra historia que es nuestro diálogo, el de los del lado de acá de la famosa, muchas veces invisible pero nunca desvanecida línea entre las clases.][10]

Crucial to understanding the possibilities of community between Gilly and Marcos is Gilly's reference to the plane. After Marcos's reflection is interrupted by the hostile flight overhead, it becomes impossible for Gilly to continue with a metalanguage that is similar—or metaphorically related—to the language of Ginzburg's essay. The plane that introduces heterogeneity and difference to their exchange also becomes the metonymic "part" that makes the "whole" discussion make sense (or non-sense). To every member of the EZLN who heard the noise of the plane, there was no need to mention it. Nor was there any need to explain the abrupt interruption of Marcos's reflection. Yet because he was writing across the invisible line between his history and that of Gilly, Marcos did mention the plane and explained the cause of the interruption. Moreover, Gilly's representation of the plane within the story of their exchange leads us to make visible and dramatic our presuppositions about the frames of reference for the thought and work of these two writers.

First appearances might lead us to believe that Marcos's and Gilly's frames of reference for their thought were impossible to bridge: Marcos's time was interrupted by planes overhead and by the urgent need to negotiate with his comrades immediate responses to the latest exigencies of war; his thought was constrained by time. It is implied, by contrast, that Gilly's contemplative time, uninterrupted by such emergencies, was by contrast unbound by time, even timeless. Marcos's space appeared as a highly social space in the mountains of Chiapas, a space marked by a history that was far removed from the spaces in which History (with a capital "H") is produced. By contrast, Gilly's writing space was presumably the isolated space of an academic study, a space for producing History far removed from the histories of other spaces. His thought was constrained by space. And one could, of course, perform a similar reading of the different times and spaces occupied by Menocchio (the rural, highly social intellectual environment of sixteenth-century Friuli) and Ginzburg (the bourgeois, highly isolating environment of the faculty of Discipline storiche in late-twentieth-century Bologna or of the Department of History at UCLA), brought into community, across the distance of four hundred years, by the Inquisition.

In both cases, a presumably "isolated" scholar imagines community with a writer and reader whose thinking is engendered by a highly social time and space full of interruptions. His purpose, in doing so, may be to escape from the confines of his study and the timelessness of his thought into the contingencies of history. Just as Marcos and Menocchio are "scholars" whose studies and knowledge actively pertain to their actions in the field, so Gilly and Ginzburg make good use of such figures as Marcos and Menocchio to enrich their engagement with the world and to bring that engagement into their studies. In the course of this study of Lorenzino and republican thought, we have asked the questions: Are these binaries—the isolated, alienated scholar versus the engaged, integrated one—self-evident divisions, or are they merely the product of a long-standing history of scholarly and binary self-perceptions that cancel from our frames of knowing the possibilities for reorganizing historical knowledge as personal, transnational, historical, and diasporic conversations?[11] As we have seen, once we step out of the study and outside the bounds of humanistic examples of tyrannicide, the possibilities for (respectfully) reorganizing political theory and historical knowledge around issues of gender struggle (or any other issues) take us on important scholarly journeys. To articulate, theorize, and historicize these possibilities has become, for me, the most compelling aspect of my research on Lorenzino and my endeavor in the following two sections of this book.

SECTION TWO

Wings for My Courage

Accept my best wishes . . . and overlooking my boldness, place the blame on *Mr. Naudé, who, having fashioned wings for my courage when he requested my works for admission into your most splendid Library*, will now have to intercede for my pardon. [emphasis mine]

[Riceva questi augurij . . . e condonando a tanto ardire v'attribuisca la colpa al *Sign. Naudeo, il qual' havendo fabricato l'ali all'ardimento mio all'hora, che fu a richiedermi l'opere mie per ricovrarle nella fioritissima Bibliotheca di Vostra Eminenza*, dovrà al presente intercedermene il perdono.]

—Arcangela Tarabotti to Cardinal Giulio Mazarin,
Lettere familiari e di complimento (1650)

The weaknesses of my scanty intellect . . . *dare to insert themselves between [frapporsi] the most famous writers, in order to enter the most flourishing Library* of such a virtuous Prince. [My works] even hope that his [Mazarin's] incorrigible sense of justice will not let anyone commit outrage to the naive offspring of a holy virgin.

[Le debolezze del mio povero ingegno . . . *ardiscono di frapporsi trà i più celebri Scrittori, per entrar nella fioritissima Bibliotheca* di cosi virtuoso Prencipe, sperando pure, che la di lui inemendabile Giustitia non lascierà far oltraggio a i semplici parti d'una Vergine Sacra.]

—Arcangela Tarabotti to Madame Anne de Gremonville,
French ambassadress in Venice, *Lettere familiari e di complimento* (1650).

Historians have traditionally told a story of republican thought that, requiring the rape of a noblewoman as a precondition of republican freedom, culminated in the French Revolution and the consolidation of republicanism as a conversation among brothers.[1] In the course of my research on Lorenzino, I have looked for a way out of this apparent historical destiny, seemingly etched in concrete in our political imaginations, imagining the possibility of an earlier moment on the road to the French Revolution, a historical perspective that included in the meaning of republicanism the voices of women—not as violated ciphers but as political writers and intellectuals of influence. In Section One I told the story of those who constructed and conserved knowledge of Lorenzino in historiography and in state archives, making visible the relationship between knowledge of tyrannicide and the political contexts in which such knowledge was conserved. Now, in this section, I intervene in the tradition of republican thought with my studies of a particular relation of knowledge and research between Arcangela Tarabotti (1604–52), a Venetian political theorist and nun who made gender central to her political reflections, and Gabriel Naudé (1600–1653), the "father" of library science and librarian of the Mazarine, one of the first modern libraries of state in Europe.

A vast physical and existential distance separated Tarabotti's convent of Sant'Anna del Castello from Naudé's Parisian library, which opened to the public in 1643. But Tarabotti's and Naudé's thinking converged in the attention they paid to the centrality of the daughter in political knowledge. Tarabotti saw the daughter as pivotal to men's construction of the *ragion di stato*, while Naudé represented the library of state, so central to negotiations of political power, as "daughter" to the librarian. Naudé, perhaps vaguely intuiting the importance of Tarabotti's perspectives to political theory, requested her works for inclusion in the Mazarine, thereby producing both "wings for her courage" and an image of her writings "taking up shelf space"—or inserting themselves ("frapporsi")—among the most famous writers of this celebrated library. I take the image of this connection between Naudé and Tarabotti to create a series of imaginary shelf lists that would document the (hypothetical) space taken up by Tarabotti's works among the writers of the Mazarine. Two areas of research and theory, in particular, guide me in this scholarly enterprise: on the one hand, the history of books and libraries, and on the other, feminist approaches to issues of historicity.

In the first area of research, Roger Chartier and other historians of writing and the book remind us: "There is no text apart from the physical support that offers it for reading, hence there is no comprehension of any written piece that does not at least in part depend upon the forms in which it reaches its readers."[2] Chartier extends this principle in two directions to suggest that (1) there is no comprehension of any text that does not at least in part depend on the physical space it occupies on an actual library shelf (or electronic screen);[3] and, at the same time, (2) there is no comprehension of any text that does not at least in part depend on intellectual habits subsequent to those in which the text was originally inscribed. As Chartier noted, the intent of any project that collects historical materials for presentation in a new context (he gives the examples of the Bibliothèque Bleue—a collection of French popular literature—and performances of Shakespeare in the United States) is to "inscribe the text into a cultural matrix that was not the one that its original creators had in mind, and by that means to permit 'readings,' comprehensions, and uses that might have been disqualified by other intellectual habits."[4] The intent of my project here is precisely that: to excerpt a series of political perspectives from the works of Tarabotti that might have modified the history of republican thought, had they not been disqualified by the intellectual habits dominating her time.

We scholars of the twenty-first century are not required to reproduce the misogynist habits and conditions that dominated the production of political knowledge in the seventeenth century. Yet as Silverblatt, Mohanty, and other feminist theorists have shown, this is precisely what we do when we ignore how such categories or habits of thought emerged as a product of those times, representing, as Benjamin lamented, a skewed and incomplete history of the winners.[5] We disregard "the ways in which our destinies as scholars join those of our 'objects' of study,"[6] continuing to subject ourselves now to those same hierarchical and unequal social conditions in which knowledge was produced then. What happens if, instead, we start from concrete social relations between women and men in order to address particular questions of "how gender imageries and relations are constituted, experienced, and struggled over in the historical processes that both form and subvert states"?[7] Instead of seeing women as outside of or restricted by social, intellectual and historical processes of state making, we might envision, in the case of Tarabotti, the space taken up by her works among the most celebrated writers of the Mazarine and, in doing so, might account for the potential impact of her contestatory perspectives.

Although Naudé fashioned wings for Tarabotti's courage as a political thinker and writer and produced an image of her works taking up shelf space among the most celebrated writers of the Mazarine, today Library of Congress classifications cloister the works of Tarabotti in much the same way that her person was cloistered in her lifetime; the works she authored have, for the most part, been classified ahistorically among works pertaining to the monastic and religious life of women. From this position on the shelf, it is difficult to activate the intellectual relations she imagined when Naudé invited her to send her works for inclusion in his library. I would like to suggest that one way to reintroduce historicity to Tarabotti's works might be to reclassify her works in the ways that she imagined, in conversation with the political thinkers of the Mazarine, reintroducing her perspectives as "integral" to republican thought and to the ways such thought was organized in a library of state. Such conversations on the library shelf, although supported by intellectual habits that came much later, restore the potential impact opened up by the convergence between Naudé's request and Tarabotti's aspirations.

SHELF LIST 1. CATALOGUERS, COMPILERS, AND THE STATE

Catalogus librorum bibliothecae publicae quam vir ornatissimus Thomas Bodleius eques auratus in Academia Oxoniensi nuper instituit (1605)
—Gabriel Naudé, *Advis pour dresser une bibliothèque* (1627)

Catalogo dei manoscritti del Card. Federico Borromeo nella Biblioteca Ambrosiana
—Arcangela Tarabotti, *Lettere familiari e di complimento* (1650)

Thomas Bodley, *Letters of T. Bodley to T. James*, ed. G. W. Wheeler (1926), and G. W. Wheeler, *The Earliest Catalogues of the Bodleian Library* (1928)

Hayden White, "The Politics of Historical Interpretation: Discipline and De-sublimation" (1982)

Enzo Bottasso, *Storia della biblioteca in Italia* (1984)

Roger Chartier, *The Order of Books: Readers, Authors, and Libraries in Europe between the Fourteenth and Eighteenth Centuries* (1994)

Arcangela Tarabotti, *Lettere familiari e di complimento*, ed. Meredith Kennedy Ray and Lynn Lara Westwater (2005)

Chartier's scholarship, rich with a sense of the historicity of learned men who intervened in the order of books, encourages us to investigate the political interests and investments of such men as Thomas Bodley,

Federico Borromeo, and Gabriel Naudé, who were instrumental in the founding and organizing of the first public libraries in Europe. The catalogs and inventories produced by or under the auspices of such men are not transparent windows into the holdings of these libraries but ideological frames that train us to classify knowledge with particular political objectives. For example, Thomas Bodley, born in 1545, followed his Anglican father into exile during the brief reign of Mary Tudor (1553–58), spending his adolescence in Germany and Switzerland. He finished his studies at Oxford, however, and taught Greek and "natural philosophy" there for some years. From 1576 to 1580 he traveled in Italy, France, and Germany before his election to Parliament in 1584 and then, over the course of the next ten years, took important diplomatic assignments in Denmark, France, and Holland. This is the profile, not of a disinterested scholar, but of a scholar with powerful political investments.

On February 23, 1598, Bodley made a formal offer to reconstruct the library that Humphrey, Duke of Gloucester, had donated, in several installments, to Oxford in the early fifteenth century and that had been dispersed. On November 8, 1602, the library, containing less than three thousand volumes, reopened for six hours a day without lighting. It had a total of 248 readers that year, with about seventeen readers using the library each day. In 1605, with the collaboration of the erudite Thomas James, Bodley published a topographic catalog of the library (then almost six thousand volumes strong). He ordered this catalog first according to the four fields into which the library was subdivided and then by authors but never exceeded the categorical framework of Konrad Gesner's *Bibliotheca universalis* (1545). The catalog of 1620 (Bodley died in 1613), now representing sixteen thousand volumes, sang the fame of the Bodleian and its rich cultural patrimony throughout Europe. We might study the rhetoric of these catalogs, not to mention the correspondence of Thomas Bodley, to understand the specific strategies by which gendered struggles over authority were transformed into "neutral" instruments of research and knowledge.[8]

A similar profile might be written of the scholar and politician Federico Borromeo, founder of the Ambrosiana Library in Milan. Born in Milan in 1564, he began his ecclesiastic career with the support of his cousin Carlo, archbishop and intimate adviser to Pius IV in the last phase of the Council of Trent. Sixtus V, the founder of the Vatican Library, elevated Borromeo to cardinal in 1587, and Clement VIII named him archbishop of Milan in 1595. A long controversy with the occupying Spanish kept Federico from performing his office from 1597 until 1601, when he returned to Milan with the idea of founding an important library. After an exceptional program of acquisitions, Borromeo opened the Ambrosiana in December 1609.⁹

As in the case of Bodley, Federico's scholarly work was not a refuge from but an integral part of his political investments. Unlike Bodley, however, who wanted the widest publicity of the Bodleian catalog, Borromeo pursued a different politics of knowledge, insisting that his librarian keep the Ambrosiana catalogs to himself. The first catalogs were subdivided according to language but not according to research fields. Authors were listed alphabetically according to their first names, making accessibility to the library depend upon the goodwill of the librarian, who alone was familiar with the library's holdings.

In the case of Gabriel Naudé, the intersection between politics and his work as an erudite book collector, librarian, and advisor to such figures as Henri de Mesme, Richelieu, and Mazarin has been extensively studied.¹⁰ Indeed, Naudé's erudite activities were, from the outset, inscribed by an interest in the politics of knowledge and books. Three of his works—*Advis pour dresser une bibliothèque* (1627), *Bibliographia politica* (1633), and *Considérations politiques sur les coups d'état* (1639)—grew directly from his service to political figures in their libraries. And the Mazarine Library, fruit of Naudé's erudite and collecting labors and open to the public in 1644, was a monument at the crossroads between politics and books. Especially in his *Bibliographia politica*, Naudé was eager to offer political rulers a sort of specialized catalog of the right books at the right time so as to obviate the chasm between theory and practice.¹¹ But in all of his "cataloguing" of knowledge, Naudé paid special attention to the concrete details that were the basis of political action and experience. Whether considering questions of power or compiling those books that "one should read to become skilled in that art [of politics]," the learned librarian was the most important resource for any man of state.¹²

We tend to locate the disciplinization of historical studies in the early nineteenth century as part of the "consolidation of the (bourgeois) nation-state."¹³ I would like to suggest that this disciplinization began rather in the seventeenth century with the foundation of such libraries as the Bodleian, the Ambrosiana, and the Mazarine and the publishing of their catalogs. Consulting the books in these (and other) catalogs is not just a straightforward task of compiling material support for our research projects; how the books got there, the political investments of collectors and directors, and the classification systems that function to strain out certain kinds of knowledge are an important part of the interpretive picture. Especially in the case of the early public libraries, printed catalogs were not only instruments for the diffusion of book culture throughout Europe but also instruments of state formation; the impulse, in these documentary projects, to appeal to the authority of the state was sublimated and transformed into a catalog.

> *Frapporsi 1. Claiming Space on the Shelf*
>
> Tarabotti's *Lettere familiari* contain ample representation of her appeals to the authority of powerful men and women of state. The authority of these political figures caused her "anxiety" because she had no choice but to trust those who carried off her works for publication and placement in libraries. In a letter to the Marchesa René Clermont-Gallerande, Tarabotti expressed "the anxiety of purgatorial souls awaiting intercession" ("quell'ansietà che l'anime purganti attendono li suffragi") because a certain gentleman had taken her works to France with the intention of publishing them and then had left her hanging without any news for thirteen months. She felt that this lack of news—and the fact that the marchesa had not responded to her two previous letters—was tormenting her "viscera" and causing her soul to die ("mi sento spirar l'anima dal dolore . . . questi particolari che mi premono nelle viscere"). Only the thought of Naudé provided any relief to her torment: "I will write to Mr. Gremonville, or rather to the librarian of the most eminent Mazarin, from whom I will receive every favor" ("scriverò al signor di Gremonville overo al bibliothecario dell'eminentissimo Mazzarino, dai quali riceverò ogni favore").[14] Later, in a letter to Anne de Gremonville, the French ambassadress to Venice, Tarabotti, as we have seen, used the term *frapporsi* to speak about her works placing themselves between the works of the most famous writers of the Mazarine Library. "The weaknesses of my scanty intellect . . . dare to insert themselves between [frapporsi] the most famous writers, in order to enter the most flourishing library of such a virtuous prince. [My

works] even hope that his [Mazarin's] incorrigible sense of justice will not allow anyone to commit outrage upon the naive offspring of a holy virgin." With just this one word, *frapporsi*, Tarabotti opened up an unexpected vista on western political thought. It as if she had found a breach—a Shakespearean chink—in the wall of paternal tyranny and imagined herself disappearing into it, slipping through and placing herself on the other side.

Unlike other seventeenth-century women, who, as we shall see, were depicted by men as animals and peasants looking in upon institutions of learning, Tarabotti depicted herself in social relation with Gabriel Naudé, the "father" to the profession of library science, a state librarian. And contrary to the "social appearance" afforded by general images of women excluded from learning and state-making organizations, Tarabotti's "intervention" or *frapporsi* among the writers of the Mazarine affords an opportunity "to discern the multiple, paradoxical and tangled relations" that constituted seventeenth-century social process.[15] Her "intervention" in the politics of a state library suggests, moreover, the importance of the history of libraries to investigations of gender and history.

SHELF LIST 2. NOSES/POLITICAL GNOSIS

Laura Terracina, *Rime* (1548)

Veronica Gambara, *Rime* (1554)

Vittoria Colonna, *Tutte le rime* (1558)

Traiano Boccalini, *Ragguagli di Parnaso* (1612)

Arcangela Tarabotti, *La semplicità ingannata* (1654)

Traiano Boccalini, *"I ragguagli di Parnaso," or, Advertisements from Parnassus* (1656)[16]

Susanna Bucci, "Come si parla della donna: I cataloghi" (1983)

Wendy Beth Heller, *Emblems of Eloquence: Opera and Women's Voices in Seventeenth-Century Venice* (2003)

Arcangela Tarabotti, *Paternal Tyranny*, ed. and trans. Letizia Panizza (2004)

Arcangela Tarabotti, *La semplicità ingannata*, critical ed., ed. Simona Bortot (2007)

Virginia Cox, *Women's Writing in Italy, 1400–1650* (2008)

In his *Ragguagli di Parnaso*, Traiano Boccalini represented the relation of distinguished women writers to the culture of academies. The Accademia degli Intronati had, for a short time, made the mistake of admitting the renowned poets Laura Terracina, Veronica Gambara, and Vittoria Colonna to their activities. For a while, the academicians were "set on fire" ("riscaldati") by the presence of these women poets and intellectuals; they became more avid for their "learned exercises" ("esercizi letterari") and "did every day publish such Poesie, as made the very Muses wonder" ("ogni giorno pubblicavano poesie tali che ne stupivano le muse stesse").[17] But soon news of this development came to the attention of Apollo as a very unpleasant smell to his nose ("Passò che alle nari di Sua Maestà [Apollo] giunse un certo odore molto spiacevole").[18] He understood "that Women's true Poetry consisted in their Needle and Spindle; and that the Learned Exercises of Women together with the Vertuosi, was like the sporting and playing of Dogs, *who after a short time end up humping each other*"[19] ("che la vera poetica delle donne era l'aco e il fuso, e gli esercizi letterari delle dame co' virtuosi somigliavano gli scherzi e i giuochi che tra loro fanno i cani, i quali dopo brieve tempo tutti forniscono alla fine in montarsi addosso l'un l'altro"). Responding to the unpleasant smell in his nose, Apollo chased away the intruders and spread great joy among those academic fellows who had fought all along to keep these feminine figures from invading their "typically masculine" activities.[20] The "nose of Apollo" was imagined as a sensor that could prevent any trespass of women in the dominion of male knowing.

Clearly, Boccalini intended, with this misogynistic anecdote, to amuse his male readers, and he is still successful today in amusing all readers, male and female. The image of these male scholars unable to focus on their "learned exercises" in the presence of learned women continues to yield material for spirited reflection on current academic sociality and intercourse and enables us to appreciate all the more Tarabotti's intervention in this world of learning and state making.[21] It is important to see this "unpleasant smell" that resulted from intellectual intercourse between men and women as a foundation of seventeenth-century political thinking with lasting legacies. Is it possible to reproduce this anecdote without inadvertently transmitting its censorious effects? What if we arrange for this anecdote to share the shelf space with another seventeenth-century anecdote about noses and gender?

Frapporsi 2. The Father's Nose (and Bowels):
The Education of Sons and Daughters

On the shelf that holds Boccalini's popular *Advertisements* is also a copy of Tarabotti's *Semplicità ingannata*, a work that theorized the conditions of deceit in which young girls grew up in seventeenth-century Venice. In this work, Tarabotti intervened in Boccalini's discourse about gender, politics, knowledge, and the nose when she imagined a day in which daughters would tear off the noses of those fathers who had deceived them and forced them to become nuns. On that day, "we would see only men deprived of that member in the middle of their faces . . . monstrously deformed" ("non si vedrebbero che uomini privi di quel membro . . . situato nel mezo della faccia . . . mostruosi in defformità").[22] The story she was telling exposed the hypocrisy of fathers who falsely professed to their daughters a "love that reached deep into the bowels," while depositing and forgetting them in convents ("La lingua mentitrice . . . pronunzia un amor sviscerato, ma la verità è che poi non si raccordano delle monache").[23]

Conventionally read as a sublimated image of the phallus, Apollo's nose, "that member in the middle of the face," seemed to function for Boccalini to disconnect women from learned culture. For Tarabotti, the same nose functioned to connect fathers to the political responsibility of educating their sons and daughters and providing them with honest examples.[24] In both cases, we might think of the nose as an important participant and marker in the production of culture and knowledge. Tarabotti's story, in particular, points to a deformation in the production of political knowledge—the father's denial of education to daughters—and reclaims a space, in the image of men without noses, for the perspectives and contributions of those daughters.

SHELF LIST 3. GENDER IN THE PUBLIC LIBRARY

Arcangela Tarabotti, *Lettere familiari e di complimento* (1650)

Zacharias Conrad von Uffenbach, *Travels* (1710)

Paula Findlen, "The Museum: Its Classical Etymology and Renaissance Genealogy" (1989)

Irene Silverblatt, "Interpreting Women in States: New Feminist Ethnohistories" (1991)

Lynn Westwater, *The Disquieting Voice: Women's Writing and Anti-feminism in Seventeenth Century Venice* (2003)

Meredith Ray, "Letters from the Cloister: Defending the Literary Self in Arcangela Tarabotti's Lettere familiari e di complimento" (2004)

Arcangela Tarabotti, *Lettere familiari e di complimento*, ed. Meredith Kennedy Ray and Lynn Lara Westwater (2005)

Meredith Ray, *Writing Gender in Women's Letter Collections of the Italian Renaissance* (2009)

In 1683, at Oxford, the Ashmolean Museum opened its doors to anyone who could pay a modest admission. Zacharias Conrad von Uffenbach, a German traveler to Oxford in 1710, reported that he had visited the museum on market day, when "all sorts of country-folk" had the same idea: "So as we could have seen nothing well for the crowd, we went down-stairs again and saved it for another day." He was disappointed that the museum no longer reserved an exclusive experience of erudition for him— "Even women are allowed up here for a sixpence." But he also generally resented the commodification of scholarship represented by the newly imposed admission fee.[25]

The Bodleian Library, open to the public since 1612, presented von Uffenbach with even more frustration. Here, at least, most people were unable to pay the steeper fee of "about eight shillings" and were unwilling to take the trouble to apply for admission. Still, people were constantly entering the building, perturbing the decorum of the scholars. Like Boccalini, who thought cultured women would turn members of the Accademia degli Intronati into a pack of sporting dogs, von Uffenbach saw women in the library as cows: "Every moment brings fresh spectators and, surprisingly enough, amongst them peasants and women-folk, who gaze at the library as a cow might gaze at a new gate with such noise and trampling of feet that others are much disturbed."[26]

Frapporsi 3. The Importance of Social Relations in Libraries to Investigations of Gender and History

Both Boccalini and von Uffenbach exemplify the unequal—not to mention misogynistic—social conditions in which literature and knowledge were produced in seventeenth-century Europe.²⁷ And both writers reveal something of the historical struggles over gender imageries emanating from those institutions of knowledge, academies and libraries, that were so instrumental to the construction of European history and to the denial of a place for women in that history.²⁸ Both passages would seem to confirm that seventeenth-century European institutions and states were indeed effective in subordinating and dominating women; animal-like or peasantlike, noisy and illiterate, women were represented as stereotypically excluded from the state-making procedures of library building, as "pawns" in the game of relations among men.²⁹ But Tarabotti's *Lettere familiari e di complimento* intervene in these stereotypical representations of excluded women, expressing especially her own interest in addressing powerful men and women of state.³⁰ Representations of her relations with two men in particular—Gabriel Naudé, librarian of the Mazarine Library, and Cardinal Mazarin, the patron of the library—help to illuminate the social spaces and paths by which Tarabotti's works might have become "integral to and indissoluble from state-making itself."³¹

In a letter to Gabriel Naudé, Tarabotti figured the visit of France's ambassador to Venice, Nicolo Bretel de Gremonville as a face-to-face visit with Naudé himself: "Your Lordship was once pleased to share the honor of your visits with me via that great Gremonville, so outstanding in the world" ("Quell'honore, che già si compiacque di compartirmi V.S. delle sue visite col mezo di quel Gran Gremonville tanto conspicuo al mondo").³² And after Naudé had requested her works for the Mazarine Library, she imagined enough familiarity with Naudé to suggest that Mazarin blame him for her "courage" ("ardire"). Naudé had, as we saw, "fashioned wings for [her] courage when he requested [her] works for

> admission" to Mazarin's library and now, he would "have to intercede for [her] pardon." In each case, Tarabotti imagined from behind the grate that her body was in contact with Naudé, the *father* of the Mazarine Library. She perceived first his physical (although mediated) visit to the convent and then his construction of "wings," a physical prosthesis for her epistolary "courage." In a sense, these wings, which provided the energy and courage to move Tarabotti's works from her convent in Venice to the shelves of a library of state, also gave me (the organizer of these shelf lists) the energy and courage to intervene here in our knowledge of republican thought.

SHELF LIST 4. CATALOG, CAPITALISM, SPATIAL ARRANGEMENTS

Plutarch, *Mulierum virtutes* (early second century)

Giovanni Boccaccio, *De mulieribus claris* (1361–62)

Laura Terracina, *Rime* (1548)

Veronica Gambara, *Rime e lettere* (1554)

Vittoria Colonna, *Tutte le rime* (1558)

Moderata Fonte, *Il merito delle donne* (1600)

Lucrezia Marinella, *La nobiltà et l'eccellenza delle donne, co' diffetti e mancamenti de gli uomini* (1601)

Maddalena Salveti, *Rime toscane* (1590)

Margherita Sarocchi, *La Scanderbeide, poema eroico* (1606)

Isabella Andreini, *Rime* (1601)

Traiano Boccalini, *Ragguagli di Parnaso* (1612)

Arcangela Tarabotti, *La semplicità ingannata* (1654)

Traiano Boccalini, *"I ragguagli di Parnaso," or, Advertisements from Parnassus* (1656)

Maria Luisa Cicci, *Poesie* (1796)

Ginevra Canonici Fachini, *Prospetto bibliografico di donne italiane rinomate in letteratura* (1824)

Pietro Leopoldo Ferri, *Biblioteca femminile italiana* (1842)[33]

Anna Maria Mozzoni, *Un passo avanti nella cultura femminile: Tesi e progetto* (1866)

Susanna Bucci, "Come si parla della donna: I cataloghi" (1983)

Patricia A. Parker, "Rhetorics of Property: Exploration, Inventory, Blazon," in *Literary Fat Ladies: Rhetoric, Gender, Property* (1987)

Emilia Biga, *Una polemica antifemminista del Seicento: La "Maschera scoperta" di Angelico Aprosio* (1989)

Roger Chartier, *The Order of Books: Readers, Authors, and Libraries in Europe between the Fourteenth and Eighteenth Centuries* (1994)

Lorna Hutson, *The Usurer's Daughter: Male Friendship and Fictions of Women in Sixteenth-Century England* (1994)

Virginia Cox, "The Single Self: Feminist Thought and the Marriage Market in Early Modern Venice" (1995)

Nancy L. Canepa, "The Writing behind the Wall: Arcangela Tarabotti's *Inferno monacale* and Cloistral Autobiography in the Seventeenth Century" (1996)

Arcangela Tarabotti, *La semplicità ingannata*, critical ed., ed. Simona Bortot (2007)

Virginia Cox, *Women's Writing in Italy, 1400–1650* (2008)

Boccalini's work *Ragguagli da Parnaso*, a catalog of pieces of information about the literary world, enjoyed the fortune of many editions and translations, with the English version of his *Ragguagli* translated as *Advertisements from Parnassus*. Although we should not conflate the modern function of the term *advertisement* with seventeenth-century usage, it is nonetheless important to explore how the commodification of pieces of information like those in Boccalini's text functioned in the development of a capitalist world system.[34] Henry Earl of Monmouth, one translator of the *Ragguagli*, understood knowledge as a linear and hierarchical process of accumulation: "One day is Master of another; and whatsoever is written to day, there will be some body who will know more tomorrow."[35] Moreover, he was concerned that his freedom to compete as a translator might be impeded by a monopoly on learning: "And if monopolizing any Earthly Commodity be an adjudged grievance; to monopolize Learning is questionless the worst of Monopolies."[36]

This kind of capitalist thinking was not peculiar to Henry Earl of Monmouth but was the currency of Boccalini's original text. The very first *ragguaglio* or "advertisement" tells how "the Society of Polititians open a Ware-house in Parnassus, wherein are sold divers sorts of Merchandize, very useful for the vertuous living of those that are learned," including "stuffing or bombast," "Humane Eyes," and "Glass Vials of Sweat associated with Learned with Pen in hand."[37] The catalogs of libraries, those instruments through which we, scholars, gain access to research materials, might be fruitfully seen against the background of this politics and commodification of knowledge and learning.

The catalog has also been used as an instrument of research to commodify and organize "knowledge" about women, as in the many catalogs of exceptional women, a genre that originated with Plutarch, was reworked by Boccaccio, and reached the height of its popularity in the seventeenth century.[38] Unlike Boccalini's "Advertisements from Parnassus," which offered a colorful catalog and repository of anecdotal knowledge to interpellate male readers, the catalog of women writers generally offered to its reading public "a laborious and cold list of names."[39] The goal was not to capture the historical details of any individual woman's life but rather to represent abstract types of feminine virtue. Famous and unknown writers, ancients and moderns, mothers and nuns all inhabited an impersonal, mythical and ahistorical Parnassus, isolated from the relations and activities of their daily lives.

Tarabotti herself tried to prove the prodigiousness of women writers, collecting and cataloguing the achievements of women writers in history. Among writers close to her own generation, she included Moderata Fonte, Lucrezia Marinella, Maddalena Salveti, Margherita Sarocchi, Isabella Andreini, Laura Terracina, Veronica Gambara, and Vittoria Colonna.[40] Although such "catalogs" of women writers are crucial to our construction today of different genealogies of thinking and knowing, it is important to understand how catalogs are actually instruments that separate thought, knowledge, and texts from thinking, knowing, and writing; from the bodies of thinkers, knowers, and writers; and from the physical books and physical spaces in which thoughts and knowledge erupt onto the page.

The seventeenth-century catalogs employed various methods to separate the intellectual accomplishments of a woman from the historicity and continuity of her life's activities. One way was to emphasize the manliness of her successes, thereby discrediting her merits as a woman.[41] Another was to underline her choice to renounce or postpone marriage or to reap the advantages of widowhood. If she had the characteristics of a "normal" woman, the compiler would exalt her moral qualities rather than her literary ones, downplaying both her exclusion from the society of women for her superior knowledge and her isolation from male circles for being a woman. To form some knowledge of women's cultural and political negotiations, we might make visible the rhetorics by means of which catalogs dehistoricized and dematerialized the activities of women intellectuals.[42]

In later centuries, details of quotidian things, activities, thoughts, desires, and disappointments might sneak into the pages of catalogs.[43] For example, the Pisan writer Maria Luisa Cicci (1760–94), confined by her father to a convent, was denied access to ink. But her ingenuity elevated her so far above such restrictions that she managed to write verses by making ink from black grapes.[44] Or the reader catches a glimpse of the poverty and social dramas of eighteenth-century Milan under Napoleonic occupation through a portrait of one of its celebrated matrons of culture, Teresa Trotti.[45] The particular conditions of how Teresa Pelli became erudite are represented in her relation with her adoptive father, the director of Florence's Biblioteca Medicea, who educated Teresa through visits to Florence's museums, libraries, and palaces.[46] But in most cases the function of the catalog was to abstract its heroines from history.

Naudé praised the virtues of collections, which, like catalogs, abstracted works from their historical settings in various codices and libraries to publish them in one volume. Naudé understood that these collections—sometimes titled "Bibliothèques" and the ancestors of our modern textbook anthologies and course readers—earned the reader time, movement, and money: "They save us . . . the trouble of searching for a host of books extremely rare and uncommon; . . . they gather together for us in one convenient volume that for which we should otherwise have to search laboriously in many places; and finally . . . they are less expensive—as it is certain that it does not require as many pence to purchase them as it does pounds to possess separately all those authors whom they contain" ("Ils nous sauvent . . . la peine de rechercher une infinité de livres grandement rares et curieuses; . . . ils nous ramassent en un volume et commodément ce qu'il nous faudroit chercher avec beaucoup de peine en plusieurs lieux; et finalement . . . ils tirent après eux une grande espargne, estant certain qu'il ne faut pas tant de testons pour les acheter, qu'il faudroit d'escus si on vouloit avoir séparément tous ceux qu'ils contiennent").[47] We can recognize in these considerations of Naudé the beginnings of our own dehistoricized endeavors to save ourselves trips to libraries by consulting online facsimiles of early printed books.

But while Naudé pointed especially to the economic savings of collections, he was quite clear that the abstracting of titles from historical collections to compile and transcribe catalogs had a political, more than economic, value. For him, after the selection of the books, the most important job of the librarian was to make the books accessible to friends, and indeed, to make new friends and new obligations to the state by means of such access. The librarian, he wrote, "should not fail to have all the catalogs transcribed." And he specified that "all the catalogs" meant those of "the great and most famous libraries—whether ancient or modern, public or private, in this country or abroad,—but also of the small private collections, which for not being known or frequented remain buried in perpetual silence" ("Il ne faut point obmettre et négliger de faire transcrire tous les Catalogues, non seulement des grandes et renommées Bibliothèques, soit qu'elles soient vieilles ou modernes, publiques ou particulières, et en la possession des nostres ou des estrangers: mai aussi des Estudes et Cabinets, qui pour n'estre cognus ny hantez demeurent ensevelis dans un perpétuel silence").[48] Political obligation would be incurred via the librarian's catalogs because "one may sometimes serve and please a friend, when one cannot provide him the book he requires, by directing him to the place where he may find a copy, as may easily be done with the assistance of these catalogs" ("C'est faire plaisir et service à un ami quand on ne luy peut fournir le livre duquel il est en peine, de luy monstrer et désigner au vray le lieu où il en pourroit trouver quelque copie, comme l'on peut faire facilement par le moyen de ces Catalogues").[49] The function of abstracting titles and "transcribing all the catalogs" was to construct and solidify relations of power among men. This was certainly the case for the work of Boccalini.

But if Boccalini's catalog of knowledge or "advertisements" confirmed the exclusion of women from processes of state making, the shelf lists I create here explore the ways in which academies and libraries emerged precisely from relations between women and men. If catalogs of women writers leave us little with which to understand the difficulty of negotiating between being a woman and being an intellectual, my shelf lists, focusing on the specific historical relation between Tarabotti and Naudé, point to one way of understanding such negotiations.

Frapporsi 4. Spatial and Temporal Location

The classification of political knowledge according to chronological and geographic criteria discourages us from grasping how older categories might have been, and often were, taken apart and reorganized to correspond to new political exigencies and historical changes. For example, my categories here are situated simultaneously in at least three places and times—in Venice in the mid-seventeenth century, in postunitary Milan, and in my own twentieth- to twenty-first-century location. I first learned of the Venetian political theorist and nun Arcangela Tarabotti in a work of critical pedagogy of 1866 entitled "One Step Ahead in Feminine Culture: Thesis and Project" (*Un passo avanti nella cultura femminile: Tesi e progetto*), by Anna Maria Mozzoni (1837–1920). An important activist, thinker, and writer in the history of Italian (and European) feminism, Mozzoni herself was in a position to grasp the historicity of categories, as she witnessed the postunification founding and organizing of state archives and libraries. Mozzoni well understood that prejudices against women and their learning were already set in place by the first modern libraries and catalogs that oriented men in the labyrinths of proliferating knowledge. She knew that learned and learning women needed alternative catalogs of women writers to guide them in their own paths of knowing. And she created such a "catalog," citing Tarabotti among a number of women poets, scholars, and theorists from the past who might serve as models of intellectual advancement to women of her day: "In 1644 from the Convent of Sant'Anna del Castello, Arcangela Tarabotti talked back to those men who hurled satiric accusations of frivolity against women. She talked back first with a powerful Antisatire and then, seven years later, with a *Defense of Women*." ("Ed Angelica Tarabotti rispondeva nel 1644 alle satiriche accuse di frivolezza, che gli uomini del suo tempo lanciavano contro la donna, con una vigorosa Antisatira, alla quale faceva seguire, sette anni dopo, una *Difesa delle Donne*.")[50]

I understood Mozzoni's catalog also as an imaginary storehouse or library, an imaginary place populated, however, in a very concrete way, by writers, books, and documents that were in continuous activity and movement. This space provided, in my imaginings, a curriculum for women but also a physical place to stand. Here women might come to understand that previous organizations of knowledge left them little space for knowing and acting in the physical world. In this space carved out by Mozzoni, women would discover that different cognitive arrangements were possible, that each woman had the license to symbolize, with the collection and placement of particular writers, books, and documents, her own participation in the making of knowledge. As I began to research the texts of Tarabotti and scholarship about her, I became more and more convinced that this political theorist/nun, encountered through the filter of Mozzoni's catalog, was giving me a historical place to stand, as her theorizing, writing, and collocation in a social world between Venice and Paris formed a prominent part of the cognitive landscape in which I was reorganizing and restructuring my thoughts and questions about Lorenzino.[51]

Venice, a maritime republic located at the crossroads between East and West and Tarabotti's city, was also an important destination of my historiographic inquiry. An information clearinghouse, an important geographic locale for the work of organizing knowledge about the New World, Venice was a crucial publishing capital and capitalist player in the new global economy. We might remember that in January 1537, when Lorenzino murdered the duke, the imperial forces of Charles V dominated much of "Italy," while Venice was still an independent republic and an important refuge for the Florentine exiles.[52] And in the 1540s, Gonzalo Fernandez de Oviedo, the official historiographer of Charles V and military governor of the fortress of Santo Domingo, sent his iguana to Ramusio, a Venetian broker of knowledge, who published parts of Oviedo's *Historia natural* with the publisher and investor in the rum triangle, Tommaso Giunti.

Historically a busy intersection for the brokering of culture and political tensions, Venice provided a fertile ground for the unique political interventions of a nun/theorist. As we work to bridge the gaps between our own historical spaces and the ones we study, we encounter such intersections that become part of our relations with the past. Standing in the space created by Mozzoni's catalog, I have found the works of Tarabotti to be one key to understanding the implications of our own research practices in the contradictory relation between women and state making.

SHELF LIST 5. WORK HABITS, MOVEMENTS, TRANSCRIPTION

François de La Croix du Maine, *Bibliothèque* (1584)

Henry Hexham, preface to the Mercator-Hondius *Atlas* (1636)

Francesco Buoninsegni, *Contro il lusso donnesco, satira menippea, con l'Antisatira di Arcangela Tarabotti in risposta* (1644)

Arcangela Tarabotti, *Che le donne siano della spezie degli uomini* (1651)

John Amos Comenius, *Orbis pictus* (1658)

Carlo Cattaneo, *Opere edite ed inedite* (1881–83)

Roland Barthes, "An Almost Obsessive Relation to Writing Instruments," interview in *Le Monde*, September 27, 1973

Anna Maria Mozzoni, *La liberazione della donna*, ed. Franca Pieroni Bortolotti (1975)

Ginevra Conti Odorisio, *Storia dell'idea femminista in Italia* (1980)

Yve-Alain Bois, "Writer, Artisan, Narrator" (1983)

Michel de Certeau, *The Writing of History* (1988; *L'écriture de l'histoire*, 1975)

Roger Chartier, *The Order of Books: Readers, Authors, and Libraries in Europe between the Fourteenth and Eighteenth Centuries* (1994)

Arcangela Tarabotti, *Che le donne siano della spezie degli uomini*, ed. Letizia Panizza (1994)

Francesco Buoninsegni and Arcangela Tarabotti, *Satira e antisatira*, ed. Elissa B. Weaver (1998)

Scholars—both past and present—are often inquisitive about their own physical movements in the social world of knowing. Michel de Certeau, for example, invokes the moment in which historians question the relation between their fields of research and the spaces in which they come to know about the past: "Interrupting their erudite perambulations around the rooms of the National Archives, for a moment they detach themselves from the monumental studies that will place them among their peers, and walking out into the street, they ask, 'What in God's name is this business? What about the bizarre relation I am keeping with current society . . . ? . . . No thought or reading is capable of effacing the specificity of the place, the origin of my speech, or the area in which I am researching. . . . My way of speaking, my patois, represents my relation to a given place.'"[53] In this passage, de Certeau theorizes history's precarious connection between "a past that is its object and a present that is the place of its practice."[54] Perambulating inside the rooms of a library or archive among "symptoms" of the past and walking out into the street to wonder about the present form at least part of this connection between object and practice.[55] But history's "objects" are also the repositories of social practices and relations of writing. They reserve a wealth of information about their own making and conservation in social contexts—past and present. So I wonder why the researcher needs to detach herself from such practices and relations to reflect on the present outside in the street.

The writings of François de La Croix du Maine, the author of an imaginary bibliothèque of 1584, tell us how a "library" is never a fixed object or monument of stone. He writes that his library grew from a practice of transcription and a passion for accounting for such transcribing and compiling activities. Writing three hours per day, filling a page each hour, he would produce one thousand pages every year. There were, consequently, "eight hundred volumes of memoirs and diverse collections, written by my hand and otherwise, and all of my invention or sought by myself, and extracts from all the books that I have read until this day, of which the number is infinite."[56] Like La Croix du Maine, I am also intrigued to understand how it is we come to know through our hands and acts of transcription. We find scholars from all times reflecting about their practices of collecting and compiling transcriptions of excerpts and extracts from books. On my own sheets of writing I often transcribe, from my readings, those words that represent the activities, relations, and movements of scholars. My pages of transcribed quotations, then, become a social space for relations of knowledge that I have had some hand in creating. In creating these pages, I participate in a scholarly tradition that was typified at least as early as the sixteenth century and was made standard in all subsequent European representations of the scholar.

"The *Study* is a place where a Student, apart from Men, sitteth alone, addicted to his *Studies*, whilst he readeth *Books*, which being within his reach he layeth open upon a *Desk*, and picketh all the best things out of them into his own *Manual*, or marketh them in them with a *Dash*, or a *little Star*, in the Margent" ("*Museum*, est locus ubi Studiosus, secretus ab Hominibus, sedet solus deditus *Studiis*, dum lectitat *Libros*, quos penes se & exponit super *Pluteum*, & excerpit optima quaeque ex illis in *Manuale* suum, notat in illis Liturâ, vel *Asterisco*, ad *Margiem*").[57] This definition of the scholar or student comes from John Comenius's seventeenth-century primer *Orbis pictus*, which introduced to young students, by means of text and woodcut illustrations, the things and experiences of the world, including the world of scholarship. Images of the study, writing, paper, printing, bookshops, libraries, bookbinding, books, and schools are introduced, through the visual sense, to young readers in order to "stir up the Attention, which is to be fastened upon things, and even to be sharpened more and more." Sharpening their attention, Comenius's book can then prepare these young students for "deeper studies."[58]

Comenius presented an image of the student as an isolated sort who compensated for his isolation with a dedication verging on obsession, keeping connected to the world via the (obsessive) transcribing or quoting of other writers' words. His manual—a product of his hand—created and contained a community of knowers in which he participated most fully. The scholar's hand was busy transcribing, quoting, making marks, dashes, and asterisks. These concrete marks were his conduit to a concrete place in the world.

In an interview published in *Le Monde* (September 27, 1973), Roland Barthes updated this image of the scholar in the context of his own "very oppressive, not to say repressive" university experience.[59] He provided one possible gloss for our seventeenth-century student's habits when he wrote: "I'm content to read the text in question, in a rather fetishistic way: writing down certain passages, moments, even words that have the power to move me. As I go along, I use my cards to write down quotations, or ideas that come to me, and . . . from then on, I'm plunged into a kind of frenzied state. I know that everything I read will somehow find its inevitable way into my work."[60]

Barthes, of course, was highly conscious of the social frame of reference for his "work habits"—it was an antiacademic movement challenging the research and rhetorical practices that resulted in the format of the dissertation and similarly structured arguments. Since most scholars made the topic of work habits taboo, Barthes was convinced of its importance: "When a great many people agree that a problem is insignificant, that usually means it is not. Insignificance is the locus of true significance."[61] Focusing on work habits, he thought, theorists would be able to move away from the argumentative format and "to reinforce the critical part of writing by fracturing the very notion of the 'subject' of the book."[62] But it is not just a question of our own work habits.

To understand our own work habits, we might investigate the work (and the workers) by means of which particular texts came to be "within our reach." There is a long social history of organization of libraries and archives that is the prehistory for the development of our obsessive, fetishistic, isolated habits. The passages that move us to *excerpt* and *mark* also propel our researching bodies to move in libraries, archives, and erudite societies. Do the content, rhetoric, and physical production of the passages that move us bear some relation to our movements in these settings? Perhaps we move toward certain texts and the quotation of particular passages in our notebooks because those passages invite us to be a part of the story of their making. As we have seen, proper research decorum would always have us remember that we are *not* the addressees of the texts and documents we study. Such texts were written for readers of *another* time to be used in *their* relations. Still, with our interest in particular texts and documents, we enter the story of their transmission. We are latter-day addressees of these texts as we use them in *our* scholarly relations. As we shape the transmission of these texts into scholarly arguments, we exercise a certain amount of will to rule. But we are also subject to the historical relations of ruling that these texts represent.

> *Frapporsi 5. Against Academic Arguments: Tarabotti and Mozzoni*
>
> The academic practice of quoting and transcribing the words of authorities was customary in seventeenth-century polemics that argued the inferiority of women. And women were certainly capable of quoting the same authorities to build up their counterarguments. But Tarabotti wanted to avoid this practice entirely. In her work *l'Antisatira*, which responded to the misogynistic arguments of Buoninsegni's satire *Contro il lusso donnesco,* Tarabotti showed how the arguments of philosophers, jurists, and theologians, constructed as they were from the conviction of male superiority, could be of little use or interest to women.[63] Although it is near impossible to avoid counterarguments in efforts to discount the value of an argument, Tarabotti saw herself rather as exposing the "deceit" ("inganno") of misogynistic arguments. To expose the "deceit" of a purportedly humorous argument that women were not humans, she wrote: "What does it matter, please tell me, that among you learned philosophers, theologians,

jurists, and mathematicians, you distort the words of God to make it seem as if the Scriptures comply with your monstrous erroneous interpretations?" ("Che importa di grazia che tra voi altri dottissimi filosofi, teologhi, legisti, matematici, andate stiracchiando le parole d'Iddio per far apparir la Scrittura conforme a vostri sensi erronei e bestiali?")[64]

Indeed, according to Tarabotti, "Most academic arguments were raving acts of madness" ("la maggior parte degli accademici ragionamenti meritino titolo di pazzie non che di deliri") that grew, on a daily basis, from "insane complaints of husbands" and their preference for "squandering their wives' dowries on gifts for prostitutes" instead of purchasing "necessities for their wives" ("Non essendo poi altro le lamentazioni degli ammogliati che follie, anzi sceleragini di coloro che, doppo aver con studiati mezzi procurata una ricca dote, si dolgono poi di dover far le spese necessarie per quelle ... per piú agiatamente poter scialacquare in adornar le meretrici").[65] Moreover, Tarabotti protested, academic rhetorics served as stratagems to keep a physical distance between women and books: "Kept far from study, [women] don't have the skills to defend themselves" ("Artificiosamente tenute lontanissime dagli studi acciò alle occasioni non sappiano o vagliano a difendersi"). And not knowing how to defend themselves, they are the ones who "appear unpleasant, guilty of every offense," while the men appear "so innocent" ("appaiono esse le malvage e ree d'ogni colpa, ed essi gl'innocentissimi").[66] If men used academic arguments to keep women far from learning, women would need different discursive structures to defend their right to learn.

        . . .

Perhaps Mozzoni was especially interested in Tarabotti because of her critique of academic argument. Like Tarabotti, Mozzoni saw the quotation of literary and historical example as part of a taxonomy of intolerance. Intellectuals, she believed, were complicit with lawmakers in their obsequiousness toward examples from tradition. "The voice of Cicero and Tribonian," wrote Mozzoni, "sounds louder to the ear of the Italian Senate than public opinion, the cry of philosophy and the unanimous vote of a whole century and a whole nation" ("La voce di Cicerone e di Triboniano suon[a] piú alto all'orecchio dell'italico senato che non l'opinione pubblica, il grido della filosofia, il voto unanime di tutto un secolo e di tutta una nazione").[67] The effect of this practice of quoting from the past was to create nothing less than ignorance of the present. Like de Certeau, Mozzoni understood that the scholar, once detached from historical quotation, would be somewhat disoriented walking out into the street. "Isn't it laughable," Mozzoni asked, "that the scholar discusses the laws of Lycurgus and the twelve tables, and then knows nothing about which institutions more or less safeguard his person and his property? Isn't it irrational that he speaks about the wars of the Titans and then is a complete stranger to the upheavals that produced Italian liberty and to the thousands of those who, on the field, from prisons and in exile prepared the way for our current cultural state?" ("Non è egli risibile che lo scolaro discuta le leggi di Licurgo e le dodici tavole, e poi non sappia da quali istitutioni è piú o meno tutelata la sua persona e la sua proprietà? Non è egli fuor di ragione che vi parli delle guerre dei Titani e poi sia completamente straniero ai rivolgimenti che produssero la libertà italiana e alle miglia[ia] di coloro che sul campo come dalle prigioni all'esilio prepararono l'attual civiltà?")[68] Tarabotti had pointed the way to this insight two hundred years earlier with her understanding of academic argument as prejudicial to women's advancement and education. She even saw the materials and instruments of writing as implicated in the prejudice against women.

SHELF LIST 6. HANDS, INSTRUMENTS OF WRITING

Lucrezia Marinella, *La nobiltà et l'eccellenza delle donne co' diffetti et mancamenti de gli huomini* (1601)

Anne Bradstreet, *The Tenth Muse Lately Sprung Up in America: Or Severall Poems, Compiled with Great Variety of Wit and Learning, Full of Delight . . . By a Gentlewoman in Those Parts* (1650)

Arcangela Tarabotti, *Che le donne siano della spezie degli uomini* (1651)

Arcangela Tarabotti, *La semplicità ingannata* (1654)

Traiano Boccalini, *Ragguagli di Parnaso* (1612); *"I ragguagli di Parnaso," or, Advertisements from Parnassus* (1656)

Susanna Bucci, "Come si parla della donna: I cataloghi" (1983)

Patricia Klindienst Joplin, "The Voice of the Shuttle Is Ours" (1984)

Daphne Marlatt, *Ana Historic* (1988)

Ann Rosalind Jones, *The Currency of Eros: Women's Love Lyric in Europe, 1540–1620* (1990)

Arcangela Tarabotti, *Che le donne siano della spezie degli uomini*, ed. Letizia Panizza (1994)

Ann Rosalind Jones and Peter Stallybrass, *Renaissance Clothing and the Materials of Memory* (2000)

Satya Brata Datta, *Women and Men in Early Modern Venice: Reassessing History* (2003)

Arcangela Tarabotti, *Paternal Tyranny*, ed. and trans. Letizia Panizza (2004)

Arcangela Tarabotti, *La semplicità ingannata*, critical ed., ed. Simona Bortot (2007)

As we saw, Traiano Boccalini understood "that Women's true Poetics consisted in their Needle and Spindle." For him, the engagement of women's hands in activities of learning could only lead to the degradation of men's erudite intercourse. Did the women offend by bringing their pens to academic meetings? By writing and taking notes as equals among men?[69] In the prologue to her poetry, Anne Bradstreet worried about the critics who would say "my hand a needle better fits."[70] And this material metaphor—a needle as a metaphor for a woman's activities—often intruded in the literature concerning women's education.[71] But it was also a metaphor for the difficulty experienced by seventeenth-century male cultural figures in classifying the many women writers who inhabited their republic of letters. If they were writers, they could not be women, and if they were women, why didn't they stick to sewing and mending?[72]

It was important for Boccalini (and his readers) to name the "Needle and Spindle"—the instruments women used to perform their sewing and mending—leaving women's writing unspoken and abstracted from the "pen and ink" and ongoing work of writing. Moreover, women's work with the "Needle and Spindle" was irreparably severed from the work of their hands with the materials of writing. The kinds of thought that might be generated in the suturing of these two material activities (a historical possibility that emerged precisely in the seventeenth century) were thereby lost to representation.[73]

> *Frapporsi 6. Hands That Take Up the Pen in Specious Reasoning*
>
> In her own writing, Tarabotti deployed the "needle and spindle" metaphor to deplore the state of girls' education. Fathers, she wrote in *La semplicità ingannata (Simplicity Deceived)*, "raise their daughters as if they lacked both reason and feeling. They hire female teachers who are ignorant, who barely know how to teach the first elements of reading, who know nothing of philosophy, law, and theology. With such imperfect instruction, the girls scarcely learn to read the ABCs. The fathers then reproach them for their stupidity, and when they see them with a pen in hand, they start yelling right away, threatening them with their lives if they will not leave their writing and attend to feminine labors of needle and spindle." ("Le allevate e nutrite come fossero senza giudicio e sentimento, e date loro per direttrice ne gl'insegnamenti un'altra femina, pur anche inerudita, e che malamente le amaestra ne' primi elementi che concernono al saper leggere, senza cognizion alcuna di filosofie, di leggi, e di teologie. In somma non apparano altra lettura che quella dell'A,B,C, imperfettamente insegnata loro. Io che 'l so il posso liberamente testificare. Se le vedete con una penna alla mano, i gridi sono in pronto, imponendo loro sotto pena dell'istessa vita che tralasciato lo scrivere attendano a' lavori feminili dell'ago e della conocchia.")[74]
>
> In the *Antisatira*, Tarabotti went beyond her censure of girls' education to lament men's training in grammar, humanities, rhetoric, logic, and philosophy as that which makes them blind to women who put down their needles for pens: "Those [men], I say, so as to seem like master teachers of the whole literary world, if by chance, they see a woman use a pen instead of a needle, they will testify, like the Gospel, against their writings with a thousand lies about how it cannot be a woman who writes." ("Perversità grande di costoro i quali, essendo sin dagli anni piú teneri allevati fra

studi di grammatica e umanità . . . , poi passano ad applicarsi alla retorica, logica, filosofia, e altre scienze. . . . Costoro, dico, per parere protomaestri di tutto il mondo litterario, se per sorte vedono da una donna invece dell'ago adoprarsi la penna, con mille invenzioni contro quei scritti attestano come Evangelo che non può essere ch'una femina scriva.")[75] Because men threaten and ignore those women who take up the pen, Tarabotti goes on to understand the needle and spindle as alternative instruments for recording our stories: "We could weave volumes of raped women" ("Si potriano tesser volumi di donne sforzate").[76]

As we have seen, attention to the instruments of writing includes attention to the hand that takes up the pen. This is the hand that participates in the making and organizing of historical knowledge, taking notes, creating files, transcribing. Paleography is sometimes considered the "handmaid" of history, but the hand is also the handmaid of history.[77] Tarabotti made this clear as she tried to disentangle the specious reasoning of the treatise *Che le donne non siano della spezie degli huomini (That Women Are Not of the Species of Men)*, the Italian translation, printed in 1647, of a Latin tract published in Frankfurt in 1594.[78] Tarabotti took each point of the treatise's argument, titled it an *illusion* or *deceit* ("inganno"), and responded with a *disillusionment* ("disinganno") that would expose and undo the damage of each "deceit."

One especially insidious deceit pertained to the hand as an instrument of writing and history. It argued, in essence, that the definition of a writing instrument was that it was "detached" from the body of the writer. "A blacksmith cannot make a sword without the help of a hammer. A writer cannot write without the medium of a pen. Nor can a tailor sew without a needle. In the same way, a man cannot procreate without the help of a woman. So a hammer does not belong to the species of the blacksmith. And a pen does not belong to the species of the writer. And a needle does not belong to the species of the tailor. In the same way, a woman does not belong to the species of the man. . . . In nature, one never finds an instrument attached to the one who uses it—the instrument is always detached. So, in the case of the blacksmith, the instrument is not the hand but something detached, that is, the hammer." ("Il fabro non può formare una spada senza l'aiuto del martello, lo scrittore non può scriver senza il mezzo della penna, né meno il sartore può cucire senza l'aco. Così l'uomo non può generare senza l'aiuto della femina. Come dunque il martello non è della spezie del fabbro, la penna dello scrittore, e l'aco del sartore; così ancora la donna non è della spezie dell'uomo. . . . non si ritrova mai naturalmente che l'instrumento sia unito con la causa efficiente ma sempre disgionto dell'istessa maniera: ché nel fabro l'instrumento non è la mano ma qualche cosa di disgionto, cioè il martello.")[79] Tarabotti deftly undid the damage of this reasoning with a question: "Why, please tell me, do you compare a woman to a hammer, a pen, a needle?" ("Perché di grazia comparate la donna al martello, alla penna, all'aco?")[80] With one stroke, she revealed the absurd use the author was making of Aristotelian notions of efficient and instrumental causes.[81] Focusing, in general, on the physical dimension of handwriting and ink, Tarabotti clearly perceived the hand of the author as an integrated part of his attack on women. "With the poison of your letters you try to kill the souls of simple women. You even try with the blackness of your ink to obscure the brightness of Christian faith and to stain the innocence and purity of women." ("Col veleno de'vostri caratteri procurate d'uccider l'anime de'semplici. Anzi tentate col nero de'vostri inchiostri d'oscurare il candido della Fede Cristiana, e di macchiar l'innocenza e purità delle donne.")[82]

SHELF LIST 7. DEBAUCHERY, ERUDITION

Seneca, *De tranquillitate animi* (before 62 A.D.)

Guy Patin, *Lettres choisies* (1649–55)

Gabriel Naudé, *Advis à Nos Seigneurs de Parlement, sur la vente de la Bibliothèque de M. le Cardinal Mazarin* (1652)

Arcangela Tarabotti, *La semplicità ingannata* (1654)

Charles Augustin Sainte-Beuve, *Portraits littéraires* (1832–39)

Gabriel Naudé, *News from France; or, A Description of the Library of Cardinal Mazarin, Preceded by the Surrender of the Library* (1907)

Robert Damien, *Bibliothèque et état: Naissance d'une raison politique dans la France du XVIIe siècle* (1995)

Gabriel Naudé, *Avvertenze per la costituzione di una biblioteca*, ed., and trans. Vittoria Lacchini (1992)

Arcangela Tarabotti, *Paternal Tyranny*, ed. and trans. Letizia Panizza (2004)

Arcangela Tarabotti, *La semplicità ingannata*, critical ed., ed. Simona Bortot (2007)

To instruct—*erudire*—to expel rudeness.[83] *To debauch*, to lead someone astray, to corrupt, to rough-hew timber into a beam.[84] Books that, in the best of worlds, make us polished and cultured also have the capacity to lead us astray, isolate, abstract us from the branch, the tree, the forest. Seneca asked: "What is the use of having countless books and libraries, whose titles their owners can scarcely read through in a whole lifetime? The learner is not instructed but burdened by the mass of them." ("Quo innumerabiles libros et bibliothecas, quarum dominus vix tota vita indices perlegit? Onerat discentem turba, non instruit.") For Seneca, the Alexandrian Library was nothing more than a monument to "learned debauchery" ("studiosa luxuria").[85] Since antiquity, scholars and philosophers have understood the potential for cultural debauchery in books and libraries. Was it a gnawing sense that the language and knowledge in books were abstracted from the hands that wrote them? What metamorphoses took place in the hands and bodies of writers once their knowledge was rough-hewn into books?

In August 1648 in Paris, Gabriel Naudé was looking forward to the public inauguration of the Mazarine Library. He invited two of his friends, a physician, Guy Patin, and a philosopher, Pierre Gassendi, to spend a private evening of revelry prior to the inauguration. On August 27, 1648, Guy Patin wrote bemusedly about this party invitation:

> Mr. Naudé has invited us to eat and sleep, all three of us, next Sunday in his house at Gentilly. He promised that only the three of us will engage in debauchery. But God only knows what kind of debauchery! Mr. Naudé, by nature, drinks only water and has never tasted wine. Mr. Gassendi is so delicate that he would never dare to drink wine and imagines that his body would burn if he were to drink any. This is why Ovid's verse—he flees from wine and abstemiously enjoys pure water—is so pertinent to both of them. As for me—next to these two men whose writings are so great I feel worthy only to dry their ink with sand—as for me, I drink very little; and still, all the

same, there will be great debauchery, but of the philosophic type, and perhaps something more, since all three of us have recovered from lycanthropy and the disease of scruples, the tyrant of conscience. Maybe we will venture as far as the edge of Naudé's biblio-sanctuary.

[M. Naudé, bibliothécaire de M. le cardinal Mazarin, intime ami de M. Gassendi comme il est le mien, nous a engagés pour dimanche prochain à aller souper et coucher nous trois en sa maison de Gentilly, à la charge que nous ne serons que nous trois et que nous y ferons la débauche: mais Dieu sait quelle débauche! M. Naudé ne boit naturellement que de l'eau et n'a jamais goûté vin. M. Gassendi est si délicat qu'il n'en oseroit boire, et s'imagine que son corps brûleroit s'il en avoit bu. C'est pourquoi je puis bien dire de l'un et de l'autre ce vers d'Ovide: Vina fugit, gaudetque meris abstemius undis. Pour moi, je ne puis que jeter de la poudre sur l'écriture de ces deux grands hommes, j'en bois fort peu; et néanmoins ce sera une débauche, mais philosophique, et peut-être quelque chose davantage, pour être tous trois guéris du loup-garou et du mal des scrupules, qui est le tyran des consciences. Nous irons peut-être jusque fort près du sanctuaire.][86]

Unfortunately, we have no record of the private carousing among the three friends because the planned public inauguration of the Mazarine Library was canceled. But I would like to consider these corporeal images of the librarian's former lycanthropy and philosophic debauchery in relation to the inauguration of a library of state, as markers of relations between bodies and politics. Patin tells us that because the three friends were recovered lycanthropes, they might have engaged in *something more* than the usual philosophic debauchery. That is, because they used to suffer delusions of transforming themselves into werewolves (with all of the bestiality such transformations entailed), their philosophic debauchery might have had bestial overtones. Ultimately, though, instead of philosophic debauchery, the potential for bestiality erupted in the political demise of the library.

The first Fronde, or uprising against Mazarin's regime, broke out on August 28, and the library became one of the first casualties of the ensuing civil war. Naudé's vigorous protests were not enough to save the library from dismemberment and sale. In 1651, Mazarin was forced to leave Paris. Parliament seized his property and eleven months later ordered the sale of the Mazarine Library. In an effort to forestall the demise of the library, Naudé wrote a letter to Parliament in 1652 in which he appealed to Parliament's "ordinary sense of justice to save the life of this daughter, or—to be more exact—this famous library. . . . the most beautiful and the best furnished of any library now in the world, or that is likely, if affection do not much deceive me, ever for to be hereafter" ("Ne puis-je mas me promettre que votre bienveillance et votre justice ordinaire sauveront la vie à cette fille, ou, pour mieux dire, à cette fameuse Bibliothèque . . . la plus belle et la mieux fournie de toutes les bibliothèques qui on jamais esté au monde, et qui pourront, si l'affection ne me trompe bien fort, y estre à l'advenir").[87]

Frapporsi 7. The Bestiality and Deceit of Political Erudition

As we saw, Tarabotti exposed the hypocrisy of fathers who falsely professed to their daughters a "love that reached deep into the bowels" ("un amor sviscerato").[88] Indeed, the viscera or bowels served to bind daughters to their deceptive fathers, creating a particular vista on political knowledge. Tarabotti wrote: "How is it possible, you deceitful fathers, that you hold in your breasts a heart so cruel that it can stand to torture the body of your daughters, who are really your viscera . . . ?" ("Com'è possibile, o ingannatori, che chiudiate in seno un cuore così crudele che soffra di tormentare il corpo delle vostre figliuole, che pur son vostre viscere . . . ?")[89] These deceits were elaborated at an age in which children's trust of their tyrannical fathers was total. Tyranny, then, was best understood from the perspective of a trusting daughter who, although connected to her father by flesh, suffered the cruelest political deceptions at his hands. Interposing the bodies of father and daughter in her knowledge of politics and culture, Tarabotti traced, from the body or the viscera of the daughter to the bowels of the father, an embodied design for reorganizing this knowledge. As we have seen, Tarabotti represented herself in the history of the Mazarine Library and in relation to this library's founder and librarian, the French bibliophile Gabriel Naudé. We might see her also as a "daughter" to his philosophic debauchery, as well as an heir to his erudition.

SHELF LIST 8. DAUGHTERS IN THE ORDER OF POLITICAL KNOWLEDGE

Jean Bodin, *Les six livres de la République* (1576)

Gabriel Naudé, "Advis à Nos Seigneurs de Parlement, sur la vente de la Bibliothèque de M. le Cardinal Mazarin" (1652)

Arcangela Tarabotti, *La semplicità ingannata* (1654)

Gabriel Naudé, *News from France; or, A Description of the Library of Cardinal Mazarin, Preceded by the Surrender of the Library* (1907)

Emilio Zanette, *Suor Arcangela monaca del Seicento veneziano* (1960)

Ginevra Conti Odorisio, *Storia dell'idea femminista in Italia* (1980)

Patricia Klindienst Joplin, "The Voice of the Shuttle Is Ours" (1984)

Elaine Scarry, *The Body in Pain: The Making and Unmaking of the World* (1985)

Emilia Biga, *Una polemica antifemminista del Seicento: La "Maschera scoperta" di Angelico Aprosio* (1989)

Francesca Medioli, *L'"Inferno monacale" di Arcangela Tarabotti* (1990)

Stanley Chojnacki, "'The Most Serious Duty': Motherhood, Gender, and Patrician Culture in Renaissance Venice" (1991)

Ginevra Conti Odorisio, *Famiglia e stato nella "République" di Jean Bodin* (1993)

Lorna Hutson, *The Usurer's Daughter: Male Friendship and Fictions of Women in Sixteenth-Century England* (1994)

Virginia Cox, "The Single Self: Feminist Thought and the Marriage Market in Early Modern Venice" (1995)

Nancy L. Canepa, "The Writing behind the Wall: Arcangela Tarabotti's *Inferno monacale* and Cloistral Autobiography in the Seventeenth Century" (1996)

Jutta Gisela Sperling, *Convents and the Body Politic in Late Renaissance Venice* (1999)

Arcangela Tarabotti, *Paternal Tyranny,* ed. and trans. Letizia Panizza (2004)

Janet Levarie Smarr, *Joining the Conversation: Dialogues by Renaissance Women* (2005)

Arcangela Tarabotti, *La semplicità ingannata,* critical ed., ed. Simona Bortot (2007)

Naudé's affection for the Mazarine was a fatherly one. He spoke of the library in procreative terms as "the work of my hands and the miracle of my life" ("l'oeuvre de mes mains et le miracle de ma vie").[90] And he prayed to Parliament that they might assist him in "saving the life of this daughter" ("sauveront la vie a cette fille").[91] Even before the sale of the library, Naudé began to grieve for the "decease of this my daughter" ("au trepas de cette mienne fille").[92] While writing daughters like Tarabotti figured themselves as the "viscera" of their cruel, deceitful fathers, "who tortured the bodies of their daughters," Naudé figured the Mazarine as a daughter to the librarian.[93] Together, in the convergence of their father-daughter figurations, Tarabotti and Naudé confirmed the political centrality of daughters to learning and the state and constructed a historical trope for understanding the constraints writers and scholars might feel today in the confines of a library and its organizations of knowledge. Naudé requested Tarabotti's works for placement in his library, whose walls, tables, shelves, and order of books conveyed something of the cruelty, deceit, and torture conventionally practiced on the bodies of seventeenth-century daughters.[94]

Frapporsi 8. Tyranny (and Freedom) from the Daughter's Perspective

Tarabotti understood tyranny (and freedom) in relation to the political status (and body) of the daughter. In her *Semplicità ingannata*, also titled *La tirannia paterna*, Tarabotti claimed that the tyranny of fathers was greater than the tyranny of Nero and Diocletian. While men condemned the power of the tyrant in their political discourses, they still promoted a *ragion di stato* that made the father's tyranny over suffering daughters one of its moral mainstays.[95] How might this suffering of daughters have gained political voice with the entry of Tarabotti's works in Naudé's library of state? Did the eventual dispersion of the Mazarine amount to a political victimization of Naudé's cherished "daughter" similar to the forced monachization experienced by Tarabotti?

For Tarabotti, the *ragion di stato* was not the "neutral" knowledge necessary for founding, conserving, and expanding a political domain but the active efforts of noble fathers to conserve their wealth and class at the expense of their daughters' servitude. Drawing attention to men's belief that "the high number of daughters was detrimental to the ledgers of state" ("stimate pregiudicar la multiplicità delle figliole alla Ragion di Stato"), Tarabotti discovered, in this same belief, men's underlying knowledge that daughters were crucial to the processes of state making.[96] In this passage from the *Inferno monacale* that Jutta Sperling has so brilliantly illuminated for us in her work, Tarabotti was able to overturn the terms of western political discourse and to see daughters at the center of this discourse from which they were generally excluded, placing daughters and their dowries at the center of men's thinking about the *ragion di stato*.[97] The emergence in this period of the public library, figured as a *daughter*, might constitute one such measure of how writers like Tarabotti actively intervened in a not-so-rational reason of state. Her self-representation as a suffering daughter may further permit us to imagine that Naudé's "daughter" of state, the Mazarine Library that was eventually sold and dismembered, could produce only a highly problematic refuge for Tarabotti's feminist concepts.

Tarabotti's representation of daughters at the center of men's thinking about the *ragion di stato* effectively shifted the balance in republican discourse, encouraging us to reread a whole history of tacit—albeit discursive—prohibitions. As feminist scholarship of the last twenty years has shown, such discursive prohibitions have permanently arranged daughters as invisible, yet indispensable, markers, shoring up relationships of power and knowledge among men. Among many scholars and theorists one could cite, Lynda Boose has pointed to the "hierarchy of value that isolates the daughter as the most absent member within the discourse of the family institution" and has shown how this hierarchy is inscribed in the "production and organization of knowledge."[98]

Lorna Hutson's brilliant study of sixteenth-century representations of "daughters" as rhetorical/discursive markers in relations of friendship and credit among men is fundamental to what I have been developing here. We can see Naudé's ordering of his library/daughter as an epistemological consequence of the sixteenth-century art "to use and order," carefully theorized and historicized by Hutson in rhetorical constructions of *oikonomia* and in textualizations of *amicitia* and service.[99] But more central to our purpose here, Hutson's critique of a historical transition from feudal to textual economies of service makes more audible the vehement charges of daughters like Tarabotti against the noisy tyranny and deceits of educated men.[100]

Tarabotti well understood that any republic, such as that defined by Bodin as the "just government by a sovereign power over a number of families and what they have in common" ("un droit gouvernement de plusieurs mesnages, & de ce qui leur est commun, avec puissance souveraine"), could not enfranchise daughters with any measure of citizenship or voice.[101] In such political conditions, Tarabotti turned her hopes to a sort of citizenship in the republic of letters with the placement of her books on the shelves of the Mazarine. There, on the shelf, she still spoke as a "daughter," as a "hidden investment" of relations of knowledge among men.[102] But there on the shelf, she would address her charges of "deceit" not only to the fathers who imprisoned their daughters in convents but also to the order of books in the library, that other "daughter" with whom she might rewrite the story of tyranny.[103]

SHELF LIST 9. BIBLIOGRAPHIC CATEGORIES AND ARMIES OF NUNS

Gabriel Naudé, *Advis pour dresser une bibliothèque* (1627)

Arcangela Tarabotti, *Lettere familiari e di complimento* (1650)

Arcangela Tarabotti, *La semplicità ingannata* (1654)

Gabriel Naudé, *Advice on Establishing a Library*, ed. Archer Taylor, trans. W. H. Alexander, J. S. Gildersleeve, H. A. Small, and T. Webb Jr. (1950)

Virginia Cox, "The Single Self: Feminist Thought and the Marriage Market in Early Modern Venice" (1995)

Satya Brata Datta, *Women and Men in Early Modern Venice: Reassessing History* (2003)

Arcangela Tarabotti, *Paternal Tyranny*, ed. and trans. Letizia Panizza (2004)

Arcangela Tarabotti, *Lettere familiari e di complimento*, ed. Meredith Kennedy Ray and Lynn Lara Westwater (2005)

Arcangela Tarabotti, *La semplicità ingannata*, critical ed., ed. Simona Bortot (2007)

Edward Muir, *The Culture Wars of the Late Renaissance: Skeptics, Libertines, and Opera* (2007)

Gabriel Naudé's treatise on libraries, *Advis pour dresser une bibliothèque*, was written in 1627 and addressed to Henri de Mesmes, a bibliophile and president of the Parliament of Paris. It was among the first works in early modern Europe to professionalize the work of the librarian, providing comprehensive guidelines for collecting books, placing them in an appropriate setting, and arranging them by subject and language. In my reading here, I am most interested in Naudé's representation of the love that was intrinsic to dynamic and hierarchical social relations in the library. For Naudé, the goal of a great library was to generate among its visitors a certain love of the state and its rulers and to produce such love through the medium of books. "Every man who seeks a book judges it to be good and, conceiving it to be so without being able to find it, is forced to esteem it curious and very rare. So that, coming at last upon it in some library, he readily believes that the owner of the library knew it as well as himself and had bought it for the same reason that prompted him to search after it. And thus he conceives an incomparable esteem both for the owner and for the library," who, as we remember, is daughter to the librarian. ("Tout homme qui recherche un livre le juge bon, et le jugeant tel sans le pouvoir trouver, est contraint de l'estimer curieux et grandement rare, de sorte, que venant en fin à le rencontrer en quelque Bibliothèque, il se persuade facilement que le maistre d'icelle le cognoissoit aussi bien que luy, et l'avoit acheté pour les mesmes intentions qui l'excitoient à le rechercher, et en suite de ce conçoit une estime nompareille et du maistre et de la Bibliothèque.")[104] According to this bibliographic dynamic, the works of Tarabotti were, at least hypothetically, the object of someone's search and a medium for promoting love and political identification with Mazarin. If not, what function would they, or could they, serve in his library?

It would be important to know the criteria by which Naudé selected the works of Tarabotti for the promotion of love and political identification with Mazarin. Tarabotti might, for example, have joined that group of writers who "have introduced new principles and upon them have established strange and unheard-of reasoning, such as had never been foreseen" ("ont introduit de nouveaux principes, et basty sur iceux des ratiocinations estranges, inouyes et non jamais préveues").[105] Her organization of political knowledge around the suffering of daughters certainly produced a novel kind of reasoning. We may know little of such authors, Naudé wrote, because the novelty of their thought inevitably leads them to be "buried under disdain" ("couvrir . . . sous le mespris").[106] Imagine it. Buried under disdain. A new Library of Congress subject category. Our ignorance of those authors like Tarabotti, who have been buried under disdain, provides the most compelling reason, according to Naudé, for understanding such authors as "very necessary" ("très-nécessaires") for the library.[107]

Naudé may also have collected Tarabotti's works with the criterion that they were the "first that have been composed upon the matter that they treat" ("les premiers qui ayent esté composez sur la matière de laquelle ils traictent").[108] Or perhaps they were collected with a more negative criterion in mind, as one of those books that are "trivial or unusual, interesting or neglected" ("triviales ou peu communes, curieuses ou négligées").[109] Such books were important to the library for the "weak wits" ("les foibles esprits") who visited, as well as for the "strong" ("les forts") who took satisfaction in "refuting" ("réfuter") such works, claiming them to be "like serpents and vipers among other living creatures, like tares in good wheat, like thorns among roses. And all this in imitation of the natural world in which these unprofitable and dangerous things help to round out the masterwork and the scheme by which it was accomplished" ("comme les serpens et vipères entre les autres animaux, comme l'ivroye dans le bon bled, comme les espines entre les roses; et ce à l'exemple du monde où ces choses inutiles et dangereuses accomplissent le chef-d'oeuvre et la fabrique se sa composition").[110] We may be tempted to conclude that Tarabotti's works were collected under the category of the "trivial," knowing what we do about the misogynist ambience in which her work was received. Still, we must remember that newness of argument was an important category of collecting for Naudé, and one that could just as well be applied to her writing.

The improvement of a library's collection depended on the circulation of "affection" and "desire": the *affection* for books felt by either the library's founder or the librarian and the *desire* held by both to augment the collection ("l'affection que l'on porte aux Livres, et le grand désir que l'on a de dresser une Bibliothèque").[111] At times, the substance of relations among statesmen was one of bibliographic love more than diplomatic exchange. In the case cited by Naudé of Richard de Bury, bishop of Durham, lord chancellor and lord high treasurer of England, the "flying rumor of our love for books now spread everywhere. The rumor spread so much that we were reported to be even languishing from our desire for them, especially old ones, and that anyone could easier obtain our favor by quartos than by money" ("amoris nostri fama volatilis jam ubique percrebuit, tantumque librorum et maxime veterum ferebamur cupiditate languescere, posse vero quemlibet per quaternos facilius quam per pecuniam adipisci favorem").[112] Books in state libraries thus acquired a currency of political eros that may have had nothing to do with the words contained within their covers. When Tarabotti wrote to Clermont-Gallerande expressing self-confidence in her ability to obtain the favor of Naudé, perhaps she was referring to his languishing for books and the ways in which her books could become an instrument of political favor.

...

Naudé advised librarians to organize their libraries as an officer might organize his troops, writing that books must be "classified and arranged according to subject matter, or in such other fashion as will facilitate their being found at specified places. I affirm, moreover, that without this order and arrangement a collection of books of whatever size, were it fifty thousand volumes, would no more merit the name of a library than an assembly of thirty thousand men the name of an army if they be not arranged in their several quarters under the orders of their officers." ("Rangez et disposez suivant leurs diverses matières, ou en telle autre façon qu'on les puisse trouver facilement et à point nommé. Je dis davantage, que sans cet ordre et disposition tel amas de livre que ce peut estre, fust-il de cinquante mille volumes, ne mériteroit pas le nom de Bibliothèque, non plus qu'une assemblée di trente mille hommes le nom d'armée, s'ils n'estoient rangez en divers quartiers sous la conduitte de leurs Chefs et Capitaines.")[113] The purpose of such military discipline, explained Naudé, was to enable a patron to make use of the library "without labor, without difficulty, and without confusion" ("sans labeur, sans peine et sans confusion").[114] Such military organization of the library/daughter, however, could only make a highly problematic atmosphere for the feminist works of daughters like Tarabotti.[115]

> *Frapporsi 9. A Bibliographic Army of Nuns*
>
> I would like to suggest that this highly gendered set of images, by virtue of which the male library patron was able to obtain easy access to the treasures of the *daughter*, produced precisely a difficult and troubled setting for the writings of Tarabotti. While Naudé brought his *daughter* of state into existence by outlawing labor, difficulty, and confusion from the order of books, Tarabotti intervened in this procreative process by dint of the labor, difficulty, and confusion of her thinking and writing, which unraveled his political accountings or *ragion di stato*. Naudé prescribed a military order of books for his *daughter* of state, but Tarabotti intervened with a completely different view of a bibliographic army. "It may be true," she wrote, "that if all of history's daughters forcibly confined in convents were to return to the world, we could form a very large army. But still, we would not devote ourselves to taking over kingdoms; we would be content to stay closed up in the rooms of our fathers' houses." ("Vero è che se tutte le Religiose involontarie fossero al secolo, potriano col loro numero formar un grandissimo esercito, ma non attenderiano a impadronirsi di regni, anzi stariano volentieri chiuse nelle paterne abitazioni.")[116]

SHELF LIST 10. THE LIBRARIAN AS POLITICAL ACTOR

Gabriel Naudé, *Considérations politiques sur les coups d'état* (1639)

Francesco Buoninsegni, *Contro il lusso donnesco, satira menippea, con l'Antisatira di Arcangela Tarabotti in risposta* (1644)

René Pintard, *Le libertinage érudit dans la première moitié du 17e siècle* (1943)

Gabriel Naudé, *Considérations politiques sur les coups d'état,* with an introductory essay by Louis Marin, "Pour une théorie baroque de l'action politique" (1989)

Irene Silverblatt, "Interpreting Women in States: New Feminist Ethnohistories" (1991)

Francesco Buoninsegni and Arcangela Tarabotti, *Satira e antisatira,* ed. Elissa B. Weaver (1998)

As we have seen, Naudé envisioned the construction of a relation between a ruler and his subjects via the experience of looking for—and finding—books in the library. A public library, therefore, must contain "all the principal authors who have written upon the great diversity of particular subjects.... It must be said also that there is nothing more to the credit of a library than that every man finds in it what he seeks." ("Tous les principaux Autheurs qui on escrit sur la grande diversité des sujet particuliers ... qu'il n'y a rien qui rende une Bibliothèque plus recommandable que lors qu'un chacun y trouve ce qu'il cherche.")[117] Naudé then develops this experiential connection between readers and authors in the library, suggesting that librarians might choose books according to their healing qualities: "It seems to me expedient to follow the practice of those physicians who prescribe the quantity of drugs according to their quality, and to state that one cannot be mistaken in collecting all those books which by quality and condition should be placed in a library" ("Il me semble qu'il est à propos de faire comme les Médecins, qui ordonnent la quantité des drogues suivant la qualité d'icelles, et de dire que l'on ne peut manquer de recueillir tous ceux qui auront les qualitez et conditions requises pour estre mis dans une Bibliothèque").[118] The library, then—a daughter born from the viscera of the librarian—also contained the physical salves (or books) that would create a bond between the prince and his subjects. In other words, the daughter and the medicinal quality of the books were called upon to mediate between knowledge and the state.

Naudé understood the librarian to be the most important political actor after the prince, best elaborating this idea in his work *Considérations politiques sur les coups d'état. Considérations politiques* was first published in Rome in 1639, with only twelve copies printed for twelve men to treasure in their cabinets.[119] Louis Du May, who reedited the work in 1673 under the title *Sciences des princes,* classified it as a Machiavellian or Tacitean work, in which the secrets of power, the mysteries of statecraft (*raison d'état*), were exposed to those who were not supposed to have any knowledge of them. With it, Naudé became a canonical reference in the history of state power.[120]

From 1631 to 1637, Naudé, an erudite libertine and theorist of state reason, was secretary/librarian in Rome to Cardinal Bagni, the papal nunzio to Paris, who died in 1637. After a brief stay with Antonio Barberini, Naudé was recalled to Paris to serve as librarian to Richelieu and then to Mazarin. In this capacity, Naudé spent almost ten years building the Mazarine Library.[121] In the course of his career, Louis Marin asks, does Naudé change from a libertine philosopher to become a "domestic servant" ("le domestique") collecting and arranging books for the statesman Mazarin?[122]

In the seventeenth century, a coup d'état was not a change of government by violent means but a government's preservation of the health of the state by an exceptional, violent action. A coup d'état was, in other words, a reversion to the originary violence that marked the foundation of a prince's power. Naudé, in his *Considérations politiques*, defined a field, a space between ceremony and violence, and in this field he developed a baroque theory of political action.[123]

When he writes about the coup d'état, Naudé focuses his attention on "the secret of state, the secret that shrouds the preparation of the coup" ("le secret d'état, ce secret qui enveloppe la préparation du coup").[124] The librarian is best prepared to understand these secrets by virtue of his intellectual imagination, which Naudé considers a blend of knowledge and action. Naudé knows he can never enter in the cabinets of the powerful to see the elaboration of a coup d'état. "But," writes Marin, "he can use his imagination to play and penetrate, to imitate the paths and reflections of the prince, to 'double' his political behavior, in order to study it. He can feign the behavior of the prince in order to understand it. This is how Naudé acted in the political theater, by virtue of intellectual play and imaginative pretending. He didn't pretend 'to be Nero, in order to find better ways to destroy humankind.' But he imagined himself interpreting Nero's plans, deciphering his acts, uncovering, with this game, all of the things Nero intended to hide with thousands of strategies."[125] Indeed, Naudé's librarian/collector plays a special role in state secrets, secluding himself in the library and entering the fictions of those who rule via documents and books: "In the secrecy of the library, in contact with the documents, the librarian," writes Marin, "playing different roles of political action, would be able to construct images of different political behaviors and the models of secrets of state."[126]

Frapporsi 10. Women, Liberty, the State

With this theory of political action, Naudé is innovative in his construction of the librarian as a figure who, entering the fiction of those who rule, interrupts the western tradition and logic of seeing culture as separate from economy and power. I would like to suggest that Tarabotti, too, was able to fashion herself as a central player in the *ragion di stato* and as a worthy neighbor to the most famous writers in the Mazarine Library, by the ways in which she, too, constructed a bridge between culture, economy, and power and between women and the state. In all of her writings, Tarabotti turned political arguments of tyranny and liberty upside down, pointing to the paradoxical ways in which men's idea of liberty meant tyranny, impoverishment, and visceral suffering for women.[127] Her *Antisatira*, in particular, provides several clues for understanding the methods she employed to reorganize knowledge of republican politics from the perspective of these logics.

Tarabotti's *Antisatira* is generally read as a dialectic response to Francesco Buoninsegni's *Contro il lusso donnesco (Against Women's Extravagance),* a work of "academic raving" ("delirio Accademico"), according to the author himself, that inveighed against the shoes, clothes and makeup of women.[128] I would like to suggest, rather, that the *Antisatira* saw beyond the historical theory that has stereotyped women to address the social relations that separated women from such categories, theories, and institutions as "ragion di stato," "economy," "culture," "politics," libraries, and so on.[129] For example, in the *Antisatira*, Tarabotti showed how economies depended on economic relations between the sexes or, more particularly, how men balanced their budgets with lust, avarice, and vanity, keeping their wives plain and their courtesans adorned. "They would like their wives to dress after the fashion of our first Mother, so that they can more easily squander in the adornment of their prostitutes" ("Vorrebbero ch'elle [le mogli] vestissero all'uso della nostra prima madre, per piú agiatamente poter scialacquare in adornar le meretrici").[130] Moreover, she insisted on pointing out the ways in which men and women imitated each other in matters of vanity, clothes, jewels, hairstyles, perfume, and makeup. And she showed how moral discourses about women depended upon the moral failings of men. "Today, we see all that Mr. Buoninsegni detests and blames on women to be regularly practiced and exercised by men" ("Tutto ciò che'l sig. Buoninsegni detesta a biasimo delle donne, tutto si vede a' giorni nostri pontualmente effettuato et esercitato dagli uomini").[131]

Challenging western "categorical splits" that would separate women from the state and culture from economy, Tarabotti argued, in particular, that jewels and other adornments had the same political significance for theories of state as the price of grain had for the conservation of liberty.[132] Her argument, which is rhetorically labored, difficult, and confusing in terms of her leaps and juxtapositions, might be understood like this: the price of grain is the economic standard for understanding jewels and adornments, money spent on courtesans, the liberty of state, and the liberty of women. She writes that men "bewail the price of grain spent on adorning [wives] with jewels. . . . But then they freely squander treasures in the purchase of disgraceful and abominable loves. . . . Cato was so right in considering the loss of Roman liberty imminent when he heard that a fish was sold for as much as an ox. But to spend in the adornment of a wife is different than spending to satisfy one's greed, and you detest feminine display with different objectives from his. He wanted to see the people of Rome kept free, and you are laying a trap for women's freedom." ("Piangono il prezzo di grano applicato in adornarvi di quelle gemme . . . e poi in comprar infami et indegni amori profonderanno liberalmente tesori . . . A gran ragione stimò vicina la perdita della romana libertà Catone allora ch'udí essersi venduto un pesce quanto un bue, ma diverso è lo spendere in adornamenti d'una moglie, dallo spendere per sotisfazione della gola, e voi con fini diversi da lui detestate le pompe feminili. Egli bramava di veder conservato libero il popolo di Roma, e voi sète insidiatori della libertà donnesca.")[133]

In this labored rhetoric of analogy, Tarabotti related terms that could be envisioned together only with great effort. On the one hand, the price of grain, wives, jewels, and oxen was related to the conservation of Roman liberty, and on the other, the price of prostitutes and fish was related to tyranny and the entrapment of women. In either set of relations, Tarabotti reinforced her conceptual challenge to the dualistic thinking that separated culture from economics and women's bodies from political knowledge. Moreover, Tarabotti revived and revisioned the historical Cato of Utica as a censor of western dualisms and as an "authority" who underwrote her concept of cultural economics and gendered states to oppose Buoninsegni's conceptual "entrapment" and "imprisonment" of women. "Not without disdain would the father of his country see the tyranny used today to imprison women. So this time, Mr. Buoninsegni, the authority of Cato turns out to be against you." ("Non senza sdegno vedrebbe quel gran padre della sua patria la tirannide oggidí usata nell'imprigionar le donne. Sí che l'auttorità di Catone, questa volta sig. Buoninsegni, rissulta contro di voi.")[134]

For Tarabotti, every authority claimed by Buoninsegni as a support to his arguments could be disclaimed from the perspective of women's bodies in the politics of states. Perhaps the most forceful example of this move was Tarabotti's political appropriation of the authority of Ferdinando de' Medici, the Grand Duke of Tuscany. Ferdinando, according to Tarabotti, would never give his favor to Buoninsegni's misogynist arguments because, as head of state, he was well aware of the crucial role played by women in the social reproduction of the state and its hierarchies: "The great Ferdinand, accustomed and dedicated to safeguarding virtue, will not want to bestow the favor of his kind patronage to a pen and a language that manage to keep busy in the reproach of that sex which, producing subjects, can only be dear and welcome to princes" ("Il gran Ferdinando, avezzo e dedito a proteggere la virtú, non vorrà compartir l'aura del suo benigno patrocinio ad una penna e ad una lingua che procura d'impiegarsi ne' biasimi di quel sesso che, generando sudditi ai principi, non può esser loro se non caro e gradito").[135]

> Tarabotti understood that women were responsible not only for biological reproduction but, more importantly, for the socialization of proper subjects for the state. Who better than women would be equipped to teach the political difficulties and confusions of citizenship, where citizens were subjected to the authority of the prince? Who more than Tarabotti was equipped to understand her own contradictory citizenship among the best writers of the Mazarine?

GENDER AND THE LIBRARY AS FICTIONS OF RESEARCH

1. *Gender Fictions in History*

In her poem "El Sueño," Sor Juana Inés de la Cruz understood knowledge as a dream.[136] Like her Venetian counterpart Tarabotti, Sor Juana challenged the categories that oppressed women, understanding them as gender fictions.[137] Again, in her response to a Peruvian gentleman who suggested she become a man, Sor Juana insisted on creating a gender fiction for herself. She came to the convent precisely "because there is no one to verify if I am a woman" ("porque si es que soy mujer ninguno lo verifique") and because there her body could be "neuter or abstract" ("neutro, o abstracto"). Indeed, the term *virgin*, describing her sex, could be applied to either woman or man ("es común de dos lo virgen").[138] Sor Juana and Suor Arcangela never knew—nor could they have known—each other, given the historical ideologies that limited their impact and permeated the social construction of categories of knowledge in libraries, archives, and academies that memorialized relations among men. But observing and registering their convergence as nuns, theorists, and creators of fictions that contested the gender ideologies of their time, we might imagine "their 'complexifying' potentials" inscribed within the legacy of seventeenth-century misogyny.[139] To research and arrange their theories and fictions on a library shelf, taking up space among the canonized writers, is not to break up and reconfigure actual institutions that conserve historical memory but "to imagine beyond the boundaries of our received categorizations" a kind of research that is no longer constrained by the limits of past relations.[140] If our sources, categories, and historical theories are permeated by a vision that "Women's true Poetry consisted in their Needle and Spindle," we find in such writers as Sor Juana and Tarabotti that "internal divisions have also left their mark" on our materials of research.[141]

2. *Fictional Space on the Shelf*

In her 1966 essay on the Puritan poet Anne Bradstreet, Adrienne Rich makes a distinction between Bradstreet's earlier poems treating such themes as the Ages of Man and Assyrian monarchs and her later poems written "in response to the simple events in a woman's life." Characterizing Bradstreet's earlier poetry as "pedestrian, abstract, mechanical," Rich wrote: "Had she stopped writing after the publication of these verses, or had she simply continued in the same vein, Anne Bradstreet would survive in the catalogues of Women's Archives, a social curiosity or at best a literary fossil."[142] Rich went on to claim that the later, more personal poems "rescue Anne Bradstreet from the Women's Archives and place her conclusively in literature."[143] In her 1979 "Postscript" to this essay, Rich regretted her "condescending references to 'Women's Archives,'" saying that such condescension exemplified "the limitations of a point of view which took masculine history and literature as its center and which tried from that perspective to view a woman's life and work."[144] No longer attempting to "rescue" Anne Bradstreet from the Women's Archives, Rich, in this reflection, rescued the Women's Archive as an important site of feminist research. To imagine a Women's Archive in which women writers share a fictional space on the shelf in the function of their relations with one another is to make visible the fictional categories and contradictions within which they wrote.

It is not clear, however, how we are to imagine this fictional Women's Archive and the fictional point of view that would take women's history and literature as its center. Are we to imagine a series of writings by individual women writers lying inert on a shelf in a vault, unable to be organized in the kind of organic relations from which most institutions of historical records were formed? Indeed, because the "facts" of conquest and colonialism implied a particular organization of social relations and knowledge, few women writers in history could either know each other or form political or social ties. How then could a Women's Archive activate a relation that never existed in history? Would there be rearranging or more writing to be done?

In the case of my research here, I have been particularly interested in arranging materials to represent the appearance of women writers in relation to the foundation of the first public libraries. For how can we separate Naudé's representation of the library as a "daughter" generated from his "viscera" from the "suffering daughter" who hoped to favor its shelves with her writing? By the same token, it is important to interpret Naudé's request for the works of Tarabotti in relation to the foundation of seventeenth-century public libraries as significant "evidence" of gender antagonisms at the heart of state making. The foundation of the first public libraries in Oxford, Paris, Milan, and Rome gives us some insight into the gendered construction of nationhood in these metropolitan capitals. To create for the works of such writers as Tarabotti (and Sor Juana and Anne Bradstreet) a fictional space on the library shelves among the canonized theorists of republican thought is to draw attention to the constructed nature of all relations of knowing, while drawing out different perspectives from within that tradition.

Nor should this kind of fictional rearrangement of materials be seen as particularly radical or disrespectful of existing taxonomies. Any experience with the history of library classifications will reassure us that existing taxonomies are in a constant state of flux and contestation. In the histories of many archives and libraries, we find that generations of librarians and archivists have been arranging and rearranging historical materials, creating taxonomic fictions to fit their own cultural needs. As the researcher walks into a library, archive, or museum, s/he is instantly aware of becoming part of these fictions. One way of making visible the fictitious categories that organize our research would be to analyze the rhetorics of inventories and catalogs of libraries, archives, and museums formed in the seventeenth century.[145] Another way of dramatizing these categories would be, of course, to write new fictions.

3. Scholarly Fictions

My project has been one of reinvisioning, in the historical record and on the shelves of the Mazarine, a place to stand in the library that does not take masculine history as the center of republican thought. What I have "found" in the course of this quest are the works of a Venetian nun, Arcangela Tarabotti, who, instead of idealizing those tyrant-slayers who followed the models of the republican tradition, exhorted tyrannical fathers to acknowledge their daughters as the mainstay of political economy. Although today Tarabotti's works are readily accessible in excellent scholarly editions and translations, when I began to be interested in this writer and intellectual I had to request her works from several different libraries. In our acts of requesting, I would like to suggest, a fiction of our selves emerges as part of the historical record.

Two copies of *La semplicità ingannata* in U.S. libraries (the Peabody Library in Baltimore and the Regenstein Library in Chicago) were too tightly bound to microfilm, a common barrier to access. I hoped that by some miracle (I could hear the echo of the words of Naudé, who spoke of the Mazarine as "the miracle of my life") I might obtain a copy of this work from the University of Pennsylvania's Van Pelt Library.

30 July 1998

Curator, Van Pelt Library
University of Pennsylvania Library
3420 Walnut
Philadelphia, Pennsylvania 19104-6206

Dear Curator,

I am very much, fervently (even desperately) hoping that you might be able to send me a microfilm of your copy of Arcangela Tarabotti, *Semplicità ingannata* (and relevant information about costs, permissions, etc.). There are several copies of this work in United States libraries, but they are all too tightly bound to microfilm. I am hoping that, by some miracle, your copy is not too tightly bound; it would be a sad case indeed, if Tarabotti's readership were restricted by the binding of her books.

Thank you very much for your attention.

      Optimistically yours,
      Stephanie Jed
      Assoc. Prof. of Italian and Comparative Literature

If the copy at the Van Pelt Library was also inaccessible, I would write to the Marciana Library in Venice. I had already requested (and received) a copy of Tarabotti's *Letters* from the Marciana, but I was reluctant to trouble the bureaucracy of a big national library like the Marciana with another request. Would that I had *wings for my courage*.

In any case, my guarded optimism paid off at the Van Pelt Library. I eventually received a digitalized copy of Tarabotti's work on a CD-ROM that was a wonder to read on my own computer.[146] But even before I received the CD-ROM, my relation to *La semplicità* was already mediated by fervent and desperate hope, by the gracious response of the Van Pelt library curator and staff, by the cost of a digitalized facsimile, and by the tightly bound copies at other libraries. There was, in addition, the anticipation of potential sadness, the sense of a miracle, and the reflection on bookbinding that still historically and materially restricted Tarabotti's readership. These are some of the tangible components of the transmission of Tarabotti's texts and of a fictional self that emerged from my desire and request to read a text of Tarabotti. Nor do I want to exclude from this fiction the sense I have of my researching self as still too tightly bound by argumentative style, still stylistically restricted to a specialized audience, unable to break free from a discursive mode to connect to my aspirations as a lyrical writer. Perhaps, through this fictional self, I have a tangible understanding of the cruelties and deceits of fathers who forced their daughters to become nuns.

Tarabotti, elaborating a theory that put daughters at the center of state making, was certain that if she dedicated this theory to princes they would reject and perhaps prohibit her work because of their own male-centered theories of state (so she dedicated this work to God). She was certain that every other male reader would abhor her theories as prejudicial to the self-interested politics of men. Tarabotti most certainly felt bound and restricted in her writing by this sense of rejection and abhorrence that surrounded her. One reader materialized the restrictions that surrounded Tarabotti's pen in an act of writing on the frontispiece of the 1654 Elzevier edition at the University of Pennsylvania Van Pelt Library. He dismissively framed and bound the fruits of her suffering when he wrote: "This woman was too partial to her own sex and much prejudiced against man." And perhaps, this reader's act of writing articulates my own sense of historical restriction as well. Part of the feminist project of producing new relations of knowing might also entail making visible such categorical restrictions and dissolving them into acts of writing and relations of power. If we readers and researchers are taxonomic fictions, we might write these fictions for all to see.

4. A Fictional Tour of the Mazarine

Although Tarabotti's published *Letters* "document" Naudé's request to place her works on the shelves of the Mazarine, there is no documentary evidence of his letter. Moreover, we know that Tarabotti's works never took up their rightful place "among the most famous writers" of this famous library during her lifetime. Today, it is true, readers may find three of Tarabotti's works in the Mazarine catalogs, but two of these—*La semplicità ingannata* and *l'Antisatira*—were confiscated from the Abbey of St. Victor and entered the Mazarine during the revolutionary period. And the third—*Il paradiso monacale*—came to the Mazarine in 1668 with the Bibliothèque royale (Tarabotti had died in 1652, Naudé in 1653, and Mazarin in 1661).[147] *La semplicità ingannata*, Tarabotti's work that decried the tyranny of fathers over daughters, may be found on a shelf list between two satires by the famous Dutch scholar Daniel Heinsius (1617) and two satires (1667) by Curio (Caelius Secundus), a Protestant professor of eloquence in Basel, while the *Antisatira*, the work that exposed the hypocrisy of male economic thinking, finds room on a shelf list between an anthology of poetry edited by Carlo Fiamma—*Il gareggiamento poetico del confuso accademico ordito* (1611)—and a didactic poem about the heavens—Jean-Edouard du Monin's *Uranologie* (1583). Tarabotti's *Paradiso monacale*, on the other hand, found shelf space with the works of other "Mystici," including the Spanish Jesuit and mystic Juan Eusebio Nieremberg and a Spanish monk, Diego Niseno, author of "El politico del cielo." All three spaces on the shelves honor, albeit posthumously, Tarabotti's wish for her works "to be placed among the most famous writers" of the Mazarine. But not one of those spaces acknowledges the significant intellectual and theoretical contribution Tarabotti made to our thinking about gender and republican politics. For this reason, fictional shelf lists were necessary to acknowledge the potential impact and resonance her works might have had in important collocations in the library. A fictional tour of this library is now in order.

. . .

"Naudé didn't want to rest before traversing Europe. To enrich his well beloved *daughter*, as he would later call her, he was ready to brave every hardship and every danger."[148] This is the myth of Gabriel Naudé's book-collecting project as it was transmitted to and reproduced in 1860, by Alfred Franklin, then director of the Mazarine. Just as literary fantasies of knights errant motivated sixteenth-century soldiers, explorers, and conquerors to enrich the Christian empire with lucrative trade ventures, so Naudé was motivated to brave the fatiguing and dangerous journeys and examinations of books to enrich his well-beloved daughter, a library of state.

This "daughter," who occupied, in Palais Mazarin, a large gallery and six rooms, first received the books intended for the library on a large table in the middle of the gallery.[149] Walking through this gallery every day on his way to chapel, Mazarin would stop to leaf through the volumes and examine the titles and chapter titles before Naudé classified and arranged them by room.[150] The first room held books of jurisprudence, philosophy, and a part of the theology collection, including Tarabotti's *Che le donne siano della spezie degli uomini*;[151] the rest of the theology books filled the sixth room. Books of chemistry, natural history, and medicine filled the second room. The third room was filled with Bibles in every language, and the fourth room housed the library's manuscripts. Room 5 was the most heterogeneous, holding books of canon law, "light literature," and political treatises, including works by Guillaume Postel, E. J. Brutus, More, Castiglione, Campanella, Botero, Naudé, and Tarabotti's *La semplicità ingannata* and *L'Inferno monacale*.[152]

The cultural sympathies of Naudé and Mazarin drew them to collect more books written in Italian than in any other language. Many of these Italian books were obscure even in Italy, their authors second- or third-rate, often quite bizarre.[153] Although political economy was a field in its infancy, prominent among the few titles in this category was Tarabotti's *Antisatira*, her work that analyzed the significance of money spent on daughters and wives in relation to republican freedom.[154] Any reader interested in questions of tyranny and republican freedom would have the opportunity to find the works of this intellectual daughter who engaged her experience as an involuntary nun in her organization of political knowledge.

SOCIAL INTERSECTION

1536–2011, between San Diego, Milan, Rome, Venice, Florence, and Paris

Sasha Harvey had been coming to the Vatican library for weeks, unable—after the kidnapping of Aldo Moro—to read anything but her newspapers.[1] One day, overcoming inertia, she put away her newspapers to meander in the reading room, pulling various items off the shelf to read. She tells us, on loose typescript pages stored in her research folders, of the complex, painful, emotional political research she was doing in Rome in the late 1970s. Research on stories—stories of Communist Party leaders; the story of her longings for one trade unionist who rarely telephoned; and her story of wanting to flee from English and belong to this faraway intellectual culture of the parliamentary Left, so firm in its stand against terrorism, so surprising in its celebration of feminism. All of these stories led her, one day, to pull Delio Cantimori's essays about humanism off of the library shelf. She was intrigued by the language of these essays, depicting particular humanists' "confusion and uncertainty" ("confusione e incertezza mentale"), their "detachment from life" ("si comincia in Italia a staccar l'uomo dalla vita"), and their desire to enter the "concrete life of the present" ("l'attualità della vita concreta").[2] Harvey's professor at home (she was pursuing a PhD at the time) approved of this interest and soon bequeathed to her the beginnings of his own research on Lorenzino de' Medici, a scholar of the classics who, in 1537, slew his cousin Alessandro, the Duke of Florence—a perfect test case for investigating Cantimori's ideas. They decided together, upon her return from Rome, that she would write a dissertation about humanistic tyrant-slayers, a sort of rhetorical grammar of conspiracy. Had she found some way of eluding the need to express her own murderous rage? Or was she about to stand trial precisely for this well-developed art of avoidance? She didn't have a clue. She just kept on trying to change the story around.

Here is one version of the story of tyrannicide Harvey kept trying to tell (in many different versions) until the end of her life. It is conserved in one of her research files: *The many passages traversed and studied led us back to the night of January 6, 1537, in which Lorenzino de' Medici murdered his cousin Alessandro de' Medici, the Duke of Florence. We entered a sumptuously ornate colonnade decorated with frescos of plundered riches and dark limousines—it was the day of my mother's funeral, and my father talked with his cronies in the limousine about high interest rates. From the colonnade, we gained access to the sacred narrative site of tyrannicide, a museum of severed heads from ancient historiography, above which were inscribed the words: LOVE OF THE FATHER[LAND] AND IMMENSE DESIRE FOR PRAISE [ALMOST ALWAYS] WIN.*[3] *There followed images of all the Greek and Roman tyrants, chaste noblewomen, and tyrant-slayers; and women offering gifts to them, as if wishing to show that they, too, were pious and understood the justice of these stories. We saw Lorenzino studying these images: the first tyrant-slayers, Harmodius and Aristogiton, glorified for their slaying of Hipparchus after he had dishonored Harmodius's sister. Lucius Junius Brutus, celebrated as the founder of Roman liberty because he expelled the Tarquin tyrants after Sextus Tarquinius had raped Lucretia. Marcus Brutus murdering Caesar to vindicate his sister's and mother's honor that had been stained by their adulterous affairs with Caesar. Lorenzino had a knowing sneer . . . We climbed through the chambers to Lorenzino's bedroom. Lorenzino was luring Alessandro to come in without bodyguards—the duke was so drunk and sleepy that he even removed his sword and dagger and let Lorenzino place these out of reach. Lorenzino went out then (we waited behind the curtain), leaving Alessandro in bed unarmed. Lorenzino returned—not with the girl but with his point man Scoronconcolo—and together they attacked the duke, finally slaying him. (We went home.) Then they fled to Venice, where Lorenzino was hailed by Filippo Strozzi as the "new Brutus." This was the confirmation he required to make his historiographic fiction sacred.*[4]

Harvey wrote this and more in her "Scene of Tyrannicide: Lorenzino de' Medici and the Imprint of Human Action." She worked on this elliptical, allusive, unargued dissertation at the conclusion of her visit to the sacred site in the early 1980s, but she never finished it. Here I have included in parentheses the words that Sasha Harvey, in her typescript, crossed out: ~~we waited behind the curtain~~ and ~~We went home~~. There is also a surprising note in the margin written in Harvey's own hand: *In your mingling of ancient and modern, you have reached no farther than Lorenzino's bedroom. Why do you cringe from discussing the many aspects of this story that are so problematic for the modern feminist reader interested in issues of social and political change?* Harvey seems to have remained "confused and uncertain" about her possible complicity in Lorenzino's act (~~we waited behind the curtain~~) and even "detached" from her own marginal question about developing a feminist perspective. Perhaps Harvey ~~went home~~ from her visit to this narrative site with scholarly ambitions as lofty as those of Lorenzino; but history—this time her own—kept breaking in. She continued to tell herself the story of Lorenzino, but other research stories kept breaking in to influence the story she was trying to tell. She began to lose herself in these other research stories and eventually became an eclectic scholar, whose life is phantasmatically present in this book.

What you have been reading here in this book is a miscellany of Sasha Harvey's research papers that lend themselves to particular structures of knowing: inventory, shelf list, and (in the final section) lexicon. Few scholars had previously looked at the loose pages of journal-like writing, which Harvey stored in the folders containing her research notes. Indeed, no one has really made much of the fact that Sasha Harvey continued to be an eclectic scholar until the end of her life. One can even see how these research notes were thinly disguised pages of prose about her life. Once in a while the research materials made their way, via the loose journal pages, into her poetry. Sometimes we find evidence of Harvey's imaginary travels (of which the above-cited passage is an example). Once in a while we find the address of an apartment in Milan or a receipt from Rome or Bologna that enables us to document her real travels.

The Department of Special Collections has conserved the research files in the order in which they were received. It has seemed to me important to respect this order for two reasons. First, the journal pages themselves rarely reveal a date. But, more importantly, the research notes, in their current order, form a sort of narrative depicting (1) Harvey's progressive efforts to escape from a sense of murderous rage into social relations of research and (2) the surrender of herself to her love of Florentine history, shortly before her death.

At the end of her life, Sasha Harvey was an isolated writer and scholar. She was inconsequential in the literary world (how would she ever become an important player, when it was so hard for her to know her desires?). She tried to work out her desires in her studies of tyrant-slayers that ended up as detours, flights to safer havens, avoidance of the issues. She endlessly searched for a more productive way to understand tyranny and the state. She loved libraries and archives and books, in general; she loved to study in them, but she also loved to study and think about librarians, archivists, scholars, editors; about the arrangement of books on the shelves and about the classification of documents in institutional categories; about the scholars who had frequented the libraries, archives, and erudite gatherings. She loved books and documents in the way Richard de Bury did, as quiet teachers who never lost their tempers and who expected no rewards or money. Sometimes, in her readings, she would feel an anxiety in the documents that reminded her of her mother, and she would capture such moments as if they were jewels.[5] She was addicted to isolating herself with her documents and books. And she was a scribbler who liked to be the master of her own scribbles in the confines of her study. She hoped, for a very long time, that her bibliophilic anxiety would manifest in the understanding of liberty and tyranny as relations of research, that indeed her efforts would result in collaborative projects. Sasha Harvey aspired wholeheartedly to engage in a relation of research like the one she studied in the pages that follow.

SECTION THREE

Gender, Erudition, and the Italian Nation

In 1819, at the age of forty, the Swiss Gian Pietro Vieusseux made Florence his adoptive city.[1] A successful businessman who traded in grains, wines, and oils, Vieusseux created in Florence a reading room of newspapers, journals, and books that came to be known as il Gabinetto Scientifico-Letterario or il Gabinetto Vieusseux.[2] By all reports, the Gabinetto was a cosmopolitan gathering place for male erudites and a space for studying the past with the purpose of forming "a moral national community" ("una comunità morale nazionale").[3] It was perhaps crucial to this purpose of nation formation that Vieusseux himself was from Geneva, Pieri from Corfù, Tommaseo from Dalmatia, Polidori from the Marche, Gar from Trentino, and so on. How might we acknowledge the contributions of a French feminist intellectual—Hortense Allart—to the formation of this national community?

According to Sestan, Vieusseux made his reading room an intellectual meeting place open only to men, like the English clubs, because he wanted to protect it from the gossip of a salon and from "crazies" like Madame Allart ("quella pazzarella di Madame Allart") and the Marchesa Carlotta Lenzoni, who might have proclaimed themselves members.[4] According to Sestan, Vieusseux "was anything but misogynist. Quite the contrary, he was a terrified celibate until the day he died. He was astute and an expert in the world of romance. He understood all too well—with a certain amount of conventional prejudice—that to let women into the reading room would be to take a risk: women could turn an intellectual circle that was also committed to serious civic work into a pointlessly social salon." ("Non che il Vieusseux fosse un misogino, tutt'altro, per quanto celibatario imperterrito fino alla morte; ma, da uomo avveduto e del mondo esperto, e specialmente del mondo romantico, capiva fin troppo bene—sia pure con qualche pregiudizio convenzionale—che ad aprire quelle sale anche al bel sesso, si correva il rischio di farne non un circolo di intellettuali intesi anche ad un serio civile lavoro, ma un salotto futilmente mondano.")[5] Let us take a brief look, then, at this serious civic work, predicated, at least in part, on the exclusion of women.

Since a school of historical method did not yet exist in Italy, almost all of the erudites were self-taught scholars.[6] Despite their different training and different historical predilections, they all seemed to share a desire to overcome their scholarly isolation, finding ways to combine history with sociability. In the space of the Gabinetto Vieusseux, for example, the erudites played at historical quotation. They played at historical facts, at trifling details of obscure medieval republics or Parisian archbishops.[7] They looked for living arrangements that would counterbalance all of the solitary time they spent in archives and libraries. In 1842, for example, Tommaso Gar wrote to the "cantankerous, misogynist" ("scontroso e misogino") Giuseppe Canestrini, informing him of his resolve to bring one of his sisters or cousins to live with him in Florence: "I'm tired of living isolated; I need domestic affections, domestic comforts. . . . If you have the same tendencies, you could become a dear member of my family, which would certainly love you as much as I love you and have always loved you." ("Sono stanco del vivere isolato; ho bisogno di domestici affetti, di domestiche comodità. . . . S'hai le stesse tendenze, tu potresti divenire un caro membro della mia famigliola, che t'amerebbe certamente come io t'amo e t'ho amato sempre.")[8]

One important project that helped the erudites of the Gabinetto Vieusseux to overcome their isolation was the *Archivio storico italiano*, a journal that aspired to construct a "national" archive in large part from the sources of Florentine and Tuscan archives and libraries. The erudites who contributed to the *Archivio* connected to each other through their interests in the history of the *comuni* and the liberties that these municipalities had afforded to the ruling merchant class. The erudites felt they belonged to this antifeudal, Guelph, bourgeois, ruling merchant class, that they were heirs to its liberties.[9] For Capponi, in particular, it was the communal period of Florence that especially prefigured the civic preeminence of the Italian nation. Florentine history was the lens and the filter through which he saw contemporary conditions, hopes, and challenges.[10]

But aside from their connection through such lofty ideas of the nation, the major compilers of the *Archivio* also made the day-by-day vicissitudes of the journal the focus of their personal conversations. For example, Canestrini wrote to Vieusseux in January of 1845 that at the archivist Francesco Bonaini's house "conversation always turns to the subject of the *Archivio storico,* to the great pleasure and amusement of Bonaini's sisters, who demonstrate a sincere interest in the journal. They know by heart all the ups and downs of the *Archivio* and its compilers, whom they seem to know so well." ("La conversazione cade sempre sull'*Archivio storico*, a grande piacere e divertimento delle sue sorelle, le quali mostrano di prendere per esso un sincero interesse, e sanno a memoria tutte le peripezie dell'*Archivio* e dei compilatori, che hanno l'aria di conoscere perfettamente.")[11] And, in general, letters among the various compilers and erudites of the Gabinetto Vieusseux connect the comings and goings of these men between past and present, the various states of disorder and confusion in which they found their archives and libraries, and their strong personality traits, ranging from cantankerous, hostile, hungry, and bad-tempered to passionate, grateful, sickly, vehement, frenzied, and brave.

ENTER ALLART

Now, in 1826, some fifteen years before the Florentine erudites began to publish the *Archivio storico italiano*, Madame Hortense Allart (1801–79) entered the space of the Gabinetto Vieusseux. She crossed the threshold, not of its reading room, of course, because that space was closed to her, but rather of the minds and hearts of the Florentine erudites. She, too, was a focal point that connected the research and ideas of these scholars and a part of their relations of writing. If in previous centuries, poets and political writers had figured *Italia* as a woman, in the space of the Vieusseux group in Florence ideas of the nation were gendered and engendered in the responses of male erudites to a learned French historian, novelist, feminist, and Italophile.[12]

Allart made two lengthy visits to Italy.[13] Her first stay lasted three years, from 1826 to 1829, during which time she resided mostly in Florence, with the exception of an eight-month visit to Rome. Allart's first visit provides a good illustration of how social relations can engender republican ideals and ideas of the nation. Appealing right from the start to the republican desires of the Vieusseux group, Allart gave birth, in June of 1826, to a beautiful baby boy whom she named Marcus Brutus, after which the "angry, most erudite, most academic Mario Pieri, a celibate, whining fifty-year-old" ("iracondo, letterarissimo, accademicissimo, Mario Pieri, celibatario, inuggiolito, cinquantenne"), wrote: "I made my visits more frequent, so that an entire day didn't pass without seeing her" ("spesseggiai le mie visite tanto, che non correva un'intera giornata senza ch'io la vedessi").[14] Perhaps inspired by the baby boy's name, Guglielmo Libri, in the days after Allart gave birth, "would come in the evenings to chat at the foot of [her] bed" ("il venait le soir au pied de mon lit causer") about the Romans—"he knew them by heart" ("Il parlait bien des Romains, les savait par coeur").[15] Indeed, the boy's name would eventually become a focus of play for the Florentine erudites, a part of their relations of writing. Niccolò Tommaseo, in a letter to Capponi of August 1834 (from Paris), played on the boy's name when mentioning his father: "I saw the father of Marcus. He resembles Cicero somewhat, but not in his style." ("Ho veduto il padre di Marcus, e somiglia un po' a Cicerone ma non nello stile.")[16] And Allart figured her dedication to Marcus (Brutus) as a playful aspect of her republican commitment to writing a history of Florence.

Back in Paris in 1829, Allart maintained her relation with Italy and the Florentine erudites by working on *Essais détachés sur l'Italie,* her *History of Florence,* and a novel, *Sextus ou le Romain des maremmes,* which was published in March of 1832 and whose hero was none other than a thinly disguised Gino Capponi. Allart wrote to Capponi in July 1837: "You dream of unity; do you despair of virtue, like Brutus?" ("Vous songiez à l'unité; désespérez-vous de la vertu, comme Brutus?")[17] But if Capponi thought of himself as a republican Brutus, Allart was instead careful to cast him in her novel as the tyrannical Sextus and to keep him desperate for the attention and love of her female protagonist, Thérèse de Longueville.

In December of 1837, upon the completion and publication of the first volume of her *History of Florence,* Allart returned to Florence and other parts of Tuscany to continue working on the second volume of her *History.* In this period, which ended in 1840, Allart especially appreciated the intellectual support she received from Capponi in the form of books, notes, conversations, and visits.[18] But during this second visit the erudites were especially connected through their sexual responses to Allart. The legal historian Pietro Capei courted Allart and made her pregnant, while Tommaseo, Vieusseux and Capponi expressed a need to keep Allart at a distance. Tommaseo wrote to Vieusseux from Paris to warn him of her "pitiful" focus on women in the preface she had written to her *History of Florence* ("una prefazione che fa proprio pietà") and of her "eager desire for Italian men" ("Desidera gli uomini bramosamente; e dice che gl'Italiani possono ormai soddisfarla").[19] And Capponi's principal problem was his fondness for her: "I have been fond of her, as you know, for thirteen years, because she is fundamentally good and has noble parts. . . . I have never touched, nor would I touch a finger of hers. And she already knows that for me it would be impossible, physically impossible. And I have told her so, and written, thousands of times, how and why. She is too good to be [my] prostitute; as my wife, God forbid. And it is necessary for me to imagine women in one of the two roles. I have never liked it any other way: I have never known how to be gallant, and my too many sins are, without exception, those of an angel or a pig, a pig not disguised as a decent man." ("Ed io che le voglio bene, come sapete, da 13 anni in qua, perchè di fondo è buona e ha nobili parti, . . . io non le ho toccato mai, né toccherei, un dito. E già la lo sa, ch'e' mi sarebbe impossibile, impossibile fisicamente; e glie ne ho dette le mille volte, e scritto, il come e il perchè. Per meretrice la vale troppo; per moglie, Dio ne guardi. ed io le donne bisogna che una delle due cose me le figuri o figurassi. Né altro modo mi piacque: galante non seppi essere mai, ed i miei troppi peccati sono, senza eccezione tutti, di angelo o di porco; di porco non travestito da uomo civile.")[20]

Rather than speak, with Benedict Anderson, about "imagined communities" constructed by print culture, I would like to chart here some of the specific lexical contours of this historical community, whose inclusions, exclusions, concepts of learnedness, and written relations with archives, libraries, and each other were instrumental in producing ideas of the Italian nation. In particular, Allart's letters to Capponi provide an opportunity for understanding how gender may have affected the enterprise of historical research and the political thinking of men in the Gabinetto Vieusseux, who were unable to fathom the likes of Allart, a "professional" writer who crossed the boundaries between history, fiction, and political theory and who aspired to be as erudite as they.[21] Taking my prompt from Petrucci's "relation of writing," I have organized and interpreted the language of this correspondence lexically, selecting terms that, in my view, make visible the gender dynamics implicit in the making of Capponi's *Storia*. To organize knowledge about members of the Vieusseux group in this manner is to understand their ideas, projects, and activities as socially or relationally constructed and to integrate Allart as an important co-producer of Italian nationalist historiography and thought.

LEXICON

Allargare (and restringere)

As we saw in the Introduction, Capponi, in the preface to his *Storia*, referred to Allart's *Histoire* as a "ristretto" or "compendium," implying that his own work was more substantial or voluminous than hers. After making mental notes about Allart's text, he began to "reduce" some passages and "lengthen" others until he found all of her ideas inside his text. This contrast between "large" and "small"—fundamentally an opposition between "his" and "hers" (though sometimes the roles were reversed)—pervaded Allart and Capponi's relationship and formed part of the lexical filter through which they saw their work. It is, therefore, easy to see how this fundamental opposition overflowed into other oppositions between "broad" and "narrow," "full" and "lacking," "slow" and "hurried," "bland" and "spicy," and so on.[22] As we shall see, these oppositions ultimately helped Capponi, Allart, and other intellectuals of the Gabinetto Vieusseux to produce a common ground despite their differences.

In August 1847, Allart protested Capponi's belittling of her *History* as a "manual," trusting that once it appeared in Italian translation everyone would acknowledge its comprehensive scope: "You say that my little history is going to appear, you call it a manual, but of all that I was able to find in your civic history I have omitted nothing. So, portray me in the true language." ("Vous dites que ma petite histoire va paraître, vous appelez cela un manuel, mais je n'ai rien omis de tout ce que j'ai pu trouver de civil dans votre histoire. Faites-moi donc paraître dans la vraie langue.")[23] It is important to note, however, Capponi was not the only one to belittle Allart's *History* by calling it a "ristretto." Allart most frequently referred to it herself as her "petite histoire de Florence."[24] This is an interesting and complicated issue. Did Capponi and Allart somehow make the smallness of her work a condition of their early conversations and exchanges?

At times, Allart described the "smallness" of her work in a positive frame. In December 1858, Capponi sent Allart a section of his history in progress that he published in the *Archivio storico italiano*.[25] Confronting his accomplishments with her own, Allart was somewhat intimidated but remained satisfied with the succinctness of her work: "Still, I am not frightened for mine, because I have written with more compact proportions, you will need more volumes" ("Cependant je ne suis pas effrayée pour la mienne, car j'ai écrit dans d'autres proportions, plus serrées, il vous faudra bien plus de volumes").[26] On another occasion she was satisfied that the less ambitious nature of her *History* had at least led her to fly higher in her work of political theory, the *Essai sur l'histoire politique*. Correcting the proofs of this *Essai*, Allart thought of Capponi and wrote to him: "It is my little history of Florence that has made me look elsewhere in these lofty directions" ("C'est ma petite histoire de Florence qui m'a fait chercher ailleurs ces hautes directions").[27]

We might imagine the "small" size of Allart's work as iconically appropriate to the "smallness" of the Florentine Republic (and il granducato toscano), whose "smallness," according to Allart, epitomized everything that could be learned about politics: "In Florence one learns politics, one finds the civic life that other nations don't have. This small patch of land, as beautiful as it is learned, always enchants me.... The events of recent years have made us understand better the excellence of these small States.... Your small provincial towns have learned people, erudite priests, publishing done within their walls; the small States spread life and knowledge among more families." ("À Florence on apprend la politique, on trouve là une vie civile que les autres nations n'ont pas. Ce petit coin, aussi beau qu'il est savant, fait toujours mon enchantement.... les événements de ces dernières années nous en fait mieux comprendre l'excellence de ces petits États. Vos petites villes de province ont des gens lettrés, des prêtres savants, des éditions à elles, faites dans leurs murs; les petits États répandent la vie et le savoir en plus de familles.")[28] In any case, Allart was convinced that her "smallness" was bound to produce "greatness" in Capponi: "I am very delighted," she wrote, "that my little and shabby history of Florence has awakened you for Florence and given you the idea to work according to your great knowledge and talent" ("Je suis très charmée que ma petite et mesquine histoire de Florence vous ait éveillé pour Florence et donné l'idée de travailler selon votre grand savoir et votre talent").[29] Together, her "smallness" and his "greatness" would be productive of a common field of political knowledge.

Amazon

According to Tommaseo, Allart "wanted to become pregnant" ("desidera di essere ingravidata"), and if "anyone asked her why she let herself be impregnated, she methodically gave a lesson in sex education" ("A chi le domandava perchè si fosse lasciata impregnare, rispose per ordine come si fa a fare un figlio"). Moreover, Tommaseo complained that any man who kept company with Allart "would have to take responsibility for the fruit of her pregnancies" ("che l'amico riconosca subito il nuovo nato per figlio").[30] But perhaps the contrary was true. Allart came purposefully to Florence to give birth to her first son, Marcus, far from Marcus's father. Similarly, Allart announced to Capponi the birth of her second son, Henri, making a literary game around the mystery of his father. He might have been as distinguished as Theseus, the father of Hippolytus, but, in any case, he was not Gino Capponi: "Thalestris, Thomyris, Myrine, and all the race of Amazons have the honor of announcing that one of them comes to give birth happily to a second son. We do not know which warrior has, on the banks of the Thermodon, given life to this other Hippolyte, but it is definitely not Gino Capponi, who would not know what to do with Amazons." ("Thalestris, Thomyris, Myrine et toute la race des amazones ont l'honneur de vous avertir qu'une d'entr'elles vient d'accoucher heureusement d'un second fils. On ne sait quel guerrier a donné sur les rivages du Thermodon la vie à cet autre Hippolyte, mais ce n'est point Gino Capponi qui ne sait faire que des amazones.")[31] It is not surprising to find Allart, a French woman of letters, figuring herself as an Amazon. Did Capponi share this view, pointing to her "virile sense"? In any case, Allart understood her career in letters to be analogous to the work of the warrior, writing in her autobiographical work *Les enchantements*: "A woman would do well to imitate [the race of Amazons], replacing the trade of warrior with a career in letters" ("Une femme peut vouloir les imiter, remplacer par les lettres le métier des armes").[32]

Archives

Allart had two interesting methodological objections to archival research. After the appearance of the first volume of her *Histoire*, she wrote to Capponi, asking him to "beware of those people who might reproach me for not speaking of the magistracies of Florence" ("Soyez en garde contre ces gens qui me reprochent de n'avoir pas parlé des magistratures de Florence"). She explained that the real history of Florence took place, not "in the depth of those archives where the magistracies were hidden" ("dans la *profondeur* des archives où vos magistratures sont cachées"), but rather "in the street, in the sunlight" ("dans la rue, au soleil"). Allart did not want to dissociate the spaces of research from the places where actors made history.³³

Five and a half years later, after the publication of her second volume, Allart responded to a publication of Capponi, "Discorsi intorno alla riforma dello Stato di Firenze (1522–1532)," published in the first volume of the *Archivio storico italiano*. Criticizing his judgment of Guicciardini's discourse as favoring the constitution of the *principato*, Allart took issue with his too-literal interpretations of Guicciardini's words. It might be possible to construe Guicciardini's words as meaning "It is necessary to oppress Florence" ("il faut opprimer Florence"), but his deeds, for Allart, spoke much louder: "That's why I don't like the study of archives. The literal meaning of those discourses will make us hate those citizens who, nevertheless were busy saving what they could." ("Voilà pourquoi je n'aime pas l'étude des archives. La lettre de ces discours fera détester ces citoyens, et pourtant ils étaient occupés à sauver ce qu'ils pouvaient.")³⁴ Here again, it seems, Allart was worried that scholars who stayed hidden in the archives with their documents were unable to see the import of history in a broader social context. Capponi and other members of the Vieusseux group shared Allart's worries about archival research. For them, though, it was not just a problem of being shut away in the dark. Archival scholars could also suffer from hunger, thirst, and passion.

For example, Bonaini's "unquenchable thirst" ("una sete inesausta") for more archival experiences and documentary details about Pisan history "stirred up . . . a frenzy of research and work" ("eccitando . . . un furore di ricerca e di lavoro").³⁵ Only his vehement passions as a suitor and then husband could compete with his scholarly passion, as the celibate Canestrini maliciously noted in a letter to Vieusseux (March 17, 1845): "Yesterday . . . I tore Professor Bonaini from the embraces of his fiancée, to her great displeasure" ("Jeri lunedì strappai il professor Bonaini dagli abbracciamenti della sua fidanzata, con molto rincrescimento di lei").³⁶ Perhaps even more frustrating, Bonaini endured long hours in the archives without the pleasures and calories of food to sustain him. Nicola Nicolini, who had observed Bonaini doing research in the Neapolitan archives, wrote: "I am amazed to see men of great genius endure the greatest exertions with a weak stomach and a sickly appearance. I could neither write a line nor look at one of our neverending folios without first fortifying myself with a plate of good maccheroni and thick Neapolitan ragù." ("Tra le cose che mi fanno maravigliare, è il vedere uomini d'alto ingegno reggere alle più grandi fatiche con uno stomaco debole e con la fisionomia infermiccia. Io non potrei scrivere un rigo né guardare uno de' nostri interminabili in-fogli, senza premunirmi con buoni maccheroni e grasso ragù alla napolitana.")[37]

Perhaps the hunger and sexual passion associated with archival frenzy made Capponi and Vieusseux (who, as we remember, excluded women from his reading room) prefer the narrative sources of history (chronicles, historiographic accounts, biographies, correspondences found more often in libraries) to the documentary sources of archives. The Florentine archives, with their "scanty indices and disorderly materials" ("scarsi e confusi gli indici, disordinate le materie"), might have unsettled Capponi, who, according to Sestan, "retreated toward history as toward a chaste and secret love, hidden from indiscreet eyes" ("ripiegava verso la storia come verso un amore casto e segreto, precluso a occhi indiscreti").[38] In any case, it followed that a minimal space was allotted in the *Archivio storico italiano* to archival sources and there were few archivists among the editors of the *Archivio*.[39] At some level, both Capponi and Vieusseux agreed with Allart's reservations about archival research.

Body parts and intellect

For Capponi and Allart and other members of their circle, Capponi's loss of eyesight and eventual total blindness were a major intellectual concern. As early as July 1838, Vieusseux wrote to Tommaseo that Capponi was making many social blunders in his efforts to conceal his blindness.[40] In the years 1839–40, three men of Capponi's circle worked for a short time assisting Capponi, each one abandoning his job to the next until a fourth, Alessandro Carraresi, took over the job of reader and secretary on December 1, 1840, and continued to serve Capponi until his death in 1876.[41] Capponi duly acknowledged the help of Carraresi's eyes in the preface to his *Storia della Repubblica di Firenze*, writing that Carraresi "will always be able to say when thinking of me, 'I was the eye for a blind man'" ("potrà sempre dire pensando a me, 'oculus fui caeco'").[42]

Regular expressions of concern for Capponi's blindness emanated, of course, also from the pen of Allart. In July 1939, concerned about

Capponi's inability to read her letters, Allart wrote: "When you will receive a letter from me, put it in your pocket and have Niccolini read it to you, so I will not be afraid of tiring your eyes and the poet is never too much trouble for his friends" ("Quand vous recevrez une lettre de moi mettez-la dans votre poche et faites-vous la lire par Niccolini, ainsi je ne craindrai pas de fatiguer vos yeux et le poète n'est pas de trop entre ses amis").[43] In subsequent letters, Allart no longer asked Capponi to write but to dictate: "Would you be so kind as to dictate a short history of Malatesta?" ("Vous seriez très aimable de me dicter une petite histoire de Malatesta"); "Are you working? Are you dictating?" ("Travaillez-vous? Dictez-vous?"). Referring to his ongoing work on the history of Florence, she wrote in July 1855: "Are you dictating some great work that has been planned for a long time?" ("Dictez-vous quelque bel ouvrage, longtemps projeté?")[44] Allart imagined one day performing, via her own embodied voice, the role of keeping Capponi connected to knowledge and to friends. She wrote in August 1842: "I am counting one day on reading to you. Since you love my voice, perhaps you will be happy to have me as a reader sometimes. When we are old, I am going to see you and read to you . . . at Varramista." ("Je lis quelquefois de l'italien tout haut en votre honneur, car je compte un jour vous faire vos Lectures. Comme vous aimez ma voix, il vous sera peut-être agréable de m'avoir parfois pour lectrice. Quand nous serons vieux, j'irai vous voir et vous lire . . . à Varramista.")[45]

Capponi imagined in similarly collaborative terms the corporeal dimension of his intellectual relation with Capei (the father of Allart's second son). In March 1843, he thought of Capei's research in relation to his heart problems, writing to him: "Scratch around those Longobard matters, when your chest is calm" ("Seguitate a razzolare, quando il petto è tranquillo, sopra quelle cose longobardiche"). For Capponi, Capei's unhealthy heart rhetorically paralleled his own diseased eyes—the composite physical foundation of their interest in Longobard matters: "Your chest and my eyes don't want to rush; and the world will wait" ("Il vostro petto ed i miei occhi non vogliono fretta; ed il mondo aspetterà").[46] By the same token, he connected Capei's scholarly accomplishments to certain improvements in health: "I love that you are taking notes, and I see that you work eagerly, an indication and cause of good health. . . . You have completed a big volume, and this will would be good for your throat and maybe even for your liver, your intestines and the rest." ("Ho caro che facciate le note, e veggo che lavorate con alacrità, indizio e causa di buona salute; e godo che terminiate con una scoperta. Avere compito un grosso volume è cosa che fa del bene alla gola, e lo farebbe quasi al fegato, agli intestini ec.")[47] Against the background of this direct relation between body and intellect, we can better understand what Capponi meant when he wrote to Capei: "I love to feel you totally immersed in the Longobards" ("Ho caro sentirvi tutto ingolfato nei Longobardi").[48]

It is always interesting to investigate our ways of knowing in relation to roles played by our bodies—our palpitating hearts, our eyes as they connect to the letters on the page, our legs in the library, our hands as we handle documents, books, writing, and note taking. Sometimes it is not just our own bodies but the body of another that informs our investigations. Among members of the Vieusseux group, Allart's body—her purported seductions, her pregnancies and childbirths, her general whereabouts—came to have rhetorical value in the context of their epistolary exchanges. But especially one body part—Allart's nose—became emblematic of the trouble these men had relating to her knowledge. As they endeavored to accomplish their serious civic work, Vieusseux, Tommaseo, and Capponi tuned in to their sense of smell and were troubled by the undeniable presence of a woman's knowing nose.[49]

In the first several months of his exile in Paris, Tommaseo expressed a fear of seeming like a pig to Allart, writing to Capponi in June 1834: "I made a frightful impression on her, which is to say in Italian I acted like a pig" ("Io feci la figura del pauroso, che in lingua italiana dicesi porco").[50] By August 13, though, in the midst of scrutinizing his own behavior, Tommaseo began to displace the blame from his own piggishness to the nose of Allart. "When a woman's nose begins to grow," he wrote to Capponi, "it is a bad sign. Now the nose of Madame Allart is much more noteworthy than her forehead or eyes." ("Quando a una donna comincia crescere il naso, cattivo segno: or il naso di Madame Allart è molto più notabile della fronte e degli occhi.")[51]

When Tommaseo and Capponi wrote letters that touched on Allart, they seemed to enjoy adding gratuitous comments about her nose to other news of her intellectual accomplishments. On May 1, 1837, after announcing the publication of Allart's *History of Florence,* Tommaseo also hastened to inform Vieusseux that Allart "makes hypotheses that are more disagreeable than her nose" ("fa delle ipotesi, che sono più antipatiche del suo naso").[52] Eleven days later, he continued to Capponi: "She is too heathen, too much a lady-philosopher, too dry, too large-nosed" ("Troppo pagana e filosofessa, e secca, e nasuta").[53] On June

24, 1837, soon after Allart had returned to Florence, Capponi, echoing Ariosto's famous description of Alcina, wrote to Tommaseo: "The nose of Madame Allart is such that envy finds no way to improve it; and you slander it, because you have disdained it. . . . A good woman, poor thing, and although it is not a good idea to get too deeply involved with her, she inspires in me so much confidence that I tell her more things than to any other woman. But I have not been able to grasp even from her whether or not you love me." ("Il naso di Mª Allart è tale, *che non trova l'invidia ove l'emende*; e voi lo calunniate perchè l'avete sprezzato. . . . Buona donna, poveretta, e benchè non sia da mescolarsi con lei omericamente, m'ispira una confidenza tale, ch'io dico a lei più cose che non ad altra donna mai. Ma nemmeno da lei ho potuto raccapezzare se mi vogliate bene o no.")[54]

Perhaps, in the end, Allart's nose, in these letters, was nothing more than a marker of insecure affections between Tommaseo and Capponi.[55] Still, the possibility remains that their inability to fathom the scholarly body of an intellectual woman resulted in their making anxious calumnies about one of Allart's body parts. As Allart worked on her *Essai sur l'histoire politique*, she wrote of the bodily bliss she experienced in relation to the books she was consulting: "I am as happy as a woman can be who is a coquette, still cold, always nursing, and who has totally immersed her body in the works of the Bibliothèque Royale that I have here in the country." ("Vous semblez craindre que je ne sois pas très contente en France. Détrompez-vous. Je le suis autant qu'une femme coquette, froide encore, toujours nourrice, et qui s'est jetée à corps perdu dans les ouvrages de la Bibliothèque Royale que j'ai à la campagne et avec lesquels je continue mon entreprise.")[56] If Capponi and Tommaseo used the shape of Allart's nose to confirm their conflicted assessment of her projects and knowledge, Allart was not hindered by the smell of their comments.

Carraresi

Alessandro Carraresi was an important figure in the life of Gino Capponi. He spent thirty-six years as Capponi's secretary, reading to him, writing for him, accompanying him, and translating for him.[57] He had little scholarly preparation for such an important role in the intellectual and political life of Florence and Italy. And although he had only a spotty preparation in French, Carraresi took over from Orlandini the job of translating Allart's *Histoire de la République florentine* into

Italian.⁵⁸ We cannot know what precise role this translation had in Capponi's elaboration of his own *Storia della Repubblica fiorentina*. As we know, Capponi was blind and relied on the assistance of Carraresi's eyes for reading and writing. Perhaps the name of Carraresi's first child—Ortensia (born in 1845)—is an indication of how much the work of Hortense played a role in their conversations?⁵⁹

Chinese

On June 15, 1837, the day after she arrived for her second extended visit to Italy, Allart sent a note to Capponi inviting him to visit the next day. The note, which alluded among other things to the great simplicity of Confucian thought, consisted of three columns of single words to be read from right to left and from top to bottom and ended with the word *Chinese*.⁶⁰ The next day she wrote again, quoting an infinitive and three nouns from her previous note—"to remember, Italians, sweetness, sadness" ("souvenir, Italiens, douceur, tristesse")—and explaining her understanding of the Chinese language: "I love Chinese because it says so much without too much explanation" ("J'aime le chinois parce qu'il dit beaucoup sans trop s'expliquer").⁶¹ Many years later, soon after Capponi had died, his daughter, Marianna Farinola, wrote to Allart, requesting Capponi's letters. Responding that she didn't save any letters, Allart added that Capponi, too, had written to her in Chinese: "I had explained to him that the Chinese had only substantives and nouns without verbs; so he wrote me in Chinese" ("Je lui avais expliqué que les Chinois n'avaient que des substantifs et des noms sans verbe; il m'écrivit ainsi en chinois").⁶² Included in the letters to Allart that we do have, there are, unfortunately, no samples of Capponi's letters "in Chinese." When she said Capponi wrote her "in Chinese," was Allart perhaps referring to the telegraphic way in which Capponi expressed, in the preface to his *Storia della Repubblica fiorentina*, his indebtedness to her work?

Coquetteries

As we saw, when Allart was able to immerse her body in the works of a library, she was "as happy as a woman can be who is a coquette."⁶³ Did she mean she could have been happier in her work had she not been a flirt? Or was she ironically representing herself as she knew her Italian friends saw her? On one occasion, Tommaseo reported Allart's intention "to flirt" with him in a letter to Capponi, quoting her as saying: "Court me. I need for you to court me. Well, I am going to flirt with you." ("Faites-moi la cour. J'ai besoin qu'on la fasse à moi. Eh bien, je vais vous faire des coquetteries.")[64] But flirtation, for him, was unthinkable except in the context of intellectual exchange: "We wouldn't be able to make love, because I cannot find topics to discuss with her" ("Ma io le scrissi che noi due non potevamo fare all'amore, perch'io non trovavo materia da discorrere seco").[65]

Allart and Capponi, on the other hand, shared so many intellectual and political interests that Allart could represent her flirtations as a duet with Capponi. She wrote: "Both of us have flirted" ("Nous nous sommes fait tous deux des coquetteries"); "You give me the desire to continue my flirtations, telling me that passion could become complete even in correspondence" ("Vous me donnez l'envie de continuer mes coquetteries, en me disant que la passion pourrait devenir entière, même par correspondance"); "Don't you remember... your uncertain heart... and my expiring flirtations?" ("Ne vous souvenez-vous pas un moment de votre coeur incertain... et de mes coquêtteries expirantes?").[66] Allart set up her novel *Sextus* around the mystery of Thérèse de Longueville, who, according to Count Rucellai, was a stereotypical French coquette. But Guido resisted this judgment with his own belief in her noble and lofty sentiments:

> [Count:] She is French, she is a coquette. She loves the dominion she exercises. You speak of her virtue. I don't believe it.
> [Guido:] A stupid virtue that makes her spend the best years of her life in solitude. Often, in the Roman countryside in the presence of nature, I have seen her eyes well up with tears. She is not a coquette; she is noble. She wakes up in men's hearts lofty sentiments that give birth to love. She has no other art.
>
> [—Elle est Française, elle est coquette; elle aime l'empire qu'elle exerce: vous parles de sa vertu, je n'y crois pas.
> —Vertu stupide, qui lui fait passer les belles années de sa vie dans la solitude. Souvent, dans nos campagnes romaines, à l'aspect de la nature, j'ai vu ses yeuxs mouiller de pleurs. Elle n'est pas coquette, elle est noble; elle éveille dans le coeur de l'homme des sentimens élevés qui font naître l'amour: elle n'a pas d'autre art.][67]

Dominate

While Count Rucellai characterizes the French coquette by the "dominion" she exercises over men, Allart's protagonist Sextus finds on his trip to France that French women in general "exercise a dominion that

Italian women don't have: they compete in Paris to dwarf the character of men" ("Il trouvait que les femmes exercent un empire qu'elles n'ont pas en Italie: elles concourent a Paris a rapetisser le caractère des hommes").[68] Pieri, Capponi, and Tommaseo were, to say the least, fixated on this perception that Allart could somehow dwarf their characters by means of her dominion. Pieri, for example, wrote in his memoirs in January 1828 that Allart, "with her intense desire to dominate, would always sacrifice morality to politics. She was one of those ambitious women who would turn the world upside down in order to rule it. She was a Semiramis, a Catherine II and even more." ("Per ismania di dominare, sagrificherebbe sempre la morale alla politica: una di quelle donne ambiziose che porrebbe il mondo a soqquadro per comandarlo: una Semiramide, una Caterina II, e più ancora.")[69] And Tommaseo warned Capponi that Allart was "pitiful in her overuse of the verbs 'to hold, to possess, and to dominate'" ("E troppo adopera i verbi tenir, possider, dominer, che in donna di vent'anni fanno stizza, e di quaranta pietà"),[70] a sure sign that she had a one-track will to subjugate them.

Tommaseo was right that Allart often used verbs of domination. In March 1829 in Florence, Allart was reviewing the progress of her friendship with Capponi from the very first time the Milanese baron Sigismondi Trechi had spoken of Capponi as a "very remarkable man" whom Allart should "not fail to subjugate" ("un homme très remarquable que je devais **subjuguer** infailliblement") to the first times she had met him in Florence before really getting to know him: "It was a conquest," she wrote, "that remained incomplete, that I left behind" ("C'était une **conquête** qui me restait à faire, je la laissais en arrière").[71] It was a conquest that for Allart was not meant to frighten Capponi but rather to strengthen their qualities in common. "The Italians say you are afraid I will dominate you? So much the better for you, because we have the same inclinations, the same nobility. I could only want something worthy of you." ("Les Italiens disent que vous avez craint que je ne vous dominasse? Tant mieux pour vous, car nous avions les mêmes penchants la même noblesse; je ne pouvais rien vouloir qui ne fût digne de vous.")[72] Allart was interested in domination in general as central to the politics of relationships.

She was interested, for example, in the way some people, like Capponi, were "sensitive to frivolous display" ("sensible à un frivole éclat"), while others (like herself) "ruled by truth" ("moi je ne pouvais **régner** que par la vérité"). She distinguished between "making a name and fame for herself" and "conquering public opinion" ("J'ai l'opinion à **conquérir**, mon nom et ma gloire sont à faire").[73] She understood scholars to have little control over their writing, and when Capponi said he was "close to dominating his work" ("l'ouvrage que vous faites *a été près d'être commandé*") she called him "conceited" ("un peu **fat**") and an "ungracious loser" ("un **vaincu** de mauvaise grâce").[74] Many things, in Allart's opinion, could subjugate humans. Political ambition subjugated her English lover Henry Bulwer-Lytton: "I die, the man I love... has let ambition conquer him" ("J'y meurs, l'homme que j'aime... s'est laissé **subjuguer** par l'ambition"). And the present moment subjugated Capponi and perhaps prevented him from sustaining his focus on history: "I don't think, as you do, that concerns of the past grow pale with time. I am not so subjugated by the present." ("Je ne pense pas comme vous que les affaires du temps passé **pâlissent**, je ne suis pas si **subjuguée** par le présent.")[75] To judge by her intense commitment to historical scholarship, perhaps the past subjugated Allart. In any case, it seems that Allart was interested in subjugation and preferred to reflect on its modalities rather than cringe from it in fear.

Dreams of the nation

Allart understood all of Capponi's dreams as nationalistic ones. He dreamt of unity, he dreamt only of the nation.[76] She was concerned that his dream might be centered on the "small, poor, horizonless" Tuscany ("Votre Toscane est petite, bornée, pauvre, sans horizon") and might marginalize the "beauty, glory, ancient and modern times" of Rome and Naples ("Rome et Naples? Ici est l'Italie, ici la beauté, ici la gloire, ici l'antiquité et les temps modernes").[77] Was she sensing early on those aspersions on the South that would plague the architects of the nation and, today, their heirs?

Erudite relations

The term *erudire*, "to instruct, to make learned," comes from the Latin root *rudis* or *rozzo:* rough, rude, boorish, ill-bred. The prefix *e-* or *ex-* creates the irony of erudition. To become erudite is not a lofty enterprise; it is to become less rough, less rude, less boorish. To become erudite, we sand down those edges that mark our connections to each other. Do we bury our rudeness or leave it behind, becoming so refined?[78] Is roughness required to make us erudite?

The cavaliere Inghirami, owner and director of a huge printing and editorial enterprise since 1819, used his roughness in the instruction of future typographers, graphic artists, engravers, and so on. As an ex-military man of the Order of Malta, Inghirami made them erudite to the sound of a drum and also, when necessary, by dint of thrashings.[79] The cantankerous, celibate erudite Canestrini was no less boorish in the pursuit of his erudition. As we saw, in 1842 Gar invited Canestrini to join his family and thereby become more refined. Although it took a few more years for the bad-tempered, misogynous Canestrini to surrender his bristly boorishness to Gar's offer of social refinement, by January 1845 he had taken up residence in Pisa with Bonaini, his mother, and his sisters and had acceded to the domesticity of erudition.[80] Erudition and national history had become a parlor game.

Indeed, Italian erudites felt that they held the European title for the power of quoting facts of the past. Tommaseo wrote to Capponi in December 1838: "Europe has only two powerful quoters: you and me" ("Due soli citatori potenti ha l'Europa, signor marchese: voi e me").[81] Florentines took great pleasure in watching Carlo Troya and Gabriele Pepe play the game "historical fact" ("fatto storico"). The game allowed each player fifteen tricky questions ("domande cornute") for each tiny fact. Troya and Pepe were so erudite in Italian stories of the Middle Ages that they would guess a fact about some silly obscure Italian republic long before using up their fifteen questions. Niccolini was always prepared for this game, keeping handy chronological tables so that he could instantly settle historical disputes that arose among the guests. And Capponi would astound his friends, reciting in order the names of the archbishops of Paris. This was not really history but high-class recreation. Still, a new nineteenth-century ethos attached great value to this historical game, which expressed the erudites' deeply lived curiosity about the past that informed their present.[82]

These same questions of erudition and national history were central to the process of redacting the *Archivio storico italiano*. Should a text like Malipiero's diary, for example, be published in Venetian dialect or in Italian? Would readers be more interested in linguistic and philological questions or in civic, moral, and political history or in neither of the above? "If the Archivio is to be for the people," Capponi wrote, "then it must be published in such a way that the people can read and understand it. If it is to be for the learned and erudite, then it must conserve in its full integrity all that it publishes." ("Se l'Archivio deve essere pel popolo, deve allora [essere] in modo che il popolo lo legga e lo intenda; se deve essere per i dotti e gli eruditi, allora deve conservare nella sua piena integrità tutto quello che pubblica.")[83] These scholarly choices were not about "showing off . . . some old manuscripts that offered more correct readings" ("l'ostentare o qualche novella e magra scrittura, o qualche più corretta lezione di antichi manoscritti").[84] To make such erudite choices was politically charged with the power of the past to make a national future.

Fear

Capponi, Tommaseo, and Vieusseux were intimate friends, willing to share their fears and embarrassments with respect to love. When, for example, Tommaseo fell in love in Paris with George Sand, he wrote to his friend Bianciardi, confessing his fear: "I could get to know her, but I am afraid. I fear devotion, not love; not her body, but her wit." ("Potrei conoscerla, ma temo: temo la pietà, non l'amore; non il corpo di lei, ma l'ingegno.")[85] When Vieusseux heard this "spicy" ("piccante") news, he imagined that he, in Tommaseo's fearful shoes, would "grovel at her feet" ("umiliarmi ai piedi di G. Sand") or would "avoid her like the devil. Cursed love!" ("la scanserei come il diavolo. Maledetto amor proprio!").[86] Tommaseo, possibly reassured by his friend's sympathetic response, first responded that Vieusseux "would do better to avoid her" ("ben fareste a fuggirla") and then denied his previously confessed fears with a stoic attitude: "I neither avoid her nor seek her out; I would see her willingly, but if no occasion arises, even better" ("Io nè la fuggo, nè la cerco; la vedrei volentieri, ma se l'occasione non s'offre, meglio").[87]

Tommaseo was probably just as happy not to seek out Allart when he first went to live in Paris as an exile in 1834. Capponi had not given him any letter or message to deliver to Allart, so he conveniently assumed this meant Capponi did not want him to visit her. Tommaseo avoided Allart's invitations, giving her "the impression of a man full of fear" ("io feci la figura del **pauroso**"),[88] until Capponi responded that Tommaseo had no reason to fear Allart on his behalf: "Go to Madame Allart's house, if you want to. I didn't want to give you a letter (do you want to know why?), for fear, fear of you; as if you resembled me!" ("Andate da madama Allart, se ne avete voglia. Non volli darvi una lettera (volete saperlo?) per paura, paura di voi; come se voi mi somigliaste!")[89] Capponi did not fear Allart, but he feared that Tommaseo would somehow stand in for him in Allart's affections. When he thought of Allart, he feared Tommaseo.

Capponi also feared his own loneliness and especially the words and thoughts born from that lack of social contact. In March 1835, Capponi wrote to Allart that he had "no one, not one person, to talk to. That makes my blood a little bitter, and that's why I write to you so harshly. In truth, I am afraid to reread my letter and I shouldn't send it. If you were a man, you would have to blow my brains out for my irreverent expressions. I fear you more being a woman." ("Je n'ai plus personne, pas un, avec qui parler. Cela m'aigrit un peu le sang et voilà pourquoi je vous écris si âprement. En vérité, **j'ai peur** de relire ma lettre, et je ne devrais pas l'envoyer. Si vous étiez homme, vous devriez me brûler la cervelle, pour mes expressions irrévérentes. **Je vous crains plus étant femme.**")[90] Capponi's fear of rereading his irreverent letter was a many-faceted fear. He had railed in his letter against the French in general for their cultural superiority and against Allart in particular for her gift of "mixing fiction and truth" ("mêler le faux et le vrai") in her novel *Sextus*.[91] But perhaps Capponi was most afraid to reread his condemnation of Allart for her happiness, productivity, and success: "You are happy; that's why I don't love you anymore, and you judge men as the world does, according to a criterion of success" ("Vous êtes heureuse; voilà pourquoi je ne vous aime plus, et vous jugez comme le monde, qui a aussi besoin du succès pour rendre justice aux hommes").[92] It is plausible to imagine from the letter's end that Capponi feared Allart's completed draft of a volume of Florentine history was implicitly a judgment on his inability to complete his own volume. "Goodbye, Madame. I congratulate you again, very cordially, on your *History of Florence*. It would give me great joy to talk to you about it, if you will forgive my rudeness of today." ("Adieu, Madame, je vous féliciterai une autre fois, bien cordialement, sur votre Histoire de Florence, dont j'aurai grande joie à vous parler si vous m'aurez pardonné mes impertinences d'aujourd'hui.")[93]

Filial relations

Allart described herself as an affectionate, independent daughter of Italy, writing from Paris in November 1829: "If I miss Italy, it is because of my deep affection, but I no longer need her. . . . I defend her, I praise her, I have filial feelings for her, I speak so highly of you distinguished men whom she has produced." ("Si je regrette l'Italie c'est par un fond d'affection, mais je n'ai plus besoin d'elle. . . . Je la défends, je la loue, je lui porte **un sentiment filial**, je vous vainte tous, hommes distingués qu'elle a produits.")⁹⁴ Implicit was her claim to be a sibling of those distinguished men.

Five days after he had noted in his *Diario intimo* that Allart was continuing to make him "useless sexual offers" ("profferte sue inutili"), Tommaseo published a review of Allart's novel *Settimia*, praising her as a "figliuola d'Italia."⁹⁵ It would seem that Tommaseo, for all of his fears and negative judgments of Allart and her work, accepted nonetheless Allart's "dignity" ("dignità") and "nobility" ("sì levata sopra il volgo") in her role as Italy's "daughter." Imagining her as a daughter, Tommaseo was able to appreciate Allart's difference from all those women philosophers and poets who were "ignorant" and "disdainful" of Italy ("il volgo delle filosofesse, e poetesse, e marchese viaggianti e sprezzanti e ignoranti l'Italia"). Seeing her as a daughter, he was also able to grasp Allart's experience of fondness for Italy as the foundation of her qualities as "a warm," "moving," and "innovative" thinker. ("Non neghiamo la verità delle querele di questa calda ragionatrice, le quali ci commovono a riverente simpatia. Nè possiamo negare al suo fare il raro merito della novità.")⁹⁶ And we might (once again) reorganize the "historiographic past" to make central—rather than disavow—the collaborative fantasies and contributions of "fathers" and "daughters" to the building of nations.⁹⁷

Florence

Allart referred metonymically to her published *Histoire de la République de Florence* as "Florence." She wanted to send copies of "Florence" to friends, Italian publishers, erudite societies.⁹⁸ "Florence" was a nickname, a metonymy that captured the intensity of her experiences of relations in the city, past and present.

French lessons

It is also important to regard Gino Capponi's relations with Hortense Allart in the context of his early experiences of the French. Capponi was only six years old in March of 1799, when the French occupied Tuscany, forcing the Grand Duke Ferdinando III into exile. Capponi's father, the Marquis Piero Roberto Capponi, felt obliged to follow his prince into exile, leaving his wife and young son defenseless against the violence of the occupying officers and soldiers. Mother and small boy must have been quite traumatized by this abandonment, as they were left to witness the beating of servants and the ravaging of their house.[99] For the six-year-old Gino, this must have been a formative experience of "Italian" shame and humiliation at the hands of the French.[100]

At the age of twenty-four, totally occupied by his studies of Latin prosody and Greek grammar, he wrote to his former tutor, the abbot Zannoni, that "shame" defended him from the "seductions" of "lighter studies" and kept him focused on his hope of becoming "a very deep grammarian." ("Spero di tornare a Firenze grammatico profondissimo. . . . La prosodia latina e la grammatica greca . . . sono la mia occupazione . . . e se qualche volta il diavolo dell'ignoranza mi tentasse a lasciarle per degli studi più ameni, non mi lascio sedurre per la vergogna di esservi tanto bue.")[101] Indeed, philology and the relation with ancient sources had political ramifications in occupied Tuscany. Del Furia, director of the Laurentian Library, once let a drop of ink fall on a manuscript. The stain became infamous when a certain French official, Paul-Louis Courier, tried to shame the honest librarian. But Del Furia was ultimately vindicated by his personal integrity and the good name of Italian literary and philological culture. A foreigner, even worse a Frenchman, still worse an unwelcome colonizer (especially in Tuscany), did not have the right to offend Italian philological pride, humiliating an Italian librarian.[102]

Years later, Capponi perhaps felt humiliated by the fact that the French Allart had completed a history of Florence before he could. When Lady Russell asked him in 1859 to recommend a book about Florentine history, Capponi, "forgetting" Allart's work, recommended Machiavelli, Varchi, and others, and he "felt shame that no modern writer had yet completed a readable history of Florence" ("non potè suggerirle altro che il Machiavelli, il Varchi e gli altri antichi, e sentì vergogna che non ci fosse una Storia moderna di Firenze compiuta e leggibile").[103] Perhaps, his mind was still reverberating with the impact of his experiences of psychological/scholarly shame at the hands of the French when he chose for his tomb the message by which he wanted to be remembered: "He wanted Italy to be avenged of her age-old humiliations" ("Volle vendicata l'Italia dalle secolari umiliazioni").[104]

Insults and compliments

Was it his humiliation at the hands of the French that made Capponi so ambivalent about the quality of Allart's historical scholarship? In any case, Capponi had a pattern of insulting Allart and then expressing regret for his rudeness. He wrote to Tommaseo in July 1835, worrying about a long pause in Allart's communications: "Perhaps she was offended by the terrible insults I wrote to her a while back? If that were true, I would feel bad . . . because I still love her a little. . . . She is writing a history of Florence. I would like for her to do a good job and I would have sent her some materials." ("Che forse Mª Allart s'ebbe a male certe insolenze, insolenze vere, ch'io le scrissi tempo fa? Se ciò fosse, mi dorrebbe . . . perch'io l'amo sempre un poco. . . . Fa una storia di Firenze. Vorrei la facesse bene, e le avrei mandato qualche cosa.")[105] Did Capponi still "love her a little" when he wrote to Tommaseo in January 1838, after the appearance of her 1837 *Histoire*, that Allart was "good but stupid" ("Buona donna, ma scempiata"), speaking of her in terms of fruit that had become "withered instead of mature" ("E' invizzita, povera creatura, piuttosto che maturata")?[106]

Writing to Pietro Capei, the father of her second son, on the occasion of the publication of Allart's *Histoire*, Capponi proved his mastery of mixing insults with compliments: "This evening Bargiacchi will bring you Madame Allart's book, a good book, much better than I would have believed, except for a very few of her usual vulgarities, and the greatest one of all at the very beginning, the dedication to women. But I find that the second part is much better than the first, and the history of internal strife and of councils that governed in the last days of the Republic is crafted with much diligence and manly judgment. . . . I will write all of this tomorrow to the beautiful author." ("Dal giovine Bargiacchi avrete stasera il libro di madama Allart: buon libro, più assai che non avrei creduto, salvo pochissime delle solite **sguaiaterie**, ed una massima, in testa del libro, la dedica *aux femmes*. Ma trovo che la parte seconda è superiore d'assai alla prima . . . ; e la storia interna dei partiti e dei consigli che governarono la Repubblica negli ultimi tempi, è fatta con molta diligenza e **senno virile**. . . . e scriverò tutte queste cose domani **alla bella autore**.")[107]

Capponi was anxious to separate out the diligence and manly judgment of the work from its (feminist) vulgarities, to press a grammatically mismatched "bella" against an appropriately masculine "autore," and to purge Allart's *Histoire* of her identity through his work of translation. Capponi was beginning to occupy Allart's *Histoire* with his feelings of admiration and disdain.

Italy and Italian

Allart took pleasure in her long evenings and long conversations with Capponi about "politics, action, and hope for the Italian nation" ("la politique, l'action, les espérances pour l'Italie").[108] She considered it an "honor" to write about Italy, and on several occasions she wrote to Capponi that she worked only for Italy, that she had never worked so hard as she had on her *Essais sur l'Italie*.[109] For Allart, the term *Italian* spoke to every dimension of her life. She reported in 1855 that her son by Capei was engaged in the "beautiful activities of a sixteen-year-old Italian: He pleases, he loves, he writes poetry, etc." ("Henri fait les belles choses d'un Italien de 16 ans, plaire, aimer, faire des vers, etc.").[110] She also claimed to use the "Italian" language to communicate "hidden matters" ("C'est ma langue pour les choses voilées"),[111] as if to say, perhaps, that her Italian friends were the best interlocutors for her secrets, or that the Italian language best "veiled" news that she was reluctant (or embarrassed) to present more openly in public (like the news of her marriage, in March 1843, to Napoléon-Louis de Méritens, which would last one year); or that writing in Italian was a resource Allart used to create a wall in her mind between matters she found obscure, unfathomable, and murky and matters that could better enjoy (in French) the light of day. As we have seen, reading aloud to Capponi in "Italian" was the bond that Allart hoped would keep her connected to him through their old age.[112] As time went on, *Italian,* for Allart, became a consummate metonymy standing in for so much of what she cherished about Italians. After the publication of Capponi's *Storia*, Allart wanted Capponi to know just how much *Italian* meant to her. She wrote in March 1875: "Your work has three things: charm, profound knowledge, and *Italian* politics, to say Italian is to say everything" ("Votre ouvrage a les trois choses: le charme, le savoir profond, et la politique *italienne, italienne* c'est tout dire").[113]

Making scenes

Allart's relations of writing with Capponi and the other erudites could become, at times, heated and dramatic. She might report that she "made a scene" ("Je fais une scène") or announce that she had "come to make a scene" ("Je viens vous faire une scène") or simply make the scene without framing it as such. The motives for this acting varied from frustration to sadness and annoyance. She was angry with Capponi for withholding some notes that would have helped her in her research and writing.[114] And when she learned that Capponi had labeled as "crazy" ("matta") the dedication of her Florentine history to "women who want reform, improvement, honor, and influence" ("Je la dédie aux femmes qui veulent une réforme, je la dédie à un principe, celui d'une amélioration dans leur sort, celui d'un honneur moins frivole et d'une carrière plus étendue"), she lashed out at him, using a verse from Racine's *Brittanicus* (IV.2) to call him an "eternal ingrate" ("Vous êtes un ingrat, vous le fûtes toujours") who "understood nothing of French women" ("Vous n'entendez rien aux femmes françaises").[115]

Allart did not limit her expressions of anger to Capponi. She also "made a violent scene" ("J'ai fait une scène violente") with Pieri "for letting her go to England to learn those mysteries and delights that she was supposed to experience first in Italy" ("pour m'avoir laissée aller apprendre en Angleterre ces mystères et ces délices que l'Italie eût dû m'enseigner"), the mysteries and delights of "love, pleasure, and ambition" ("l'amour, la volupté, et l'ambition").[116] Perhaps Allart acted out with her erudite friends at least sometimes because she thought of them all playing characters on the stage. In August 1842 she wrote to Capponi, announcing the imminent appearance of her Florentine history, "trembling at the thought of her Florentine reading public" ("Je tremble en pensant à mon public de Florence") and figuring herself as Racine's princess Monime captivated by Mithridates' (wishfully Capponi's) attentions.[117]

Mixing

Allart perceived her work, life, and loves as parts of a whole and preferred mixing them to keeping them separate. She hoped to "meet some man who was able to mix political interests with love" ("J'aurais voulu rencontrer quelqu'homme d'un pays libre qui pût **mêler** les intérêts politiques à l'amour"), and she thought that Capponi would become more successful as a writer if he were to "mix some Italian woman into his scientific patriotism" ("**Mêlez** quelque femme italienne à ce patriotisme scientifique").[118] While Capponi, as we saw, had "no talent for mixing the false and the true," Allart was able to work simultaneously on works of fiction, historiography, and political philosophy.[119] Tommaseo wrote to Capponi with impatience about this mixing of genres: "First, she writes the history of Florence, then, a work on women" ("Ora scrive la storia di Firenze, poi un'opera sulla donna").[120]

Organization/classification

Although Allart could not "resist the appeal" ("Je ne puis résister à leur appel") of the supporters of Saint-Simon who called for improvement in the social conditions of women, she did not align herself with them because she took issue with their classifications of knowledge ("**Je ne me range pas** avec eux, car je trouve de grands empêchements à leurs **classifications**, etc.").[121] Indeed, Allart carefully considered how specific organizations of knowledge were related to facts, theories, and political positions, claiming that she never organized her ideas according to a preexisting argument; rather, she would contemplate her ideas, arrange them, and deduce from them a position.[122] Only after writing her *Essais sur l'Italie* could Allart "dream of a theory for the organization" of the new Italian nation ("J'y voudrais mettre *une théorie* sur l'**organisation** que je rêve pour l'Italie").[123] Writing of her *Essai de l'histoire politique*, Allart wrote in August 1840 that she had not uncovered any new facts but that her "arrangement" of those facts was new and original ("Je trouve les faits partout mais pas mon impression ni mon arrangement").[124] In short, Allart considered her organizations of knowledge different and original. And because of her unique arrangements and classifications, Allart did not want to be compared to others: "Above all," she wrote to Capponi on one occasion, "don't compare my letters to others you receive at the same time . . . classify me separately" ("Surtout **ne comparez pas** mes lettres à celles que vous recevez en même temps . . . **classez-moi** *à part*").[125]

Past and present

Ernesto Sestan's essay "Lo stato maggiore del primo 'Archivio storico italiano' (1841–1847)" was drafted during the Nazi-fascist invasion of Florence and published in the first postwar issue of the *Archivio storico italiano* in 1945–46, those years of few resources and upheaval in which the old historical journal wearily resumed publication. Giovanni Spadolini was touched by what he perceived as "the constant autobiographical tone" ("la costante nota autobiografica") in Sestan's essay.[126] An antifascist scholar's experience of fascist occupation colored his scholarly perceptions of and attractions to an intellectual enterprise of one hundred years earlier. *Stato maggiore*, the corps of officials assigned to help the central military authority or the commanders of troop formations in the study and resolution of military problems.[127]

Did Sestan perceive the corps of editors of the *Archivio storico* as paramilitary officials assigned to shore up the cultural authority of Florence in the march toward Italian nationalism?

The question of how the past inhabits the present (and, just as important, how the present shapes our view of the past) was, of course, a central concern for Capponi as well. Sometimes, according to Sestan, current problems might send Capponi to the past to find clues for understanding the present ("Un problema attuale lo porta a ripercorrere a ritroso il passato e a ricercarvi di quel problema, gli addentellati, i sostegni, le tentate soluzioni"). At other times, revisiting the past, he might come across a figure or fact that seemed to have determined a present situation ("S'imbattono, nel passato, in qualche figura o fatto . . . che sembri aver determinato una situazione attuale"). Capponi would become "impassioned" about these connections, "taking apart and reassembling" the materials of history "in a continuous counterpoint between past and present" ("Ci si appassiona, ci lavora attorno, scomponendo e ricomponendo in un continuo e sottile gioco di contrappunto fra presente e passato").[128]

Allart certainly captured this sense of counterpoint in her fictional Capponi, the Tuscan Sextus, who, in his younger years, wrote as one torn between an idealized past and a complicated present, preferring "rustic nature" to "our modern political situation" ("J'aimais mieux la nature agreste que notre situation politique et les modernes") and finding beauty only in the ancients.[129] The failure to find any satisfaction in the present brought a sense of shame to Sextus and a desire to dissimulate this feeling in veneration of the past. "I determined to bury my shame and my life in the Maremma, the true sojourn of a modern Roman. I carried back my thoughts to my ancestors. I erected altars to them. I was the last priest of the temple." ("Je résolus d'ensevelir ma honte et ma vie dans les Maremmes, vrai séjour d'un romain moderne; je reportais ma pensée vers mes aïeux; je leur dressais des autels; j'étais le dernier prêtre du temple.")[130]

As time went on, Sextus found ways to reconcile past and present. Through the study of history, he began to take apart and reassemble his judgments. He "came to judge the moderns more fairly," finding "beauty" in the history of Italy and especially in the first communes of the Middle Ages, which were "worthy of the ancient federations" ("Devenu plus juste envers les modernes, l'histoire d'Italie me parut plus belle que je ne l'avais trouvée d'abord: les premières fédérations du moyen âge, dignes des fédérations antiques").[131] He felt a sense of responsibility toward these worthy ancestors, placing himself in a male lineage that connected past to present: "Nations revive because of men. I was a man. I was Italian. I resolved to do for my country all that was in my power." ("Les nations se relèvent par les hommes: j'étais Italien; je résolus de faire pour mon pays tout ce qui était en mon pouvoir.")[132] A sense of the past was impinging on Sextus's obligations, in the present, to create a nation.

In her creation of the fictional Sextus, Allart embodied her idea of Capponi as an "heir of the great citizens of the Florentine republic whose history she was in the process of writing" ("Héritier de tant de grands citoyens dont j'écris l'histoire"). Following the suggestion of the women in Capponi's house, she looked for the "secret of his character" in relation to his ancestors ("J'ai cherché quelquefois chez eux le secret de votre caractère, et si les femmes de votre maison ne m'égarent, il y a bien du rapport").[133] For example, Allart thought Niccolò Capponi (1473–1529), who embodied the political talent and qualities of the noble Florentines of the past, might help her to decipher Gino's character. By the same token, Niccolò's descendant Gino, would be, in Allart's mind, the most qualified to explain to her the Florentine noble citizens of the fifteenth and sixteenth centuries.[134] She expressed frustration after several years of waiting for him to take up the job: "Work on your ancestors, for devil's sake, and brag to me from the rooftops about their relations of justice, impartiality" ("Occupez-vous de vos aïeux de par le diable, et vantez-moi par-dessus les toits, sous le rapport de la justice, de l'impartialité").[135]

For Allart, Gino Capponi was a "unique mixture" ("Vous êtes un mélange singulier") of a past that never faded and a present that gave shape to historical memory.[136] Her arrivals in Florence were "completely imbued with memories of the Florentine republic" ("Florence où j'arrive fort pénétrée de tous les souvenirs de la République").[137] And she preferred the old chronicles to the historiographic classics because they retained their "original fragrance that one could still smell in Florence" ("Moi j'ai essayé de garder la naïveté, le parfum natal des vieilles chroniques. On l'a senti à Florence, où ces chroniques sont admirées").[138] As she studied the 1476 Pazzi conspiracy, Allart wrote to Capponi, mixing her present concern for Capponi's health with the fate of the fifteenth-century conspirators: "I don't believe in your liver ailment. You need action, air, success. . . . I worked all day today on the Pazzi. They healed their liver ailment, surely you don't have to get hanged." ("Je ne crois pas à votre mal au foie, c'est de l'action, de l'air, du succès qu'il vous faut.... J'ai travaillé toute la journée sur les Pazzi, ils ont guéri leur mal de foie; il ne faut pourtant pas se faire pendre.")[139]

At times, the fusion of present feeling with history allowed Allart to speak freely of her affairs of the heart, as when she wrote to Capponi that she was involved in a "tender correspondence with Spain... not with Charles V, but you understand" ("Je suis dans une tendre correspondance avec l'Espagne... c'est encore là qu'est resté mon coeur; non pas à Charles Quint, mais vous comprendrez").[140] At other times she readily acknowledged this fusion as restrictive: "My history in Florence was restricted by this: one man enraptured me (Libri), another pleased me (Antonio Bargagli), and a third touched my soul (Charles Didier). Not one of them knew it." ("Mon histoire à Florence s'est bornée à ceci: Un homme m'a ravie [Libri], un homme m'a plu [Antonio Bargagli], un homme a touché mon âme [Charles Didier]: aucun ne l'a su.")[141] Allart therefore worried that Capponi's work on his history could likewise be obstructed by feelings about current events: "Give me your news. I believe you are very agitated and busy with events. Florence born again to civic life—may it not prevent you from recalling the past, and let's see your first volume." ("Donnez-moi de vos nouvelles, je vous crois très agité et occupé des événements. Voici Florence qui renaît à la vie civile, que cela ne vous empêche pas de rappeler le passé, et voyons votre premier volume.")[142]

Placing copies of the Histoire de la République de Florence *in Florence*

Although not "subjugated" by the Florentine present, Allart was regularly occupied, in the present, by the time-consuming task of physically placing copies of her *Histoire de la République de Florence* in the hands of Florentine readers. One obstacle to this transmission (or manumission) of Allart's *Histoire* was the concern of publishers and booksellers about losing money on the book. The Florentine bookseller and typographer Giuseppe Molini had promised to order one hundred copies, but he worried about taking a loss on his promise and was "requesting copies a dozen at a time" ("il ne demande que douzaine par douzaine"). The Parisian publisher of Allart's *Histoire*, realizing that Allart's target audience was primarily in Florence, sent Molini forty copies anyway, incurring some financial risk of his own ("Delloye plus aventureux lui a envoyé 40 exemplaires à tout hasard").[143] Allart understood the worry of the French booksellers about "uncertain payments" ("l'incertitude des paiements") and the difficulty of "making [her] fortune by intellectual work" ("Un homme ne peut espérer de faire sa fortune avec son travail intellectuel") in a city where booksellers did nothing "to facilitate the printing, sale and promotion of a book" ("À Florence . . . il n'y a . . . pas d'activité dans la librairie qui facilite l'impression d'un ouvrage, sa vente et sa célébrité").[144] She hoped to alleviate this concern by promising to subsidize the distribution of her book, sacrificing her own earnings from the book and "assuring a profit" to the Italian booksellers ("Au lieu de gagner par mon livre, j'ai promis 500 francs de contribution; les exemplaires vendus en Italie achèveront d'assurer au libraire un bénéfice").[145]

Allart also tried to enlist Capponi in the promotion of her work in Florence. In September 1841, seventeen months before the publication of her *Histoire* (on February 11, 1843), Allart began to play with the idea that Capponi might help her to materially publicize her work. She suggested to Capponi that the sale of copies of her *Histoire* in Italy would enhance the reputation of his family in France: "The glory of the Capponi in France is at stake, so please take care of it" ("La gloire des Capponi en France y est fort intéressée, occupez-vous en donc je vous prie").[146] And asking for some pointers as to how to write a "manifeste," Allart sent Capponi a theatrical "Manifesto!" announcing her history metaphorically as an architrave resting directly on the tops of three Herculean columns, her erudite friends in Florence (and playfully figuring Capponi and herself as Dante's Paolo and Francesca): "Sensitive Italians! A lady timidly presents to you the history of your glorious Florence. The cruel Capponi—so many sweet thoughts, so much desire!—encouraged this beautiful lady to write history so much that she gave her heart to that ancient, famous, humane Capponi family. The more gracious and courteous Pieri (always a precious memory) entertained the lady with pleasant conversations. But the fine, sublime Niccolini—also cruel but less so than the mischievous friend—recalled this very lofty lady to her love of a perfect republic. Now, resting on these three Hercules, the daring woman hopes to find Florence supportive and indulgent." ("Italiani sensibili! Una signora vi presenta timidamente l'istoria della vostra gloriosa Firenze! Una signora che il crudele Capponi—*Quanti dolci pensier, quanto disio!*—sempre incoraggiò a scrivere l'istoria, sì chè il cuore di questa bella si dette a' quelli Capponi antichi, famosi e umani. Il Pieri, più grazioso e cortese (rimembranza sempre cara!) tratenava la signora con suavi discorsi, ma il nobile, sublime Nicollini, crudele anche lui ma meno del amico briccone, richiamava questa gentilissima al amore d'una repubblica perfeta. Adesso, appoggiata sopra questi tre Ercoli, l'audace donna spera di trovar Firenze favorevole e debole.")[147] Capponi requested a more serious brochure.

Three months later, Allart asked Capponi to correct and tidy up the text of a more serious French-language "Manifeste" that described the chronological limits of her history, the historiographic sources she used, and its bargain price. She was mortified to learn that Capponi was no longer willing to help promote her book in Florence. First, he had helped to persuade Allart to market her *Histoire* at a low price so that it would sell ("Vous me dites d'abord que si on fait une édition bon marché, on en placera davantage"). Now that this inexpensive edition was nearing completion, Capponi was saying that she needed no help, a cheap edition "would sell by itself" ("Vous dites que cela ira tout seul"). "Nothing in the world," Allart protested, "sells by itself, especially a foreign work. Make the Manifeste, as we agreed. Otherwise, [my book] will not be successful. In a year, I must sell one printing made in Italy in French and a translation in Italian. Otherwise I will not be happy." ("Rien dans le monde ne va tout seul, surtout pour un ouvrage étranger. Faites le *Manifeste* come nous étions convenus.... Autrement rien ne réussira. Il me faut dans l'année une édition faite en Italie en français, et une traductione en italien. Autrement je ne serai pas contente.")[148] Even after the completion of a book, scholars need the continued supportive relations of peers.

Once Allart's *Histoire* was printed, the obstacle of censorship could still hypothetically keep Allart's scholarship from reaching her Florentine reading public. This was a potential difficulty that Allart also hoped to finesse with Capponi's support and complicity. On the same day (February 10, 1843) that the Italian publisher Molini sent fourteen copies of Allart's *Histoire* for review by the censors, Allart wrote to Capponi with this idea: "Here's something we could do. We could send, on behalf of the author, a copy to the grand duke." ("Voici ce qu'on pourrait faire. On pourrait envoyer de la part de l'auteur un exemplaire au Grand-Duc.") She imagined the social paths by which her work would arrive in Leopoldo II's hands—Capei or Torrigiani would ask Count Ginori to deliver her *Histoire* to the grand duke. ("On peut lui dire que je le prie de remettre l'ouvrage au Grand-Duc. Chargez de cela Capei ou Torrigiani; Capei fera mieux parce qu'il sait faire ce qu'il veut.") The count would remember their pleasant exchange when she had asked his permission to work in the Pitti Library. ("J'ai connu un chevalier Ginori . . . qui m'a donné un permission pour travailler à la Bibliothèque Pitti. . . . Ce chevalier Ginori était agréable . . . il était de ma cour.") And the grand duke's pleasure at seeing that her work was "on the side of public power" would "assure the work against any odds." ("Il ferait passer l'ouvrage; le Grand-Duc aime les Médicis, et l'ouvrage lui plaira car il est pour le pouvoir public . . . Ceci est une bonne idée qui assure l'ouvrage contre tout.")[149] Here again, Allart was acutely aware that the success of her book would depend on a network of social relations—that is, friends and fellow scholars working sincerely on her behalf.

Capponi's imagination, however, took him in other directions. He was convinced that Allart's suggestion to deliver her *Histoire* to the grand duke was a "ridiculous" idea ("Ebbi dall'autore una ridicolissima lettera, nella quale voleva si presentasse il libro al Granduca, a fine di salvarlo dalla censura; che intendete bene sarebbe fare peggio"), and he feared that her "usual vulgarities"— particularly the dedication of the *Histoire* to women ("le solite sguaiaterie, ed una massima, in testa del libro, la dedica *aux femmes*")—would make the work more vulnerable to censorship and would create "difficulties for its uncensored distribution" ("potrebbe lo smercio libero avere difficoltà"). Only a translation that purged Allart's work of its stupidities ("sciocchezze"), according to Capponi's fearful perspective, would easily pass the censors ("una traduzione, facilmente espurgata, passerebbe a piene vele").[150] Although Capponi's fears of censorship proved to be groundless, his "approval" of her work was still the sine qua non of her Florentine readership. ("Delloye m'apprend que la censure n'a mis nulle opposition. . . . Puisque la censure permet, il me semble qu'on n'aura rien à retrancher. C'est à votre approbation, à vous que je devrai celle du public à Florence.")[151] And, in any case, no matter what happened, Allart hoped Capponi would personally deliver copies of her "Florence" to "La Colombaria," the learned society over which he presided, and to two women—a French sculptress living in exile in Florence, Félicie de Fauveau, and Capponi's own daughter, Marianna Farinola. Allart especially wanted to get her work in the hands of women: "Women must give me a little support. And the work is dedicated to them." ("Je vous prie aussi d'envoyer un exemplaire de Florence à la Divine Félicie, via Santo Spirito. Et d'en donner un aussi à la Colombaria. Je vous prie d'intéresser pour moi Mme la Marquise Farinola, votre fille, personne lettrée e très spirituelle, dit-on. Les femmes me doivent un peu d'appui. Et l'ouvrage leur est dédié.")[152]

Political relations with books

In her foundational and richly researched book, *Eve's Proud Descendants: Four Women Writers and Republican Politics in Nineteenth-Century France,* Whitney Walton analyzes the lives of George Sand, Marie d'Agoult, Hortense Allart, and Delphine Gay de Girardin and shows how their public identities as writers who embraced republicanism "undermine[d] the masculine gendering of . . . sustained rational endeavor and its public presentation." Moreover, in their practices of social independence and erudition, Walton explores how these writers were able to "eliminate the dependent, ignorant, domestic wife and mother who was the justification for the independent, educated, republican patriarch and citizen."[153]

Walton's idea of politics as "a practice, a network of power relations, as well as a body of theory" reveals how these four writers were not simply trying to "wedge" themselves into a masculine-gendered tradition of thinking about liberty and tyranny. Rather, they were all, to some degree, political theorists, who changed the tradition of political historiography by making relations of power, gender, and knowledge a central aspect of historiographic inquiry and republican politics.[154] Prior to their intervention, the women in republican stories from the past were primarily mothers of male protagonists or objectified sisters, aunts, and daughters who were raped or vilified by a tyrant and then passed from male scholar to male scholar in a seamless, unmarked manumission.[155] Now, in nineteenth-century France, the hands of women writers, scholars, and theorists reworked these stories with competence, making themselves protagonists of the transmission of political thought and historiography. From this perspective, any study of the history of republicanism that ignores their interventions and relations of power seems lacking in historicity.

Allart made a place for herself in this republican tradition by virtue of her scholarly method. As Walton noted, Allart's method in her works of political historiography was to "amass historical data, examine and test different philosophies, and compile this material into books intended to further the science of statecraft."[156] In this sense, her method was not that distant from her predecessors in the tradition of political thought, writers, for example, like Machiavelli or Gabriel Naudé, who researched and collected examples of political behavior in their libraries (one personal, one public) in order to serve a prince.[157]

What distinguished Allart's work from theirs was her unique social relation to men's books and libraries. To consult the books she needed, Allart often depended on the favor of men who owned or had access to significant libraries. Her relations of dependence did not prevent her, however, from realizing her aspirations as a political theorist.[158] If thinking about politics and thinking about love took place in parallel universes for most male political thinkers, Allart's relations with the books of men she loved enabled her to integrate these two universes and to construct a different space for thinking and writing about politics that was based on this integration.[159]

On December 21, 1841, Allart wrote to Sainte-Beuve, describing the company she kept with books and thereby writing herself into a political tradition that had perhaps started with Machiavelli's famous letter to Vettori of December 10, 1513. Like Machiavelli, who returned home at the end of the day to converse with his Roman authors, the independent, educated Allart returned home in the evening to be received by her books. And just as Machiavelli put on the clothes of an ancient man in an ancient court, Allart envisioned herself as "a man in his own home" ("Tout était calme, tout rappelait doucement l'homme à son foyer domestique"). But the similarities end there. Allart refers to her books as "all the wise men who are my true lovers" ("j'ai là autour de moi tous ces sages qui sont mes vrais amants"). Would she converse with these lovers for four hours in the quiet of the night, as Machiavelli did? It is hard to know, but such a long conversation would have kept her from enjoying "the tender breathing of [her] sleeping child" ("Je n'entends que la tendre respiration de mon enfant endormi"). Although Allart affirms that "one lives well alone with one's books" ("qu'on vit bien seule avec ses livres!"), she imagines that "she would have liked to share" this life with the addressee of her letter, Sainte-Beuve ("J'aurais bien aimé de vous faire partager ces douceurs. . . . Nous eussions goûté ensemble les sciences et la solitude").[160]

Indeed, Allart had no choice but to share her scholarly life with the men she depended on for access to political and historical knowledge. Her personal collection of books was adequate to identify her interests, but she required the books of others to complete her research projects. She was not a book collector, nor was she guaranteed admission to libraries or erudite societies. Rather, Allart insinuated herself in the transmission of political thought via her love of books and learning that brought her close to powerful men of learning with significant libraries. Many of Allart's scholarly undertakings were political projects collaboratively conceptualized in love for these men and their books.[161]

In June 1855, Allart was rereading her memoirs and remembering with special nostalgia her second trip to Florence (in 1837). In her *Enchantements de prudence* of that year, she had noted Capponi's bibliographic generosity: "In the mornings, he would send me books and write to me, in the evenings, he would come." ("Dans son âme, un fond de grandeur et de bonhomie.... Le matin il m'envoyait des livres et m'écrivait, le soir il venait.")[162] Now, about seventeen years later, she wrote to Capponi, puzzling about the nature of their relationship, which she called, in French, "notre long commerce," to emphasize, among other things, their passing back and forth of books: "I remember our long exchange, your books at my orders, your kind notes, our philosophy. It was a long friendship, nothing more, why? I don't know and I will not explain it in my memoirs." ("Je me souviens de notre long commerce, de vos livres à mes ordres, de vos aimables billets, de notre philosophie. Ce fut une longue amitié, rien de plus, pourquoi? Je ne sais, et je ne l'expliquerai pas dans mes mémoires.")[163] His books and her orders were an inseparable duo that implied, among other things, love and power.

If Capponi was unable to relate to Allart as a scholarly woman who gave birth, nursed, and cared for children as she continued with her scholarly, state-building projects, he may have derived some sense of comfort from Allart's requests for books. There was no fear of impotence on this account, and Allart's reliance on his bibliographic generosity provided the safest adhesive for their attachment to each other. In March 1939, expecting her second son at any time, Allart was able to finish her *Essai sur l'histoire politique*, thanks to the books in Capponi's library.[164] Much later, she would acknowledge that this work was also "begun under your eyes and with your books" ("Ceci fut commencé sous vos yeux, et avec vos livres").[165] Other typical requests and acknowledgments included: "You have forgotten, Mr. Marquis, to send me Guicciardini ... and I am too proud to ask for it again" ("Vous avez oublié, Monsieur le Marquis, de m'envoyer Guicciardini ... et je suis trop fière pour le redemander"); and "I thank you a thousand times for your books, because without you, I would not have been able to start working" ("Je vous remercie mille fois pour vos livres car sans vous je n'aurais pu commencer encore mon travail").[166]

Allart's letters to Capponi provide details of the sources and editions that were common to their histories of Florence.[167] But beyond this important information about the books they shared per Allart's orders, we find in Allart's letters her hopes and fantasies that Capponi's books, passed back and forth, might somehow serve as a conduit to transmit her contentment, productivity, and political engagement to him. In February and March of 1838, Allart wrote to Capponi, requesting important works of Florentine political historiography—Machiavelli, *Istorie fiorentine;* Iacopo Nardi, *Istoria della città di Firenze dal 1494 al 1532;* and Bernardo Segni, *Istorie fiorentine dall'anno 1527 al 1555.* Later, returning Capponi's copy of Machiavelli's *Istorie fiorentine* (among other books), Allart imagined the returned books on the shelf attracting a muse to organize his library as a place of creative inspiration: "Put everything back in your library, I hope that a hand directed by Apollo will come there one day to take and put things back with fantasy; and that the fine arts and genius will take hold of Palazzo Capponi" ("Faites remettre tout cela dans votre bibliothèque, j'espère qu'une main dirigée par Apollon y viendra un jour prendre et remettre à sa fantaisie, et que les beaux Arts et le génie s'empareront du Palais Capponi"). At the very least, the returned books would usher in to Capponi's "private life and interests" ("cette vie privée et . . . ces intérêts tout privés") a little of Allart's "abandon" ("Ayez seulement un peu d'abandon, chose que vous n'avez point assez, et laissez-moi faire").[168]

A few months later, Allart, luxuriating in a house near Siena that had a library of five thousand volumes, wrote to Capponi about the happiness and sense of power that he surely derived from his proximity to a library.

> Living here in a library, I attribute your great knowledge a little to your libraries, because it seems to me so much to have the universe under one's hand and to be able to continually traverse it. When I am tired of Florence, I go in the library, where I take down every sort of book, travels, philosophy, Mably, Lairon, Montaigne, Cook, Burke, Blair, whatever. I am happy in this muddle. I don't understand why you are sad—there are two reasons that make it inexplicable for me: 1. your library, 2. Italian music. Two things that, in my opinion, are enough for everything, the one as action, the other as emotion.
>
> [En vivant ici dans une bibliothèque, j'attribue un peu votre grand savoir à vos bibliothèques, car c'est beaucoup il me semble d'avoir l'univers sous sa main et de pouvoir sans cesse le parcourir; quand je suis fatiguée de Florence, je vais dans la bibliothèque où je prends toute espèce de choses, voyages, philosophie, Mably, Clairon, Montaigne, Cook, Burke, Blair, que sais-je? Je me plais dans ce fouilli[s]. Je ne comprends pas pourquoi vous êtes triste à cause de deux raisons qui me le rendent inexplicable: 1. votre bibliothèque; 2. la musique italienne. Deux choses qui à mon avis suffisent à tout, l'une comme action, l'autre comme émotion.][169]

Libraries and books, in the experience of Allart, could become conduits to political action and bonds of loyalty and friendship.[170]

Preface

On March 11, 1875, Allart wrote to Capponi that the French newspapers were already praising Capponi's newly released *Storia della Repubblica di Firenze*. As soon as she received her own copy, she would immediately write again with her impressions of the work. For the moment, she wrote, "I hear that you mention me in the preface in the most amiable and friendly way. I am very impatient." ("On dit qu'il est question de moi dans la préface de la façon la plus aimable et la plus amicale. Je suis très impatiente.")[171]

Process

As we know, Capponi's process was a slow one . . . in which Allart, for thirty years, regularly intervened, encouraging Capponi to bring his *Storia* to completion. The material support of her historiographic writing and her encouragement were both instrumental in the production of Capponi's *Storia*.

Protection

Allart believed that if she portrayed her work as "little" and in need of protection, Capponi might be inspired to be "big" and protective of it. On various occasions, Allart asked Capponi to "protect my little work" ("protégez mon petit travail") or to "protect my, or rather your, Republic" ("protégez ma République ou plutôt la vôtre").[172] Perhaps Capponi did "protect" Allart's *Histoire* in Florence by embracing her work within his own. All kinds of discrimination may be "ideologically justified" under the term *protection*.[173]

Rules

Capponi and Allart had very different relations to social norms and rules around marriage. Capponi was happiest abiding by the rules, while Allart left her husband after only one year: "You say that we aren't happy when we break the rules and that we know it, you and I. But you haven't broken the rules, because you have remained a widower by your tender devotion, I believe, to your children; and I have found ordinary happiness only by leaving my rough husband, whom I married imprudently, because I have never suffered except by the rules." ("Vous dites qu'on n'est pas heureux sortir de la règle, et que nous le savons vous et moi. Mais vous n'êtes pas sorti de la règle puisque vous êtes resté veuf par un tendre dévouement, je crois, à vos enfants; et moi je n'ai retrouvé mon bonheur ordinaire qu'en quittant ce rude mari que j'avais pris imprudemment, car je n'ai souffert jamais que par la règle.")[174]

Study as consolation

At age fifty-four, Allart wrote to Capponi that she "preferred study to everything" ("Je préfère l'étude à tout"). Having left love "without regret rather with joy" (J'ai laissé l'amour sans regret, plutôt avec joie"), she could now truly savor the "sweet" life of philosophy ("il n'est rien de si doux, de si animé; la vie ne plaît bien qu'avec la philosophie").[175] But indeed, even at a younger age (thirty-six years), she had always found study to be her greatest consolation. In the summer of 1837, as her feelings of love for Bulwer were first taking hold, she wrote to Capponi that she had no trouble focusing on her history of Florence: "Study is the greatest happiness in life. Even love without study becomes tedious." ("L'étude est le plus grand bonheur de la vie et l'amour même sans l'étude devient un ennui.")[176] Tears were no longer a problem at this juncture, because Allart "loved history" ("Je ne crois pas pleurer, car je suis forte, et j'aime l'histoire"). She no longer needed Gino Capponi to console her, because Gino's ancestor, the historiographer and politician Neri di Gino Capponi (1388–1457), was better at "drying her tears" ("C'est Neri Capponi qui les essuierait et non pas vous"). Immersed in "thought," she was happy to send off love with a "bon voyage" and a one-way ticket ("*La pensée* est de mon âge, l'amour s'enfuit, adieu, bon voyage, n'y revenez plus").[177] By the time she was forty-three, in the midst of a bitter diatribe against the enslavement of marriage and its humiliating laws, Allart wrote to Capponi that, aside from seeing her "Florence" translated in Italian, "study alone" could console her. ("L'étude seule m'a consolée. . . . J'aurais été consolée si j'avais su que Capponi ait fait traduire ma Florence.")[178]

Translation

Aside from his reference to a translation of Allart's *Histoire* in the preface to his *Storia*—"Mr. Alessandro Carraresi had completed a translation of this book" ("Di questo Libro il signore Alessandro Carraresi ... aveva compito una traduzione")—Capponi never gave Allart any consolation with respect to her desire to see her *History* translated in Italian.[179] On March 1, 1843, two and half weeks after Allart's *Histoire* was published, Capponi informed Pietro Capei of his interest in finding someone to translate the work. Capponi believed that Allart's *Histoire* in translation would be "useful" ("credo sarebbe utile lavoro"), but he never directly communicated this belief to Allart.[180] Indeed, Capponi kept Allart in the dark all along about his efforts to have her work translated into Italian. At first, he entrusted the translation to Francesco Silvio Orlandini, who translated the first volume but then left this project for his studies of Foscolo.[181] Capponi's secretary, Alessandro Carraresi, completed the translation that Capponi used as the springboard for his own *Storia*, but no one informed Allart of Carraresi's work.[182] If she had known, she might have insisted on receiving more credit.

On several occasions, Allart communicated to Capponi that she could not be happy without an Italian translation of her voluminous work, which, after all, represented a period of love and happiness among the Florentine erudites.[183] But it seems that her repeated inquiries were received as leaves in the wind. In May of 1843, beginning to grow anxious, Allart asked Capponi again for at least some "assurance" of his efforts: "I would be very delighted to be translated into Italian, but I fear that the project has already been abandoned, assure me on this subject" ("Je serais très charmée d'être traduite en italien, mais j'ai peur que le projet ne soit déjà abandonné, rassurez-moi à ce sujet").[184] By January of 1846, Allart was reduced to begging for some kind of attention to the matter: "You write little. But I beg you to answer this question by return courier: What became of the translation of my small history of Florence?" ("Vous écrivez peu. Mais je vous prie de répondre courrier par courrier à cette question: Qu'est devenue la traduction de ma petite histoire de Florence?")[185]

Despite his silences on the matter, Allart continued to remind Capponi that she still cared about the translation, sending him corrections to pass on to the translator and expressing her belief that once the errors were eliminated "the translation will be better than the original"

("La traduction sera meilleure que l'original; on en ôtera les fautes").[186] After reading a piece by Capponi regarding the Council of Seventy and the organization of the magistracies, Allart reflected that her *Histoire* was like "a rough canvas of cloth for scrubbing the floor" in comparison to his "fine cloth of India" ("Il me semble que vous avez travaillé une toile fine de l'Inde, et moi dans mon *Histoire* un gros canevas à torchons"). "Still," she wrote, "I believe that if you have it translated, my *Histoire* will be good for introducing and indicating to others where one must search, showing a comprehensive view of republican history that one doesn't find in any part" ("Cependant je crois que si vous la faites traduire, cette Histoire sera bonne pour introduire à d'autres et indiquera où l'on doit fouiller, en fesant [sic] voir un ensemble de l'histoire républicaine qui n'est nulle part").[187] Ten years after the publication of her *Histoire*, Allart still hadn't given up hope of an Italian translation. She understood the translation of her *Histoire* to be a natural sequel to the bibliographic kindness Capponi had shown prior to its publication.[188] Now that the work was published, Allart urged Capponi to continue to think of her in relation to procuring a translation: "Think of me and of the translation" ("Pensez à moi et à la traduction").[189] Capponi never revealed to Allart the intensity of thought he gave to this project.

Tyranny

When Allart reflected on tyranny, the tyranny of her brief marriage came to mind more quickly than the tyrannies of Nero and Diocletian or Alessandro de' Medici. Just as Tarabotti had, from personal experience, so passionately articulated her experience of fathers' tyranny over daughters, Allart was able to know, from her brief experience, about the tyranny of husbands over wives. Leaving her husband of one year, she wanted to give to all women "the example of a woman who leaves her tyrant" ("Il me restait à donner cet exemple d'une femme qui quitte son tyran"). Indeed, Allart's experience of the slavery of marriage was the key to understanding her hatred of all tyranny. To marry was "to be handed over to a man like a black slave from Santo Domingo." ("Que veut donc le femme? . . . Elle veut n'être pas livrée à l'homme comme un esclave noir de Saint-Domingue.")[190] Allart diverged far from a humanistic understanding of tyranny, exposing, with this simile, some of the continuities and contradictions between anticolonial and feminist discourse in this period.

Vanity

Early on in their relationship, Allart became aware that Capponi complained to his friends of her "vanity" ("Je sais que vous avez fort parlé avec eux de ma vanité").[191] In return, she articulated at length, in her novel *Sextus*, the characteristics of "male vanity." Thérèse de Longueville was incensed that the Capponi-like protagonist of her novel, Sextus, "was offering her that Italian love, quick as lightning, nourished neither by time or reflection" ("Il lui offrait cet amour des Italiens, prompt comme l'éclair, que le temps ni la réflexion n'ont nourri"). He was not really getting to know her and was courting her, instead, with "insipid conversations" ("les conversations insipides") and "that frivolous tone that had become habitual for him" ("ce ton léger qui lui était devenu habituel"). She tore up Sextus's profession of love, criticizing him but blaming the culture that produced his condescension toward women: "A Roman treats all women with the same tone. The fault is in the country, not in him." ("Un romain traite toutes les femmes sur le même ton; le tort est au pays, pas à lui.") Needless to say, "Sextus was wounded. His male vanity suffered. He did not understand, at first, the goodness and dignity of her response." ("Sextus fut blessé: sa vanité d'homme souffrit; il ne comprit pas d'abord la bonté et la dignité de cette réponse.")[192]

What we share

What Capponi and Allart shared was fundamentally what we scholars all share, lending each other books, transcribing each other's words, consulting books and documents in common, corresponding with each other, and sharing fields of study. Tommaseo even noticed the sharing of poor-quality paper and ink of print materials that tire our collective eyes and bear witness to the "pale and fleeting words and ideas" passed from scholar to scholar ("La carta e l'inchiostro che adoperiamo alle stampe affatica gli occhi ed è quasi prima stracciata che usata, segno e confessione di parole e d'idee sbiadite e fugaci").[193] And perhaps, to the extent that we share fields of interest, we may also share a common biography.[194] Ultimately, these practices, materials, and lives are shared across time, as we scholars become interested in past relations of knowledge.

In the specific case of sharing between Allart and Capponi, as we have seen, Capponi found himself with all of Allart's thought inside *his* history of Florence. At the same time, Allart also acknowledged the large role that Capponi played in the production of *her* history.[195] As she was working on her *Histoire* in September of 1840, Allart found herself writing in her manuscript: "Malatesta, Malatesta, as if I were writing a letter to Gino Capponi" ("Je dis dans mon manuscrit: Malatesta, Malatesta, comme si j'écrivais une lettre à Gino Capponi"). She needed him to share with her the history of Malatesta Baglioni that was missing from her notes and her memory ("Je crois qu'on trouve tout cela dans vos notes, mais je ne les ai pas ici").[196] And three months after the appearance of her *Histoire*, Allart confessed to Capponi that some of the words and sentences in her history of "our little Republic" ("notre petite République") were his words and sentences transcribed from their conversations ("Vous m'avez dit à peu près ce que j'ai écrit dans mon *Histoire*; il y a des mots, des phrases qui sont de vous").[197]

There were also times, of course, when Allart and Capponi shared only impertinences and a sense of disconnection.[198] We have seen how Capponi was unable to reconcile the "diligence and virile sense" he found in Allart's *Histoire* with her dedication to women.[199] On her side, Allart often felt disconnected from Capponi's scholarly views about Florentine history. Sometimes, with a strong proprietary sense, she insisted to Capponi that her volume of her history was hers ("J'aurais voulu aussi mon vol. de mon histoire à moi").[200] And she sorrowfully acknowledged that sometimes, historiographic texts "have had a different effect on me than on you" ("Hélas! que de choses m'ont fait un autre effet qu'à vous"). She was unsure, at these times, if the Florentine republic belonged to him or to her ("Protégez ma République ou plutôt la vôtre").[201] She protested "the division . . . between our sexes" ("Et voilà le partage qu'on a fait entre nos sexes!") that made Capponi see her differently than he would see her "if [she] were a man" ("Vous dites cela, parce que vous êtes homme et moi femme, car si j'étais homme vous me trouveriez austère").[202] His history and hers. Her republic and his. Men's and women's views. The "sguaiaterie" of women and the virile sense of men all combined in their scholarship to vex the sharing of their common field of study and passion for Florentine history. Still, during the long course of their exchanges of books, conversations, impertinences, and letters, Allart and Capponi had indeed constructed a history in common that, as Allart predicted early on, would pass through "flirtation" and end in "friendship" ("Nous nous sommes fait tous deux des coquetteries et nous avons fini par l'amitié").[203] It was their history of Florence.

Withholding

Allart's learned friends were often generous with their conversation and bibliographic support, but they also withheld texts and support at strategic moments. In March of 1832, Allart asked Sainte-Beuve to please assure the success of her recently published novel, *Sextus*, by writing a signed review of it. Sainte-Beuve, however, obliged her by writing an unsigned note, saying that the novel was unfeeling and had no charm ("n'a rien qui charme et ressemble trop à la sécheresse").[204] And we saw that after Allart had requested advanced publicity about her *Histoire*, Capponi told her that he would do nothing to promote the work.[205] Was there some unwritten rule that kept these otherwise gracious men from supporting her role as a player in their field?

Frequently, in her letters to Capponi, Allart complained that she was excluded from news of important bibliographic matters. If Capponi didn't notify her of the publication of texts she had read in manuscript, she would end up providing an outdated bibliography.[206] Once he gave her a significant unpublished document, only to scoop her by publishing it first.[207] Having received the first volume of the *Archivio storico* in March 1843, a year after its publication and a month and a half after the publication of her *Histoire*, Allart was incensed that her "teacher" ("mon Maître") Capponi had never shared the "notes" he had published in the journal; they "would have been a great help and aid" to Allart, as she was preparing her work for publication ("Vous ne me dites pas qu'il y a des notes de vous qui auraient été d'un grand secours et aide pour moi!").[208]

Women of Italy

The Academy of Arezzo had invited Allart to be a member of its society, and on the day of her reception in October of 1837, Allart read to the assembled body "some pages on women" ("quelques pages sur les femmes").[209] As she prepared her comments, Allart wrote to Capponi wondering why she had never been admitted to the Florentine Società Colombaria, the academy over which Capponi had presided since he was nineteen years old. Capei thought she was "worthy of membership" ("M. Capei me juge digne d'être correspondant"), and Allart was especially keen to be invited, "in order to spread French ideas on women in your Italian academies" ("pour répandre dans vos académies d'Italie les idées de la France sur *la femme*"). It was, moreover, in men's interest ("c'est l'intérêt de l'homme") for a new "intellectual aristocracy to replace the old," allowing women to occupy academic positions. ("Une aristocratie intellectuelle se prépare à remplacer l'ancienne. La femme pourra s'y placer et . . . ainsi atteindre aux places et aux Académies.") No longer would the "honor" of women be tied to their chastity (and their dishonor to prostitution); women's honor, like men's, would consist in the merits of their deeds and achievements. ("L'honneur de la femme doit changer. . . . Il doit consister comme le vôtre dans un ensemble de faits.")[210]

Allart used her identity as a "woman of letters" to situate women in the world of politics, and this identity accompanied Allart to her grave—the words "femme de lettres" adorned her tombstone.[211] She wrote of women and society in her *La femme et la démocratie de nos temps*, and she dedicated her *Histoire de la République de Florence* to women.[212] Specifically concerned about the obstacles to progress faced by Italian women, Allart wrote: "You [Italians] are lagging way behind on this question, [a backwardness] made all the worse because you have the most intelligent women in Europe" ("Vous êtes très en arrière en Italie sur cette question, ce qui est d'autant plus mal que vous avez les femmes les plus intelligentes de l'Europe"). She was "tempted" to remain in Italy for the sole purpose of dedicating her scholarly efforts to them ("Si je restais en Italie je ferais tous mes efforts pour elles, et je suis presque tentée d'y rester pour cela").[213] Ultimately, Allart's dedication to women was an irreconcilable aspect of her relation to Capponi and of their collaboration on a work of nationalist historiography.

CONCLUSION

In contrast to Capponi, who, more precisely, ended his *History of the Florentine Republic* in 1532, when Duke Alessandro de' Medici officially took power in Florence, Allart ended her history in 1537, when Lorenzino de' Medici assassinated the duke. She wrote: "As if republics always ended with requisite and regular events, a new Brutus, Lorenzino de' Medici, conspired single-handed against Duke Alessandro, his cousin. But this new Brutus, vicious, puny, treacherous, devoured by ambition, playing the coward around the duke, already known for his stormy youth, capable of a great scheme but of abject crimes, was as different from the ancient Brutus as Duke Alessandro was from Caesar." ("Comme si les républiques à leur fin, avaient des faits habituels et nécessaires, un nouveau Brutus, Lorenzino de Médicis . . . va conspirer seul contre le duc Alexandre, son cousin. . . . Ce nouveau Brutus, vicieux, chétif, perfide, dévoré d'ambition, jouant le poltron près du duc, connu déjà par sa jeunesse orageuse, capable d'un grand dessein, mais de crimes abjects, est aussi différent de l'ancien Brutus, que le duc Alexandre l'était de César.")[214] In this passage, Allart takes this sixteenth-century Brutus from his traditional role as a vindicator of republican freedoms and casts an ironic light on the republican male model of nationalism that accepted the figure of "Brutus" as a prepackaged and universal essence of masculinity, perpetually capable of overthrowing a "tyrant."[215] As if men always thought in the same vicious, puny, cowardly ways about republicanism, she wrote skeptically, Florence came to an end "in the midst of political discussions and torture of republicans, who pursued knowledge of lofty freedom but were unable to attain it" ("au milieu des débats politiques d'une école fameuse, et au sein des supplices qui domptèrent seuls ces républicains. Ils ne purent atteindre la science et la haute liberté qu'ils étudiaient").[216]

Notwithstanding this pessimistic view that scholarly aspirations to liberty afforded little protection against the political excesses of power, Allart was determined to pursue and promote her scholarly passions for the history of Florence and for the erudite men who aspired to produce a new nation from this history. Tommaseo could complain that she crossed borders between feminism and history, working simultaneously on her *History of Florence* and her 1836 work *La femme et la démocratie de nos temps*.[217] And Capponi might despair that "there [was] no woman left in her" on account of too much "sophistry" ("La s'è tanto invecchiata nel sofisma, che almeno per me, di donna non v'è più nulla").[218] Refusing to honor such behind-her-back complaints, Allart persisted in her scholarly work, crossing borders between fiction, erudition, feminism, and even motherhood, and contributing materially and relationally to the production of a political past for the future Italy.

National archives and libraries deftly suppressed the significant role played by a French feminist, novelist, and historian in the relations of writing and spaces of research of the Vieusseux group. Still, the Florentine world of literati and their conceptions of nation and disciplinary boundaries were disturbed by this woman "of such unbridled intelligence," to use the words of Sestan, "by her flirtatious ways verging on open-mindedness, by her effervescent fantasy, by her tumultuous and chaotic culture, by her sudden enthusiasms for the most eccentric ideas, by her generous heart that—notwithstanding her 'suffragettisme' ante litteram—was quite amenable to the enticements of men" ("quel mondo di letterati fu messo in agitazione da quella donna dall'ingegno sbrigliato, dalla civetteria spinta fino alla spregiudicatezza, dalla fantasia spumeggiante, dalla cultura tumultuosa e caotica, dagli entusiasmi repentini per le idee più strampalate, dal cuore generoso e assai cedevole—nonostante il suo 'suffragettismo' ante litteram—alle lusinghe degli uomini").[219] The study of figures such as Allart can help us to restore historicity to ideas of the Italian nation and to our investigations of a prenationalist past. Her "tumultuous culture" and "generous heart" certainly intervened between Capponi and the production of his historiographic studies and in the relational space of the Vieusseux group. Indeed, her "unbridled intelligence" also agitates us, challenges our conceptions of erudition as a separate realm from fantasy, and invites us to see relations of writing as crucial to our understanding of the production of history.

Afterword

As we have seen, Lorenzino's assassination of Alessandro de' Medici in 1537 was not an isolated episode of political violence; rather, it fit into a series or a humanistic tradition of tyrannicides that extended from the first tyrant-slayers, Harmodius and Aristogiton, to republican thinkers of the seventeenth, eighteenth, and nineteenth centuries and beyond. This series or tradition was and is still characterized by a rhetoric of comparison and repetition. How does Lorenzino compare to Brutus? How does Alessandro compare to Phalaris or Holofernes? Is there a violated, Lucretia-like noblewoman on the scene? The tyrant-slayers and their supporters have always been particularly eager to justify these episodes of political violence by reproducing the narratives of learned men who enacted their ideals of liberty on the stage of politics. To study and collect knowledge about this tradition without questioning its social formation, then, is to reproduce and acquiesce to the conditions, categories, terms, and paradigms of its existence, as if this tradition of understanding violence and learning deserved some special honor because of its continued reproduction. My challenge in this book has therefore been to organize research about Lorenzino and republican politics in such a way as to question the social formation of this tradition. I have endeavored to honor this tradition and, at the same time, to trouble its conditions, categories, terms, and paradigms. My project has been one of reorganizing knowledge about the republican tradition to acknowledge the conditions in which we live today as feminist scholars.

I have been inspired in this overarching argument of reorganizing knowledge and in the experimental organization of this book by the work of Anna Maria Mozzoni (1837–1920), an important feminist critic of the Italian national project, who saw how terms, theories, traditions, concepts, institutions, and ideologies all formed part of a taxonomic code that, in her view, discouraged the troubling of its categories of knowledge. This code, which wrote women primarily in terms of introspection and psychology, would need to be completely destroyed and rewritten if women (and other untolerated groups) were to take their place as social subjects in a real democracy.

In the course of her critiques of the family, taxonomies, intolerance, nationalism, colonialism, and prejudicial laws, Mozzoni, as we saw in Section Two, was especially critical of the obsequiousness toward tradition that she found in intellectuals, scholars, and lawmakers. Especially intellectuals (and in this case, she refers specifically to male intellectuals) tune out the present by immersing themselves in literary and historical examples. The repetition of examples from the past, Mozzoni suggested, was the cause of continued intolerance in the present; over time, past examples of slavery and feudalism have gathered force as a stone gathers moss, until the force of example has acquired the force of law. For this reason, Mozzoni claimed, the citation of examples from the past, contrary to every truism about history we have been taught, has never served any purpose at all. To think that the example of history could be useful, she wrote, was "to pretend that a people could free itself from foreign domination by dint of legal demonstrations" ("sarebbe come pretendere che un populo si sbarazzi da uno straniero dominio a furia di legali dimostrazioni").[1]

With this comparison between the rhetoric of historical examples, a rhetoric so central to Italy's ideology of civic humanism, and the political inefficacy of "legal demonstrations," Mozzoni hints at an important critique of our work as literary scholars of the past and our relation to current injustices. She is more explicit in her exhortation to develop new categories and new institutions that will reflect the conditions of emancipated women ("Il secolo che aspira al conquisto d'ogni ragionevole libertà non troverà esorbitante che la donna cerchi e studii il modo per dove iniziare la propria").[2] She writes of a different kind of intellectual organization generated from the ability to begin with immediate conditions before moving to more abstract speculation ("[Le donne] passerebbero senza fatica 'dal noto all'ignoto, dal concreto all'astratto'").[3] She asks us to see every aspect of social organization in relation to household economies of power and gender constructions. As Carlo Cattaneo observed, she was one of those women who took the risk of expressing new insights derived from her contact with the "dust of the laws" ("polvere dei codici").[4] One of those insights was that systems of knowledge contributed to the production of a politics of prejudice in postunification Italy and that it was important to refigure such systems ("ciò accusa una viziatura di sistema forse più che non passione di dominio o gelosia di proprietà").[5]

The organization of categories to justify or produce discrimination, ostracism, and oppression, according to Mozzoni, has been crucial, in every historical moment, to the persistence of intolerance. In her critique of the Civil Code that was proposed to regulate the new Italian nation, she wrote in 1884:

> The most excruciating injustices to devastate humankind and the most enormous philosophic errors were born from the mania for classifications. Classifications have created prejudices; prejudices, in their turn, have generated outcasts and slaves. Prejudices have led to contempt for the slave and have given rise to false and unfair biases against differently colored races, biases that unluckily persist even among many whose profession it is to understand justice. From classifications and prejudices, deep hatreds were born and lasting international conflicts, as if the person who lives on one bank of a river or on one side of a mountain differs essentially from the person who inhabits the other bank or the other slope.
>
> [Dalla manìa delle classificazioni nacquero le più strazianti ingiustizie che hanno desolato l'umana progenie, e gli errori più cubitali della filosofia. Le classificazioni crearono i pregiudizii; i pregiudizii a loro volta generarono i Paria e gli Iloti; consigliarono lo sprezzo dello schiavo; suggerirono false ed inique prevenzioni sulle diverse razze colorate, che sgraziatamente perdurano presso molti che fanno anche professione d'intendersi alla giustizia. Dalle classificazioni donde i pregiudizii, nacquero gli odii profondi, e le lunghe ire internazionali, quasi l'uomo che abita l'altra sponda di un fiume, o l'altro versante di una montagna, essenzialmente differisca dall'uomo che abita la prima sponda ed il primo versante.][6]

In the case of Italian Risorgimento activities and thought, categorizing activities affected not only the construction of the new state, its legislation and social relations, but even and particularly the organization of knowledge. The organization of national libraries and archives in this period still influence the way we think about Italy's cultural past and the way we conduct our literary and historical studies. To align the organization of our own work to reflect a politics of tolerance and antiracist, antihomophobic practices, we might examine our own positions and agency in the reproduction, undoing, and reconfiguring of archival and social taxonomies and rhetorics. It is my hope that the focus, in this book, on three central instruments of intellectual cognition and epistemology—archival inventory, library shelf lists, and lexicon—may be one small step in this direction.

Appendix

I. TEXTS AFFIXED TO *THE SCENE OF TYRANNY*

The hand is important at the scene of the assault.
spada sword passione παθειν patior (I suffer)
ξιφος sword spada
ξιφος εγχειριδιον spada pugnale
        εγχειριδιον χειρ hand
        pugio
        pugnale
        pugna fist
        pux with a clenched fist

Plutarch's Brutus made his way toward the Senate on the Ides of March, hiding an εγχειριδιον/**pugnale** under his clothes. In Suetonius, the instrument of assassination was the **pugio**: the conspirators came upon Caesar with **pugio**nibus/**pugna**li.

✍ ✍ ✍

Caesar's hand reached for a writing stylus to stab Casca and force his way from the hands of the conspirators. They were coming at him from every side with daggers drawn ("strictis pugionibus"). With his left hand, Caesar stretched his hem down to his heels. Covering the lower parts of his body, at least he would fall to the ground with less shame. (Suetonius)

✍ ✍ ✍

Lorenzino said to his henchman: Baccio, I have in my room a person of great distinction, my enemy, whom you must help me to kill. If he is a friend of the duke, don't even think about it. Just act with your hands.
— That's what I'll do, even if it is the duke himself.
Lorenzino had a happy expression:
— You guessed. He cannot escape our hands. Let's go.

✍ ✍ ✍

After slaying the duke, Lorenzino wrote: "I was afraid to go around Florence to notify key people that I had slain the duke. The duke had bitten my hand, and blood was running in extraordinary quantity from the wound. Seeing the blood, everyone would understand what had happened. I wanted to keep the deed secret for a while to insure a more positive outcome."

✍ ✍ ✍

Giovanni "the tailor" noticed Lorenzino's wounded hand and wrote a letter to Charles V's governor in Milan: *He was **wounded**, and it seems that he was fleeing from Florence and he left with the greatest fear ... and I think I heard that said messer Lorenzo. And I think I heard, as I said, that he has killed the lord duke of Florence, and so, hearing this news that is of greatest importance to his imperial majesty, I thought of sending this mail to you only for this news.*

✍ ✍ ✍

The hand is important at the scene of writing.

Giovanni's hand was hurried and scrawling, the margins unjustified. He was in such a hurry to send this news to Caracciolo, he could not wait for the ink to dry. Quick—write it, seal it, send it. The signs of this haste are the grains of 16th century sand, applied by Giovanni to dry the ink. Because of his haste, the sand remained stuck in the ink and is still there today sparkling on the paper. The past, after all, is still passing ...

> Reverendissimo et Illustrissimo Monsignor mio Osservandissimo
> Questa mia esola per avisare vostra signoria Reverendissma cum alli 7 del presente passo per qui imposta messer Lorenzo de Medici nepotte di messer ottaviano de medici il quale era ferite e mi pare che se ne fugiva

da fiorenza esene andava cum grandissima paura di sortte che alli otti che fu eri evenute uno in questa terra che va cercando ditto messer Lorenzo e me pare de intendere che ditto messer Lorenzo, E me pare de intendere como ho ditte che ha morto il signor ducha di fiorenza e cosi intendende tal nova, la quale e di grandissima importanza ala maesta Cesarea me parse de espedire questa posta solamente per tal nova a vostra signoria Reverendissima ne poterá avisare allo Illustrissimo signor Marges dil guasto, si a quela li pare

E piu ho inteso como el Reverendissimo cibo e intrato ne la fortezza in compagnia di uno fiolo Bastardo di ditto signor ducha cosí non diro altro solum che di mano in mano daro aviso a vostra signoria Reverendissima e a quelo li basso le mane e mi offero et raccomando in bologna a di viiij di Gienaro MDxxxvij

Di Vostra Signoria Reverendissima et Illustrissima umile servitore

Giovanni Antonio ditto il sarto

Lorenzino read classical stories of tyrannicide and justified his gory murder of the duke by comparing Alessandro to ancient tyrants who raped noblewomen, murdered their own mothers, and cut down the noble citizens. I always understood I was a new reader in this chain. But now, for the first time, my transcribing hand was related to his murderous hand.

I became aware of my own hand scribbling away in my notebook, becoming part of the archival atmosphere in which I wrote. Now the sparkling sand—the vehicle that conveyed Giovanni Antonio's haste—became a sort of conveyor of memories between my subjectivity as a scholar and the public, historical, social dimensions of my research. Lorenzino's fear, his wounded hand, his haste, Giovanni's hasty and anxious hand, and my own shaky and anxious transcribing hand became part of such categories as "Chancery of the State of Milan," "Florence," "the post," etc. The past, after all, was still passing . . . the f-act of the sand sparkling in the ink caught me in the act of carousing in the archive, framed by the memories I was collecting.

II. TEXTS AFFIXED TO *MYOPIC POLITICS*

Pier Paolo Boscoli was a leader of a 1512 conspiracy against Giuliano, Giulio, and Giovanni de' Medici. "He was devoted to literature, although his excessive blondness made it almost impossible for him to see."

Luca della Robbia sat with Boscoli on the night before he was decapitated, recording his last thoughts: "I was pleased to write down everything Pier Paolo Boscoli told me in that night before his execution, so that his example of willpower and strength of character would not be lost together with his body. He was such a good, noble and generous citizen, a young man of about 32 years. He was blond and beautiful and he had an air of kindness, but he was shortsighted."

Julius Caesar, in a 1582 Italian translation of Plutarch's *Life of Brutus,* said that "fat men with good eyesight didn't worry him so much as pale, thin men. He was referring to Brutus and Cassius." The translator, Lodovico Domenichi, translated the Greek term *kometas*, meaning "long-haired," as "di buona vista" (having good eyesight). Presumably, Brutus and Cassius, by contrast, did not have had such good eyes. They had a pallid, yellow (albino?) aspect ("tous oxrous"). Shakespeare's Caesar was equally troubled by the "lean and hungry look" of Cassius and the fact that Cassius used his eyes too much in reading.

How acute was the eyesight of Lorenzino? The historian Rudolf von Albertini claimed that Lorenzino's erudition caused Lorenzino and an entire generation of humanistic opponents to Medicean rule to see through a literary filter: "The years of exile, that most of them had spent in literary work . . . had made a full evaluation of the Italian and Florentine political situation impossible. Memories and hopes, little by little removed from reality, had assumed a literary hue."

Capponi's loss of eyesight and eventual total blindness were a major intellectual concern of his entire group of scholarly friends. In July 1838, Vieusseux wrote to Tommaseo that Capponi was making many social blunders in his efforts to conceal his blindness. In July 1839, concerned about tiring Capponi's eyes by her letters, Allart wrote: "When you will receive a letter from me, put it in your pocket and have Niccolini read it to you. . . . The poet is never too much trouble for his friends." In subsequent letters, Allart no longer asked Capponi to write or to work but to dictate: "Would you be so kind as to dictate a short history of Malatesta?" "Are you working? Are you dictating?" Alluding to his *History of Florence,* she wrote in July 1855: "Are you dictating some great work that has been planned for a long time?"

"Much visual deterioration is due to our unwillingness to look at the details of our situation. Our vision becomes fuzzy, in order to protect ourselves" (Meir Schneider, *Yoga for Your Eyes*).

III. TEXTS AFFIXED TO *CATEGORIES OF KNOWLEDGE*

Gonzalo Fernández de Oviedo (1478–1557), official historiographer of Charles V and military governor of the fortress of Santo Domingo, wrote of the iguana, a creature then unknown in Europe.

- It is difficult to know if the iguana belongs to the category of animal or fish.
- There are many ways to cook the iguana and its eggs.
- The iguana is such a quiet animal—it neither screams nor moans nor makes any sound, and it will stay tied up wherever you put it, without doing any damage or making any noise, for ten or twenty days and more without eating or drinking anything. Some say, on the contrary, that if you give the iguana a little cassava or grass or something similar, it will eat it. But I have had some of these animals sometimes tied up in my house, and I never saw them eat, and I had them watched day and night, and in the end, I never knew nor was able to understand what they were eating in the house, and everything that you give them to eat remains whole.

Oviedo connected his commodification of this creature to another kind of commerce, the European trade in exotic specimens and facts, a commerce that would enable Europe to secure cultural, and not just economic, domination over the newly encountered civilizations.

- Two of the bigger iguanas were brought to me, and we ate part of one in my house, and the other I had put away, tied up, to send to Venice to the Magnificent Mr. Joan Baptista [Ramusio], chancellor of the Signoria, and it was tied to a post on the patio of this fortress of Santo Domingo for more than forty days, during which time, it never ate any of the many things it was given; and I was told that these animals ate only earth, and I had a hundred pounds of dirt put in a barrel as the iguana's provisions, so that there would be no lack of it at sea. And I hope that while I am correcting these treatises, ships will arrive to let us know if the iguana arrived alive in Spain and with what nourishment.
- When I arrived in Spain in 1546, however, I found out from the one who took the animal that it had died at sea.

IV. TEXTS AFFIXED TO *WINGS FOR MY COURAGE*

In August 1648 in Paris, Gabriel Naudé, the father of library science, was looking forward to the public inauguration of his Mazarine Library. He invited two of his friends, a physician Guy Patin and a philosopher Pierre Gassendi, to spend a private evening of revelry prior to the inauguration. Guy Patin wrote bemusedly about this party invitation: *Mr. Naudé has invited us to eat and sleep, all three of us, next Sunday in his house at Gentilly. He promised that only the three of us will engage in debauchery. But God only knows what kind of debauchery! Mr. Naudé, by nature, drinks only water and has never tasted wine. Mr. Gassendi is so delicate that he would never dare to drink wine and imagines that his body would burn if he were to drink any. This is why Ovid's verse—he flees from wine and abstemiously enjoys pure water—is so pertinent to both of them. As for me –next to these two men whose writings are so great I feel worthy only to dry their ink with sand—as for me, I drink very little; and still, all the same, there will be great debauchery, but of the philosophic type, and perhaps something more, since all three of us have recovered from lycanthropy and the disease of scruples, the tyrant of conscience. Maybe we will venture as far as the edge of Naudé's biblio-sanctuary.*

Arcangela Tarabotti blamed her father for her cruel imprisonment in a convent and Mr. Naudé for her "boldness." He had "fashioned wings for her courage when he requested her works for admission to the flourishing Mazarine Library." In her mind, she helped Naudé to place her works—"the weaknesses of her scanty intellect," as she called them—"among the most famous writers of the Mazarine," hoping that no one would "commit an outrage against the simple births of a holy virgin." She organized political knowledge around the suffering of daughters.

We have no record of the biblio-debauchery among the three friends, because the planned public inauguration of the Mazarine Library was canceled. The first Fronde, or uprising against Mazarin's regime, broke out on August 28, and the library became one of the first casualties of the ensuing civil war. Naudé's vigorous protests were not enough to save the library from dismemberment and sale. He spoke of the library in procreative terms as *the work of my hands and the miracle of my life.* And he prayed to Parliament to assist him in *saving the life of this daughter.*

Naudé figured the Mazarine as a daughter to the librarian, and writing daughters like Tarabotti figured themselves as the *viscera* of their fathers, *cruel, deceitful fathers who tortured the bodies of their daughters.* Together, Tarabotti and Naudé constructed a historical trope for understanding the constraints women writers and scholars might feel today in the confines of a library and its organizations of knowledge. Naudé requested Tarabotti's works for placement in his library, whose walls, tables, shelves, and order of books conveyed something of the cruelty, deceit, and torture conventionally practiced on the bodies of seventeenth-century daughters.

V. TEXTS AFFIXED TO *THE NOSE KNOWS*

How do our ways of knowing relate to our palpitating hearts, our eyes as they connect to the letters on the page, our legs in the library, our hands as we handle documents, books, writing, and note taking? Or how does the body of another inform our investigations? Hortense Allart's body, for example—her purported seductions, her pregnancies and childbirths, her physical whereabouts—came to have rhetorical value in the writings of many Florentine erudites who knew her. Especially her nose became emblematic of the trouble they had relating to her as an intellectual. Vieusseux, Tommaseo, Capponi, and others were very tuned in to their sense of smell as they endeavored to accomplish their serious civic (and masculine) work. Allart's knowing nose was an undeniable glitch in their otherwise seamless project.

In the first several months of his exile in Paris, Tommaseo did not call on Allart. He wrote to Capponi in June, 1834: "Because you didn't want me to visit the . . . titillating woman, she complained, and I made a frightful impression on her, which in Italian we say 'I acted like a pig.'" Tommaseo continued to record his piggish comments to Allart, writing in his diary on July 9: "This evening at Allart's place, I said harsh and foolish things." By August 13, he was taking stock of his behavior—"I mistreat her often, and then afterwards I feel badly about it." But he also began to displace the blame from his own piggishness to the nose of Allart. "When a woman's nose begins to grow," he wrote to Capponi, "it is a bad sign. Now, the nose of Madame Allart is much more noteworthy than her forehead or eyes."

Tommaseo and Capponi related news of Allart's intellect to news of her nose. On May 1, 1837, Tommaseo wrote: "Hortense Allart has published a volume of the *History of Florence* with a truly pitiful preface.... She eagerly lusts after men and says that by now Italians can satisfy her.... Then she makes hypotheses that are more disagreeable than her nose." Several days later, he continued: "She is too heathen, too much a lady-philosopher, too dry, too large-nosed." On June 24, 1837, Capponi wrote to Tommaseo: "The nose of Madame Allart is such that it arouses no envy no matter how she tries to repair it; and you slander it, because you have disdained it.... A good woman, poor thing.... I tell her more things than to any other woman. But I have not been able to grasp even from her whether or not you love me."

Allart's nose was nothing more than a marker of insecure affections between Tommaseo and Capponi. Still, the possibility remains that their inability to fathom the scholarly body of an intellectual woman defaulted in anxious calumnies about one of Allart's body parts. As Allart worked on her *Essai sur l'histoire politique*, she wrote of the bliss of immersing her whole body in a library: "I am as happy as a woman can be who is a coquette, still cold, always nursing, and who has totally immersed her body in the works of the Bibliothèque Royale." If Capponi and Tommaseo used the shape of Allart's nose to confirm their conflicted assessment of her projects and knowledge, Allart was not hindered by the smell of their comments.

Fathers without Noses

There was once a boy whose father did nothing to guide him to the path of virtue and health. Indeed the father's neglect sent him down the road of sin. The boy behaved so badly that once justice caught up with him he was condemned to die. When the woeful moment arrived, his last wish before making the awful passage was to be allowed to kiss his father. Everyone was moved to pity by this request and expected to see in such a pitiful spectacle some kind of loving gestures deriving from paternal and filial affection. The poor convict, embracing his father, angrily tore off his nose with his teeth. This was his sign that he would die innocent, because if his crimes had brought him to the gallows, only the father, who had neglected his upbringing, was to blame for his miserable end.

I myself can attest to the truth that boys are nourished with bad models and raised with a thousand deceits and obscene stories. . . . Ask one of these children, who is still babbling as much as saying whole words: "What will happen to your sisters?" And that genius for deceit handed down to him by his parents will instantly compel him to say: "They will be nuns, because I want to be rich." . . . And the parents take pleasure in hearing him express such an evil and greedy prejudice . . . Today, fathers deceitfully deprive their daughters of the sweet and free air of the sky, when they force them to become nuns. If all of these daughters were to tear off the nose from the face of their fathers, as that poor condemned man did, we would see only men deprived of that member in the middle of their faces, monstrously deformed.

(Arcangela Tarabotti, *La semplicità ingannata*)

The Smell of Scholarly Women

The Accademia degli Intronati had, for a short period of time, made the mistake of admitting the renowned poets Laura Terracina, Veronica Gambara, and Vittoria Colonna to their activities, but soon news of this development came to the attention of Apollo "as a very unpleasant smell to his nose." He understood "that Women's true Poetry consisted in their Needle and Spindle; and that the Learned Exercises of Women together with the Vertuosi, was like the sporting and playing of Dogs, which after a while ends in getting upon one another's backs." Apollo chased away the intruders, to the great joy of all those academic fellows who had fought all along to keep these feminine figures from invading their "typically masculine" activities.

Boccalini, *Advertisements from Parnassus* (originally published in Italian in 1637)

Notes

The following are abbreviations used in the notes:
CI   Niccolò Tommaseo and Gino Capponi, *Carteggio inedito dal 1833 al 1874,* ed. Isidoro Del Lungo and Paolo Prunas (Bologna: N. Zanichelli, 1911–32).
CSM Archivio di Stato, Milan, Cancelleria dello Stato di Milano
LIGC Hortense Allart de Méritens, *Lettere inedite a Gino Capponi,* ed. Petre Ciureanu (Genoa: Tolozzi, 1961).

INTRODUCTION

1. I often recall and rethink the experience of this seminar. Now, many years later, I can see how much the field of the history of writing and the idea of "social relations of writing," as they have been defined in Italy by such brilliant scholars as Petrucci and Nardelli, are infused by Gramsci's insight that intellectual work can be understood only in the context of social relations: "The most widespread methodological error has been, I think, to have looked for a distinctive criterion in intellectual activities and not, on the contrary, in the whole complex of relations in which such activities are situated" ("L'errore metodico piú diffuso mi pare quello di aver cercato questo criterio di distinzione nell'intrinseco delle attività intellettuali e non invece nell'insieme del sistema di rapporti in cui esse ... vengono a trovarsi nel complesso generale dei rapporti sociali"). Antonio Gramsci, *Quaderni del carcere,* ed. Valentino Gerratana (Turin: Einaudi, 1975), 3:1516 (translation my own).
2. Luciano Canfora, *The Vanished Library: A Wonder of the Ancient World* (Berkeley: University of California Press, 1990), 184–85.
3. Ibid., 50.

4. I am here translating and paraphrasing the impassioned story told by Mario Rosa, "I depositi del sapere: Biblioteche, accademie, archivi," in *La memoria del sapere: Forme di conservazione e strutture organizzative dall'antichità a oggi*, ed. Pietro Rossi (Bari: Laterza, 1988), 185.

5. I am here translating and paraphrasing the story told by Rosa, "I depositi," 186, and Maria Moranti and Luigi Moranti, *Il trasferimento dei "Codices urbinates" alla Biblioteca vaticana: Cronistoria, documenti e inventario* (Urbino: Accademia Raffaello, 1981), 78.

6. Moranti and Moranti, *Il trasferimento*, 87 n. 98.

7. Ibid., 85–86.

8. Ibid., 86 and document 136.

9. See Adrienne Rich, "Notes toward a Politics of Location," in *Blood, Bread, and Poetry: Selected Prose, 1979–1985* (New York: Norton, 1995).

10. Avery Gordon's *Ghostly Matters: Haunting and the Sociological Imagination* (Minneapolis: University of Minnesota Press, 1997) has definitely given me license to explore the many "detours" this book has taken as signposts pointing to alternative epistemologies.

11. See Joan Wallach Scott, "The Evidence of Experience," *Critical Inquiry* 17, no. 4 (1991): 773–97; and Natalie Zemon Davis, *Women on the Margins: Three Seventeenth-Century Lives* (Cambridge, MA: Harvard University Press, 1995). Scott's essay has had a profound impact on my endeavor to restore scholars to "critical scrutiny as active producers of knowledge" (788). I would like to think that my small contribution to this enterprise is my exploration of our relations to each other as scholars, archivists, librarians, and theorists via our physical and discursive connections to books, writing, libraries, and archives. Davis's book and indeed all of her books have made it possible to imagine how the scholar, as storyteller, "can move into the way others remember the past and change it merely by introducing an unexpected detail into a familiar account" (7).

12. Jack Goody and Ian Watt have been tremendously influential in their reflection of this legacy. See their essay "The Consequences of Literacy," in *Literacy in Traditional Societies*, ed. Jack Goody (New York: Cambridge University Press, 1968), 60. The logical "abstractions" of our work, they write, and the "compartmentalization" of our knowledge "restrict the kind of connections" we can make between our studies, on the one hand, and our "social experience and immediate personal contexts," on the other: "The essential way of thinking of the specialist in literate culture is fundamentally at odds with that of daily life and common experience; and the conflict is embodied in the long tradition of jokes about absent-minded professors."

13. Scholars and theorists from Walter Benjamin to Hayden White have drawn our attention to the ideological and rhetorical aspects of the organization of history. My reorganizing project is indebted to their work and also to the work of Reynaldo Ileto, who has illustrated a method for reading against the grain of archival categories, and Irene Silverblatt, who urges us to see the construction of archival categories as a part of historical process. Reynaldo C. Ileto, "Outlines of a Non-linear Emplotment of Philippine History," in *Reflections on Development in Southeast Asia*, ed. Lim Teck Ghee (Singapore: ASEAN Economic Research Unit, Institute of Southeast Asian Studies, 1988), 130–59, reprinted, with minor

changes, in *The Politics of Culture in the Shadow of Capital*, ed. Lisa Lowe and David Lloyd (Durham: Duke University Press, 1997), 98–131; Irene Silverblatt, "Interpreting Women in States: New Feminist Ethnohistories," in *Gender at the Crossroads of Knowledge: Feminist Anthropology in the Postmodern Era*, ed. Micaela di Leonardo (Berkeley: University of California Press, 1991), 140–74.

14. Tarabotti published her response to Naudé's invitation in her *Lettere di complimento*, but as far as I have been able to ascertain, Naudé's invitation is not extant. Arcangela Tarabotti, *Lettere familiari e di complimento* (Venice: Guerigli, 1650).

15. See Rosa, "I depositi," 171, who dates the first modern catalogs in the first decades of the sixteenth century and distinguishes them from previous inventories or lists of books whose primary function was to register personal property; Roger Chartier, *The Order of Books: Readers, Authors, and Libraries in Europe between the Fourteenth and Eighteenth Centuries* (Stanford: Stanford University Press, 1994), 69–70; Paula Findlen, "The Museum: Its Classical Etymology and Renaissance Genealogy," *Journal of the History of Collections* 1, no. 1 (1989): 61; Enzo Bottasso, *Storia della biblioteca in Italia* (Milan: Editrice Bibliografica, 1984), 49–53. Bottasso cites G. W. Wheeler, *The Earliest Catalogues of the Bodleian Library* (Oxford: Oxford University Press, 1928). See also John Huxtable Elliott, *The Old World and the New, 1492–1650* (Cambridge: Cambridge University Press, 1970), 32–38.

16. Silverblatt, "Interpreting Women in States," 154. Silverblatt underlines the importance of "accounting for," rather than "naturalizing," the "ideologies and institutions," such as bibliographic and archival orders of knowledge, that are "progeny of human encounters" between women and men.

17. Ibid., 156.

18. Of course, I use *gender* advisedly as a shorthand term that, in my opinion, best embodies Tarabotti's insistent attention to relations of power between women and men. The term *gender*, as we use it today, connotes (among other things) precisely such relations of power. See Simona Bortot's excellent introduction, "La penna all'ombra delle grate," to her recent critical edition of Tarabotti's *La semplicità ingannata* (Vicenza: Il Poligrafo, 2007), 21–167. Bortot begins with this quote from the *Paradiso monacale*: "Iddio Benedetto ama tutte le Creature, ma particolarmente la Donna, e poi l'huomo, bench'egli non lo meriti."

19. Chartier, *Order of Books*, viii.

20. Silverblatt, "Interpreting Women in States," 166.

21. Hortense Allart de Méritens, *Histoire de la République de Florence* (Paris: Delloye, 1843). Allart had also published an earlier version of this work in 1837 (Paris: Moutardier).

22. Gino Capponi, *Storia della Repubblica di Firenze* (Florence: G. Barbèra, 1875), 1:v-vi.

23. Ernesto Sestan, *La Firenze di Vieusseux e di Capponi*, ed. Giovanni Spadolini (Florence: Leo S. Olschki, 1986), 121.

24. Capponi had all along appreciated the "virile" quality of Allart's writing. He wrote to his friend Capei in March 1843, at the time of the publication of Allart's *History*: "Trovo che la parte seconda è superiore d'assai alla

prima . . . ; e la storia interna dei partiti e dei consigli che governarono la Repubblica negli ultimi tempi, è fatta con molta diligenza e senno virile." Gino Capponi, *Lettere di Gino Capponi: E di altri a lui raccolte e pubblicate*, 6 vols., ed. Alessandro Carraresi (Florence: Le Monnier: 1884–90), 2:120–21. Cf. below Section Three, "INSULTS and compliments" and p. 162.

25. Sestan, *La Firenze*, 121, reminds us that the *Storia della Repubblica di Firenze* was the only historical work that Capponi completed.

26. See Marco Tabarrini, *Gino Capponi, i suoi tempi, i suoi studi, i suoi amici. Memorie raccolte da Marco Tabarrini* (Florence: G. Barbèra, 1879), 273, 309.

27. This relational space, according to Petrucci, may be characterized by a community of secretaries (as in the case of Thomas Aquinas); by a social commitment to the renovation of "Roman" handwriting (as in the case of the Florentine humanists); or by a contest for control between authors and the publishing industry (as in the early nineteenth century). But in each case the author is understood as a social figure whose writing expresses, as much as the creative/intellectual spirit inherent in a text, the meaning that writing and text production had in a particular sociohistorical moment. Moreover, the relation of writing may bear a symbolic or metaphorical relationship to the content of any given text. See Armando Petrucci, "La scrittura del testo," in *Letteratura italiana*, ed. Alberto Asor Rosa, vol. 4, *L'interpretazione* (Turin: Einaudi, 1985), 285–308. I am also very much indebted, in the conception and interpretive work of this book, to two other essays by Petrucci that address issues of power and hierarchy evident in all relations of writing but especially on the pages of public documents: "L'illusione della storia autentica: Le testimonianze documentarie," in *L'insegnamento della storia e i materiali del lavoro storico* (Messina: Società degli Storici Italiani, 1984), translated by Charles Radding as "The Illusion of Authentic History: Documentary Evidence," in *Writers and Readers in Medieval Italy: Studies in the History of Written Culture,* ed. Charles Radding (New Haven: Yale University Press, 1995), 236–50; and "Pouvoir de l'écriture, pouvoir sur l'écriture dans la renaissance italienne," *Annales ESC* 4 (1988): 823–47.

28. Pettruci, "La scrittura," 285.

29. Sestan, *La Firenze*, 125.

30. My reading here would be impossible without Petre Ciureanu's rich introduction and scholarly edition of Allart's letters to Capponi, Hortense Allart de Méritens, *Lettere inedite a Gino Capponi*, ed. Petre Ciureanu (Genoa: Tolozzi, 1961), hereafter cited as *LIGC*. He ends his introduction: "Che si conceda, nel concludere, di rivendicare, per queste lettere al Capponi, un giudizio più equo su Hortense Allart e di formulare il voto che il suo nome non venga dimenticato nella storia dei rapporti culturali italo-francesi del XIX secolo" (xciii). I see my work as furthering Ciureanu's project, drawing attention to Italian-French cultural relations and gender relations as fundamental to the making of the Italian nation.

31. Hortense Allart de Méritens, *Les enchantements de prudence par Mme P[rudence] de Saman,* new ed. (Paris: Calmann Lévy, 1877), 239.

32. I also want to acknowledge here that in the preparation of this book I

have spent excessive amounts of time transcribing others' words in the company of dictionaries (English, Italian, French, Latin, and Greek) and have found these activities (typing, writing, and "thumbing" through dictionaries) to be both painstaking and exhilarating—painstaking for the solitary nature of scholarly work, exhilarating for the unexpected relations of research that always come into play.

33. Indeed, I have found that the conventional alphabetical ordering of my lexicon, ideological in its own right, was nonetheless effective in extracting Allart from the interstices of Capponi's *Storia* and making visible, rather, her partnership in the production of a nationalist Florentine history.

34. Silverblatt, "Interpreting Women in States," 163.

35. For the texts affixed to this and each of the other artpieces, see the Appendix.

SECTION ONE

1. Giovanni Antonio, called "il Sarto," to Marino Caracciolo, January 9, 1537, CSM, folder 20, 268.

2. After sending news of his sighting of Lorenzino, Giovanni Antonio continued to send letters reporting the movements of the anti-Medici Florentine exiles through Bologna to various destinations. In one such letter of February 13, Giovanni Antonio reported that Lorenzino had passed through Bologna again on January 30, this time "disguised": "On the 30th of last month, the one who killed the Duke of Florence, namely Lorenzino de' Medici, mounted here in Bologna in the mail coach disguised and went toward Romagna, I don't know where. As news comes in, I will not fail to inform you." ("Alli 30 dil passato quelo ch' amazo il duca di fiorenza cioe lorenzino de medici monto imposta camufato qui in bologna e se ne ando in Romagna non so dove sia andato de mano in mano non mancaro ad avisare.") CSM, folder 20, 277.

3. See Maria Pia Bortolotti's unpublished note of May 1987, "Carteggio delle Cancellerie dello Stato di Milano," in the reading room of the Archivio di Stato in Milan; Damiano Muoni, *Archivi di Stato in Milano: Prefetti o direttori, 1488–1874* (Milan: C. Molinari, 1874); and Nicola Raponi, "Per la storia dell'Archivio di Stato di Milano: Erudizione e cultura nell' 'Annuario' del Fumi (1909–1919)," *Rassegna degli Archivi di Stato* 31, no. 2 (1971): 313–34.

4. This episode in Florentine history is famous in literature and drama, having been treated by Marguerite de Navarre, Thomas Kyd, Cyril Tourneur, James Shirley, Vittorio Alfieri, Alexandre Dumas, Alfred de Musset, George Sand, and others. The scholarly literature on Lorenzino is vast (even without considering the extensive literature on Musset's *Lorenzaccio*) and includes Eride Baldoni, *Lorenzino de' Medici e l'Apologia* (Ancona: Atima, 1950); Joyce G. Bromfield, *De Lorenzino de Médicis à Lorenzaccio: Étude d'un thème historique* (Paris: M. Didier, 1972); Lorenzino de' Medici, *Apologia e lettere*, ed. Francesco Erspamer (Rome: Salerno, 1991); Luigi Alberto Ferrai, *Lorenzino de'Medici e la società cortigiana del Cinquecento* (Milan: U. Hoepli, 1891); Ferruccio Martini, *Lorenzino de' Medici e il tirannicidio nel Rinascimento* (Florence: G. B. Giachetti, 1882); Siro Attilio Nulli, *L'emulo di Bruto (Lorenzino de' Medici)*

(Milan: Athena, 1932); Manfredi Piccolomini, *The Brutus Revival: Parricide and Tyrannicide during the Renaissance* (Carbondale: Southern Illinois University Press, 1991); Roberto Ridolfi, *Lorenzino, sfinge medicea* (Florence: SP 44, 1983).

5. For the classical "sources" of the sexual politics enacted here, see below, Folder 6, "Sexual Politics and Imperial Documentation Projects."

6. Louis Althusser, "Ideology and Ideological State Apparatuses," in *Lenin and Philosophy, and Other Essays* (New York: Monthly Review Press, 1972). We shall see, throughout this chapter, the prominence of the figure of Brutus in the organization of knowledge about Lorenzino.

7. Cf. Gramsci's notion of traditional intellectuals who believe that they represent "a historical continuity uninterrupted by even the most complex and radical changes in social and political structures." Gramsci, *Quaderni del carcere*, 3:1514–15 (translation my own).

8. I am grateful to Prof. Kirstie McClure, who encouraged me to ask these questions when she invited me to speak about my research at the Pembroke Center Roundtable on Resistance and Revolution held at Brown University in March 1989.

9. Although Giovanni Antonio writes that Lorenzino was "wounded" (without specifics), historiographic accounts, as we saw, and Lorenzino himself specify that Alessandro wounded Lorenzino's hand by biting down hard on his thumb. See Jacopo Nardi, *Istorie della città di Firenze*, ed. Agenore Gelli (Florence: F. Le Monnier, 1858), bk. 10, 2:283 ("Lorenzo ponendogli la mano alla bocca, lo ributtò rovescio sopra il letto; ma il duca lo prese co' denti nel dito grosso della sinistra mano gridando: *donami la vita*, aperse la bocca, onde ritirando la mano si possette Lorenzo valere della persona sua. E così tra l'uno e l'altro uccisero il duca ... [Lorenzo] dalla finestra pose mente se poteva essere stato udito di fuori il fatto rumore ... Ma nell'appoggiarsi, ... lasciò tutta macchiata la sponda di quella del sangue proprio che gli usciva della mano morsa; che fu poi il primo indizio dello eccesso seguito"); Benedetto Varchi, *Storia fiorentina* (Milan: Società Tipografica de' Classici Italiani, 1804), bk. 15, 5:271–72 ("E perchè egli [il duca] non potesse gridare, [Lorenzo] fatto sommesso del dito grosso e dell'indice della mano sinistra gl'inforcò la bocca dicendo, Signore non dubitate; allora il duca aiutandosi quanto poteva il più gli prese co' denti il dito grosso, e lo strigneva con tanta rabbia ... nè mai gli lasciò quel dito, ch'egli gli teneva rabbiosamente afferrato co' denti"); Paolo Giovio, *Istorie del suo tempo*, trans. Lodovico Domenichi (Venetia: Giovan Maria Bonelli, 1560), bk. 38, 2:500 ("Co i denti gli afferrò il dito grosso della man manca, et gliel ruppe" ["levae manus pollicem dentibus apprehendit atque perfregit"]); Filippo de' Nerli, *Commentari dei fatti civili occorsi dentro la città di Firenze dall' anno 1215 al 1537*, 2 vols. (Trieste: Colombo Coen Tipi, 1859), bk. 12, 2:241 ("Il Duca si rizzò per difendersi, e co' denti, non avendo altre armi, prese Lorenzo per un dito della mano"); Frate G. D. (possibly Donato Giannotti), "A Paolo del Tosco," in *Lettere di principi*, ed. Girolamo Ruscelli (Venetia: Giordano Ziletti, 1577), 3:164v ("Et il Duca li prese co i denti un dito grosso della mano, et mordevalo tanto forte"); Bernardo Segni, *Storie fiorentine* (Milan: Società Tipografica de' Classici Italiani, 1805), bk. 7, 2:124 ("Il Duca ... rizzatosi, e

gridando, *ah traditore*, prese un dito a Lorenzo colla bocca"); and "Lettera di Lorenzo di Pierfrancesco de' Medici a Francesco di Raffaello de' Medici," in *Aridosia-Apologia: Rime e lettere*, ed. Federico Ravello (Turin: UTET, 1921), 200 ("Il sangue, che mi usciva in quantità straordinaria di una mano che mi era stata morsa"). Biting the body of a conspirator is a recurring motif. When Francesco Salviati was hanged and lowered from a window of Palazzo della Signoria (for his participation in the Pazzi conspiracy), he bit into the breast of Francesco Pazzi, who was hanging beside him. We don't know why—Francesco was already dead when he took the bite. Was it by chance or out of rage? Strangled by the noose, he opened his eyes ferociously and held onto his companion with his teeth. ("Cum deiceretur . . . sive id casus aliquis sive rabies dederit, ipsum illud cadaver dentibus invadit alteramque eius mamillam, vel cum laqueo suffocatus est, apertis furialiter oculis, mordicus detinebat.") Angelo Poliziano, *Della congiura dei Pazzi: Coniurationis commentarium*, ed. Alessandro Perosa (Padua: Antenore, 1958), 44–45. The two most chewed-upon conspirators in literary history, of course, are Brutus and Cassius, eternally bitten and clawed by Satan in Dante's circle of traitors (*Inferno*, 34.55–60).

I am indebted here and in what follows by the ways Irene Silverblatt theorizes the historicity of archival research and by Walter Benjamin's reflection on Ranke, "Theses on the Philosophy of History," in *Illuminations*, ed. Hannah Arendt, trans. Harry Zohn (New York: Schocken Books, 1969), 255: "To articulate the past historically does not mean to recognize it 'the way it really was' (Ranke). It means to seize hold of a memory as it flashes up at a moment of danger. . . . The danger affects both the content of the tradition and its receivers. The same threat hangs over both: that of becoming a tool of the ruling classes." In my research, I have been especially concerned to use this "moment of danger" in which Lorenzino passes by to make visible and historicize the various agencies, including my own, through which political knowledge is organized. Silverblatt, "Interpreting Women in States," esp. 150–56.

10. See Lorenzino, "Apologia," in *Apologia e lettere*, 207–9.

11. See Petrucci, "Pouvoir de l'écriture," 831–32; Petrucci, "L'illusione," 82–83.

12. The relation between facts, actions, things, and the construction of knowledge in writing, central to thinking about historiography, politics, philosophy, and science, is treated by, among others, Bacon, Galileo, Hume, Kant, Vico, Hobbes, Leibniz, and such early modern epistemologists as Aldrovandi, Gesner, and Kircher. In my research I have been especially interested in the collection and construction of sixteenth-century facts of history, literature, and the natural world. The sixteenth-century literary genre "il fatto d'arme" is of particular interest and merits a study of its own. Hayden White has guided my thinking about "facts" and discourse from the outset. See, in particular, Hayden V. White, *Tropics of Discourse: Essays in Cultural Criticism* (Baltimore: Johns Hopkins University Press, 1978) and "The Politics of Historical Interpretation: Discipline and De-sublimation," *Critical Inquiry* 9, no. 1 (1982): 113–37. My thinking is also indebted to Paula Findlen, *Possessing Nature: Museums, Collecting, and Scientific Culture in Early Modern Italy* (Berkeley: University of California Press, 1994); to Daphne Marlatt's novel *Ana Historic*, 2nd ed. (Con-

cord, Ontario: House of Anansi Press, 1997), 31, in which a "f-act" is defined as "the f stop of act, a still photo in an ongoing cinerama"; and to Dorothy Smith, whose books include *Texts, Facts and Femininity: Exploring the Relations of Ruling* (London: Routledge, 1993), *The Everyday World as Problematic: A Feminist Sociology* (Boston: Northeastern University Press, 1989), and *The Conceptual Practices of Power: A Feminist Sociology of Knowledge* (Boston: Northeastern University Press, 1991). The "I" here is not the same as my biographical "I" but rather that persona who, though influenced by my life experiences, is constructed by my training and experiences of research.

13. Cf. Gramsci's idea of the relationship between intellectuals and "the world of production" as "'mediated' in varying degrees by the whole social fabric, by the complex of superstructures, of which the intellectuals are, precisely, the 'functionaries.'" Gramsci, *Quaderni del carcere*, 3:1518. My project here is, in part, to document and make concrete this process of mediation. Like Giovanni Antonio, I have become a functionary of this mediation.

14. Several scholars have worked in this intersection. I have been helped, in particular, by Roland Arthur Greene, *Unrequited Conquests: Love and Empire in the Colonial Americas* (Chicago: University of Chicago Press, 1999); and Timothy Hampton, *Fictions of Embassy: Literature and Diplomacy in Early Modern Europe* (Ithaca: Cornell University Press, 2009).

15. Delio Cantimori, "Il caso di Boscoli e la vita del Rinascimento," *Giornale critico della filosofia* 8 (1927): 241–55; and "Rhetoric and Politics in Italian Humanism," trans. Frances A. Yates, *Journal of the Warburg Insititute*, 1, no. 2 (1937): 83–102. For a brief history of the *Journal of the Warburg Institute*, see Elizabeth McGrath, "Journal of the Warburg and Courtauld Institutes: A Short History," n.d., http://warburg.sas.ac.uk/journal/historyjwci.htm. I would also like to draw attention to the fact that Cantimori researched the "case" of Boscoli, in part, by drawing on documents published in 1842 in the very first issue of the *Archivio storico italiano;* Luca della Robbia, "Narrazione del caso di Pietro Paolo Boscoli e di Agostino Capponi (1513)," ed. F. Polidori, *Archivio storico italiano*, 1st ser., 1 (1842): 275–309. The Florentine eruditi who founded this nation-building journal are the subject of Section Three of this book. Cantimori, as we shall see, understood this Risorgimento period of Italian history as an heir to the Renaissance and a precursor to fascism.

16. I am interested, in particular, in how fascist (and antifascist) scholars read Renaissance texts for insight into their present times, and, conversely, how fascist politics may have directed these scholars to focus on aspects of Renaissance texts that had never before seemed pertinent. See Natalie Zemon Davis's investigation of Lucien Febvre's scholarly relation to Rabelais in the 1940s and of the vicissitudes of the *Annales* historians under the German occupation of France as a model for the work that still needs to be done in this area: "Rabelais among the Censors (1940s, 1540s)," *Representations* 32 (1990): 1–32. I also had the extraordinary opportunity to participate, with professors Davis, Jane Newman and Dianella Gagliani, in a 1997 MLA panel entitled "Humanism under Fascism," in which Davis shared her research on the vicissitudes of the Bibliothèque d'Humanisme et Renaissance under the Vichy regime.

17. The scholarship on fascist historical films is extensive and important.

See among other works, Gian Piero Brunetta, *Cinema italiano tra le due guerre: Fascismo e politica cinematografica* (Milan: Mursia, 1975); Marcia Landy, *Fascism in Film: The Italian Commercial Cinema, 1931–43* (Princeton: Princeton University Press, 1986); Riccardo Redi, ed., *Cinema sotto il fascismo* (Venice: Marsilio, 1979).

18. The figure of Cantimori is a complex one whose relation to fascism has been extensively studied. See, among other works, Eric Cochrane and John Tedeschi, "Delio Cantimori: Historian," *Journal of Modern History* 39, no. 4 (1967): 438–45; Giovanni Miccoli, *Delio Cantimori: La ricerca di una nuova critica storiografica* (Turin: Einaudi, 1970); Michele Ciliberto, *Intellettuali e fascismo: Saggio su Delio Cantimori* (Bari: De Donato, 1977); Bruno V. Bandini, ed., *Storia e storiografia: Studi su Delio Cantimori*, Atti del convegno tenuto a Russi (Ravenna) il 7–8 ottobre 1978 (Rome: Editori Riuniti, 1979); Patricia Chiantera-Stutte, *Res nostra agitur: Il pensiero di Delio Cantimori, 1928–1937* (Bari: Palomar, 2005); Nicola D'Elia, *Delio Cantimori e la cultura politica tedesca: 1927–1940* (Rome: Viella, 2007); Paolo Simoncelli, *Cantimori e il libro mai edito: Il movimento nazionalsocialista dal 1919 al 1933* (Florence: Le lettere, 2008). My knowledge of Cantimori's biography comes primarily from Miccoli, *Delio Cantimori;* Ciliberto, *Intellettuali e fascismo;* and Michele Ciliberto, "Cantimori e gli eretici: Filosofia, storiografia e politica tra gli anni venti e gli anni trenta" (152–93), and his roundtable response (232–39) in Bandini, *Storia e storiografia*. See also Eugenio Garin, *Intellettuali italiani del XX secolo* (Rome: Editori Riuniti, 1974); and Piero Craveri, "Delio Cantimori," in *Dizionario biografico degli italiani* (Rome: Istituto della Enciclopedia Italiana, 1960–), www.treccani.it/Portale/elements/categoriesItems.jsp?pathFile=/sites/default/BancaDati/Enciclopedia_online/C/BIOGRAFIE_-_EDICOLA_C_113455.xml.

19. See Ciliberto, "Cantimori e gli eretici," 182, 235: "Politica e storiografia sono poli d'una medesima ricerca, che trascorre, in modo spontaneo, dall'uno all'altro campo, cercando contemporaneamente di salvaguardare l'autonomia di entrambi," and "Ignorare la sua 'politica' significa disconoscere alcuni caratteri peculiari della sua 'storiografia.'" In the writing of this book, I have thought it important to include several allusions to my own political experiences and commitments in order to underline this connection between politics and historical perspective. In this section, for example, my experience, in 1992, of writing a column of media criticism for *Lies of Our Times* directly influenced my analysis of documents pertaining to Lorenzino.

20. For critical scholarship on fascist journals, see especially Luisa Mangoni, *L'interventismo della cultura: Intellettuali e riviste del fascismo* (Bari: Laterza, 1977), and Anna Panicali, *Le riviste del periodo fascista: Un saggio introduttivo* (Messina: G. D'Anna, 1978).

21. Quoted in Mangoni, *L'interventismo*, 70, and in Ciliberto, "Cantimori e gli eretici," 175–76.

22. *Vita nova*, 1926, quoted in Ciliberto, "Cantimori e gli eretici," 166–67.

23. "Il tipo italiano nel cinema," *Cinema Illustrazione*, October 12, 1938.

24. *Vita nova*, 1935, quoted in Ciliberto, "Cantimori e gli eretici," 168.

25. Anna Panicali, "L'intellettuale fascista," in *Cinema sotto il fascismo*, ed. Riccardo Redi (Venice: Marsilio, 1979), 43.

26. Ibid., 43.
27. See Delio Cantimori, review of *La vita come ricerca*, by Ugo Spirito, *Giornale critico della filosofia italiana* 18 (1937): 360.
28. Ibid., 366.
29. Cantimori, "Il caso di Boscoli," 241.
30. Niccolò Machiavelli, *Istorie fiorentine*, 7.34.
31. Della Robbia, "Narrazione," 290.
32. Cantimori, "Il caso di Boscoli," 241, 242.
33. Ibid., 245.
34. Ibid., 248, 255.
35. Ibid., 254.
36. Ibid., 255.
37. Later in life and from his perspective as a Communist Party member, Cantimori looked back at the confusion surrounding his adherence to fascism, writing: "What *confusion* . . . I had entered the fascist party in 1926 . . . I was full of mental *confusion* and almost without any excuses: in fact, I had even read *The Liberal Revolution* . . . and my father's subscription to Salvemini's l'*Unità* . . . Still, I was convinced that fascism had made and was making the true Italian revolution, [one that] was destined to become a European revolution; and I believed it was necessary to work on that path . . . I had often read *Avanti!* and once in a while *Il Comunista* . . . and still I was convinced that the right path for Italy was that of the fascists: what mysterious stupidity . . . in other words, I was not in the dark about the most noteworthy alternatives to fascism . . . So, it was not because I didn't know. Of course, I didn't know everything. I'm not about to analyze how and why I started off on that path, nor will I say that the *confusion* I had in my head was the fault of Gentile, Croce, De Sanctis, Hegel, Mazzini, Gioberti, Gioacchino Volpe, Lutero, Burckhardt, Sorel." ("Che zuppa . . . Ero entrato nel partito fascista nel 1926 . . . Ero pieno di confusione mentale e quasi senza scusanti: infatti avevo pur letto Rivoluzione liberale . . . e l'Unità di Salvemini alla quale era abbonato mio padre; . . . Tuttavia, ero convinto che il fascismo aveva fatto e stava facendo la vera rivoluzione italiana, che doveva diventare rivoluzione europea; e ritenevo che bisognasse lavorare su questa strada . . . avevo letto spesso l'Avanti! e qualche volta Il Comunista . . . eppure, ero convinto o credevo d'esser convinto che la strada giusta fosse per l'Italia quella dei fascisti: che mistero di stoltezza . . . insomma non ero all'oscuro di alcune delle più note alternative al fascismo . . . Dunque, non era perché non sapessi. Certo, non sapevo tutto. Non starò a fare l'analisi del come e del perché mi ero messo su quella strada, né mi metterò a dire che la confusione che avevo in testa era colpa di Gentile, Croce, De Sanctis, Hegel, Mazzini, Gioberti, Gioacchino Volpe, Lutero, Burckhardt, Sorel.") Delio Cantimori, *Conversando di storia* (Bari: Laterza, 1967), 137–38, quoted in Ciliberto, "Cantimori e gli eretici," 154.
38. Cantimori, "Il caso di Boscoli," 247.
39. Delio Cantimori, "Osservazioni sui concetti di cultura e storia della cultura," in *Scritti vari pubblicati dagli alunni della R. Scuola Normale Superiore di Pisa* (Pacini: Mariotti, 1928), 35–36.
40. In 1937, Cantimori began to assign a more positive value to the re-

public of letters than the one he had assigned to the literary world of Olgiati and Boscoli in 1926, writing: "Rhetoric and politics were for the Florentine humanists one and the same thing since both were founded upon ethics. And from these political passions, the Florentine humanists returned to 'rhetorical' problems but always with a political preoccupation." Cantimori, "Rhetoric and Politics," 101. As Cantimori focused on the "process by which the 'rhetoric' and literature of the humanist tradition [became] political action in pursuit of an idea" (86), his own rhetoric surpassed the schism between "culture" in the republic of letters and "action."

41. Jean A. Gili, "Film storico e film in costume," in Redi, *Cinema sotto il fascismo*, 135.

42. Ibid., 135.

43. *Cinema Illustrazione*, December 5, 1934, 15.

44. Ibid., 15.

45. Gianfranco Gori, *Patria diva: La storia d'Italia nei film del ventennio* (Florence: La Casa Usher, 1988), 13.

46. *Cinema*, o.s., 5, no. 86 (January 25, 1940): 48–49.

47. I am quoting directly from the film that I viewed privately in Rome with my friend and colleague Dianella Gagliani, courtesy of the Biblioteca Nazionale di Cinema. Cf. Machiavelli, *Il principe*, bk. 8: "Bene usate si possono chiamare quelle [crudeltà] . . . che si fanno ad un tratto, per necessità dello assicurarsi, e di poi non vi si insiste dentro, ma si convertiscono in più utilità de' sudditi che si può."

48. Mussolini, in his entry "Fascismo" that appeared in the 1932 edition of the *Enciclopedia italiana di scienze, lettere ed arti* (Milan: Istituto Giovanni Treccani, 1932), 14:847–51, was famously unwilling to fix fascism within any ideology. He wrote: "Il fascismo è prassi ed è pensiero, azione a cui è immanente una dottrina . . . La mia dottrina . . . era stata la dottrina dell'azione."

49. *Condottieri*, dir. Luis Trenker, Giacomo Gentilomo, and Werner Klingler (1937). I viewed this film, as well, at the Biblioteca Nazionale di Cinema in Rome.

50. Luis Trenker, "Le mie idee sul film," *Cinema*, no. 25 (1937): 10.

51. Cf. Landy, *Fascism in Film*, especially ch. 4.

52. "Il tipo italiano nel cinema."

53. Ibid.

54. "Registi, storia e film," *Cinema*, o.s., 5, no. 86 (January 25, 1940): 48.

55. Libero Solaroli, "La Terza Cines indossa la camicia nera," *Cinema nuovo* 2, no. 8 (April 1, 1953): 213–14.

56. Cantimori, "Osservazioni," 38.

57. Cantimori, review of *La vita come ricerca*, 359. Later in the review, Cantimori made explicit his agreement with this perspective (366): "E' vero che occorre liberare la scuola (e con essa la cultura tutta intiera) dal 'l'umanismo storico e letterario consolidato come modello intangibile attraverso i secoli' . . . [e] 'gli esempi e l'opera dei classici a cui è tanto difficile accostarsi con animo non gelido.'"

58. Ibid., 367. Cantimori, here, is quoting Spirito.

59. Ibid., 366.

60. Machiavelli, *Istorie fiorentine*, 7.33. I want to draw particular attention to the term *litterato*. When Girolamo Olgiati found himself naked before his executioner, he spoke in Latin, because he was, according to Machiavelli, *litterato*. *Litterato*, a term we associate today with literary elites, referred more specifically, in fifteenth-century Florence, to a world that was dominated or lettered by Latin culture. Other types of literacy—such as the ability to write Italian for commercial, diplomatic, and generally nonclassical purposes—would not mark a person as *litterato*. Even Leonardo da Vinci, today perceived as the quintessential Renaissance man, considered himself to be illiterate—*omo sanza lettere*—because he knew no Latin. His was not a world without writing but a world written or lettered by other, nonhumanistic codes. It is important to understand the humanistic codification of political violence, not as a screen isolating humanists from authentic political activity, but as a particular political strategy in its own right, a strategy of suppression. Humanists are ambitious to dominate the political world with Latin or classical culture and to suppress nonhumanistic modes of thinking and writing about political violence.

61. For a modern historian's account of the assassination of Galeazzo Maria, see Vincenzo Ilardi, "The Assassination of Galeazzo Maria Sforza and the Reaction of Italian Diplomacy," in *Violence and Civil Disorder in Italian Cities*, ed. Lauro Martines (Berkeley: University of California Press, 1972), 72–103.

62. Machiavelli, *Istorie fiorentine*, 7.33. Tyrants heap cruelty and violence on their mothers to eliminate the evidence of their origins and any legitimate threat to their power. Julius Caesar dreamed of raping his mother. The soothsayers understood this dream to mean that Caesar would some day subjugate the world. Since, in the dream, his mother was lying under him, 'mother' could only mean 'earth,' who is the mother of all things. Suetonius, *Le vite de dodici cesari di Gaio Suetonio,* trans. Paolo del Rosso (Venice: Hieronymo Calepino, 1550), 7: "Stando ancora in Roma tutto confuso per un sogno fatto da lui la notte passata (conciosia che gli fusse paruto di usare con la madre) [nam visus erat quietem stuprum matri intulisse] gli fu dato dalli Indovini grandissima speranza, interpretando che cio significava l'aver lui a soggiogare il mondo, concio fusse cosa, che la madre quale egli sognando s'haveva veduta in cotal guisa sottoposta, non significava altro, che la terra, la quale è tenuta madre di tutte le cose." Cf. Isidore of Seville (*Etymologies*, 9.3, *Patrologia Latina* 82), who distinguishes between kings who rule and tyrants who "hold the land": *Per me reges regnant et tyranni per me tenent terram.*

Nero was so disturbed by what he perceived as Agrippina's "unbridled desire" ("sfrenato desiderio") for power that finally, he resolved to have her killed. Nero's captain invented a ship designed to break apart at sea, but Agrippina survived the shipwreck. When Nero sent a band of henchmen to murder his mother in a straightforward way, Agrippina made a last request before surrendering to their violence. She screamed and prayed for the sword to be buried in her womb: "Strike it—here, here you must strike, here, I say in this womb that gave birth to such a monster." Tacitus, *Gli annali de' fatti e guerre de' Romani*, trans. Giorgio Dati (Venice: ad instantia de' Giunti di Firenze, 1563), 156–58 (bk. 14): "sfrenato desiderio" is the translation of the Latin *ardore;* "gridò, feriscilo, pregandolo che nel ventre di lei ascondesse il crudo ferro, et poi sog-

giunse qui qui dovete ferire, qui dico in questo ventre che partorì tal monstro."
(Dati embellishes considerably the original Latin text: "iam [in] morte[m] centurioni ferrum destringenti protendens uterum "ventrem feri" exclamavit multisque vulneribus confecta est").

Alessandro's treatment of his mother was considered to be a sure sign of his tyranny. She was poor and needed everything, but he hated her so much that he was unwilling to provide her even with food. Jacopo Nardi, "Orazione," in *Orazioni scelte del secolo XVI*, ed. Giuseppe Lisio (Florence: Sansoni, 1997), 108: "L'ha sì grandemente in odio, che pur del vitto necessario non si degna di sovvenirla, sendo lei di tutti li bisogni poverissima." The exiles had hoped to make a very strong case around the duke's mother by bringing her in person to Naples to show the emperor the cruelty of his future son-in-law. But Alessandro, hearing of this plan, put an end to the miseries of his mother by having her poisoned. Scipione Ammirato, *Istorie fiorentine* (Florence: Stamperia Nuova d'Amador Massi e Lorenzo Landi, 1641), bk. 31, 431. Even if he could not quell the anger of legitimate cousins who resented being ruled over by a bastard, he could at least destroy reminders of his illegitimate birth. The Florentines would have to learn to allow a man of obscure origins to tyrannize their state. Varchi, *Storia fiorentina*, bk. 14, 5:140: "uno, ch'ei non sapevano chi egli si fosse, né di cui nato, a tiranneggiare la patria loro."

"So that no one would doubt that he was a tyrant, Alessandro took away every vestige of civic life from Florence, even its name 'republic,' and as if, in order to be a tyrant, it were necessary to be more evil than Nero, more hateful and lustful than Caligula, and more cruel than Phalaris, Alessandro tried to exceed their crimes. Beyond his cruelties against citizens . . . he exceeded the cruelty of Nero in having his mother killed; because Nero did it for fear of losing his state and his life . . . but Alessandro committed such an outrage only for pure cruelty and inhumanity." ("Perché non si avesse a dubitare s'egli era tiranno, levata via ogni civiltà e ogni reliquia e nome di repubblica, e come se fusse necessario per esser tiranno non esser meno empio di Nerone, nè meno odiatore degli uomini e lussurioso di Caligola, nè meno crudele di Falari, cercò di superare le sceleratezze di tutti; perchè, oltre alle crudeltà usate ne' cittadini . . . superò nel far morire la madre l'empietà di Nerone; perchè Nerone lo fece per timore dello stato e della vita sua . . . ma Alessandro commesse tale sceleratezza solo per mera crudeltà et inumanità.") Lorenzino, "Apologia," in *Apologia e lettere*, 207–8. Nero, Galeazzo, and Alessandro cruelly killed their mothers, but we might be just as shocked, as we shall see in Section Two, by those fathers who just as cruelly commit their young daughters to convents.

63. Paul Ricoeur, "The Work of Resemblance," in *The Rule of Metaphor* (Toronto: University of Toronto Press, 1977), 173–215.

64. According to the juristic tradition that culminated in the treatises on tyranny of Coluccio Salutati (1400) and Bartolus of Sassoferrato (ca. 1350), the laws concerning ambition were designed to keep a check on tyranny. There were two principal ways to exercise tyranny—with oppressive behavior (*ex parte exercitii*) or illegitimate authority (*ex defectu tituli*). If a ruler were a tyrant by reason of his oppressive behavior, two Roman laws would apply. If a ruler afflicted his subjects with corporal punishment, kept the city divided as

an obstruction to justice, or imposed new taxes and revenues, he would come under the jurisdiction of the law concerning public force (*lex julia de vi publica*) and the law concerning ambition (*lex julia de ambitu*). The law concerning public force would condemn a tyrant to exile and strip him of his civil rights. Like any disgraced person, he would lose his rank and authority. Under the law concerning ambition, a tyrant could also come up against capital punishment. See Bartolus a Saxoferrato, *Opera quae nunc extant omnia* (Basileae ex officina episcopiana, 1589), "De Tyrannia," in vol. 10, *Consilia, Quaestiones et Tractatus*, par. 33, 325. I consulted the translation of this treatise by Ephraim Emerton in *Humanism and Tyranny: Studies in the Italian Trecento* (Cambridge, MA: Harvard University Press, 1925). See also Coluccio Salutati, *Il trattato "De tyranno" e lettere scelte*, ed. Francesco Ercole (Bologna: Zanichelli, 1942).

In the case of the ruler who exercised tyranny by unlawfully usurping authority or extending his term of office, jurists would also have recourse to the law concerning ambition (Bartolus a Saxoferrato, *Opera*, par. 40, p. 326). *Ambitus*, in the time of the Roman republic, was a technical term used to denote the physical "going around" of political candidates who were seeking to win votes by means of bribery and corruption. *The lex julia de ambitu*, enacted by Caesar in 49 B.C.E., was only the last of several attempts at controlling such corruption, and his version is the law that remained on the books.

Although, in Shakespeare's *Julius Caesar*, Brutus's accusation of ambition against Caesar is skillfully parried by Mark Antony, it should be noted that in Roman history, Caesar was suspected of ambition from the beginning of his career. Among his many other crimes of ambition, these were especially remembered: he conspired (66/65 B.C.E.) to usurp the dictatorship along with Marcus Crassus, Publius Sulla, and Lucius Autronius, who were afterwards condemned for ambition. During the consulship of Marcus Claudius (51 B.C.E.), he was accused of having granted Roman citizenship to the settlers of Novum Comun because of his ambition and not by sanction of the law. He made himself consul (refusing successors); he made himself dictator for life and censor. He named himself emperor and father of the country. He allowed his statue to be placed among those of the kings. He sat in the highest and most honored place at the theater. He allowed temples and altars to be dedicated in his honor and his statue to be placed among those of the gods. And although he refused the crown three times from the hand of Mark Antony, it was generally thought that Caesar ambitiously longed to be addressed as king. Thus the Sibylline prophecy that only a king could defeat the Parthians precipitated plans for the slaying of Caesar, for his coronation was imminent. Cf. Suetonius *Life of Julius Caesar* 76–79. Ambition seems to generate murderous feelings, but the murderers are also ambitious.

65. Sanctio to Caracciolo, January 12, 1537, CSM, folder 12bis, 28.

66. Speciano to Caracciolo, January 12, 1537, CSM, folder 14, 9.

67. See, for example, Filippo Archinto, governor of Rome, to Caracciolo, July 18, 1537, CSM, folder 20, 95.

68. Speciano to Caracciolo, January 14, 1537, CSM, folder 14, 18.

69. Landriano to Caracciolo, January 17, 1537, CSM, folder 13bis, 71.

70. When Caracciolo wrote to Salviati, hoping to enlist his efforts in the

support of imperial dominion, the imperial postal agents were unable to find him. Salviati wrote: "If Ridolfi and I had received the other letters you say you sent, we would not have delayed in responding, but those letters were delivered to us neither in Rome before our departure nor upon our arrival in Florence, where we think you probably addressed them" (autograph letter from Salviati to Caracciolo, February 17, 1537, CSM, folder 13, 426) ["Se il Reverendissimo de Ridolfi o io havessimo receute le altre lettere che Vostra Signoria Reverendissima ci dice ... haverci scritte ... non haremo tardato a risponderli ... ma né in Roma avanti el partire nostro ci furon date, né ancora arrivati in Firenze, dove pensiamo più presto le indirizasse"]. Another imperial correspondent reinforced the exclusion of men like Salviati from the imperial loop by claiming that Salviati and Ridolfi were at least partly to blame for the death of Alessandro and that Caracciolo was naive to write to him at all. Speciano to Caracciolo, January 16, 1537, CSM, folder 14, 27: "essendo statta non senza loro causa la morte d'uno genero dello imperatore."

71. Salviati to Caracciolo, February 17, 1537, CSM, folder 13, 426 (autograph).

72. Ibid.

73. Landriano to Caracciolo, January 14, 1537, CSM, folder 13bis, 64.

74. Plutarch, *Vite di Plutarco cheroneo de gli huomini illustri greci et romani*, trans. Lodovico Domenichi et al. (Venetia: Appresso Felice Valgrisio, 1582), 201. Domenichi translated *kometas*, meaning "long-haired," as "di buona vista" (having good eyesight), perhaps to underline the weak vision of tyrant-slayers.

75. Shakespeare, *The Tragedy of Julius Caesar*, ed. Barbara A. Mowat and Paul Werstine, Folger Shakespeare Library (New York: Washington Square Press, 1992), 1.2.209–11: "Yet if my name were liable to fear, / I do not know the man I should avoid / So soon as that spare Cassius. He reads much."

76. Plutarch, *Vite di Plutarco*, 196, 197. Cf. Shakespeare, *Julius Caesar*, 4.3.293, 315–16: "here's the book I sought for so"; "Let me see, let me see; is not the leaf turned down / Where I left reading? Here it is, I think."

77. Scipione Ammirato, *Istorie fiorentine* (Florence: L. Marchini and G. Becherini, 1826), bk. 29, 9:136.

78. Della Robbia, "Narrazione," 284. Polidori annotates Boscoli's shortsightedness, citing Giovanni Cambi: "Il Cambi dice: 'Era bianchastrino, e tanto biondo che gl'impediva 'l vedere.' Sulla conseguenza che il cronista inferir sembra dalla biondezza, non occorre qui disputare."

79. Rudolf von Albertini, *Firenze dall repubblica al principato: Storia e coscienza politica* (Turin: Einaudi, 1970), 211.

80. Later, in Section Three, we will see how Gino Capponi also participated in this typology of "myopic politics."

81. Françoise Waquet, "Qu'est-ce que la république des lettres? Essai de sémantique historique," *Bibliothèque de l'École des Chartes* 147 (1989): 475. Quoted also in Elizabeth L. Eisenstein, *The Printing Press as an Agent of Change* (Cambridge: Cambridge University Press, 1985), 137 n.

82. Marin Mersenne is described by Waquet, "Qu'est-ce que la république des lettres?" 492, as a "grand négociant des Lettres," "comme le centre de

tous les gens de lettres par le commerce continuel qu'il entretenoit avec tous, et tous avec luy." As Waquet notes (490), Thomas Sprat writes in 1667 in *The History of the Royal Society* that the Royal Society admitted members from all countries: "For by this means, they will be able to settle a constant intelligence throughout all civil nations, and make the Royal Society the general Banck, and free-port of the world." Members of the Accademia del Cimento vowed to establish "una libera comunicazione di diverse adunanze sparse, come oggi sono, per le più illustri e più cospicue regioni d'Europa; le quali con l'istessa mira di giugnere a fini sì rilevanti, aprendosi a vicenda un sì profittevol commercio" (490–91).

83. Marc Fumaroli, "La république des lettres," *Diogène* 143 (1988): 140.

84. Fumaroli notes that Boccaccio's 1341 *Life and Customs of Petrarch [De vita et moribus Francisci Petrarchi poetae]* and the *Lives* of Vespasiano da Bisticci, Vasari, and Giovio provided the scholarly community with moral examples and models of scholarly discipline. Ibid., 143.

85. Ibid., 142.

86. Waquet, "Qu'est-ce que la république des lettres?" 491.

87. Ibid. Cf. how necrologies allowed the registering of deaths occurring in different years on the page commemorating a particular day in the year. Armando Petrucci, *Writing the Dead: Death and Writing Strategies in the Western Tradition* (Stanford: Stanford University Press, 1998).

88. See Paolo Rossi, "Sulle origini dell'idea di progresso," in *Immagini della scienza*, quoted in Waquet, "Qu'est-ce que la république des lettres?" 490, and Elliott, *Old World*. See esp. ch. 2 of Elliott, *Old World,* 37ff., and Folder 4 below for an example of how "scientific" method can work in tandem with imperial politics.

89. Waquet, "Qu'est-ce que la république des lettres?" 481.

90. Ibid., 484. Waquet also paraphrases Erasmus, *De conscribendis epistolis* (490): "Rien ne pouvait ruiner un tel corps;" and cites Richelieu (484), who defined the Republic of Letters as "tous les gens de lettres en gros. C'est le corps des gens de lettres."

91. Ibid., 490 (Waquet is paraphrasing Erasmus) and 488–89 (Waquet is citing Chapelain's 1652 letter to Nicolas Heinsius, written amid the war and anarchy then reigning in Paris).

92. The day of the wedding was not an auspicious one, as it coincided with a solar eclipse. But Alessandro disdained those who believed that the disposition of the heavens had anything to do with earthly affairs. Lorenzino had given thought to the wedding festivities of the duke as a possible occasion for murdering the duke. The marriage of Alessandro to Margherita d'Austria, the daughter of Charles V, took place in June of 1536, and Lorenzino's gift was his play, the *Aridosia*. As director, producer, and designer of the sets, Lorenzino fantasized making a faulty design and causing the set to cave in, killing all the spectators. But this plan didn't work out. See Nerli, *Commentari*, bk. 12, 2:238: "e benchè s'usasse molta diligenza, perchè quella solennità si facesse in buon punto, ad ogni modo spregiando il duca quella qualunque si sia osservazione della disposizione de' cieli, si fecero quelle nozze intorno all'eclisse del Sole,

cosa, che in quel tempo fu assai notata e molto biasimata." See Nulli, *L'emulo di Bruto*, 113.

93. See Federico Chabod, *Lo stato e la vita religiosa a Milano nell'epoca di Carlo V* (Turin: Einaudi, 1971), 11, 19. See also the draft of a proclamation to the magistrates of Cremona, advising them to be on the lookout for deserters to the French cause. CSM, folder 18, April 19, 1537: "Essendo pervenuto a nostra notitia che in molti loci del stato di Milano se fanno diverse pratiche per levare fanti in servitio di franza."

94. Regarding reports of mutinies, see, for example, CSM, folder 16, "Ammutinamento degli Spagnoli," and CSM, folder 20, 95, Filippo Archinto, governor of Rome, to Caracciolo, July 18, 1537: "Molta gente de Infanteria spagnola passa per Roma ... per manchamento de pagha et st[r]ettezza del vivere li piu arditi soldati de ditta natione, intendendo che in lombardia li lor compagni di essa natione per via de mutino riccaveno cio che voleno, si sono disposti contra tutti li editti del vicerè fugirsene alla volta del campo in lombardia.... Del che ne seguono dui desordini grandi, l'uno abbandonare il Regno in tempo de tanto bisogno, l'altro ad augmentare il desordine in lombardia ... uno de questi soldati ... me certificava gia erano piu de $^m/_2$ [due mila] li fugiti et sbandati et ogn'hora piu crescevano."

95. Chabod, *Lo stato*, 52–53 and n. 2, quotes this letter of November 25, 1537, from Gómez Suárez de Figueroa, Spanish ambassador in Genova, to Caracciolo (ASM, Doc. dipl., 23 [I°] f. 322). See also Federico Chabod, *Storia di Milano nell'epoca di Carlo V* (Turin: Einaudi, 1961), ch. 3, "Oro di Milano, oro di Castiglia, oro d'America"; and Elliott, *Old World*, 82, who quotes a letter of 1570 from the governor of Milan to Philip II: "These Italians, although they are not Indians, have to be treated as such, so that they will understand that we are in charge of them and not they in charge of us."

96. Rosa, "I depositi," 183.

97. Herodotus 5.92: και εκολουε αιει οκως τινα ιδοι των ασταχυων υπερεχοντα, translated as *Herodoto Alicarnaseo Historico delle guerre de Greci et de Persi* by Mattheo Maria Boiardo (Venetia, 1533), 178: "Percotea con una verga tutte le belle spiche che l'altre sopra avanzavano" ("With a rod, he was striking all of the best ears of grain that grew above the others").

98. Aristotle *Politics* 3.8.

99. φασι γαρ τον περιανδρου ειπειν μεν ουδεν ... αφαιρουντα δε τους υπερεχοντας των σταχυων ομακυσαι την αρουραν; translated as *Gli otto libri della republica che chiamono politica di Aristotile* by Antonio Brucioli (Venetia: Alessandro Brucioli e i frategli, 1547), 64v. The reference to Dionysius comes from Antonio Brucioli, *Dialogi* (Vinegia: Gregorio, 1526), bk. 1, dialogue 7, li.

100. Livy *Ab urbe condita* 1.54, translated as *Le deche di T. Livio Padovano delle historie romane* by Iacopo Nardi (Venetia: Nella stamperia degli heredi di Luc'Antonio Giunti Fiorentino, 1547), 17: "si dice, che con una bacchetta, andava abbattendo, et gettando a terra, i piu belli, et sopra gli altri eminenti capi d'i papaveri, che vi fussero ... Sesto, poscia che sotto sifatti occulti segni, comprese chiaramente la volonta et consiglio del padre, uccise tutti i principali cittadini della terra."

101. Machiavelli, referring to tyrants, tended to prefer the term *principe* to *signore* or *tiranno*.

102. Girolamo Savonarola, "Trattato circa el reggimento e governo della città di Firenze," in *Prediche sopra Aggeo con il Trattato circa el reggimento e governo della città di Firenze*, ed. Luigi Firpo (Rome: Angelo Belardetti, 1965), tr. 2, ch. 2.

103. Filippo Cavriani, *Discorsi del signor Filippo Cavriana Sopra i primi 5 libri di Tacito* (Florence: Filippo Giunti, 1597), 522. Here *Aristobolo* represents a slightly altered memory of *Trasibolo*.

104. Gabriel Naudé, *Considérations politiques sur les coups d'état*, with an introductory essay by Louis Marin (Paris: Ed. de Paris, 1989), 52.

105. The numerous references to this motif include Frontinus *Stratagemata* 1.1.4; Diogenes Laertius *Lives of Eminent Philosophers* 1.7.100; Ovid *Fasti* 2.703–7; Valerius Maximus, *Dei detti et fatti memorabili*, trans. Giorgio Dati (Rome: Antonio Blado d'Asola, 1539), 8.4.

106. Francesco Maria Molza, "Orazione contro Lorenzino de' Medici," in *Lorenzino de' Medici, Scritti e documenti per la prima volta raccolti*, ed. Carlo Téoli (Milan: G. Daelli e comp., 1862), 138. Statues are important in narratives of tyrannicide. Pliny tells us that the first statues or images of the tyrant-slayers, Harmodius and Aristogiton, appeared in Athens in the year 509 B.C., the same year in which the Tarquins were expelled from Rome (Pliny *Natural History* 34.8.17). The appearance of statues, far from announcing the birth of an image, represents the codification of that image (or story), an organization of already existing fragmentary details.

In December 1476, before slaying Galeazzo Maria Sforza, the Duke of Milan, Giovannandrea Lampognano, "turned to a statue of Saint Ambrose and said: 'O patron of our city, you know our intention and the reason we want to put ourselves in so much danger'" ("si volse ad una statua di S. Ambrogio e disse: 'O padrone di questa nostra città, tu sai la intenzione nostra e il fine a che noi voliamo metterci a tanti pericoli'"). Machiavelli, *Istorie fiorentine*, 7.34.

Donatello's statue of Judith about to cut off the head of Holofernes used to stand in the house of Piero de' Medici. But some months after Charles VIII invaded Italy and forced the Medici to leave Florence (November, 1494), the statue was removed and placed near Michelangelo's David outside the Palazzo della Signoria. One can still read today the words inscribed for the occasion: "The citizens placed the statue here as a sign of their public safety" ("Exemplum Salutis Publicae Cives posuere"). See Giorgio Vasari, *Le vite de' più eccellenti pittori scultori ed architettori* (Florence: Sansoni, 1878), 2:405. This episode is cited by Jacob Burckhardt, *The Civilization of the Renaissance in Italy* (New York: Harper and Row, 1958), 1:79. Every threat to the public safety is concentrated in the tyrant's head and eliminated by means of his decapitation. Perhaps the Florentines thought that after the expulsion of the Medici the removal of Donatello's *Judith and Holofernes* to a site of public significance would have an apotropaic effect and keep the Medici away. Sometimes statues are addressed. Sometimes they appear in dreams. Sometimes they speak. Sometimes they are mutilated. Sometimes they are moved. But almost always they are involved in expressing the intention and the reason of what is about to take place: the liberation of a city from the tyrant.

One morning in 1534, Romans woke up to find several ancient statues of the Arch of Constantine (and other areas of Rome) headless. Pope Clement, enraged by this act of vandalism, commanded that the author of the crime be immediately hanged without trial. Cardinal Ippolito de' Medici, suspecting his cousin Lorenzino, defended him, saying that Lorenzino was just a crazy youngster and that, in the tradition of his forefathers, he was obsessed with antiquity. With great effort, he was able to check the pope's anger, calling Lorenzino a disgrace and shame to his family. Varchi, *Storia fiorentina*, bk. 15, 5:266: "Trovandosi una mattina nell'arco di Costantino, e in altri luoghi di Roma molte figure antiche senza le loro teste, Clemente montò in tanta collera, che comandò che chiunche fosse colui, che tagliate l'avesse, eccettuato solo il cardinal de' Medici, dovesse esser subitamente senz'altro processo appiccato per la gola; il qual cardinale andò a scusare al Papa Lorenzo come giovane, e desideroso, secondo il costume de' loro maggiori, di cotali anticaglie, e con gran fatica potè raffrenar l'ira sua, chiamandolo l'infamia, e 'l vituperio della casa de' Medici." Perhaps, Lorenzino was here "imitating" what he had read in Thucydides, bk. 6, about Alcibiades' mutilation of the Hermae.

In any case, Lorenzino managed to escape from Rome with two official proclamations issued against him. "Lorenzino can never again set foot in Rome," proclaimed the city council. "Whoever kills Lorenzino in Rome will not be punished but rewarded," proclaimed the Roman Senate. And Francesco Maria Molza, a man of great eloquence and wisdom in Greek, Latin, and Tuscan letters, delivered an oration against Lorenzino in the Roman academy, cutting him to the quick in Latin to the best of his knowledge and abilities: "This predator of monuments . . . this public thief of memory . . . has profaned the gods" (ibid., 266–67). [S'ebbe nondimeno a partir di Roma Lorenzo, ed ebbe due bandi pubblici, uno dai Caporioni, che non potesse stare in Roman mai più, l'altro dal senatore, che chiunche l'uccidesse in Roma, non solo non dovesse esser punito, ma premiato; e messer Francesco Maria Molza uomo di grand'eloquenza e giudicio nelle lettere Greche, Latine e Toscane, gli fece un'orazion contra nell'accademia Romana, trafiggendolo latinamente quanto seppe e potette il più.]

Molza characterized Lorenzino's escapade as the work of a "parricide" ("parricida"). At the same time, he likened Lorenzino to a tyrant. His "unbridled lust" ("sfrenata libidine") for antiquities had left the city poisoned and "contaminated by so many rapes, so much pimping and adultery" ("da tanti stupri, da tanta ruffaneria, da adulterj contaminata"). For Molza, Lorenzino had violated sacred rites ("violò i riti più sacri") and made mock of the Roman deities ("gli stessi Dei immortali restarono profanati"), and the Roman Academy needed to work quickly to "cut back this pestiferous plant so that it would no longer creep and grow wildly" ("questa pestifera pianta, acciocchè più lungamente non serpa e transcorra, recidete per tempo")! But Molza's warning went unheeded, and Lorenzino was allowed to continue growing "wild" ("orrida fiera"). Molza, "Orazione," 138–39, 146–49.

Lorenzino, according to Giovio's account, felt himself "pierced in every part of his body" by Molza's venomous attack. He was beside himself with a shame that produced such intense pain he knew he would never find relief. So he decided to do something even more monstrous. The greatness he would achieve by slaying the duke might cover the ignominious stain on his honor he had incurred from the statue scandal (Giovio, *Istorie,* bk. 38, 2:510). ["Egli, sentendosi d'ogni parte trafitto da queste armi velenose, et per la vergogna, che si gli levava contra, sentendo insanabil dolore [suoque pudore excito insanabilem sentiens dolorem], prese un consiglio, veramaente assai più scelerato del primo . . . per oscurare, et coprire con la novità et grandezza di questo la fama, ch'era già scorsa per tutto di quello altro."] Cf. Paolo Giovio, *Le iscrittioni poste sotto le vere imagini de gli huomini famosi le quali a Como nel Museo del Giovio si veggiono,* trans. Hippolito Orio Ferrarese (Florence: Lorenzo Torrentino, 1552), 199: "Lorenzo usci talmente di se stesso temendo, che l'oratione fattagli contra da costui non gli fosse d'eterno biasmo, et per la vergogna del fatto; che con l'animo colmo d'amarezza et di crudeltà, si consigliò di voler'uccidere il Duca di Firenze suo amico singolare, per vedere di cancellare con la novità di tanta sceleragine l'ignominiosa macchia, che per ciò egli portava nell'honor suo."

Archaeological guidebooks of Rome do not give any explicit clues to understanding the statue scandal. The Arch of Constantine, they say, was one of the "least offended" ("manco offeso") of the Roman monuments, one of the best preserved against the destructiveness of time and barbarians. Still, the sculptures of the prisoners used to have heads ("si veggono i prigioni . . . iquali haveano la testa"). Bernardo Gamucci, *Le antichita della citta di Roma* (Venice: Giovanni Farisco, 1580), 48. Giovio (*Istorie,* bk. 38, 2:510) noted that Lorenzino, before fleeing Rome, had "buried the booty" ("sotterrato ch'egli hebbe la preda") of his reckless escapade. See, among others, Filippo de' Rossi, *Ritratto di Roma antica* (Rome: F. Moneta, 1645), 173; Stefano du Perac, *I vestigi dell'antichità di Roma raccolti et ritratti in perspettiva* (Rome: Carlo Losi, 1773), table 16. I was unable to find, either in the Archivio di Stato or in the Archivio Storico Capitolino of Rome, any trace of the public proclamations against Lorenzino. Carlo Ginzburg generously shared the news of an archaeologist who had discovered some inscriptions on the top of the Arch of Constantine. Cf. Rosaria Punzi, "Fonti documentarie per una rilettura delle vicende post-antiche dell'arco di Costantino," in *Arco di Costantino tra archeologia e archeometria,* ed. Patrizio Pensabene and Clementina Panella, 2nd ed. (Rome: "L'Erma" di Bretschneider, 2001).

107. Shakespeare, *The Tragedy of Richard the Second,* Folger Library General Reader's Shakespeare (New York: Pocket Books, 1962). Cf. also Kierkegaard, who introduces *Fear and Trembling* with this epigraph from Johann Georg Hamann: "What Tarquinius Superbus spoke in his garden with the poppies was understood by his son, but not by the messenger." Soren Kierkegaard, *Fear and Trembling and The Sickness unto Death,* trans. and introd. Walter Lowrie (New York: Doubleday Anchor Books, 1954).

108. Cf. Hayden White, "Method and Ideology in Intellectual History: The Case of Henry Adams," in *Modern European Intellectual History: Reappraisals and New Perspectives,* ed. Dominick LaCapra and Steven L. Kaplan (Ithaca: Cornell University Press, 1982), 288, reprinted as "The Context in the Text: Method and Ideology in Intellectual History," in Hayden White, *The Content of the Form: Narrative Discourse and Historical Representation* (Baltimore: Johns Hopkins University Press, 1987).

109. *Humanism* is understood here in a technical sense as a term for the particular activities of editing, reproducing, studying, and transmitting classical texts performed by scholars of Greek and Latin literature in fifteenth- and sixteenth-century Italy. It is my understanding that our modernday humanistic activities are descended from those of the first humanists, even when we focus our attention on nonclassical literature. See, in particular, Augusto Campana, "The Origin of the Word 'Humanist,'" *Journal of the Warburg and Courtauld Institutes* 9 (1946): 60–73, and Paul Oskar Kristeller, *Renaissance Thought: The Classic, Scholastic, and Humanist Strains* (New York: Harper and Row, 1961). Here I use the term *class* to refer to the group of individual subjects who understand the code of humanism to be "natural" and not specific to their own social practices. See Althusser, "Ideology," 170–77, and White, "Method and Ideology," 289. For a social history of fifteenth-century Florentine humanists, see Lauro Martines, *The Social World of the Florentine Humanists, 1390–1460* (London: Routledge and Kegan Paul, 1963). For a more extended examination of the relation between this specific topos of the tyrant in the field and humanistic scholarly practices, see Stephanie Jed, "The Scene of Tyranny: Violence and the Humanistic Tradition," in *The Violence of Representation: Literature and the History of Violence*, ed. Nancy Armstrong and Leonard Tennenhouse (London: Routledge, 1989), 29–44.

110. For this relation between sign systems and Peirce's concept of the "self-analyzing habit," see Teresa de Lauretis, *Alice Doesn't: Feminism, Semiotics, Cinema* (Bloomington: Indiana University Press, 1984), 158–86.

111. Piccolomini to Caracciolo, May 30, 1537, CSM, folder 20, 146.

112. Lope de Soria to Caracciolo, January 5, 1537, CSM, folder 12, 137.

113. Lope de Soria to Caracciolo, January 15, 1537, CSM, folder 12, 146; "entiendo que andaran vestidos a la Italiana."

114. Ibid., 147. Parts of this letter were written in cipher (here indicated by brackets) and deciphered in the Cancelleria.

115. CSM, folder 12, 140.

116. Ibid.

117. Much later, another "functionary" of Duke Cosimo and Charles V, Francesco Bibboni, will be out and about in Venice looking for an opportunity to kill Lorenzino (and finding that opportunity on March 13, 1547). See "Morte di Lorenzo, di Pier Francesco de' Medici: Racconto tratto da una relazione del Capitano Francesco Bibboni che l'uccise," in Carlo Morbio, ed., *Codice Visconteo-Sforzesco, ossia Raccolta di leggi, decreti e lettere famigliari dei duchi di Milano* (Milan: Società Tipografica de' Classici Italiani, 1846), 527–29.

118. Lope de Soria to Caracciolo, January 5, 1537, CSM, folder 12, 135.

119. See, in particular, Antonio Alvarez-Ossorio Alvariño, "The State of Milan and the Spanish Monarchy," in *Spain in Italy: Politics, Society, and Religion, 1500–1700*, ed. John Marino and Thomas Dandelet (Leiden: Brill, 2007); and Gian Luigi Beccaria, *Spagnolo e spagnoli in Italia: Riflessi ispanici sulla lingua italiana del Cinque e del Seicento* (Turin: Giappichelli, 1968).

120. Bernal Díaz del Castillo, *Historia verdadera de la conquista de la Nueva España*, ed. Joaquín Ramírez Cabañas, 2 vols. (Mexico City: Editorial Porrúa, 1960), 1:260; Bernal Díaz del Castillo, *The Discovery and Conquest of Mexico,*

1517–1521, ed. and introd. Irving Leonard, trans. A. P. Maudslay (New York: Farrar, Straus and Giroux, 1979), quoted in Irving A. Leonard, *Books of the Brave: Being an Account of Books and Men in the Spanish Conquest and Settlement of the Sixteenth-Century New World*, introd. Rolena Adorno (1949; repr., Berkeley: University of California Press, 1992), 43.

121. In particular, the studies of Leonard, Rabasa, and Alvar present a compelling argument that literary fantasies of knights errant, Amazon kingdoms, and enchanted islands "exerted a profound influence on contemporary conduct, morality and thought patterns." Leonard, *Books of the Brave*, 13–14. Compare Leonard, introduction to Díaz del Castillo, *Discovery and Conquest*, xi–xviii; José María Rabasa, "Fantasy, Errancy and Symbolism in New World Motifs: An Essay on Sixteenth Century Spanish Historiography," PhD diss., University of California, Santa Cruz, 1985; Manuel Alvar, "Fantastic Tales and Chronicles of the Indies," in *Amerindian Images and the Legacy of Columbus*, ed. René Jara and Nicholas Spadaccini (Minneapolis: University of Minnesota Press, 1992), 163–82. I was fascinated to observe that in the Marciana Library one nineteenth-century librarian suppressed this social-historical connection between the literary topoi of chivalry and the conquest of the New World by extracting materials pertaining to geography and the New World from their original context among chivalric verses and verses pertaining to European wars. For vicissitudes of the Venetian archives during the periods of Napoleonic and Austrian occupation, see Claudio Povolo, *Il romanziere e l'archivista: Da un processo veneziano del'600 all'anonimo manoscritto dei Promessi sposi* (Venice: Istituto Veneto di Scienze, Lettere ed Arti, 1993).

122. Leonard, introduction to Díaz del Castillo, *Discovery and Conquest*, xiv; Leonard, *Books of the Brave*, 20–21, 25–26.

123. Gonzalo Fernández de Oviedo, *Historia general y natural de las Indias*, ed. Juan Pérez de Tudela Bueso (Madrid: Atlas, 1959), bk. 2, ch. 7, 2:32. I first became interested in this anecdote when I read of it in Elliott, *Old World*, 32–38. For an excitingly original and important reading of Oviedo in relation to literary and colonial discourses, see Roland Greene, "Petrarchism among the Discourses of Imperialism," in *America in European Consciousness, 1493–1750*, ed. Karen Kupperman (Chapel Hill: University of North Carolina Press, 1995). For another reading of this episode of the iguana in a different context, see Stephanie Jed, "The Tenth Muse: Gender, Rationality and the Marketing of Knowledge," in *Women, "Race," and Writing in the Early Modern Period*, ed. Margo Hendricks and Patricia Parker (London: Routledge, 1994), 195–208, reprinted in *Feminism and Renaissance Studies*, ed. Lorna Hutson (London: Oxford University Press, 1999). I am especially grateful to Watson Branch, who, when he heard me speak of Oviedo's perception that the iguana lived on dirt, identified the bits of Old World knowledge that this story articulated and generously shared these connections: (1) When asked by the king how he was faring, Hamlet responds (act 3, scene 2): "Excellent, i' faith; of the chameleon's dish: I eat the air"; (2) Sir Thomas Browne, in *Pseudodoxia epidemica*, 6th ed. (1672), bk. 3, ch. 21, writes of the chameleon: "There generally passeth an opinion that it liveth only upon air, and is sustained by no other aliment" (http://penelope.uchicago.edu/pseudodoxia/pseudo321.html); and (3) Edmund Goldsmid cites,

in his *Un-Natural History, or Myths of Ancient Science* (Edinburgh, 1886), Isaac Schoockius's 1680 tract "On Chameleons," which refutes Pliny's and Tertullian's understanding that the chameleon lived on air (http://web.archive.org/web/20051221164921/www.herper.com/ebooks/library/biofort/AncientMyths.pdf).

124. Oviedo, *Historia general*, bk. 12, ch. 7, 2:35.

125. Here, I borrow Dorothy Smith's interpretive approach in *Texts, Facts and Femininity*, 21–28.

126. This dynamic was characterized, in general, by a tension between the standardizing effects of the imperial bureaucracy and the diversity of cultures within its jurisdiction. The exacerbation of these cultural and economic differences within Europe was such as to provoke (decades later) the Spaniard Cristóbal Suárez de Figueroa to lament that because of imperial dependence on Genoese bankers, Spain had become "the Indies of the Genoese." Elliott, *Old World*, 96.

127. Marica Milanesi, introduction to Giovanni Battista Ramusio, *Navigazioni e viaggi*, ed. Marica Milanesi, 6 vols. (Turin: Einaudi, 1978–85), 1:xxi.

128. Ibid., xxiii.

129. Cf. Daniel Defert, "The Collection of the World: Accounts of Voyages from the Sixteenth to the Eighteenth Centuries," *Dialectical Anthropology*, 7, no. 1 (1982): 16.

130. Antonello Gerbi, *Nature in the New World: From Christopher Columbus to Gonzalo Fernández de Oviedo*, trans. Jeremy Moyle (Pittsburgh: University of Pittsburgh Press, 1985), 152–53, 201–4.

131. Ibid., 169. For a different treatment of the episode of the iguana, see Elliott, *Old World*, 32–38.

132. Cited in Gerbi, *Nature*, 412–13, and in Ramusio, *Navigazioni e viaggi*, 2:961.

133. Ramusio, *Navigazioni e viaggi*, 2:962.

134. For background and bibliography on "Lamenti" and other genres of nonerudite verses, see Arnaldo Segarizzi, *Bibliografia delle stampe popolari italiane* (Bergamo: Istituto Italiano di Arti Grafiche, 1913); Caterina Santoro, ed., *Stampe popolari della Biblioteca Trivulziana* (Milan: Castello Sforzesco, 1964); Alberto Di Mauro and Alessandro Gregorio Capponi, *Bibliografia delle stampe popolari profane dal fondo Capponi della Bibiloteca Vaticana* (Florence: Olschki, 1981). These nonerudite verses represented Alessandro as being at his own state funeral, denouncing Lorenzino's act of betrayal and addressing Charles V and each and every Florentine who remained loyal after his assassination. Nonerudite publications also represented Alessandro in stories and anecdotes as a just ruler. See Alessandro Ceccheregli, *Delle attioni et sentenze del S. Alessandro de' Medici primo duca di Fiorenza* (Venice: Gabriel Giolito de' Ferrari, 1564), reprinted in *Scelta di curiosità letterarie inedite o rare dal secolo XIII al XVII*, Dispensa 66 (Bologna: Gaetano Romagnoli, 1865).

135. Lorenzo Ghibellini da Prato, *Il lamento che fa in fra se Lorenzino de' Medici che amazzò l'iIllustrissimo Signor Alessandro de Medici Duca primo di Fiorenza* (Florence: Giovanni Baleni, 1584).

136. Ibid. Cf. Timothy Hampton, "'Turkish Dogs': Rabelais, Erasmus, and

the Rhetoric of Alterity," *Representations* 41 (1993): 58–82. My thanks to Prof. Margit Frenk for referring me to the following study of the phenomenon of renouncing Christian faith: Lucia Rostagno, *Mi faccio turco: Esperienze ed immagini dell'islam nell'Italia moderna* (Rome: Istituto per l'Oriente C. A. Nallino, 1983).

137. The connection between the "heads" of grain and the human head—be it a head of state or a head of a citizen—is not a casual one. For the head of state, cf. Savonarola, "Trattato," tr. 2, ch. 1, 453: "li membri vanno drieto al capo, e con gran difficultà insurgono contra il capo. E nel governo del tiranno è molto difficile a fare uno capo contra di lui: però che lui sempre vigila a spegnere li uomini che poteriano fare capo." The very term for brain, *cerebrum*, and the name of the goddess of corn and fertility, Ceres, share the same Old Latin root, *cereo* (later *creo*, to create). And according to Greek tradition, the head was the storehouse of seed. For the Greeks, the soul and the seed of new life were in the head, just as humans were likened to corn in the mysteries of Eleusis. Cf. Richard Broxton Onians, *The Origins of European Thought* (New York: Arno Press, 1973), 125–26: "The flower or fruit of a plant, i.e. what contained the seed, was called its 'head.' Thus Homer describes a warrior wounded: 'As in a garden a poppy droops aside its head . . . being heavy with fruit and the moisture of spring, so [the wounded warrior] bowed he aside his head laden with the helmet." Earth produced for Demeter's daughter, "the flower-faced maid," a wondrous narcissus, and from its root "grew a hundred heads." Onians, *Origins of European Thought*, 113–15, referring to Homer *Iliad* 8.306ff, and *Hymn to Demeter* 8ff.

The Florentines connected the political head with a vegetal image. The term *cipolla* (onion) was used to mean the head of a person in the context of decapitation, as in "They cut off the onion of Mr. Donato del Ricco" ("A messer Donato del Ricco fu tagliata la cipolla"), Giovanni di Pagolo Morelli, *Ricordi*, ed. Vittore Branca (Florence: Le Monnier, 1956), 326; or "Make him place his onion by his feet" ("Di fargli porre a' piedi la cipolla"), Lorenzo Lippi, *Il Malmantile racquistato* (Venice: Antonio Zatta e figli, 1788), 5.48, quoted in *Grande Dizionario della Lingua Italiana* (Turin: UTET, 1961–78), vol. 3, "cipolla." My thanks to Prof. Margit Frenk for bringing this detail to my attention.

138. Timoleon received signs from Ceres and Persephone that they would protect him and his project to liberate Syracuse from tyranny (Plutarch, *Life of Timoleon*). The murder of the democratizing Gracchi brothers was understood as a desecration of the Roman temple dedicated to Ceres, and the Sybilline books advised the Romans to placate the venerated Ceres in whatever way they could (Valerius Maximus *Factorum et dictorum memorabilium, libri novem* 1.1). Cassius condemned his own son for aspiring to tyranny. He had him beaten and killed and then consacrated all of his possessions to Ceres (5.8). And Nero was mistaken in his feeling of security on the day of Ceres' festival, leaving his own garden and going to the games without a guard. For Scevino carried a "sacred dagger" ("pugionem sacrum") for the assault, and Pisone waited at the temple of Ceres for a signal to call the Romans to freedom (Tacitus *Gli annali* 15).

139. Niccolò Machiavelli, *Discorsi sopra la prima Deca di Tito Livio*, ed.

Sergio Bertelli (Milan: Feltrinelli, 1981), 3.6: "Un'altra cagione ci è ... che fa gli uomini congiurare contro al principe, la quale è il desiderio di liberare la patria stata da quello occupata. Questa cagione mosse Bruto e Cassio contro a Cesare; questa ha mosso molti altri contro a' Falari, Dionisii ed altri occupatori della patria loro. Né può da questo omore alcuno tiranno guardarsi, se non con diporre la tirannide. E perché non si truova alcuno che faccia questo, si truova pochi che non capitino male; donde nacque quel verso di Iuvenale:

Ad generum Cereris sine caede et vulnere pauci
descendunt reges et sicca morte tiranni."

Mario Bonfantini's 1963 Ricciardi edition reads: "Né può da questo amore alcuno tiranno guardarsi." The verses of Juvenal are as cited in the Feltrinelli text and come from Satire 10.112–13.

140. Juvenal, *Saturae*, with commentaries by Domizio Calderino and Giorgio Valla (Venetia: Theodorus de Ragazonibus, 1491). The "sine caede et sanguine" variant quoted by Calderino and Valla is also recorded by W. V. Clausen, the editor of the Oxford edition of Juvenal (*A. Persi Flacci et D. Iuni Iuvenalis "Saturae"* [Oxford: Clarendon Press, 1959]). Salutati, in *Il trattato "De tyranno"* (17), had reframed these same lines of Juvenal into a discussion of the frequency of such murders, conferring upon them a sort of proverbial status. Salutati also cites the "sine caede et sanguine" variant, which seems to have been common in late antiquity. In his commentary on Virgil's *Georgics* 2.498, Servius also transmits the "sine caede et sanguine" variant and lays the groundwork for the reception of these verses as a maxim: "licet alii dictum hoc velint ex generali venire sententia, quod omnis magnitudo imperii periculis subiacet, unde etiam Iuvenalis ait ad generum Cereris sine caede et sanguine pauci descendunt reges et sicca morte tiranni." Servius, *Servii grammatici qui feruntur in Vergilii Bucolica et Georgica commentarii*, ed. Georgius Thilo (Hildesheim: Georg Olms, 1961), vol. 3, pt. 1, 266–67.

141. Marc Shell, *The Economy of Literature* (Baltimore: Johns Hopkins University Press, 1978), 12–13.

142. Benvenuto Cellini, *La vita di Benvenuto di M. Giovanni Cellini fiorentino scritta (per lui medesimo) in Firenze*, ed. Carlo Cordié (Milan: Ricciardi, 1960), 669–87: At the time of Alessandro's assassination, Benvenuto Cellini was making a medal portraying the duke. Lorenzino was always present when Cellini came to call upon his patron. Cellini invited him to collaborate in the design of the object: "Messer Lorenzo, here, since he is so learned and so creative, will give me some ideas for a terrific reverse of the medal" ("Misser Lorenzo qui mi darà qualche bellissimo rovescio come persona dotta e di grandissimo ingegno"). Lorenzino was delighted to accept the invitation and responded in Sybilline language about an earth-shaking idea he had for this "reverse": "I am unable to think about anything else besides coming up with a reverse that will be worthy of his Excellency. . . . I will figure it out as soon as I can, and I hope to do something which will amaze the world." ("Io non pensavo a altro se non a darti un rovescio che fussi degno di sua eccellenza. . . . Io lo farò il più presto ch'io posso, e spero far cosa da far maravigliare il mondo.")

Because Lorenzino took somewhat longer than expected, Cellini wrote to a friend in Florence, Niccolò da Monte Aguto, asking him to remind Lorenzino of his promise. Niccolò responded that when he asked "that crazy, melancholy philosopher Lorenzino" ("quel pazzo malinconico filosofo di Lorenzino") about the project, Lorenzino reiterated that "day and night, he thought of nothing else and that he would do it as soon as he possibly could" ("giorno e notte non pensava ad altro e che egli lo farebbe più presto ch'egli avesse possuto").

A "learned and creative" Lorenzino became, in the minds of people who knew him, "that crazy, melancholy philosopher Lorenzino." His delay aroused suspicion in those who distrusted him. Was he just awaiting the appropriate moment for slaying the duke? Sure enough, when the appropriate moment arrived, Lorenzino's act erupted upon the scene as the "most beautiful reverse" he had promised.

Cellini was having a pleasant dinner with friends in Rome when the news arrived of the death of the duke. Right then, an ugly she-mule came leaping by with Francesco Soderini on her back. Laughing loudly and wildly in the street, he said: "This is what your Lorenzino promised you, the reverse of that evil tyrant's medal." ("Così passatoci la cena piacevolmente, l'altro giorno al tardi venne la nuova a Roma della morte del duca Lessandro. . . . In questo veniva a saltacchione in su una mulettaccia quel misser Francesco Soderini. Ridendo per la via forte all'mpazzata, diceva:—Quest'è il rovescio della medaglia di quello iscellerato tiranno, che t'aveva promesso il tuo Lorenzino de' Medici.")

Concerning the tax on grain, see Segni, *Storie fiorentine*, bk. 8, 2:120.

143. Melissa Meriam Bullard, *Filippo Strozzi and the Medici: Favor and Finance in Sixteenth-Century Florence and Rome* (Cambridge: Cambridge University Press, 1980), 161. See also Alessandro Bardi, "Filippo Strozzi (da Nuovi Documenti)," *Archivio storico italiano*, 5th ser., 14 (1894): 3–78.

144. Strozzi's open opposition to the duke, the emperor's son-in-law, must have been an important motivating factor in the imperial embargo.

145. Bullard, *Filippo Strozzi*, 163.

146. Ibid., 164–65.

147. See Varchi, *Storia fiorentina*, bk. 14, 5:60. This connection between Strozzi and Perillo was also noted by Nulli, *L'emulo di Bruto*, 33. Cf. also Lorenzino, who wrote in his "Apologia" (*Apologia e lettere,* 208–9) that Alessandro "superò la crudeltà di Falari di gran lunga; perchè dove Falari punì con giusta pena Perillo del crudele invento per tormentare e far morire gli uomini miseramente nel Toro di bronzo, si può credere che Alessandro l'avrebbe premiato ... poi che lui medesimo escogitava e trovava nuove sorte di tormenti e di morti, come murare gli uomini vivi in luoghi così angusti, che non si potessino nè voltare nè muovere."

148. Hayden White, "Method and Ideology," 306–7, writes: "Food, clothing, and shelter may be basic 'economic' necessities, but what is considered the *proper* kind of food, appropriate clothing, and humanly adequate shelter varies from culture to culture. Moreover the provision of these necessities in any given culture is governed by rules and laws which have their justification in an extra-economic domain, specifically that in which the meaning of what is to be considererd as proper, appropriate, is produced." This essay has been central to my interpretation of grain in historiography and commerce.

149. Machiavelli, *Discorsi*, 3.26. Livy *Ab urbe condita* 1.57–58. Cf. the translation of Livy "in lingua toscana" by Iacopo Nardi (*Le deche di T. Livio*).

150. Thucydides *The Peloponnesian War*, 6.54; a detailed summary of the sources for the history of Harmodius and Aristogiton is given by Sture Brunnsåker, *The Tyrant-Slayers of Kritios and Nesiotes: A Critical Study of the Sources and Restorations*, 2nd ed. (Stockholm: Svenska Institutet, 1971). Cf. the translation of Thucydides "in lingua Thoscana" by Francesco di Soldo Strozzi, *Gli otto libri di Thvcydide Atheniese delle guerre fatte* . . . (Venetia: Baldassar de Costantini, 1545).

151. Aristotle *Politics* 5.10. Cf. the translation of Aristotle "in vulgare italiano" by Brucioli, *Otto libri della repubblica*. Marcus Junianus Justinus, *Nelle historie di Trogo Pompeio. Nouamente in lingua toscana. tradotto: [et] con somma diligentia [et] cura stampato* (Venetia: N. Zopino e Vincentio, 1524), 15v–16.

152. Cf. Stephanie Jed, "Making History Straight: Collecting and Recording in Sixteenth-Century Italy," *Bucknell Review* 35, no. 2 (1992): 104–20.

153. Caracciolo to Ridolfi, Salviati, Strozzi (rough copy), January 14, 1537, CSM, folder 13, 417.

154. Suetonius *Life of Julius Caesar* 50. Cf. the translation of Suetonius "in lingua Toscana" by Rosso, *Le vite de dodici cesari*, 24: "Cesare . . . fu innamorato di Servilia di Marco Bruto"; "Terza figliuola di Servilia, della quale era opinione che essa Servilia ne havesse accomodato Cesare."

155. Salutati, *Il trattato "De tyranno,"* 36: "Et quod filius fuerit, qui sciunt Cesari cum matre Bruti lascivie fuisse consuetudinem, et qui legunt cesariana cede dictatorem, cum ipsum stricto in se videret gladio irruentem, dixisse grece, . . . 'καὶ σὺ τέκνον.'" Suetonius, *Le vite de dodici cesari*, 36 (Suetonius, *Life of Julius Caesar*, 82): "disse in greco a Marco Bruto, che gli correva addosso: Et tu figliuolo."

156. Machiavelli, *Discorsi*, 3.26: "Lo eccesso fatto contro a Lucrezia tolse lo stato ai Tarquinii; quell'altro, fatto contro a Virginia, privò i Dieci dell'autorità loro. Ed Aristotile intra le prime cause che mette della rovina de' tiranni, è lo avere ingiuriato altrui per conto delle donne o con stuprarle o con violarle o con rompere i matrimonii."

157. "Lust," in the humanistic tradition, was a requisite characteristic of tyrants and proof of their tyranny. As we saw, the first term Machiavelli used to describe Galeazzo Maria was *libidinoso* (*Istorie*, 7.33; cf. p. 41 and n. 62 above). According to Cicero, *libido* is that *cupiditas effrenata* which is characterized by irrationality and violence and which is best understood against the background of its opposite, the male-gendered "rational desire" (βούλησις or will) of the Stoics. See Cicero, *Tusculan Disputations* 4.6.12, quoted in Jung, *Symbols of Transformation*, trans. R. F. C. Hull (Princeton: Princeton University Press, 1967), 130 n. 24. It will take many centuries of women writing and theorizing to undermine the power of this rhetorical construct. Cf. Geneviève Fraisse, *Reason's Muse: Sexual Difference and the Birth of Democracy* (Chicago: University of Chicago Press, 1994), 10–11.

Of Augustine's various subcategories of libido, Jung tells us, some are characteristic of both the tyrant and his slayers: "There is a lust for revenge, which is called rage; a lust for having money, which is called avarice; a lust for victory at all costs, which is called stubbornness; a lust for self-glorification, which is called boastfulness. There are many and varied kinds of lust, some of which are specifically named, others not. For who could easily give a name to the lust for domination, which . . . is nevertheless very powerful in the minds of tyrants?" See Jung, *Symbols of Transformation*, 130.

Arrogance, or *superbia*, becomes the mother of lechery, when the tyrant is "cheered by others' disgraces. He would like to shame every man, so that glory belongs only to him. And because of the wild fantasies of wickedness and fears that eat him up inside, he looks for pleasures as salves for his afflictions. This is the reason tyrants are always lecherous and addicted to the pleasures of the flesh" (Savonarola, "Trattato," tr. 2, ch. 2, 456). ["Si allegra delle ignominie del prossimo per tal modo, che vorria che ogni uomo fussi vituperato, acciò che lui restassi glorioso. E per le gran fantasie e tristizie e timori, che sempre lo rodono dentro, cerca delettazioni come medicine delle sue afflizioni: e però si truova rare volte, o non forse mai, tiranno che non sia lussurioso e dedito alle delettazioni della carne"]. "Because of his arrogance, every citizen walks on tenterhooks. Because of his greed, everyone's wealth is up for grabs. Because of his lechery, the chastity and modesty of women are in danger. For every occasion, the tyrant retains pimps and panders who find various ways to trap other men's women and daughters. Often, in big banquet rooms, there are hidden passageways. The women, who don't realize what is happening, are lured down these passageways and caught in the trap; not to mention that the tyrant is, in many cases, addicted to sodomy, so that no good-looking boy is safe" (465). [Ogni cittadino sotto di lui sta in pendente per la sua superbia; ogni ricchezza sta in aria per la sua avarizia; ogni castità e pudicizia di donna sta in pericolo per la sua lussuria: e ha per tutto ruffiani e ruffiane, li quali per diversi modi le donne e figliuole d'altri conducono alla mazza, e massime nelli conviti grandi, dove molte volte nelle camere hanno vie occulte, dove son condotte le donne, che non se ne avedano, e ivi rimangano prese al laccio; lasciando stare la sodomia, alla quale è molte volte dedito per tal modo che non è garzone di qualche apparenza che sia sicuro.]

Alessandro's lust was as great as his faith in Lorenzino, whom he used as a pimp to get to all kinds of women—be they nuns or worldly women, maidens or married women, widows, noble or low-born women, young or elderly women (Varchi, *Storia fiorentina*, bk. 15, 5:267). ["Così colle donne religiose, come colle secolari, o pulzelle, o maritate, o vedove, o nobili, o ignobili, o giovani, o attempate, ch'elle si fossono."] Accompanied by Lorenzino, Alessandro would scale the walls of convents and feed his insatiable appetite inside. On the night of his death, they visited the Carmelite convent of Santa Maria degli Angeli, where Lorenzino's sisters happened to be staying while their mother tended her sick son Giuliano in the family villa at Cafaggiuolo. On that particular night, "by some chance," Alessandro was not permitted any escapades with nuns or lay guests of the convent. The walk back to the ducal palace was tiring, so they stopped in at Lorenzino's house for a rest and went up to his room, where he hoped to satisfy his desire with a particular noblewoman (Nardi, *Istorie della città*, bk. 10, 2:282). ["Trovandosi la madre di Lorenzo nella sua villa di Cafaggiuolo con Giuliano suo figliuolo minore ammalato, avendo lasciato due figliuole in serbanza nel munistero di santa maria degli Angeli dell'ordine Carmelitano, e trovandosi per questo la casa vacua e molto acconcia al suo disegno; e tornando il duca da quello monasterio nel quale ei teneva conversazione, over per certo accidente non aveva potuto quella notte avere l'entratura; e tornandosi dal detto luogo si perviene prima alla casa di Lorenzo che al palagio del duca; si che essendo stracco del loro cammino, e forse mal contento dell'animo, se ne entrò insieme con Lorenzo in casa e camera di quello."]

After Triton raped the bathing women at Tanagra, the citizens offered him large quantities of wine until he fell into a stupor. They cut off his head and displayed his headless body at the temple of Dionysus (Onians, *Origins of European Thought*, 111; reference given to Pausanias 9.20.4f.). We also find this connection between lust and drink in Aristotle, who warns tyrants about indulging in too much drink, "for a drunken and drowsy tyrant is soon despised and attacked; not so he who is temperate and wide awake" (Aristotle *Politics* 5.11.1314b). See also the Vulgate version of the Book of Judith (12:16, 13:3) in which Judith defends her honor against the burning desire of Holofernes (ardens in concupiscentia eius). Holofernes is so delighted at the pleasure of dining with Judith that he drinks more wine than he has ever drunk before. At the end of the evening, they remain alone in the tent, Holofernes lying in his bed in a drunken stupor ("nimia ebrietate sopitus"), Judith standing before him and praying that God may grant her courage to carry out her deed. Did Alessandro de' Medici drink to excess on his last evening of revelry? Historiographers focus less on the parties than on the lust that impaired Alessandro's reason. Lorenzino, like Judith, murdered a drowsy tyrant whom he had lulled to sleep in the expectation of sexual pleasure. Like Judith, he thought of cutting off the head of Alessandro to apprise the Florentines of their opportunity to take back the city from tyranny, but Lorenzino, in his "Apologia" (*Apologia e lettere*, 223–24), was worried that the Florentines would not believe him: "se io gli avessi levata la testa (chè quella si poteva celare sotto un mantello), dove avevo io a indirizzarmi.... Chi mi averebbe creduto? Perchè una testa tagliata si trasfigura tanto."

158. "Minuta al Signor Don Lupe," January 11, 1537, CSM, folder 12, 141 (mistakenly numbered 134).

159. Lope de Soria to Caracciolo, CSM, folder 12, 144.

160. Ibid.

161. Varchi, *Storia fiorentina*, bk. 14, 5:66.

162. Ibid., 5:67.

163. Ibid., 5:67–69.

164. Ibid., 5:74.

165. Landriano to Caracciolo, January 11, 1537, CSM, folder 13bis, 62.

166. Segni, *Storie fiorentine*, bk. 7, 2:66: "si disse allora, e poi s'ando verificando la fama, che il Duca, indegnato contro di lei, la fece avvelenare; perchè avendola pochi giorni innanzi a una festa richiestala dell'onor suo, gli dinegò, e ancora con parole villane, e seppesi, che il ministro di questa sceleratezza era stato Vincenzo Ridolfi figliuolo del Rosso, che con quelle donne cenando, aveva servito a questo empio uffizio per compiacere al Duca."

167. It might give us pause to notice that this type of "honor killing" is still reported in the news and only occasionally prosecuted as murder. See, for ex-

ample, Dan Bilefsky, "How to Avoid Honor Killing in Turkey? Honor Suicide," *New York Times,* July 16, 2006.

168. Varchi, *Storia fiorentina,* bk. 14, 5:106.

169. Ibid., 5:107. It would be interesting to trace the history of interest in Luisa Strozzi. In February 1827, Carlo Botta wrote to Gino Capponi, a touch exasperated that no one was able to tell him the truth of Luisa's death: "Possibile che non abbiate nulla da dirmi sulla Luisa, figliuola che fu di Filippo Strozzi e moglie di Luigi di Giuliano Capponi, cioè se sia stata fatta avvelenare dal duca Alessandro, o da' suoi parenti per sottrarla dalla libidine di esso Duca!" Capponi, *Lettere,* 1:213. In the 1840s, no fewer than four operas were composed (by Pietro Combi, Pietro Cotini, Antonio Ronzi, and Gualtiero Sanelli) to commemorate Luisa's story. See also Giovanni Rosini, *Luisa Strozzi: Storia del secolo XVI* (Pisa: Niccolò Capurro, 1833). It would seem that her story was significant for the production of nationalist culture.

170. Sanctio to Caracciolo, January 13, 1537, CSM, folder 12bis, 32.

171. Ibid., 33. Lorenzino, as we have seen, fashioned himself as a vindicator of the honor of a chaste noblewoman, and several commentators, recognizing this role, hailed him as a "new Brutus." A certain Frater G. D. (Donato Giannotti?) wrote from Rome on March 15, 1537, that Lorenzino was worthy of being called "Bruto secondo." He liked to say that, like Brutus, he was better at using books than arms ("io so meglio adoperare i libri, che l'arme"), and he preferred to teach Alessandro about power by sharing his knowledge of Tacitus ("usava ancora Lorenzo di dichiararli Cornelio Tacito mostrandoli la vita di quelli Imperatori, et ammaestravalo a conservarsi nello stato"). "A Paolo del Tosso," in Ruscelli, *Lettere di principi,* 3:163, 163v. Varchi (*Storia fiorentina,* bk. 15, 5:274) and Segni (*Storie fiorentine,* bk. 8, 2:132) reported that when Lorenzino arrived in Venice, Filippo Strozzi warmly received him, calling him "Brutus" ("Filippo . . . l'abbracciò, e chiamatolo lor Bruto") and "liberator of the state" ("chiamandolo per nome di Bruto e di liberatore della patria"). Others, like Filippo de' Nerli, Paolo Giovio, and Hortense Allart (as we shall see in Section Three of this book), focused more on the differences between Lorenzino and Brutus. Did Lorenzino slay the duke in order to "resemble liberators and Brutuses"? Or did so many examples from ancient and modern histories "drive him crazy"? Nerli, *Commentari,* bk. 12, 2:241: "E' da considerare in questo caso . . . o egli il fece per gloria e per assomigliarsi a' liberatori della patria ed a' Bruti, ed agli altri tanto dagli scrittori celebrati, che hanno con gli esempi loro già fatti impazzar molti, ed infiniti ne hanno fatti mal capitare, come ne sono piene di esempi le storie antiche e moderne." Giovio, *Istorie,* bk. 38, 2:509: "Alcuni altri . . . interpretavano d'altro modo, pensando loro, che Lorenzo non per disiderio di ritornare la sua patria in libertà, ma mosso da incredibil malignità et da pazzia di animo crudele si fosse condotto a fare quella ribalderia." Lucius Junius Brutus always hid the true nature of his character and pretended to be "crazy" until the right moment came for the liberation of Rome. Livy, *Le deche di T. Livio,* 17v (1.56): "Accommodatosi per tanto con l'imitatione alla mattezza: lasciando se medesimo, et l'altre sue cose in preda del Re, non rifiutò ancho d'essere chiamato Bruto: accio che nascondendosi sotto l'ombra di cotale cognome, quell'animo liberatore del popolo Romano, aspettasse il tempo suo."

Nardi translates the Latin phrase "ad imitationem stultitiae" as "l'imitatione alla mattezza." Shakespeare's Brutus took after his ancestor, this more ancient Brutus, when he said to Cassius: "Be not deceived. If I have veiled my look, / I turn the trouble of my countenance / Merely on myself." *Julius Caesar*, 1.2.43–45. Lorenzino also hid the true nature of his character. Segni, *Storie fiorentine*, bk. 8, 2:130: "solitario e di coperta natura." Plutarch's Marcus Brutus was psychologically unstable, of a "melancholy nature." Plutarch, *La Vita di Bruto*, in *Vite de Plutarco*, 217: "maninconico da natura." Lorenzino, a "learned and creative" man ("persona dotta e di grandissimo ingegno"), became, as we have seen, "that crazy melancholy philosopher" ("quel pazzo malinconico filosafo di Lorenzino") because he was so slow in making good on his promises. Cellini, *La vita*, 669, 685. Others also nicknamed Lorenzino "the Philosopher" because he was "ingenious, articulate, and serious, and he had a melancholy nature, a pale face, and a very sharp intellect" (Nerli, *Commentari*, bk. 12, 2:239). ["Di natura malinconico, nel viso pallido, di cervello acutissimo, e molto ingegnoso, di buona lingua, di grave aspetto, tantochè intra'giovani suoi pari . . . lo chiamavano come si dice per soprannome il Filosofo."] To go along with his melancholy nature, Lorenzino was "lean, puny, and sneered instead of laughing" (Varchi, *Storia fiorentina*, bk. 15, 5:265) ["era scarso della persona, e anzi mingherlino che no, e . . . non rideva ma ghignava"]. Shakespeare's Cassius also smiled "in such a sort / As if he mocked himself, and scorned his spirit / That could be moved to smile at any thing." *Julius Caesar*, 1.2.215–17.

172. This and the following terms reproduce a part of the artpiece *The Scene of Tyranny*.

173. Isidore, *Etymologies*, 18.6, Patrologia Latina 82: "*spatha* a *passione* dicitur verbo Graeco, quoniam παθειν Graece dicitur *pati*, unde et *patior*, et *patitur* dicimus.

174. Plutarch, *Vita di Marco Bruto*, in *Vite di Plutarco*, 205-7.

175. Suetonius, *Le vite de dodici cesari*, 36 (Suetonius *Life of Julius Caesar* 82): "Cesare alhora messo mano ad uno stiletto di rame da scrivere, gli passo un braccio, et fatto forza d'uscir loro delle mani, fu impedito da un'altra ferita che gli fu data: et come egli s'accorse, che da ogni banda i congiurati gli venivano addosso co' pugnali, s'avvolse la veste intorno al capo, et con la mano sinistra si tiro giu il lembo di quella infino a talloni, accio che coprendosi le parti inferiori del corpo, venisse a cadere in terra con manco vergogna."

176. See Machiavelli, *Discorsi*, 3.26; Livy *Ab urbe condita* 1.57–58.

177. Plutarch, *Vita di Marco Bruto*, in *Vite de Plutarco*, 197 (*Life of Brutus* 1).

178. Ibid.

179. Lorenzino, "Lettera," 200. Cf. n. 9 above.

180. The Latin *tradere* "has, at the same time, two meanings—to transmit or hand over something to someone (e.g. a legacy or culture) and to deceitfully deliver something to the enemy." Manlio Cortelazzo and Paolo Zolli, *Dizionario etimologico della lingua italiana* (Bologna: Zanichelli, 1988), 'tradire.'

181. The work in this section is especially informed by Paolo Valesio's brilliant essay on translation and ideology, "The Virtues of Traducement: A Sketch of a Theory of Translation," *Semiotica* 18, no. 1 (1976): 1–96.

182. Aurora Levins Morales, *Medicine Stories: History, Culture, and the Politics of Integrity* (Cambridge, MA: South End Press, 1998), 15.

183. Marlatt, *Ana Historic*, 55.

184. Richard Rouse, "Latin Paleography and Manuscript Studies in North America," in *Un secolo di paleografia e diplomatica (1887–1986)*, ed. Armando Petrucci and Alessandro Pratesi (Rome: Gela, 1988), 308.

185. Ibid., 327.

186. Ibid.

SOCIAL INTERSECTION: 1565–1995

1. Adolfo Gilly, Subcomandante Marcos, and Carlo Ginzburg, *Discusión sobre la historia* (Mexico City: Taurus, 1995), 38. Translations of Gilly and Marcos are my own. Carlo Ginzburg, "Clues: Roots of an Evidential Paradigm," in *Clues, Myths, and the Historical Method*, trans. John and Anne Tedeschi (Baltimore: Johns Hopkins University Press, 1989), originally published as "Spie: Radici di un paradigma indiziario," in *Crisi della ragione*, ed. Aldo Giorgio Gargani (Turin: Einaudi, 1979), and then as "Morelli, Freud and Sherlock Holmes: Clues and Scientific Method," *History Workshop Journal* 9 (1980): 5–36.

2. Gilly, Marcos, and Ginzburg, *Discusión*, 70–71.

3. Ibid., 45.

4. Ibid., 64.

5. Carlo Ginzburg, *The Cheese and the Worms: The Cosmos of a Sixteenth-Century Miller*, trans. John and Anne Tedeschi (New York: Penguin Books, 1982), xxiii, originally published as *Il formaggio e i vermi: Il cosmo di un mugnaio del '1500* (Turin: Einaudi, 1976).

6. Gilly, Marcos, and Ginzburg, *Discusión*, 55.

7. I have filled in some of the details for readers who don't remember the details of Ginzburg's essay.

8. Gilly, Marcos, and Ginzburg, *Discusión*, 16.

9. Ginzburg, "Clues," 119.

10. Gilly, Marcos, and Ginzburg, *Discusión*, 26.

11. See Gayatri Spivak, "Scattered Speculations on the Question of Cultural Studies," in *Outside in the Teaching Machine* (New York: Routledge, 1993), 278. Cf. also Dipesh Chakrabarty's critique of modernity as a frame of knowing constrained by the historic time presupposed by any single tradition that, by necessity, privileges the voices of those who have propelled that tradition over and above the voices of those who were moving in a different direction. Chakrabarty suggests that we might instead accept the heterogeneity of cultures and allow for different voices to "go many different places" in different temporal trajectories. "Then there would be no way of talking about the cutting edges, the avant-garde, the latest that represents the future, the most modern, and so on. Without such a rhetoric and a vocabulary and the sentiments that go with them, . . . many of our everyday political strategies in the scramble for material resources would be impossible to pursue." Dipesh Chakrabarty, "The Time of History and the Times of Gods," in *The Politics of Culture in the*

Shadow of Capital, ed. Lisa Lowe and David Lloyd (Durham: Duke University Press, 1997), 50.

SECTION TWO

1. For a feminist critique of this story, see Carla Lonzi, "Sputiamo su Hegel" [1970], in *Sputiamo su Hegel: La donna clitoridea e la donna vaginale* (Milan: Rivolta Femminile, 1977), excerpted in translation in Paola Bono and Sandra Kemp, *Italian Feminist Thought: A Reader* (Oxford: B. Blackwell, 1991), 40–59; Libreria delle donne di Milano, *Non credere di avere dei diritti: La generazione della libertà femminile nell'idea e nelle vicende di un gruppo di donne* (Turin: Rosenberg e Sellier, 1987), translated by Teresa de Lauretis as *Sexual Difference: A Theory of Social-Symbolic Practice* (Bloomington: Indiana University Press, 1990); Benedetta Craveri, *Madame Du Deffand and Her World* (Boston: D. R. Godine, 1994); Lynn Avery Hunt, *The Family Romance of the French Revolution* (Berkeley: University of California Press, 1992); Carole Pateman, *The Sexual Contract* (Stanford: Stanford University Press, 1988); Joan Wallach Scott, *Only Paradoxes to Offer: French Feminists and the Rights of Man* (Cambridge, MA: Harvard University Press, 1996).

2. Chartier, *Order of Books*, 8. For a history of bibliography as "one sector in a complex system of social communication" and its relevance to the seventeenth-century organization of libraries, see Luigi Balsamo, *La bibliografia: Storia di una tradizione* (Florence: Sansoni, 1984), 5 and ch. 5. For a complex treatment of the history of libraries in relation to philosophy, rhetoric, and research methods, see the work of Alfredo Serrai and, in particular, *Dai "loci communes" alla bibliometria* (Rome: Bulzoni, 1984). See also Luce Giard and Christian Jacob, eds., *Des Alexandries I: Du livre au texte* (Paris: Bibliothèque Nationale de France, Paris, 2001).

3. The digital or electronic text may promote an entirely different relationship of reading and research from that promoted by the book in codex form (cf. Chartier, *Order of Books*, 90–91), but this new relationship eliminates neither the physical space of reading nor the reader's embodied acts of reading. Chartier writes: "Reading brings the body into play" and invokes throughout his book the physical, relational space between reader, text, and "physical support" (8). Since the publication of Roland Barthes' seminal essay "De l'oeuvre au texte" in 1971, most theorists have accepted his hierarchical distinction between "the work" as (merely) "a fragment of substance, occupying a part of the space of books (in a library, for example)," and "the text" as "a methodological field" that somehow supersedes the physical activities (or labor) of writing, reading, and book production. See Roland Barthes, "From Work to Text," in *Image, Music, Text*, trans. Stephen Heath (New York: Hill and Wang, 1977), 156–57. My work in this section aims to restore the physical space and relationship of reading to the theoretical enterprise. For an important critique of Barthes' distinction, see Kathy E. Ferguson, "Work, Text, and Act in Discourses of Organization," *Women and Politics* 7, no. 2 (1987): 1–21. For further discussion of the important implications of digital publishing, see, among others, David Scott Kastan, "From Codex to Computer; or, Presence of Mind," in *Shakespeare*

and the Book (Cambridge: Cambridge University Press, 2001), and Jerome J. McGann, *The Textual Condition* (Princeton: Princeton University Press, 1991), 88–98.

4. Chartier, *Order of Books*, 15.

5. Silverblatt, "Interpreting Women in States"; Chandra Talpade Mohanty, "Under Western Eyes: Feminist Scholarship and Colonial Discourses," in *Third World Women and the Politics of Feminism*, ed. Chandra Talpade Mohanty, Ann Russo, and Lourdes Torres, 51–80 (Bloomington: Indiana University Press, 1991). See also Mohanty's revisiting of this foundational essay in *Feminism without Borders: Decolonizing Theory, Practicing Solidarity* (Durham: Duke University Press, 2003), http://site.ebrary.com/lib/dukelibraries/Doc?id=10198322; Benjamin, "Theses on the Philosophy."

6. Silverblatt, "Interpreting Women in States," 142.

7. Ibid., 154.

8. In these summaries of the histories of the Bodleian and the Ambrosiana, I am paraphrasing/translating from Bottasso, *Storia della biblioteca*, 49–51. Bottasso cites Wheeler, *Earliest Catalogues;* and Thomas Bodley, *Letters of Sir Thomas Bodley to Thomas James*, ed. G. W. Wheeler (Oxford: Clarendon Press, 1926). Cf. Balsamo, *La bibliografia*, 50–51.

9. Bottasso, *Storia della biblioteca*, 54, 67–68.

10. See, among others, Robert Damien, *Bibliothèque et état: Naissance d'une raison politique dans la France du XVIIe siècle* (Paris: Presses universitaires de France, 1995); James V. Rice, *Gabriel Naudé, 1600–1653* (Baltimore: Johns Hopkins University Press, 1939); Gabriel Naudé and Jules Mazarin, *Considérations politiques sur la Fronde: La correspondance entre Gabriel Naudé et le cardinal Mazarin*, ed. Kathryn Willis Wolfe and Phillip J. Wolfe (Paris: Papers on French Seventeenth Century Literature, 1991); Domenico Bosco, preface to Gabriel Naudé, *Bibliografia politica* (Rome: Bulzoni, 1997); Louis Marin's introductory essay "Pour une théorie baroque de l'action politique," in Naudé, *Considérations politiques;* Vittoria Lacchini, introduction to Gabriel Naudé, *Avvertenze per la costituzione di una biblioteca*, ed. Vittoria Lacchini (Bologna: Editrice CLUEB, 1992).

11. See Bosco, preface to Naudé, *Bibliografia politica*, 10: "Compiendo un'operazione analoga a quella dell'Advis pour dresser une bibliothèque, Naudé fornisce un catalogo minuzioso di libri e letture, construendo una sorta di biblioteca ideale dell'uomo politico. . . . Strano rapporto quello tra politica e libro, come tra tutte quelle cose in cui pratica e grammatica sembrano contendersi il campo. . . . La Bibliografia è l'elogio della storia che attende di essere fatta esperienza." Cf. Balsamo, *La bibliografia*, 75, who sees this work of Naudé as the first modern disciplinary bibliography because Naudé composed it in Cervia far from his personal books or from any library and because it was not just a list or catalog but a guide to the use of the books cited.

12. See the entry "politique" in Pierre Richelet, *Dictionnaire françois: Contenant les mots et les choses: plusieurs nouvelles remarques sur la langue françoise; ses expressions propres, figurées [et] burlesques, la prononciation des mots les plus difficiles, le genre des noms, le regime des verbes; avec les termes les plus connus des arts [et] de sciences; le tout tiré de l'usage et des bons auteurs*

de la langue françoise (Geneva: Widerhold, 1680), quoted in Bosco, preface to Naudé, *Bibliografia politica*, 20: "[Naudé] giudica i libri di molti autori e indica quelli che bisogna leggere per rendersi abili in quest'arte."

13. Hayden White, "Politics of Historical Interpretation," 117, reprinted in White, *Content of the Form*. In what follows, I have taken the liberty of appropriating White's words concerning the "instrument of interpretation" to understand catalogs as instruments of research: "The purity of any interpretation can be measured only by the extent to which it succeeds in repressing any impulse to appeal to political authority in the course of explanation of its object of interest. This means that the politics of interpretation must find the means either to effect this repression or to so sublimate the impulse to appeal to political authority as to transform it into an instrument of interpretation itself." White, "Politics of Historical Interpretation," 114–15.

14. Tarabotti, *Lettere familiari*, 219–20 [221]. Tarabotti's letters were first published in 1650 by Gueriglij in Venice. My page citations here will refer first to this edition and then, in brackets, to the recent excellent edition by Ray and Westwater: Arcangela Tarabotti, *Lettere familiari e di complimento*, ed. Meredith Kennedy Ray and Lynn Lara Westwater (Turin: Rosenberg e Sellier, 2005).

15. Silverblatt, "Interpreting Women in States," 158.

16. I have consulted the edition of this work published in Venice in 1637 by Gueriglij, the same printer who published Tarabotti's letters in 1650. Henry Earl of Monmouth (among others) translated Boccalini's work into English; he titled his translation *"I ragguagli di Parnaso"; or, Advertisements from Parnassus: in two centuries* (1656; repr., London: Thomas Guy, 1674). Francesca Medioli cites an apocryphal sequel to Boccalini's *Ragguagli* (Amsterdam, 1653) that further documents the intervention of Tarabotti's work in the world of learning and state making with a dedication expressing appreciation of her merits and sympathy for the travails of her "infernal cloister." Arcangela Tarabotti, *L'"Inferno monacale" di Arcangela Tarabotti*, ed. Francesca Medioli (Turin: Rosenberg e Sellier, 1990), 176: "Ad Arcangiola Tarabotta. Ancorché la virtù vostra sia da noi non poco stimata ed abbia in Parnaso applauso corrispondente al vostro merito, noi, per consiglio dei nostri deputati e revisori de' libri non abbiamo voluto accettare il libro vostro, intitolato Paradiso claustrale. . . . Et in verità noi non sappiamo come possano accordarsi queste due parole sapendo molto bene che ne' chiostri sono solite di abitare l'invidia, la discordia, la persecutione et altre cose più proprie dell'Inferno. Onde meglio avreste fatto voi a intitolare il vostro libro Inferno claustrale."

17. Boccalini, *"I ragguagli di Parnaso"; or, Advertisements*, 22; cf. Traiano Boccalini, *Ragguagli di Parnaso e scritti minori*, ed. Luigi Firpo (Bari: G. Laterza, 1948), www.bibliotecaitaliana.it/exist/ScrittoriItalia/show-text.xq?textID=mets.sio58, *Ragguaglio* 22, 1:66.

18. Ibid.

19. Here, I modified the Earl of Monmouth's translation of the italicized words, which reads, "which after a while end in getting up on one another's backs." *Ragguaglio* 22, 1:66. I am indebted to Susanna Bucci, who first introduced me to this passage in her important essay "Come si parla della donna: I cataloghi," in *La condizione della donna nel XVII e XVIII secolo*, by Fiorenza

Taricone and Susanna Bucci (Rome: Carucci, 1983), 197 n. 20. See also Virginia Cox's discussion of this anecdote in her *Women's Writing in Italy, 1400–1650* (Baltimore: Johns Hopkins University Press, 2008), 198. For Cox, Boccalini's quips were "more instrumental in associating female literacy with sexual immodesty in the minds of the Italian elites than the sober discussions of educational theorists."

20. Here I am translating/paraphrasing Bucci, "Come si parla," 197 n. 20.

21. For a discussion of how the presence of learned women like Tarabotti might have distracted men from their civic duties in the particular case of the Venetian Accademia degli Incogniti, see Wendy Beth Heller, *Emblems of Eloquence: Opera and Women's Voices in Seventeenth-Century Venice* (Berkeley: University of California Press, 2003), 51–52: "It was only by instructing women on those virtues appropriate to their gender (e.g., silence and chastity)—as opposed to those virtues appropriate for themselves (e.g., eloquence and courage)—that men could engage in the civic service so necessary for the well-being of the Republic."

22. Tarabotti, *La semplicità ingannata*, 1.245. All references are to Bortot's edition. Tarabotti's fantasy of disfiguring the father's nose also intervened in the intermittent early modern thought that somehow cutting off women's noses was an appropriate punishment (and/or deterrent) for women participating (by "choice" or by force) in adulterous relationships. See Valentin Groebner and Pamela Selwyn, "Losing Face, Saving Face: Noses and Honour in the Late Medieval Town," *History Workshop Journal* 40 (1995): 1–15; Guido Ruggiero, *The Boundaries of Eros: Sex, Crime, and Sexuality in Renaissance Venice* (New York: Oxford University Press, 1985), 35, 122. I am grateful to the press reader who reminded me also of the werewolf Bisclavret, who, in Marie de France's *Lais*, bites off the nose of his "adulterous" wife. See Paul Creamer, "Woman-Hating in Marie de France's Bisclavret," *Romanic Review* 93, no. 3 (2002): 259–74.

23. Tarabotti, *La semplicità ingannata*, 1.240.

24. Cf. ibid., 241. Tarabotti's fantasy of disfigured noses of fathers comes at the end of the story, well known in Tarabotti's time, of a young man who, neglected by his father, behaved so badly that he was condemned to die. The young man's last request was to be allowed to kiss his father, but instead the "poor convict, embracing his father, angrily tore off his nose with his teeth. This was his sign that he would die innocent because if his crimes had brought him to the gallows, only the father, who had neglected his upbringing, was to blame for his miserable end." ("Il misero condennato, abbracciato il padre, strappogli co' denti rabbiosamente il naso, con ciò dando segno che moriva innocente, perché se bene i suoi misfatti l'aveano ridotto al patibolo, solo il padre con la sua trascurata educazione era in colpa del di lui miserabil fine.")

25. This anecdote is presented and analyzed by Findlen, "Museum," 72.

26. Ibid. Two hundred years of accumulated "disturbance" might account for the measure of "indignation" and "regret" expressed by the guardians of "Oxbridge" when, in 1928, Virginia Woolf dared to walk on its turf and open a door to the library. See Virginia Woolf, *A Room of One's Own* (London: Hogarth Press, 1929), ch. 1.

27. Silverblatt, "Interpreting Women in States," 143.
28. Ibid., 154.
29. Ibid., 155–56.
30. See Meredith Ray, "Letters from the Cloister: Defending the Literary Self in Arcangela Tarabotti's Lettere familiari e di complimento," *Italica: Bulletin of the American Association of Teachers of Italian*, 81 (Spring 2004): 24–43, and *Writing Gender in Women's Letter Collections of the Italian Renaissance* (Toronto: University of Toronto Press, 2009).
31. Silverblatt, "Interpreting Women in States," 156.
32. Tarabotti, *Lettere familiari*, 184 [194].
33. Ferri wrote that he was the first "to turn his thought and cares to a feminine national library" and to devote a physical part of his own library to this project. Pietro Leopoldo Ferri, *Biblioteca femminile italiana* (Padua: Crescini, 1842), prefatory pages: "Nessuno prima di me volto aveva il pensiero e le cure ad una femminile nazional Biblioteca"; Canonici Fachini's catalog of women writers (1824) was a defense of Italian women in response to an English work that maligned them, Lady Morgan's *L'Italie* (1821). Ginevra Canonici Fachini, *Prospetto bibliografico di donne italiane rinomate in letteratura* (Venice: Alvisopoli, 1824). Both scholars abstracted women writers and intellectuals from their social relations in order to construct an explicitly nationalist instrument of research.
34. As Lorna Hutson has argued, "If the printed text of prose fiction is perceived as an advertisement of gifts intended to initiate a service relation, it becomes possible to read questions of masculine authorship as involved in a wider redefinition of credit relations between men." Women writers, by this token, would not be "capable of song or sonnet," as Woolf lamented, precisely because they were not interpellated by this system of male credit relations: "If being capable of song or sonnet was also proof of eligibility for political service, then our question about gender turns on larger issues . . . about the function of the printed text as the advertisement of those skills now redefining relations of service and friendship between men." Cf. Lorna Hutson, *The Usurer's Daughter: Male Friendship and Fictions of Women in Sixteenth-Century England* (London: Routledge, 1994), 12, 115–16.
35. Henry Earl of Monmouth, "The Translator's Epistle to his Countrymen the Readers," in Boccalini, *"I ragguagli di Parnaso"; or, Advertisements*.
36. Ibid.
37. Ibid., "The First Information" [*Ragguaglio 1*].
38. This section is indebted throughout to Bucci, "Come si parla."
39. Ibid., 143.
40. Tarabotti, *La semplicità ingannata*, 2.295–307.
41. Angelico Aprosio discredited Tarabotti in precisely this way: "La Signora Avversaria è dotata di vivacissimo ingegno. Non è intelletto da femina, ben sì da maschio." Emilia Biga, *Una polemica antifemminista del Seicento: La "Maschera scoperta" di Angelico Aprosio* (Ventimiglia: Civica Biblioteca Aprosiana, 1989), 140, quoted by Bortot in Tarabotti, *La semplicità ingannata*, 22.
42. My own efforts at making visible these rhetorics follow the lead of Patricia Parker in her important essay "Rhetorics of Property: Exploration, In-

ventory, Blazon," in *Literary Fat Ladies: Rhetoric, Gender, Property* (London: Methuen, 1987), 126–54.

43. Bucci, "Come si parla," 184.
44. Canonici Fachini, *Prospetto bibliografico*, 184.
45. Bucci, "Come si parla," 186–87.
46. Ibid., 191–92.
47. Gabriel Naudé, *Advice on Establishing a Library*, ed. Archer Taylor, trans. W. H. Alexander, J. S. Gildersleeve, H. A. Small, and T. Webb Jr. (Berkeley: University of California Press, 1950), 29; Gabriel Naudé, *Advis pour dresser une bibliothèque, présenté à Monsiegneur le président de mesme* (Paris: J. Liseux, 1876), 39–40, quoted in Chartier, *Order of Books*, 65–66.
48. Naudé, *Advice*, 11 [Fr., *Advis pour dresser*, 16].
49. Naudé, *Advice*, 12 [Fr., *Advis pour dresser*, 17].
50. Anna Maria Mozzoni, *Un passo avanti nella cultura femminile: Tesi e progetto* (Milan: Tipografia Internazionale, 1866), 15.
51. Ginevra Conti Odorisio, Francesca Medioli, Emilia Biga, Elissa Weaver, Letizia Panizza, and Emilio Zanette had already been charting Tarabotti's political and theoretical importance for some time when I first became curious about her. See Ginevra Conti Odorisio, *Donna e società nel Seicento: Lucrezia Marinelli e Arcangela Tarabotti* (Rome: Bulzoni, 1979) and *Storia dell'idea femminista in Italia* (Turin: ERI, 1980); Medioli's scholarship in her edition of Tarabotti's *L'Inferno monacale*; Biga, *Una polemica antifemminista*; Elissa Weaver, "Arcangela Tarabotti," in *Italian Women Writers: A Bio-Bibliographical Sourcebook*, ed. Rinaldina Russell (Westport, CT: Greenwood Press, 1994); Letizia Panizza's scholarship in her edition of Tarabotti's *Che le donne siano della spezie degli uomini* (London: Institute of Romance Studies, 1994); and Weaver's scholarship in Francesco Buoninsegni and Arcangela Tarabotti's *Satira e antisatira*, ed. Elissa B. Weaver (Rome: Salerno, 1998). I was privileged to participate in 1997 in the Tarabotti conference Weaver organized, whose papers, including my own "Arcangela Tarabotti and Gabriel Naudé: Libraries, Taxonomies, and *Ragion di Stato*," were published in *Arcangela Tarabotti: A Literary Nun in Baroque Venice*, ed. Elissa B. Weaver (Ravenna: Longo, 2006). Emilio Zanette authored the first modern monograph on Tarabotti: *Suor Arcangela, monaca del Seicento veneziano* (Venice: Istituto per la Collaborazione Culturale, 1960).
52. For Tarabotti's view of the myth of republican Venice, see Nancy L. Canepa, "The Writing behind the Wall: Arcangela Tarabotti's *Inferno monacale* and Cloistral Autobiography in the Seventeenth Century," *Forum Italicum* 30, no. 1 (1996): 2, 7; and Virginia Cox, "The Single Self: Feminist Thought and the Marriage Market in Early Modern Venice," *Renaissance Quarterly*, 48 (1995): 536–37 and n. 65.
53. Michel de Certeau, *The Writing of History*, trans. Tom Conley (New York: Columbia University Press, 1988), 56.
54. Ibid., 36.
55. Ibid.: "When historians refer to their own practices and examine their postulates in order to innovate, therein they discover constraints originating well before their own present, dating back to former organizations of which their work is a symptom."

56. François de La Croix du Maine, the author of an imaginary bibliothèque of 1584, quoted in Chartier, *Order of Books*, 77–78.

57. Johann Amos Comenius, *The Orbis pictus*, trans. Charles Hoole (Detroit: Singing Tree Press, 1968), 120.

58. Ibid., xv.

59. Roland Barthes, "An Almost Obsessive Relation to Writing Instruments," in *The Grain of the Voice: Interviews, 1962–1980* (New York: Hill and Wang, 1985), 181. See also Jean-Louis Rambures, *Comment travaillent les écrivains: Entretiens avec Roland Barthes et al.* (Paris: Flammarion, 1978); and Yve-Alain Bois, "Writer, Artisan, Narrator," *October* 26 (1983): 27–33.

60. Barthes, "Almost Obsessive Relation," 181.

61. Ibid., 177.

62. Ibid., 182.

63. Arcangela Tarabotti, *Antisatira*, in Buoninsegni and Tarabotti, *Satira e antisatira*, 84, 86: "Qual maraviglia . . . che sparlar delle donne con auttorità di filosofi, di leggisti, d'oratori, e poeti, e fino con stiracchiamenti della Sacra Scrittura, se quasi tutti coloro che scrivono e hanno scritto son uomini?"; "essendo quasi tutti gli scrittori uomini, toccarebbe sempre alla donna esser biasimata e rimaner oppressa dalle loro dottrine, ch'appresso però di noi non rissultano di niuna fede."

64. Arcangela Tarabotti, *Che le donne siano della spezie degli uomini*, ed. Letizia Panizza (London: Institute of Romance Studies, 1994), 20.

65. Tarabotti, *Antisatira*, 60, 61.

66. Ibid., 66. Cf. Tarabotti, *La semplicità ingannata*, 2.288: "benissimo operate, secondo la vostra politica, in tenerci lontane dall'operazioni scientifiche dell'intelletto, come quelli che conoscendo ch'agiunte le scienze alla naturale e spiritosa disposizione delle donne, arriverebbono ad usurparvi gli onori e guadagni, che con mezi illeciti acquistate."

67. Quoted in Franca Pieroni Bortolotti, *Alle origini del movimento femminile in Italia: 1848–1892* (Turin: Einaudi, 1963), 76.

68. Quoted in ibid., 63.

69. See Heller, *Emblems of Eloquence*, 52 n. 16, for the question of female attendance at Academy meetings.

70. Anne Bradstreet, *The Works of Anne Bradstreet*, ed. Jeannine Hensley (Cambridge, MA: Harvard University Press, 1967), "Prologue."

71. Ann Rosalind Jones, *The Currency of Eros: Women's Love Lyric in Europe, 1540–1620* (Bloomington: Indiana University Press, 1990), 23–24.

72. I am grateful to my colleague Nicole Tonkovich for help in the articulation of this conundrum.

73. Jones has worked on this suturing project in the above-cited chapter of her book and in more recent work. See especially Ann Rosalind Jones and Peter Stallybrass, *Renaissance Clothing and the Materials of Memory* (Cambridge: Cambridge University Press, 2000).

74. Tarabotti, *La semplicità ingannata*, 2.283–84. Cf. Lucrezia Marinella's denunciation of men's fear of women's interest in reading and writing: "Ma poco sono quelle, che dieno opera a gli studi, overo all'arte militare in questi nostri tempi, percioche gli huomini, temendo di non perdere la signoria, et di

divenir servi delle donne, vietano a quelle ben spesso ancho il saper leggere et scrivere." *La nobiltà et l'eccellenza delle donne co' diffetti et mancamenti de gli huomini* (Venetia: Gio Battista Ciotti, 1601), 32, quoted in Satya Brata Datta, *Women and Men in Early Modern Venice: Reassessing History* (Aldershot: Ashgate, 2003), 166.

75. Tarabotti, *Antisatira*, 73–74,

76. Tarabotti, *La semplicità ingannata*, 2.320–21. Cf. the story of Philomela, who wove the story of her rape by Tereus after he had cut out her tongue. See also the very important and influential essay by Patricia Klindienst Joplin, "The Voice of the Shuttle Is Ours," *Stanford Literature Review* 1 (1984): 25–53.

77. As we saw in Section One, the hand is important at the scene of the assault and at the scene of writing. And we saw how the novelist Daphne Marlatt investigated the resonance of the term *handmaiden* when Annie mused on Mrs. Richards's use of the term. Annie—and Marlatt—suggest that the sexual hands of the father were historically implicated in Mrs. Richards's decision to move far away from England. Moreover, those hands of the father, to some degree, were causally related to the hand his daughter was now using to write from her new home; to the hand of Annie, who was researching and writing a history; and to the hand of Marlatt, who was writing a novel. For Tarabotti, as well, it was the hands of fathers that sacrificed daughters to paternal interests, confining them inside the walls of convents. Seeing daughters as central to state making, Tarabotti condemned these paternal hands as public agents of deceit.

78. For an incisive introduction to the work and a comprehensive discussion of the circulation of the original treatise, its translation, and its authorial attributions, see Panizza's scholarship in Tarabotti, *Che le donne*, especially xv–xxiv.

79. Tarabotti, *Che le donne*, 17–18.

80. Ibid., 18.

81. Ibid., 17 and n. 10.

82. Ibid., 6.

83. Cf. Comenius, *Orbis pictus*, xiii: "Instruction is the means to expel rudeness."

84. *The American Heritage Dictionary of the English Language* (Boston: Houghton Mifflin, 2004), "debauch."

85. Seneca *De tranquillitate animi* 9.4–5, in Lucius Annaeus Seneca, *Moral Essays*, trans. John W. Basore (London: W. Heinemann, 1958), 2:246–47. Damien cites this passage, adding at the end: "A quoi bon 'cette débauche culturelle'?" Damien, *Bibliothèque et état*, 17.

86. Guy Patin, *Lettres de Gui Patin, 1630–1672* (Paris: Champion, 1907), 616–17, quoted in Charles Augustin Sainte-Beuve, *Portraits littéraires*, ed. Gérald Antoine (Paris: R. Laffont, 1993), 688. In his capacity as conservator of the Bibliothèque Mazarine (1840–1848), Sainte-Beuve was, of course, directly interested in the preservation of this legend about the Mazarine's founder. How might such bits of "knowledge" that circulate among erudites (including Hortense Allart, who had a literary and amorous connection to Sainte-Beuve) condition the interested relations of these same scholars to politics and books? (Patin quotes Ovid *Metamorphoses* 15.323.)

87. Gabriel Naudé, *News from France; or, A Description of the Library of Cardinal Mazarin, Preceded by the Surrender of the Library*, trans. Victoria Richmond and John Cotton Dana (Chicago: A. C. McClurg, 1907), 63–64, originally published as *Advis à Nos Seigneurs du Parlement, sur la vente de la Bibliothèque de M. le Cardinal Mazarin*, in *Recherches sur les bibliothèques anciennes et modernes, jusqu'à la fondation de la Bibliothèque Mazarine, et sur les causes qui ont favorisé l'accroissement successif du nombre des livres*, ed. Louis Charles François Petit-Radel (Paris: Rey et Gravier, 1819), 272–73.

88. Tarabotti, *La semplicità ingannata*, 1.240.

89. Ibid., 1.209.

90. Naudé, *News from France*, 62 [Fr., *Advis à Nos Seigneurs*, 272].

91. Naudé, *News from France*, 63 [Fr., *Advis à Nos Seigneurs*, 273].

92. Naudé, *News from France*, 63 [Fr., *Advis à Nos Seigneurs*, 272].

93. Tarabotti, *La semplicità ingannata*, 1.209.

94. Cfr. Scarry's discussion of the conversion of the space and contents of rooms into agents of pain. Elaine Scarry, *The Body in Pain: The Making and Unmaking of the World* (New York: Oxford University Press, 1985), 40–41.

95. Tarabotti, *La semplicità ingannata*, 1210: "Più de' maggiori Tiranni del mondo, più dico de' Neroni, e Diocletiani, voi [padri] meritate gli eterni cruccii, poich'essi, cruccidando e tormentando crudelmente i corpi de' santi martiri non pregiudicavano loro punto nell'anima.... Non havean lume di fede Christiana... Ma voi Tiranni d'Averno,... Christiani di nome e Diavoli d'operationi, pretendete d'esser partecipi della divina volontà all'hora, che vivamente l'offendete."

96. Tarabotti, *L'"Inferno monacale,"* 93: "Se stimate pregiudicar la multiplicità delle figliole alla Ragion di Stato, poi chè, se tutte si maritassero, crescerebbe in troppo numero la nobiltà et impoverirebber le case col sborso di tante doti." Cf. Tarabotti, *La semplicità ingannata*, 2.275: "Se stimate che'l numero grande d'esse figliuole pregiudichino alla Ragion di Stato, poiché, se si maritassero tutte, troppo crescerebbe la nobiltà e s'impoverirebbero le case, con lo sborso di tante doti, pigliate la compagnia che vi è stata destinata da Dio senza avidità di danari, ch'ad ogni modo a comperar schiave come fate voi le moglieri sarebbe più decente che voi sborsaste l'oro e non ch'esse profondessero tesori per comperarsi un patrone."

97. Jutta Gisela Sperling, *Convents and the Body Politic in Late Renaissance Venice* (Chicago: University of Chicago Press, 1999), 32 and n. 83. Sperling's study (especially ch. 1) demonstrates how the dowry system, taking into account both dowry inflation and the lower dowries paid to convents for "involuntary nuns," delivered higher inheritances for brothers. For the question of how dowry inflation increased the financial power of married women, see Cox, "Single Self," 533–34; and Stanley Chojnacki, "'The Most Serious Duty': Motherhood, Gender, and Patrician Culture in Renaissance Venice," in *Refiguring Women: Perspectives on Gender and the Italian Renaissance*, ed. Marilyn Migiel and Juliana Schiesari (Ithaca: Cornell University Press, 1991), 137 and n. 13.

98. I am grateful to one of the press readers for pointing me to Lynda E. Boose and Betty S. Flowers, *Daughters and Fathers* (Baltimore: Johns Hopkins University Press, 1989), here quoted from the introduction, 2, 4.

99. Hutson, *Usurer's Daughter*: "The art to 'use and order' is thus fundamental to the definition of *oikonomia*, or 'household' as a kind of knowledge, and that kind of knowledge bears a startling resemblance to what we would define as 'economy' in a liberal sense, such as when we speak of the 'economy' of a well-made artefact, or of a text. Oikonomia is thus the science which defines itself as the effective use of the possession (*oikos*)" (33); "Transformations in the expressive medium of masculinity and of masculine social relations found their way into . . . the English prose fiction of the 1560s and 1570s as the formal and thematic expression of concern about the pervasive textualization of the signs of masculine honour, and of the signs of credit and trust between men" (88).

100. Ibid., 87: "A humanistic vision of how the benefits of friendship might operate through persuasive communication (*amicitia*) was expressed in the story of how a daughter could, by liberally educated men, be clandestinely given in marriage against the wishes of her powerful but less literate kindred and friends."

101. Jean Bodin, *Les six livres de la Republique* (Geneva: Gabriel Cartier, 1608), 1.1. For Naudé's interest in Bodin, see Damien, *Bibliothèque et état*, 218–21. Cf. Ginevra Conti Odorisio, *Famiglia e stato nella "République" di Jean Bodin* (Turin: G. Giappichelli, 1993), 39: "Bodin . . . introduce la nozione di sovranità assoluta nel dominio politico, cercando di renderla conciliabile con quella dei padri di famiglia . . . E questo poteva venire solo in un modo, limitare l'autorità pubblica dei padri, rendendoli uguali agli altri e ugualmente sudditi al sovrano, ma rafforzando l'autorità privata all'interno della famiglia, dando loro tutto l'appoggio e le garanzie della forza sociale." It could be interesting to trace the revolutionary "equality" and "fraternity" of men under the power of the sovereign to this moment in which Tarabotti spoke out against it. Cf. also Joplin, "Voice of the Shuttle," 34, who suggests that such a "political hierarchy" would require the "violent appropriation of the woman's [and I would specify "daughter's] power to speak."

102. Cf. Hutson's discussion, in reference to Xenophon, of the husband's "mastery" of the household as a "necessarily hidden investment." Hutson, *Usurer's Daughter*, 48.

103. Cf. Joplin's discussion of the potential afforded by "communities of women." Joplin, "Voice of the Shuttle," 48. It would be interesting to examine Tarabotti's consciousness of this potential, starting from her idea of a women's press as a source for the alleviation of the suffering and difficulty experienced by women writers. With regard to the publication of her *Paradiso monacale*, she wrote: "S'allora . . . fossi stata consapevole, com'ora sono, che in questa città si ritrovasse una stamparia non da altri esercitata che da sole donne, io non a-verei sofferto che per mano virile ei fosse stato impresso." Tarabotti, *Antisatira*, 74–75 and n. 148. Cf. Zanette, *Suor Arcangela*, 396. Very important to this issue of relations among daughters and for her assembly of a "community" of women writers is Janet Levarie Smarr, *Joining the Conversation: Dialogues by Renaissance Women* (Ann Arbor: University of Michigan Press, 2005). Smarr's research in this book provides an important and fascinating context for theorizing Tarabotti's identification with other women writers and her possible internal dialogues with the learned women who preceded her.

104. Naudé, *Advice*, 18 [Fr., *Advis pour dresser*, 24–25]. Cf. Hutson, *Usurer's Daughter*, 48. Hutson exposes the ideological load of this seemingly innocuous activity of looking and finding in the library/daughter in her discussion of the passage in Xenophon's *Oikonomikos* in which Ischomachus and his wife reorder the household after she has failed to find something he needed. He shows her how to place things "so that their knowledge of where everything was would quickly bring it to hand. This, the figure of woman as agent of rhetorical retrieval, or 'readiness for use' would seem to be the last link in the conceptual chain which identifies *oikonomia* as that 'science' (*episteme*) which positions men . . . in a state of . . . readiness to 'sette their mindes and diligence to do theyr frendes any good, for the commonwealth.'"

105. Naudé, *Advice*, 24 [Fr., *Advis pour dresser*, 33].

106. Naudé, *Advice*, 23–24 [Fr., *Advis pour dresser*, 33]: "Il ne faut aussi obmettre tous ceux qui ont innové . . . car c'est proprement flatter l'esclavage et la foiblesse de notre esprit, que de couvrir le peu de connoissance que nous avons de ces Autheurs sous le mespris qu'il en faut faire, à cause qu'ils se sont opposez aux Anciens."

107. Naudé, *Advice*, 24 [Fr., *Advis pour dresser*, 33].

108. Naudé, *Advice*, 25 [Fr., *Advis pour dresser*, 34].

109. Naudé, *Advice*, 25 [Fr., *Advis pour dresser*, 35].

110. Naudé, *Advice*, 26 [Fr., *Advis pour dresser*, 36].

111. Naudé, *Advice*, 48 [Fr., *Advis pour dresser*, 66].

112. Naudé, *Advice*, 49 [Fr., *Advis pour dresser*, 67].

113. Naudé, *Advice*, 63 [Fr., *Advis pour dresser*, 86–87].

114. Naudé, *Advice*, 64 [Fr., *Advis pour dresser*, 87].

115. Cf. Tarabotti, *La semplicità ingannata*, 2.264: "Non così si santificano, ma così si perdono quell'anime, alle quali voi organizate il corpo." Reflection on this military conceit for the organization of culture might be fruitfully developed in relation to Edward Muir's important book, *The Culture Wars of the Late Renaissance: Skeptics, Libertines, and Opera* (Cambridge, MA: Harvard University Press, 2007). According to Muir, Giovanni Francesco Loredan, founder of the Accademia degli Incogniti and patron of Tarabotti, wrote, in part, "to further his anti-Habsburg program" (69). Ferrante Pallavicino, another member of the Incogniti, was highly critical of the Habsburg political and military domination of Italy (86–89). In relation to the politics of Loredan and the Accademia degli Incogniti, see also Mario Infelise, "Libri e politica nella Venezia di Arcangela Tarabotti," *Annali di storia moderna e contemporanea* 8 (2002): 31–45.

116. Tarabotti, *La semplicità ingannata*, 2.275.

117. Naudé, *Advice*, 16–17 [Fr., *Advis pour dresser*, 22–24]. Cf. Chartier, *Order of Books*, 64.

118. Naudé, *Advice*, 19 [Fr., *Advis pour dresser*, 26], .

119. See Marin, "Pour une théorie," 7. Here and subsequently, I am freely translating/paraphrasing Marin's important essay.

120. Ibid., 8–9.

121. Ibid., 10.

122. Ibid., 13 n. 20. In relation to Naudé's travels, Marin refers to René Pin-

tard, *Le libertinage érudit dans la première moitié du 17e siècle* (Paris: Boivin, 1943), 367ff.: "En déduire... les symptômes d'une folie bibliomaniaque et aussi une mutation de Naudé qui cesserait d'être philosophe et libertin pour devenir le 'domestique' d'un homme d'Etat?"

123. Marin, "Pour une théorie," 19–21.

124. Ibid., 22.

125. Ibid., 45: "Mais il est possible par transmutation de le faculté imaginative, de jouer à y pénétrer, de mimer les démarches et les réflexions du prince, de 'doubler' les comportements politiques pour les étudier, de les feindre pour les comprendre. C'est ainsi que Naudé monte sur la scène politique par le jeu intellectuel, la feinte de l'imagination, l'expérience mentale. Non pas s'imaginer 'être Néron pour mieux trouver les moyens de perdre et d'exterminer le genre humain,' mais s'imaginer interpréter son dessein, déchiffrer son action, mettre à nu, par ce jeu, ce qu'il s'efforçait tous les jours de voiler avec mille sortes d'artifices."

126. Ibid., 53: "dans le secret de la bibliothèque, au contact du document, il aura construit les images des divers comportements politiques, les modèles des secrets d'état en jouant les divers mouvements des actions politiques."

127. Cfr. Silverblatt, "Interpreting Women in States," 158: "To apprehend reality requires creative thinking, conceptual images that penetrate the generalities of social appearance to discern the multiple, paradoxical, and tangled relations that constitute social process."

128. Buoninsegni, *Satira*, 38: "Un sogno d'infermo, un delirio accademico, una lamentazione d'ammogliati..." Cfr. Tarabotti, *Antisatira*, 60.

129. Cf. Silverblatt, "Interpreting Women in States," 162: "The same intellectual tradition that refused colonial peoples a place in history denied women theirs. This denial is ensconced in historical theory where women were stereotyped as history's passive objects, as well as in the historical practice of archive-building."

130. Tarabotti, *Antisatira*, 61.

131. Ibid., 69.

132. Silverblatt, "Interpreting Women in States," 156: "No longer envisioning women (or gender configurations) as 'affected by,' and thus apart from, state-making procedures, challenges representations that have sapped women of their historical souls. And this, in turn, encourages us to rethink the categories we use to grasp historical process. For couldn't the 'impact of the state on women' be yet another resurrection of Western conceptual dualisms, of categorical splits of social living into self-contained realms of economy versus ideas, power versus culture, state versus gender?"

133. Tarabotti, *Antisatira*, 89.

134. Ibid., 89–90 and n. 181. As Weaver points out in this note, Cato of Utica, Dante's symbol of liberty, was more present in Tarabotti's mind than Cato the Censor, to whom Buoninsegni was referring.

135. Ibid., 104.

136. See Octavio Paz, foreword to Jacques Lafaye, *Quetzalcóatl and Guadalupe: The Formation of Mexican National Consciousness, 1531–1813* (Chi-

cago: University of Chicago Press, 1976), xiv: Sor Juana's originality (in "El Sueño") consists "in the very subject of her poem: the dream of knowledge and knowledge as dream. Not a single poem in the whole history of Spanish poetry, from its beginnings to the present, has that subject for its theme."

137. Cf. Joplin's discussion, in "Voice of the Shuttle," 42, of how Philomela "may see just how arbitrary cultural boundaries truly are; she may see what fictions prepared the way for her suffering."

138. Juana Inés de la Cruz, *A Sor Juana Anthology*, trans. Alan S. Trueblood (Cambridge, MA: Harvard University Press, 1988), 26–33 (poem 48). See also Stephanie Merrim, ed., *Feminist Perspectives on Sor Juana Inés de la Cruz* (Detroit: Wayne State University Press, 1991), 22, 143; and Stephanie Merrim, *Early Modern Women's Writing and Sor Juana Inés de la Cruz* (Nashville: Vanderbilt University Press, 1999), 29–30.

139. Silverblatt, "Interpreting Women in States," 163. Cf. also Joplin's idea of potential in her consideration of Philomela's weaving. Joplin, "Voice of the Shuttle," 47: "The end of the tale represents an attempt to forestall or foreclose a moment of radical transition when dominance and hierarchy might have begun to change or to give way."

140. Silverblatt, "Interpreting Women in States," 163.

141. Ibid., 162: "As feminist theory has so well instructed, neither colonials nor colonized spoke in one voice; these internal divisions have also left their mark on sources."

142. Adrienne Rich, "Anne Bradstreet and Her Poetry," in Bradstreet, *Works of Anne Bradstreet*, xiii. Rich's essay was written for the first printing of this edition in 1967. See also Jed, "Tenth Muse."

143. Rich, "Anne Bradstreet," xvii.

144. Ibid., xxi. Rich's "Postscript" to this essay, which first appeared in 1979 in *On Lies, Secrets and Silence* (New York: Norton, 1979), is now appended to the 1967 essay.

145. See Parker, "Rhetorics of Property," 130–31; see also Serrai, *Dai "loci communes,"* 12–14 and 21–26, who analyzes and theorizes the syllogistic relation that often obtains between the cataloguer and the researcher, whose ways of knowing, in an ideal but problematic scenario, are structured by the same contents and hierarchical order as the documents being looked for. As Serrai suggests, bringing into play the experience of the researcher can change this rhetorical relation, making possible an "authentic" growth of knowledge (26).

146. Interestingly, the copy owned by the Van Pelt Library seems to be the one considered by scholars to be a "pirate edition" of 189 pages. It matches the description of the Marciana edition (Misc. 2825.3) in every respect except that the printer's mark is a *fleur de lis* type figure (not a figure of "stelline irregolari disposte a rombo," as described by Bortot). See Tarabotti, *Che le donne*, x, n. 8, and Arcangela Tarabotti, *Paternal Tyranny*, ed. and trans. Letizia Panizza (Chicago: University of Chicago Press, 2004), 30; Bortot, "Nota al testo," in Tarabotti, *La semplicità ingannata*, 156–58; Weaver, "Arcangela Tarabotti," 30 n. 13.

147. I am grateful to Dr. Isabelle de Conihout, conservateur en chef, fonds

anciens of the Mazarine, who generously shared with me, in a personal e-mail, information about the dates of acquisition of Tarabotti's works and copies of the shelf lists in which her works appear.

148. The "fictional" tour represented here closely translates and/or paraphrases the information presented in Alfred Franklin, *Histoire de la Bibliothèque Mazarine depuis sa fondation jusqu'à nos jours* (Paris: A. Aubry, 1860), 23–24: "Naudé ne voulait pas se reposer avant d'avoir parcouru l'Europe. Pour enrichir sa *fille* bien aimée, comme il l'appellera plus tard, il se sentait prêt à braver toutes les fatigues et tous les dangers" (emphasis is Franklin's).

149. Ibid., 30–31, 43.

150. Ibid., 43.

151. Ibid., 31. I am fictionally placing Tarabotti's works in the appropriate rooms.

152. Ibid., 32–34. The fifth room, containing works of a political nature, may have been hospitable to these titles among others.

153. Ibid., 172: "La langue italienne y occupe le première place." It is important to emphasize here the preeminence of Italian culture in the first French library of state, just as we shall emphasize, in Section Three, the prominence of a French feminist scholar and theorist in Italian nationalist thought.

154. Ibid., 185–86: "L'économie politique est une science trop récente pour avoir une bibliographie bien curieuse."

SOCIAL INTERSECTION: 1536–2011

1. I don't want to leave "Sasha Harvey" out of this study. She is named for the great honor (and confidence in my work) that Roy Harvey Pearce showed me in 1982 when he associated my scholarship with that of his dear friend Sigurd Burckhardt. It is my hope that this research might return the honor to Roy Pearce, his work, and his vision. In any case, "Sasha Harvey" is a fictional figure who, in a sense, emerged from my research. She may be a different manifestation of the concept of "ghostly matters" so brilliantly developed by Avery Gordon in her book of that name. I imagine Harvey's papers to be housed in the University of California–San Diego Archive for New Poetry. I don't know why she had to "die," but I think her death may have helped me complete this book.

2. See Section One, nn. 33–34.

3. According to Bernardo Segni, these were the words that Lorenzino had written on a card and placed on the head of the dead duke: *Vincit amor Patriae laudumque immensa cupido*. Segni, *Storie fiorentine*, bk. 7, 131.

4. According to a (fictional) curator of Special Collections, Sasha Harvey sold her papers to the University of California–San Diego library some months before her death in August 2006. In their description of Harvey's papers, the scholars who had prepared a critical edition of her poetry had barely mentioned these "research notes." And since the mention of these notes was so brief and the description of the poetry manuscripts and typescripts so long, I had naturally assumed that the "research notes" were inconsequential. I had been invited to write a book about Sasha Harvey's life for a series on contemporary women poets. I suppose that's what I wanted. It was an honor, after all. And there were

files and files of "research notes" among Harvey's collected papers, each file accompanied by pages of Harvey's own prose. She was doing research on tyrant-slayers, but other stories, seemingly parenthetical to this project, kept breaking in. One story of a Venetian nun who theorized the suffering of daughters in relation to a French librarian. Another story of a French feminist historian who wrote a history of Florence. What I didn't know was that I would eventually become one of the parentheses in Sasha Harvey's research. My own research life, taking off after her death, was one last parenthetical story to add to her files.

5. In the year 2000, Sasha Harvey met the Egyptian writer Nawal El Saadawi, who spoke of capturing every reminder of her own mother "as a jewel" and encouraged Sasha to turn her research notes into a novel. Sasha discovered with great disappointment that, because she was inept at writing dialogue, she would never become a novelist.

SECTION THREE

1. The background information in this section comes from the essay "Gian Pietro Vieusseux," in Sestan, *La Firenze*, 3–24. For an excellent collection of essays on the formation of this "moral national community," see Albert Ascoli and Krystyna Von Henneberg, *Making and Remaking Italy: The Cultivation of National Identity around the Risorgimento* (Oxford: Berg, 2001).

2. Sestan, *La Firenze*, 6, 9.
3. Ibid., 22.
4. Ibid., 12–13.
5. Ibid., 13.
6. Ibid., 72.
7. Ibid., 96–97 and n. 7. Cf. p. 157 below.
8. Ibid., 70–71. The epithets describing Canestrini are from the pen of Sestan, who cites Gar's letter in *La Firenze*.
9. Ibid., 122–23. According to Sestan in *La Firenze*, Capponi regarded Florentine history as "un'ocasione per analizzare la natura, le virtù e i vizi di quel mobilissimo e apertissimo patriziato borghese, mercantile, antifeudale, guelfo infine, a cui egli sentiva di appartenere con i suoi maggiori."
10. Ibid., 118–19, 110: "Le 'libertà' cittadine erano poi il presupposto di quel vigor di vita, di quel primato civile d'Italia per alcuni secoli, che ora si rimpiangeva." Historians like Capponi "s'imbattono, nel passato, in qualche figura o fatto, che solleva, per analogia di situazioni, di aspirazioni, un qualche problema attuale o che sembri aver determinato una situazione attuale; ci si appassionano, ci lavorano attorno . . . scompongono e ricompongono in un continuo e sottile gioco di contrappunto fra presente e passato."
11. Ibid., 81 n. 217.
12. On figuring Italia as a woman, see Margaret Brose, "Petrarch's Beloved Body: 'Italia mia,'" in *Feminist Approaches to the Body in Medieval Literature*, ed. Linda Lomperis and Sarah Stanbury (Philadelphia: University of Pennsylvania Press, 1993).
13. Biographical information, unless otherwise noted, comes from Petre Ciureanu's excellent introduction to *LIGC*. See also Whitney Walton, *Eve's*

Proud Descendants: Four Women Writers and Republican Politics in Nineteenth-Century France (Stanford: Stanford University Press, 2000); Bonnie G. Smith, *The Gender of History: Men, Women, and Historical Practice* (Cambridge, MA: Harvard University Press, 1998); Helynne Hollstein Hansen, *Hortense Allart: The Woman and the Novelist* (Lanham, MD: University Press of America, 1998); Juliette Decreus, *Henry Bulwer-Lytton et Hortense Allart, d'apres des documents inédits* (Paris: M. J. Minard, 1961); Lorin A. Uffenbeck, "The Life and Writings of Hortense Allart (1801–79)," PhD diss., University of Wisconsin–Madison, 1957.

14. Sestan, *La Firenze*, 121 n. 57. Sestan supplies the epithets in his description of Pieri's first encounters with Allart and also cites Pieri's first annotations after the birth of Marcus. See Mario Pieri, *Vita scritta da lui medesimo* (Florence: Le Monnier, 1850), 2:51.

15. Allart, *Les enchantements*, 106.

16. Tommaseo to Capponi, August 13, 1834, CI, 1:160.

17. Allart to Capponi, July 18, 1837, LIGC.

18. Allart, *Les enchantements*, 263, See also Allart to Capponi, January 1838, LIGC: "Vous aurez une grande part à mon second volume avec vos conversations et vos livres."

19. Tommaseo to Vieusseux, May 1, 1837, quoted in CI, 1:556 n. 2.

20. Capponi to Tommaseo, November 19, 1838, CI, 2:102–3.

21. Although I concur, in every respect, with Bonnie Smith's characterization of Allart as one of those "amateur" historians upon whom the professionalization of history depended, I also want to vindicate Allart's "professional" status as a scholar who earned money from her writing and acknowledge her material contributions to Capponi's *Storia*. B. Smith, *Gender of History*, 10.

22. In a letter of January 25, 1857 *(LIGC)*, Allart wrote to Capponi about her *Essai sur l'histoire politique, depuis l'invasion des barbares jusqu'en 1848* (Paris: J. Rouvier, 1857): "I should have completed my book where I had started it, in Florence; I would have **broadened** my project and my ideas through our conversations, you would have given me what is **lacking** in the work." ("J'aurais dû achever mon livre où je l'avais commencé, à Florence; j'aurais élargi mon plan et mes idées par vos conversations, vour m'auriez donné ce qui manque à l'ouvrage.") See also Allart to Capponi, December 27, 1858, LIGC: "It rests entirely with you to go fast if you want, because you are **full** of the topic. I had to learn everything and you know everything.... Let's go, Polyeucte, without delay, and when your work slacks off, take up and read me again to blush at your **slowness**. I hope that this new year 1859 your first volume will appear." ("Il ne tient qu'à vous d'aller vite si vous voulez, car vous êtes plein du sujet, j'avais tout à apprendre et vous savez tout. Allons, Polyeucte, pas de retard, et quand le travail languit, reprenez-moi, relisez-moi pour rougir de votre lenteur.") It was Mario Pieri (1776–1852) who expressed the contrast between his own icy blandness with respect to Allart's warm and lively spiciness. She brought to his life "that pepper and that salt that was lacking" ("**quel pepe e** ... **quel sale** che le mancava") and "that useful excitement and refreshing warmth that kept the heart and mind from dying before the chill of death crept in" ("quell'utile agitazione e quel **calore** vivifico, a non

lasciar morire il cuore e la mente innanzi che morte v'insinuasse il suo **gelo**"). Pieri, *Vita scritta,* 2:45,

23. Allart to Capponi, August 29, 1847, *LIGC;* cf. Allart to Capponi, May 21, 1875: "Vous appelez mon travail un extrait mais tout ce qui est civil je l'ai donné."

24. Allart to Capponi, January 22, 1846 ("Qu'est devenue la traduction de ma petite histoire de Florence?"), January 6, 1847 ("Capei m'a dit que vous faisiez continuer la traduction de ma petite *Histoire de Florence*"), and October 15, 1849 ("J'ai essayé d'exposer ces idées là en écrivant cette petite histoire de Florence"), all in *LIGC*. In one interesting exception to this general rule (May 23, 1843), Allart deprecates her *History* as "big" and "rough" in opposition to Capponi's work, which she regards as "fine" and "delicate." See p. 179.

25. The essay in question was Gino Capponi's "Un brano della Repubblica di Firenze (1351–1358)," *Archivio storico italiana*, n.s., 7, pt. 2 (1858): 60–92. Cf. Allart to Capponi, December 27, 1858, and note, *LIGC:* "Vous me faites un envoi très beau. Peste!"

26. Allart to Capponi, December 27, 1858, *LIGC*. See also another letter to him, dated May 21, 1875 (after the appearance of Capponi's *Storia*), *LIGC:* "Vos guerres sont trop détaillées, il me semble, et je les avais évitées exprès."

27. Allart to Capponi, July 21, 1855, *LIGC*.

28. Ibid.

29. Allart to Capponi, December 27, 1858, *LIGC*.

30. Niccolò Tommaseo, *Diario intimo,* ed. Raffaele Ciampini (Turin: Einaudi, 1946), 90.

31. Allart to Capponi, March 23, 1839, *LIGC*. Henri Diodati was born on March 21, 1839, and he died, at age twenty-three, on July 19, 1862. Ciureanu notes that Allart did not indicate the name of the father, Pietro Capei, on the baptismal certificate (introduction to *LIGC,* lxxii). Capponi took the initiative to inform Capei of the birth of his son: "Sapete che l'Ortensia partorì un maschio: sta bene, ma il bambino è un po' debole." Capponi to Capei, March 1, 1843, in Capponi, *Lettere,* 2:120–22. Allart explicitly indicated Capei as the father of Henri in only one of her letters to Capponi (July 6, 1855, *LIGC*): "Write me. And tell Capei also to write me. His son Henri engages in the beautiful activities of a sixteen-year-old Italian. He pleases, he loves, he writes poetry, etc." ("Écrivez-moi. Et dites à Capei de m'écrire aussi. Son fils Henri fait les belles choses d'un Italien de 16 ans, plaire, aimer, faire des vers, etc.")

32. Allart, *Les enchantements,* 269. I cite Walton's translation of this passage in *Eve's Proud Descendants,* 118–19. Walton notes that d'Agoult also addressed Allart as a "proud amazon."

33. Allart to Capponi, October 12, 1837, *LIGC*.

34. Allart to Capponi, May 16, 1843, *LIGC:* "Il n'accorde en paroles que pour retirer an fait. . . . Relisez je vous prie ce discours avec cette interprétation et voyez s'il n'est pas ainsi: Oui il faut opprimer Florence, mais, mais ceci, cela, il empêche tout."

35. Sestan, *La Firenze,* 88.

36. Quoted in ibid., 88–89 n. 248.

37. Quoted in ibid., 88 n. 246.

38. Referring to the Florentine archives, Marco Tabarrini, *Vite e ricordi d'italiani illustri de secolo XIX* (Florence: Barbèra, 1884), 170, wrote: "Neppure chi li custodiva a solo fine di contenderli agli studiosi, sapeva quello che ci fosse. Scarsi e confusi gli indici, disordinate le materie; chi vi si rinveniva era bravo." Quoted in Sestan, *La Firenze*, 59. Sestan's comment on Capponi is from Sestan, *La Firenze*, 108.

39. Ibid., 30–31: "Se gli archivisti mancavano, ragione principale era che nella mente del Capponi fonti storiche sono principalmente quelle narrative (cronache, relazioni, biografie, corrispondenze epistolari, magari anche statuti); tutte cose che si trovano pituttosto nelle biblioteche che negli archivi. Fra le sei serie in cui, inizialmente, si prevedeva diviso l'ASI, solo la quarta è timidamente dedicata a 'carte diplomatiche ed atti pubblici anteriori al XVII secolo'; ma anche—prosegue—'statuti e provvisioni; istruzioni date agli ambasciatori, corrispondenze dei medesimi, ecc.' . . . Allora, che farsene degli archivisti? A queste predilezioni del Capponi . . . si accompagnava l'istinto editoriale del Vieusseux, il suo senso dei gusti del pubblico: un volume di carte medioevali, chi lo leggerebbe? Lo consulterebbero, al più, degli specialisti; e il Vieusseux vuole il periodico che attiri perché sia letto."

40. Vieusseux to Tommaseo, July 7, 1838, quoted in *CI*, 2:39 n. 3, and in *LIGC*, 127, n. 1: "Egli in società non riconosce che al suono della voce: ed il desiderio di dissimulare il suo deplorabile stato gli fa fare un mondo di spropositi."

41. The three previous "readers" were F. L. Polidori, Antonio Gallenga, and Ascanio Tempestini. See Guglielmo Macchia, "Il segretario di Gino Capponi: Alessandro Carraresi (1819–1902)," *Nuova rivista storica* 40, no. 2 (1956): 299.

42. Capponi, *Storia*, 1.vii.

43. Allart to Capponi, July 14, 1839, *LIGC*. Much later (September 24, 1874), Allart worried that maybe it was too much to ask friends to take dictation in French: "Dictez pour moi en italien."

44. Allart to Capponi, September 26, 1840, February 10, 1843, and July 6, 1855, all in *LIGC*.

45. Allart to Capponi, August 8, 1842, *LIGC*.

46. Capponi to Capei, March 1, 1843, in Capponi, *Lettere*, 2:121.

47. Capponi to Capei, May 12, 1843, in Capponi, *Lettere*, 2:128.

48. Capponi to Capei, May 14, 1843, in Capponi, *Lettere*, 2:203.

49. Cf. Tabarrini to Vieusseux, 1847 (quoted in Sestan, *La Firenze*, 94): "Sono parecchi mesi che non tocco libri e fogli che non puzzino di politica."

50. Tommaseo to Capponi, June 1834, *CI*, 1:137. Tommaseo continued to record his piggish comments to Allart in his diary: "La sera dalla Allart dico durezze e sciocchezze." Tommaseo, *Diario intimo*, 200. Again, he wrote: "Io la strapazzo sovente, e poi dopo me ne sa male." Tommaseo to Capponi, August 13, 1834, *CI*, 1:160.

51. Tommaseo to Capponi, August 13, 1834, *CI*, 1:157.

52. Tommaseo to Vieusseux, May 1, 1837, quoted in *CI*, 1:556 n. 2.

53. Tommaseo to Capponi, May 12, 1837, *CI*, 1:556.

54. Capponi to Tommaseo, June 24, 1837, *CI*, 1:563–64 (*Orlando furioso*, Canto VII.12).

55. Or to connect women's noses to a more general epistemological reflection, see Fraisse, *Reason's Muse*, 1–2. Fraisse cites the case of the librarian/journalist Sylvain Maréchal, who published a fictitious law defending a woman's right to keep her nose in a book. Fraisse's book, as Catharine Stimpson notes in her preface (vii), transgresses conventional scholarly borders, making "connections between epistemology (ways of knowing) political theory and politics (ways of organizing a commonwealth), texts and literature (ways of self-representation), psychology (ways of acting and fantasizing about our actions)." A woman's nose, in the context of these connections, formed part of the fantasies of men as they organized their ways of knowing the body politic.

56. Allart to Capponi, August 25, 1840, *LIGC*.
57. Macchia, "Il segretario," 298.
58. Ibid., 299 and n. 1, 302 and n. 1. Capponi's second daughter, who died in 1844 at the age of thirty, was also named Ortensia.
59. Ibid., 300.
60. Allart to Capponi, June 15, 1837, *LIGC*.
61. Allart to Capponi, June 16, 1837, *LIGC*.
62. Allart to Marianna Farinola, April 29, 1876.
63. Allart to Capponi, August 25, 1840, *LIGC*.
64. Tommaseo to Capponi, August 13, 1834, *CI*, 1:160
65. Ibid.
66. Allart to Capponi, March 25, 1829, November 20, 1829, and February 25, 1830, all in *LIGC*.
67. Hortense Allart de Méritens, *Sextus ou le Romain des Maremmes suivie d'Essaies détachés sur l'Italie* (Paris: Heideloff et Campe, 1832), 14.
68. Ibid., 208.
69. Mario Pieri, *Memorie* [Biblioteca Riccardiana, Ms. 3558], January 27, 1828 entry, vol. 5, p. 2, quoted in Ciureanu's introduction to *LIGC*, xviii.
70. Tommaseo to Capponi, May 12, 1837, *CI*, 1:556, .
71. Allart to Capponi, March 25, 1829, *LIGC*.
72. Allart to Capponi, March 7, 1835, *LIGC*.
73. Allart to Capponi, March 25, 1829, *LIGC*.
74. Allart to Capponi, November 20, 1829, *LIGC*.
75. Allart to Capponi, January 21, 1832, *LIGC*.
76. Allart to Capponi, July 18, 1837 ("Vous songiez à l'unité") and December 8, 1874 ("vous, Monsieur, qui n'avez jamais songé qu'à la patrie"), both in *LIGC*.
77. Allart to Capponi, July 18, 1837, *LIGC*.
78. Fumaroli, "La république des lettres," 140: "Être initié aux lettres, c'est sortir du rang des rudes, c'est erudire, c'est accéder à l'humanitas et éventuellement à l'urbanitas." See also Section Two, Shelf List 7: "Debauchery, Erudition."
79. Sestan, *La Firenze*, 42–43.
80. Ibid., 70–71, 81 n. 217. See p. 142 above.
81. Tommaseo to Capponi, December 15, 1838, *CI*, 2:111, quoted in Sestan, *La Firenze*, 96 n. 6.
82. Here I am translating/paraphrasing Sestan, *La Firenze*, 97 and n. 7.

83. From a summary of the November 17, 1843, meeting of the editorial board of the *Archivio storico italiano* conserved in the Archivio della Deputazione Toscana di Storia Patria under the title "Consulte dell Archivio storico italiano," 73–75, quoted in Sestan, *La Firenze,* 78 and n. 202.

84. Editorial comment by Capponi published in *Archivio storico italiano, appendice* 3 (1843): 72, quoted in Sestan, *La Firenze,* 84–85.

85. Tommaseo to Bianciardi, quoted in Raffaele Ciampini, *Vita di Niccolò Tommaseo* (Florence: G. C. Sansoni, 1945), 238.

86. To be exact, the news was "piccante" to Sainte-Beuve, who had heard from Allart that Tommaseo had fallen in love with Sand. Vieusseux's letter to Tommaseo, January 10, 1835 (Biblioteca Nazionale Centrale di Firenze, Carte Tommaseo, box 147, file 12), in which he imagines his hypothetical love for Sand in relation to the reading of her book *Le prince,* is quoted in Ciureanu, *Saggi,* 96–97.

87. Tommaseo to Vieusseux, January 23, 1835 (Biblioteca Nazionale Centrale di Firenze, Carte Tommaseo, box 147, file 18), quoted in Ciureanu, *Saggi,* 97.

88. Tommaseo to Capponi, June, 1834, *CI,* 1:137: "Io non cercai di lei perchè parevami non amaste ch'io la cercassi: e perchè non amaste ch'io cercassi la donna della donna pruriginosa, quella se ne lamentò, ed io feci la figura del **pauroso**." Cf. p. 151 above. Still a few years later, Tommaseo continued to be fearful especially about Allart's historical writing, and since he always feared the worst, he was sometimes pleasantly surprised. In May 1837 he wrote to Capponi that Allart's *History of Florence* was "colorless and dry, but less awful than I feared." Tommaseo to Capponi, May 12, 1837, *CI,* 1:556: "La Storia di Firenze è scolorita e arida, ma meno cattiva di quel ch'io temevo."

89. Capponi to Tommaseo, July 16, 1834, *CI,* 1:149.

90. Capponi to Allart, March 24, 1835, in Capponi, *Lettere,* 1:389–90 (also given in full as Letter 40 in *LIGC*).

91. Ibid., 1:388–89: Capponi confessed that he, too, had written a novel that he would never think of publishing because he, unlike Allart, had no talent for mixing fiction and truth: "Je n'ai point le talent de mêler le faux et le vrai."

92. Ibid., 1:389.

93. Ibid., 1:390.

94. Allart to Capponi, November 20, 1829, *LIGC*.

95. Tommaseo, *Diario intimo,* July 26, 1836, 251; Tommaseo, review of *Settimia,* by Hortense Allart, *L'Italiano,* July 31, 1836, quoted in Ciureanu's introduction to *LIGC,* lvii.

96. Tommaseo, review of *Settimia.*

97. Cf. B. Smith, *Gender of History,* 67: "Disavowing the historiographic past of amateurism, one takes a stand on the side of professionalism, which in its procedures, practices, methodology, writing, fantasies, and organization has built historical science out of gender by contrasting male depth and female superficiality, significant male events and trivial female ones, male transcendence and female embodiment as part of professionalism's gains. Enforcement of this hierarchy was precisely the originary point of historiographic trauma for women, and one perpetuated not just in politics and the economy but in professionalization."

98. Allart to Capponi, October 6, 1842 ("Delloye va envoyer Florence à Molini"), and February 17, 1843 ("Je vous prie aussi d'envoyer un exemplaire de Florence à la Divine Félicie... Et d'en donner un aussi à la Colombaria"), both in *LIGC*.

99. Tabarrini, *Gino Capponi*, 6–7: "Il palazzo Capponi è occupato da ufficiali e da soldati francesi, i quali bastonano il cuoco, fanno violenze ai domestici, sciupano i mobili, ordinano e non pagano." See also the entry "abbandonare" in Alessandro Manzoni and Gino Capponi, *Saggio di vocabolario italiano secondo l'uso a Firenze compilato in collaborazione a Varramista nel 1856*, ed. Guglielmo Macchia (Florence: Le Monnier, 1957), 88–89: "separarsi, ma **con danno di chi rimane.—Abbandonare** lo studio, il lavoro; **la moglie, i figliuoli, la famiglia... *Le spighe trebbiate abbandonano i loro chicchi*. E' un pensiero che non mi abbandona mai**" (emphasis mine). I am especially interested in this last contrast: "The threshed ears of corn abandon their kernels. It is a thought that never abandons me." In the context of the entire entry, Capponi may be saying: fathers (ears of corn) may abandon their children (kernels). But my thoughts are more reliable, never leaving me alone.

100. Documenting the formation of Capponi's studious character, Capponi's mother gives us some terms for imagining a possible relation between his traumatic experience and his approach to French culture. In June of 1799, after three months of her husband's absence, the Marchesa Maddalena wrote to him: "Il caro Gino sta bene e si conserva molto buono e studioso; fa progressi nel latino e nella geometria, e parla il francese benino, essendosi esercitato coi nostri ospiti, quando li ha trovati da me." Tabarrini, *Gino Capponi*, 8.

101. Capponi to Giovambatista Zannoni, December 19, 1808, in Capponi, *Lettere*, 1:3.

102. I am here translating and paraphrasing Sestan's account of this incident in *La Firenze*, 40–42 and nn.

103. Tabarrini, *Gino Capponi*, 304. Capponi must have also felt some "shame" for 'forgetting' to mention Allart's work, but perhaps it is even more important to note how Capponi, immediately after expressing this feeling of "shame," resolves to finish his own history of Florence: "On that day, he renewed his intention to complete the work he had begun" ("Da quel giorno, rinnovò il proposito di condurre a termine il lavoro incominciato").

104. Ibid., 343.

105. Capponi to Tommaseo, July 10, 1835, *CI*, 1:278. Clearly unconcerned about Allart's feelings and his friend's worries, Tommaseo responded on September 14, 1835, adding to his friend's terrible insults (*CI*, 1:305): "She has no aptitude for history. She is slipshod and useless" ("Per istorie non è nata. Abborracciona e vana").

106. Capponi to Tommaseo, January 21, 1838, *CI*, 2:19. Cf. Capponi to Tommaseo, November 6, 1838, *CI*, 2:97: "Poverina! La m'invizzisce ogni giorno."

107. Capponi to Capei, March 1, 1843, in Capponi, *Lettere*, 2:120–21.

108. Allart, *Les enchantements*, 145.

109. Allart to Capponi, March 31, 1830 ("Je renonce si peu à l'honneur

d'écrire sur votre pays, que je n'ai travaillé que pour cela tout l'hiver. L'ouvrage sera prêt pour Octubre ou je meurs. J'en suis fatiguée: j'y travaillerai tout l'été") and March 7, 1835 ("Il y avait des morceaux sur l'Italie... dont je voudrais votre avis. Jamais je n'ai tant travaillé"), both in *LIGC*. Cf. B. Smith, *Gender of History*, 57: "Amateurs were assiduous in writing the histories of other countries, mining these narratives especially for the ingredients of citizenship and sound political rule."

110. Allart to Capponi, July 6, 1855, *LIGC*.
111. Allart to Capponi, May 16, 1843, *LIGC*.
112. See p. 150 above.
113. Allart to Capponi, March 15, 1875, *LIGC*.
114. Allart to Capponi, October 6, 1842, *LIGC*, and March 29, 1843, *LIGC*. Cf. B. Smith, *Gender of History*, 66: "Many [women historians] had trouble getting basic information they needed to pursue their writing." See also the lexical entry for "Withholding" below.
115. Capponi to Capei, June 16, 1837, *Lettere*, 1:438: "a crazy dedication to reformed women" ("una matta dedica aux femmes réformées"); Allart, *Histoire de la République* (1843), v; Allart to Capponi, November 13, 1837, *LIGC*.
116. Allart to Capponi, June 16, 1837, *LIGC*.
117. Allart to Capponi, August 8, 1842, *LIGC*: "Votre Monime n'est point fâchée."
118. Allart to Capponi, March 25, 1829, and March 31, 1830, both in *LIGC*.
119. Cf. p. 159 and n. 91 above. Allart to Capponi, March 7, 1835, *LIGC*: Allart refers, in one breath, to her novel *Settimia* and her pamphlet *La femme et la démocratie de nos temps*, both in press, as well as the beginnings of her work on "a history of Florence."
120. Tommaseo to Capponi, August 13, 1834, *CI*, 1:158.
121. Allart to Capponi, January 21, 1832, *LIGC*.
122. Hortense Allart to Charles Augustin Sainte-Beuve, March 14, 1832, in Hortense Allart de Méritens, *Nouvelles lettres á Sainte-Beuve, 1832–1864*, ed. Lorin A. Uffenbeck (Geneva: Librairie Droz, 1965), 1: "On suppose que j'ai arrangé mes idées pour ma position, je les avais avant."
123. Allart to Capponi, June 16, 1831, *LIGC*.
124. Allart to Capponi, August 29, 1840, *LIGC*.
125. Allart to Capponi, November 20, 1829, *LIGC*.
126. Giovanni Spadolini, preface to Sestan, *La Firenze*, ix. According to Spadolini, this essay, "il più toccante per la costante nota autobiografica,... fu steso durante l'invasione nazifascista di Firenze e pubblicato solo nel 1945–1946, con la prima faticata ripresa dell'antica storica rivista, grazie allo sforzo dell'editore Olschki, in un numero doppio che somma due anni, in proporzione alla povertà dei mezzi e allo sconvolgimento dei tempi."
127. "Stato maggiore," in *Enciclopedia universale Garzanti* (Milan: Garzanti, 1995).
128. Sestan, *La Firenze*, 109–10.

129. Allart, *Sextus*, 39 and 40: "Rien de ce que je trouvais de beau chez les anciens ne se trouvait chez les modernes."

130. Ibid., 41.

131. Ibid., 45.

132. Ibid., 45.

133. Allart to Capponi, July 21, 1837, *LIGC*. See also the passage from Sestan, *La Firenze*, 122–23, quoted in n. 9 above.

134. Allart to Capponi, July 21, 1837, *LIGC*: "Votre lettre m'arrive quand je cherchais comment rendre ce caractère de Niccolò Capponi.... Une foule d'hommes de talent rendaient alors la politique intéressante, jamais Florence n'eut tant de savoir. Vous, le descendant de ces hommes, aidez-moi, expliquez-moi leur caractère."

135. Allart to Capponi, January 11, 1842, *LIGC*. Cf. July 21, 1837: "Vous, le descendant de ces hommes, . . . n'admirez pas les Capponi et je ne comprends pas pourquoi."

136. Allart to Capponi, July 21, 1837, *LIGC*. In effect, Allart's relation to past and present were forged in contrast to Capponi's. Cf. Allart to Capponi, January 21, 1832, *LIGC*: "Je ne pense pas comme vous que les affaires du temps passé pâlissent, je ne suis pas si subjuguée par le présent."

137. Allart to Capponi, March 14, 1826, *LIGC*.

138. Allart to Sainte-Beuve, October 15, 1845, in Allart, *Nouvelles lettres*, 47.

139. Allart to Capponi, January 1838, *LIGC*.

140. Allart to Capponi, January 22, 1846, *LIGC*. Allart was referring to her correspondence with her longtime lover, the British politician and diplomat Henry Bulwer-Lytton. When she first became involved with Bulwer, Allart considered herself to be as "chaste as the Roman Lucretia." But the figure of Lucretia could not accommodate the kind of political partnership Allart hoped to create with the passionate statesman, Bulwer. All that she had learned and studied of political history "among the brilliant spirits of Italy" had better prepared her, perhaps, to take on the persona of Aspasia, the intellectual mistress and adviser to Pericles, an attribution later assigned to her by George Sand. See Walton, *Eve's Proud Descendants*, 119 and n. 73.

141. Allart, *Les enchantements*, 110.

142. Allart to Capponi, March 27, 1859, *LIGC*.

143. Allart to Capponi, March 29, 1843, *LIGC*.

144. Allart to Capponi, September 24, 1841, *LIGC;* "Essais sur la Toscane," in Allart, *Sextus*, 437.

145. Allart to Capponi, September 24, 1841, *LIGC*.

146. Ibid.

147. Allart to Capponi, October 15, 1841, *LIGC* (errors in spelling and grammar are Allart's). Cf. B. Smith, *Gender of History*, 47: "Few of these [women] scholars articulated their connection with history as part of a burning vocational drive inherent in their natures; rather, history came later, as part of the development of a female persona set in a network of complex relationships."

148. Allart to Capponi, February 25, 1842, *LIGC*. .

149. Allart to Capponi, February 10, 1843, *LIGC*.

150. Capponi to Capei, March 1, 1843, in Capponi, *Lettere*, 2:120–22.
151. Allart to Capponi, March 29, 1843, *LIGC*.
152. Allart to Capponi, February 17, 1843, *LIGC*.
153. Walton, *Eve's Proud Descendants*, 11.
154. Ibid.
155. See Section One above. See also B. Smith, *Gender of History*, 67: For women historians, "important cognitions were based on trauma, fear, danger, and degradation—cognitions which ... provided reliable information. These then hardened into a set of procedures, unwritten rules, and rituals for writing history."
156. Walton, *Eve's Proud Descendants*, 152.
157. On more than one occasion—for example, Allart to Capponi, July 1 or 8, 1838, *LIGC,* and Allart, *Histoire* (1843), 412—Allart quoted Machiavelli's letter to Vettori (April 9, 1513) in which he claimed that Fortune, denying him the tools to work with silk or wool, profits or losses, had destined him to think and speak about politics ("la fortuna ha fatto, che non sapendo ragionare nè dell'arte della seta, nè dell'arte della lana, nè dei guadagni nè delle perdite, e' mi conviene ragionare dello stato, e *mi bisogna o botarmi di star cheto, o ragionare di questo*"). Allart, it would seem, identified with Machiavelli's fate inasmuch as she, too, devoted herself to politics in every aspect of her life and work. The intellectual and political trajectory from Machiavelli to Naudé to Allart might be materially traced in the friendship between Allart and Sainte-Beuve, who was named curator of the Mazarine Library on August 8, 1840, and who remained in this office until he resigned in March of 1848 after being accused of embezzling one hundred francs. Cf. Sainte-Beuve, *Portraits littéraires*, cx–xcvi. Sainte-Beuve's portrait of the Mazarine's founder (655–56) included himself as heir to "the founder, the librarian and great bibliographer Naudé, whose stamp is everywhere, whose spirit is represented in each instant in the choice of books ... I, the last to come and the most unworthy of his descendants, want to earn my title as heir." ("Mais tous ces hôtes passagers ... que sont-ils auprès du fondateur même, je veux dire le bibliothécaire de Mazarin et le grand bibliographe d'alors, ce Gabriel Naudé dont le cachet est là partout sous nos yeux, dont l'esprit se représente à chaque instant dans le choix des livres ... moi, le dernier venu et le plus indigne de sa postérité directe, je veux gagner mon titre d'héritier.") For Sainte-Beuve, the space of the Mazarine was pervaded by the power, passion, and influence of Naudé, who had chosen the books and passed down an understanding of relations with books as political. Allart and Sainte-Beuve met in the spring of 1831. Their "liaison" probably began in August of 1841, and they met for the last time in 1850. See Uffenbeck's introduction to Allart, *Nouvelles lettres,* xi–xv. Like Capponi, Sainte-Beuve lifted passages from Allart's letters for use in his own writing. He would attribute these quotations to "un de mes lecteurs les plus serieux," "une personne d'esprit," "une femme d'esprit," and so on. Uffenbeck's introduction to Allart, *Nouvelles lettres,* ix n., and Walton, *Eve's Proud Descendants*, 90.
158. Among her works of political historiography and theory, we might count *Histoire de la République de Florence* (1836 and 1843), *Histoire de la République d'Athènes* (1866), *La femme et la démocratie de nos temps* (1836), and *Essai sur l'histoire politique* (1857).

159. One might use this key of integrated thinking to understand Allart's difficulties with her lover Henry Bulwer-Lytton. While Allart was attracted to the mixing of love with politics, Bulwer kept his love for Allart and his political ambition on parallel tracks: "Il ne voulait au monde que le Parlement et l'amour . . . sa vie serait consacrée à moi et à cette ambition politique" (Allart, *Les enchantements*, 184). After all, how was he to realize his political ambition as a member of Parliament and, at the same time, take up residence with his lover in France? Although he briefly lived with Allart in Paris in 1832, taking up a position there in the British Embassy, and he promised, at other times, to leave England to live with her (see Allart, *Les enchantements*, 224, 236), Bulwer "feared" absenting himself from the House of Commons to see Allart. (Allart, *Les enchantements*, 214: "Il craint de me voir et manquer la Chambre.") He tormented himself with the idea that he would have to choose between Allart and Parliament, and when he realized that she was attracted to him precisely because he was a politician, he agonized about losing Allart's affections if he were to lose the elections (Allart, *Les enchantements*, 225, discussed also by Walton, *Eve's Proud Descendants*, 150–51): "Il me disait: – Si je ne suis pas nommé, vous ne m'aimerez plus; vous aimez le Parlement. – . . . Moi je voulais finir ce supplice, et qu'il choisît entre le Parlement et moi. Mais avec mes goûts, l'homme qui devait me plaire n'était-il pas celui qui choisirait le Parlement? Aussi crut-il garder tous deux." Allart knew that she could be with Bulwer in England only if she could "maintain her sanity" with projects of research and writing of her own. (Allart, *Les enchantements*, 238: "Il fallait ne revoir l'Angleterre qu'avec une occupation forte qui me tînt raisonnable"). She was "too much of a man herself" to let her own political and erudite passions be absorbed into another man's ambition (Allart to Anna Woodcock, August 19, 1832, in Petre Ciureanu, *Hortense Allart e Anna Woodcock con lettere inedite* [Genoa: Tolozzi, 1961], 50: "Je suis trop homme moi-même pour disparaître ainsi devant l'ambition d'un homme"). Cf. also B. Smith, *Gender of History*, 47: "Amateur women often acknowledged that their sexual relationships were a school for the mind, a way of internalizing or appropriating their lovers' intellectual drives. . . . [Allart's] travels with Henry Bulwer-Lytton provided her with first-hand accounts of politics in England and Belgium for her historical writing. Her lovers and other male intimates were the ones who first persuaded her to drop the successful novels she had been writing late in the 1820s and early in the 1830s and to pursue exclusively the 'virile' study of history."

160. Allart to Sainte-Beuve, December 21, 1841, in Hortense Allart de Méritens, *Lettres inédites à Sainte-Beuve (1841–1848)*, ed. Léon Séché (Paris: Soc. du Mercure de France, 1908), 33–34. Cf. Allart to Capponi, April 15, 1860, *LIGC*, in which Allart shares with Capponi her reflections on Cicero's letters. In response to Capponi's "Studi sopra le lettere di Cicerone"—first published in 1860 (the same year he was named as senator of the new Italy) in the *Archivio storico italiano*, n.s., 11, no. 2 (1860): 30–53—Allart analyzes Capponi's political assessments and interpretations of Cicero, situating them in relation to her own work on the *Letters* (published later as *Timide essai sur la correspondance sublime de Cicéron* [Sceaux: Charaire, 1876]). Unlike Petrarch, whose relation with Cicero's *Letters* was a private and exclusive one, Allart is interested in opening up the relational possibilities, in engaging Capponi and politics via the

Letters of Cicero. Here again, Allart's passionate engagement with books open a pathway to her relations with politics and men and make a place for herself in the humanistic tradition of political thought.

161. Cf. B. Smith, *Gender of History*, 47.
162. Allart, *Les enchantements*, 263.
163. Allart to Capponi, June 25, 1855, *LIGC*.
164. See Allart to Capponi, March 8, 1939, *LIGC*.
165. Allart to Capponi, July 5, 1856, *LIGC*.
166. Allart to Capponi, November 17, 1828, *LIGC*.
167. See, for example, Allart to Capponi, October 12, 1837 and March 8, 1939, in which Allart lists the books she is returning, still using, would like to borrow, both in *LIGC*.
168. Allart to Capponi, February-March 1838 (Letters 62 and 63), *LIGC*.
169. Allart to Capponi, June 7 or 14, 1838, *LIGC*.
170. See also Walton, *Eve's Proud Descendants*, 120. Walton cites Delphine de Girardin's 1847 play *Cleopatra*, in which Cleopatra ordered military action to restore the Library of Alexandria and in doing so earned the loyalty of her erudite subjects.
171. Allart to Capponi, March 11, 1875, *LIGC*.
172. Allart to Capponi, July 1, 1857, and October 6, 1842, both in *LIGC*. Cf. Allart to Capponi, February 17, 1843, "Protégez-moi là-bas."
173. Anna Maria Mozzoni, *La liberazione della donna*, ed. Franca Pieroni Bortolotti (Milan: G. Mazzotta, 1975), 22. Bortolotti noted that Anna Maria Mozzoni "was afraid of the word 'protection' [tutela]: every discriminatory law has been ideologically justified by the necessity of 'protecting' the health of women." To productively critique bourgeois society, one would have to eliminate words like "defense" of women or "protection" of women. (Mozzoni "aveva paura della parola 'tutela': non c'è legge discriminatoria che non sia stata ideologicamente giustificata dalla necessità di 'tutelare' la salute delle donne." "Appena si parla di 'difesa' o di 'tutela' della donna, la questione femminile non serve piú a una critica consapevole e socialista della società borghese.")
174. Allart to Capponi, October 21, 1857, *LIGC*.
175. Allart to Capponi, July 6, 1855, *LIGC*.
176. Allart to Capponi, July 21, 1837, *LIGC*.
177. Allart to Capponi, October 12, 1837, *LIGC*.
178. Allart to Capponi, March 3, 1844, *LIGC*: "Comment peut-on croire qu'un être libre et capable de liberté acceptera une loi qui la soumet comme une esclave si le mari le veut. Vous, penseurs, imaginez-vous un être libre ainsi avili; voyez donc qu'il faut changer cette loi."
179. Capponi, *Storia*, v.
180. Capponi to Capei, March 1, 1843, in Capponi, *Lettere*, 2:121.
181. Allart, hearing of this work from Capei, expressed concern about Orlandini's competence and eagerness to meet him. Allart to Capponi, June 21, 1844, *LIGC*: "Capei me dit que M. Orlandini a déjà traduit un vol[ume] de mon *Histoire de Florence*. Qu'est-ce que M. Orlandini? Quel homme de goût! J'espère que vous le connaissez!" Two and a half years later, Allart registered

her understanding that work on the translation was still in progress (Allart to Capponi, January 6, 1847, *LIGC*): "Capei m'a dit que vous faisiez continuer la traduction de ma petite *Histoire de Fl[orence]*."

182. Cf. Allart to Capponi, March 29, 1843, and n. 3, *LIGC*: "La traduzione fu affidata poi ad Alessandro Carraresi, che la condusse a buon fine, ma essa non fu pubblicata. Servì invece al Capponi come punto iniziale per l'elaborazione della sua *Storia della Repubblica di Firenze*, come dice lui stesso nella 'Prefazione' dell'opera"; Allart to Capponi, October 24, 1853, and n. 6, *LIGC*: "La traduzione, affidata dal Capponi ad Alessandro Carraresi, era già terminata, ma si vede che Hortense non lo sapeva."

183. Allart to Capponi, February 25, 1842 ("Il me faut dans l'année une édition, faite en Italie en français, et une traduction en italien. Autrement je ne serai pas contente"), October 6, 1842 ("Je ne serai contente que quand il en aura aussi paru une édition en italien), and March 29, 1843 ("Je vous remercie et suis charmée de votre idée d'une traduction. Faites qu'on s'y mette tout de suite, je ne serai contente qu'alors"), all in *LIGC*.

184. Allart to Capponi, May 23, 1843, *LIGC*.

185. Allart to Capponi, January 22, 1846, *LIGC*.

186. Allart to Capponi, May 16, 1843, *LIGC*; cf. also June 21, 1844, and January 6, 1847, which mention lines Allart would like to add and lists of corrections she would like Capponi to give to the translator.

187. Allart to Capponi, May 23, 1843, *LIGC*. Cf. n. 24 above.

188. Allart to Capponi, October 24, 1853, *LIGC*: "M. Polidori avait bien voulu, m'a-t-on dit, commencer par vos conseils, une traduction de mon Histoire de Florence.... Il me donnerait par son travail, un peu de valeur, surtout si vous vouliez, vous Polyeucte, me continuer à ce sujet, votre première bienveillance."

189. Allart to Capponi, March 29, 1843, *LIGC*.

190. Allart to Capponi, May 18, 1844, *LIGC*; Allart, *Les enchantements*, 311. See also Allart to Sainte-Beuve, March 31, 1845, in *Lettres inédites à Sainte-Beuve*, 95: "Depuis mon mariage, je hais surtout la tyrannie."

191. Allart to Capponi, October 15, 1829, *LIGC*.

192. Allart, *Sextus*, 93–96. Cf. Tarabotti's political critique of men's vanity in her *Antisatira* (discussed above in Section Two, Frapporsi 10, "Women, Liberty, the State").

193. Quoted in Giulia Barone and Armando Petrucci, *Primo, non leggere: Biblioteche e pubblica lettura in Italia dal 1861 ai nostri giorni* (Milan: G. Mazzotta, 1976), 14.

194. After reading Polidori's *Life of Pieri*, Allart wrote to Capponi that Pieri's biography was, in some aspects, the same as her own. Allart to Capponi, October 24, 1853, *LIGC*: "Je l'ai lue avec beaucoup d'intérêt.... Je vous dirai même que j'ai cru lire, en un point, ma propre biographie."

195. Allart to Capponi, January 1838, *LIGC*. "Vous aurez une grande part à mon second vol avec vos conversations et vos livres."

196. Allart to Capponi, September 26, 1840, *LIGC*.

197. Allart to Capponi, May 16, 1843, *LIGC*. Phrases like "our little republic," "our Florence," and "our readings" are frequent in Allart's letters. See,

for example, also in *LIGC,* December 15, 1851 ("notre petite République de Florence"), October 24, 1853 ("nos lectures"), June 25, 1855 ("notre longue commerce" and "notre philosophie"), and July 21, 1855 ("notre Florence").

198. See pp. 159 and 162 above.

199. See p. 162 above.

200. Allart to Capponi, August 10–15, 1838, *LIGC.*

201. Allart to Capponi, October 6, 1842, *LIGC.*

202. Allart to Capponi, July 4, 1838, *LIGC.*

203. Allart to Capponi, March 25, 1829, *LIGC;* see also Allart to Capponi, June 25, 1855, *LIGC:* "Ce fut une longue amitié, rien de plus, pourquoi?"

204. Allart to Sainte-Beuve, March 25, 1832, and n. 2 in Allart, *Nouvelles lettres.*

205. See p. 170 above.

206. Allart to Capponi, February 10, 1843, *LIGC:* "Je n'ai jamais eu l'Archivio, mai j'avais lu tout cela en manuscrit, vous me l'aviez donné. Je n'ai pas dit qu'on avait imprimé la loi des Gonfalons, à quoi bon? c'est d'hier et je ne l'ai su que déjà sous presse."

207. Allart to Capponi, February 25, 1842, *LIGC:* "Je suis très mécontente de vous, sans parler de ce document que vous me donnez comme inédit, et que vous faites paraître avant moi!"

208. Allart to Capponi, March 29, 1843, *LIGC.*

209. Allart, *Les enchantements,* 262.

210. Allart to Capponi, October 17, 1837, *LIGC.* Cf. Allart to Tommaseo, August 19, 1836 (Biblioteca Nazionale Centrale di Firenze, Carte Tommaseo, box 48, file 87), quoted in Ciureanu's introduction to *LIGC,* lix: "Vous êtes dans cette vieille morale de la chasteté qui a inventé les filles publiques."

211. Ciureanu's introduction to *LIGC,* lxxxviii.

212. Allart, *Histoire* (1843), v. See p. 164 above.

213. Allart to Capponi, October 17, 1837, *LIGC.*

214. Allart, *Histoire* (1843), 543. Capponi, after the end of the Republic, continued to summarize Florentine history up to his own time.

215. Many thanks to Prof. Susan Larsen for this interesting insight.

216. Allart, *Histoire* (1843), 545.

217. Tommaseo to Capponi, August 13, 1834, *CI,* 1:158: "Ora scrive la storia di Firenze, poi un'opera sulla donna."

218. Capponi to Tommaseo, November 19, 1838, *CI,* 2:103.

219. Sestan, *La Firenze,* 121 n. 57.

AFTERWORD

1. Anna Maria Mozzoni, *La donna e i suoi rapporti sociali* (Milan: Tipografia Sociale, 1864), 171, .

2. Mozzoni, *La donna,* 33.

3. Bortolotti, *Alle origini,* 62.

4. Carlo Cattaneo, *Opere edite ed inedite di Carlo Cattaneo,* 3 vols. (Florence: Le Monnier, 1881–83), 1:358.

5. Mozzoni, *La donna,* 33.

6. Mozzoni, *La donna,* 181–82.

Bibliography

Albertini, Rudolf von. *Firenze dalla repubblica al principato: Storia e coscienza politica.* Turin: Einaudi, 1970.
Allart de Méritens, Hortense. *Les enchantements de prudence par Mme P[rudence] de Saman.* New ed. Paris: Calmann Lévy, 1877.
———. *Essai sur l'histoire politique, depuis l'invasion des barbares jusqu'en 1848.* Paris: J. Rouvier, 1857.
———. *La femme et la démocratie de nos temps.* Paris: Delaunay, 1836.
———. *Histoire de la république de Florence.* Paris: Moutardier, 1837.
———. *Histoire de la république de Florence.* Paris: Delloye, 1843.
———. *Lettere inedite a Gino Capponi.* Ed. and introd. Petre Ciureanu. Genoa: Tolozzi, 1961.
———. *Lettres inédites à Sainte-Beuve: (1841–1848).* Ed. Léon Séché. Paris: Soc. du Mercure de France, 1908.
———. *Nouvelles lettres á Sainte-Beuve, 1832–1864.* Ed. Lorin A. Uffenbeck. Geneva: Librairie Droz, 1965.
———. *Sextus ou le Romain des Maremmes suivie d'Essaies détachés sur l'Italie.* Paris: Heideloff et Campe, 1832.
———. *Timide essai sur la correspondance sublime de Cicéron.* Sceaux: Charaire, 1876.
Althusser, Louis. "Ideology and Ideological State Apparatuses." In *Lenin and Philosophy, and Other Essays.* New York: Monthly Review Press, 1972.
Alvar, Manuel. "Fantastic Tales and Chronicles of the Indies." In *Amerindian Images and the Legacy of Columbus,* ed. René Jara and Nicholas Spadaccini. Minneapolis: University of Minnesota Press, 1992.
Alvarez-Ossorio Alvariño, Antonio. "The State of Milan and the Spanish Monarchy." In *Spain in Italy: Politics, Society, and Religion, 1500–1700,* ed. John Marino and Thomas Dandelet. Leiden: Brill, 2007.

Ammirato, Scipione. *Istorie fiorentine.* Florence: Stamperia Nuova d'Amador Massi e Lorenzo Landi, 1641.

———. *Istorie fiorentine.* Florence: L. Marchini and G. Becherini, 1826.

Aristotle. *Gli otto libri della republica che chiamono politica di Aristotile.* Trans. Antonio Brucioli. Venice: Alessandro Brucioli e i frategli, 1547.

Ascoli, Albert Russell, and Krystyna Clara Von Henneberg. *Making and Remaking Italy: The Cultivation of National Identity around the Risorgimento.* Oxford: Berg, 2001.

Baldoni, Eride. *Lorenzino de' Medici e l'Apologia.* Ancona: Atima, 1950.

Balsamo, Luigi. *La bibliografia: Storia di una tradizione.* Florence: Sansoni, 1984.

Bandini, Bruno V., ed. *Storia e storiografia, studi su Delio Cantimori.* Atti del convegno tenuto a Russi (Ravenna) il 7–8 ottobre 1978. Rome: Editori Riuniti, 1979.

Bardi, Alessandro. "Filippo Strozzi (da nuovi documenti)." *Archivio storico italiano,* 5th ser., 14 (1894): 3–78.

Barone, Giulia, and Armando Petrucci. *Primo, non leggere: Biblioteche e pubblica lettura in Italia dal 1861 ai nostri giorni.* Milan: G. Mazzotta, 1976.

Barthes, Roland. "An Almost Obsessive Relation to Writing Instruments." In *The Grain of the Voice: Interviews, 1962–1980.* New York: Hill and Wang, 1985.

———. "From Work to Text." In *Image, Music, Text,* trans. Stephen Heath. New York: Hill and Wang, 1977. Originally published as "De l'oeuvre au texte," *Revue d'esthetique* 3 (1971): 225–32.

Bartolus a Saxoferrato. *Opera quae nunc extant omnia.* Basileae ex officina episcopiana, 1589.

Beccaria, Gian Luigi. *Spagnolo e spagnoli in Italia: Riflessi ispanici sulla lingua italiana del Cinque e del Seicento.* Turin: Giappichelli, 1968.

Benjamin, Walter. "Theses on the Philosophy of History." In *Illuminations,* ed. Hannah Arendt, trans. Harry Zohn. New York: Schocken Books, 1969.

Biga, Emilia. *Una polemica antifemminista del Seicento: La "Maschera scoperta" di Angelico Aprosio.* Ventimiglia: Civica Biblioteca Aprosiana, 1989.

Bilefsky, Dan. "How to Avoid Honor Killing in Turkey? Honor Suicide." *New York Times,* July 16, 2006.

Boccalini, Traiano. *Ragguagli di Parnaso.* 1612. Reprint, Venice: Gueriglij, 1637.

———. *"I ragguagli di Parnaso"; or, Advertisements from Parnassus: in two centuries.* Trans. Henry Earl of Monmouth. 1656. Reprint, London: Thomas Guy, 1674.

———. *Ragguagli di Parnaso e scritti minori.* Ed. Luigi Firpo. Bari: G. Laterza, 1948. Scrittori d'Italia Laterza, www.bibliotecaitaliana.it/exist/ScrittoriItalia/show-text.xq?textID=mets.sio58.

Bodin, Jean. *Les six livres de la République.* Geneva: Gabriel Cartier, 1608.

Bodley, Thomas. *Letters of Sir Thomas Bodley to Thomas James.* Ed. G. W. Wheeler. Oxford: Clarendon Press, 1926.

Bois, Yve-Alain. "Writer, Artisan, Narrator." *October* 26 (1983): 27–33.

Boose, Lynda E., and Betty S. Flowers. *Daughters and Fathers.* Balti-

more: Johns Hopkins University Press, 1989.
Bortolotti, Franca Pieroni. *Alle origini del movimento femminile in Italia: 1848–1892*. Turin: Einaudi, 1963.
Bottasso, Enzo. *Storia della biblioteca in Italia*. Bibliografia e biblioteconomia 16. Milan: Bibliografica, 1984.
Bradstreet, Anne. *The Works of Anne Bradstreet*. Ed. Jeannine Hensley. Cambridge, MA: Harvard University Press, 1967.
Bromfield, Joyce G. *De Lorenzino de Médicis à Lorenzaccio: Étude d'un thème historique*. Études de littérature étrangère et comparée 64. Paris: M. Didier, 1972.
Brose, Margaret. "Petrarch's Beloved Body: 'Italia mia.'" In *Feminist Approaches to the Body in Medieval Literature*, ed. Linda Lomperis and Sarah Stanbury. New Cultural Studies. Philadelphia: University of Pennsylvania Press, 1993.
Browne, Sir Thomas. *Pseudodoxia Epidemica*. 6th ed. 1672. http://penelope.uchicago.edu/pseudodoxia/pseudodoxia.shtml.
Brucioli, Antonio. *Dialogi*. Venice: Gregorio, 1526.
Brunetta, Gian Piero. *Cinema italiano tra le due guerre: Fascismo e politica cinematografica*. Milan: Mursia, 1975.
Brunnsåker, Sture. *The Tyrant-Slayers of Kritios and Nesiotes: A Critical Study of the Sources and Restorations*. 2nd ed. Stockholm: Svenska Institutet, 1971.
Bucci, Susanna. "Come si parla della donna: I cataloghi." In *La condizione della donna nel XVII e XVIII secolo*, by Fiorenza Taricone and Susanna Bucci. Rome: Carucci, 1983.
Bullard, Melissa Meriam. *Filippo Strozzi and the Medici: Favor and Finance in Sixteenth-Century Florence and Rome*. Cambridge: Cambridge University Press, 1980.
Buoninsegni, Francesco, and Arcangela Tarabotti. *Satira e antisatira*. Ed. Elissa Weaver. Rome: Salerno, 1998.
Burckhardt, Jacob. *The Civilization of the Renaissance in Italy*. New York: Harper and Row, 1958.
Campana, Augusto. "The Origin of the Word 'Humanist.'" *Journal of the Warburg and Courtauld Institutes* 9 (1946): 60–73.
Canepa, Nancy L. "The Writing behind the Wall: Arcangela Tarabotti's *Inferno monacale* and Cloistral Autobiography in the Seventeenth Century." *Forum Italicum* 30, no. 1 (1996): 1–23.
Canfora, Luciano. *The Vanished Library: A Wonder of the Ancient World*. Berkeley: University of California Press, 1990.
Canonici Fachini, Ginevra. *Prospetto bibliografico di donne italiane rinomate in letteratura*. Venice: Alvisopoli, 1824.
Cantimori, Delio. "Il caso di Boscoli e la vita del Rinascimento." *Giornale critico della filosofia* 8 (1927): 241–55.
———. *Conversando di storia*. Bari: Laterza, 1967.
———. "Osservazioni sui concetti di cultura e storia della cultura." In *Scritti vari pubblicati dagli alunni della R. Scuola Normale Superiore di Pisa*. Pacini: Mariotti, 1928.

———. Review of *La vita come ricerca,* by Ugo Spirito. *Giornale critico della filosofia italiana* 18 (1937): 356–70.
———. "Rhetoric and Politics in Italian Humanism." Trans. Frances A. Yates. *Journal of the Warburg Insititute* 1, no. 2 (1937): 83–102.
Capponi, Gino. "Un brano della Repubblica di Firenze (1351–1358)." *Archivio storico italiano,* n.s., 7, pt. 2 (1858): 60–92.
———. *Lettere di Gino Capponi: E di altri a lui raccolte e pubblicate.* 6 vols. Ed. Alessandro Carraresi. Florence: Monnier, 1884–90.
———. *Storia della Repubblica di Firenze.* Florence: Barbèra, 1875.
———. "Studi sopra le lettere di Cicerone." *Archivio storico italiano,* n.s., 11, no. 2 (1860): 30–53.
Catalogo dei manoscritti del Card. Federico Borromeo nella Biblioteca Ambrosiana. Milan: Biblioteca Ambrosiana, 1988.
Catalogus librorum bibliothecae publicae quam vir ornatissimus Thomas Bodleius eques auratus in Academia Oxoniensi nuper instituit. Oxoniae: Apud Iosephum Barnesium, 1605.
Cattaneo, Carlo. *Opere edite ed inedite di Carlo Cattaneo.* 3 vols. Florence: Le Monnier, 1881–83.
Cavriani, Filippo. *Discorsi del signor Filippo Cavriana sopra i primi 5 libri di Tacito.* Florence: Filippo Giunti, 1597.
Ceccheregli, Alessandro. *Delle attioni et sentenze del S. Alessandro de' Medici primo duca di Fiorenza.* Vinegia: Gabriel Giolito de' Ferrari, 1564. Reprinted in *Scelta di curiosità letterarie inedite o rare dal secolo XIII al XVII,* Dispensa 66 (Bologna: Gaetano Romagnoli, 1865).
Cellini, Benvenuto. *La vita di Benvenuto di M. Giovanni Cellini fiorentino scritta (per lui medesimo) in Firenze.* Ed. Carlo Cordié. Milan: Ricciardi, 1960.
Certeau, Michel de. *The Writing of History.* Trans. Tom Conley. New York: Columbia University Press, 1988.
Chabod, Federico. *Lo stato e la vita religiosa a Milano nell'epoca di Carlo V.* Turin: Einaudi, 1971.
———. *Storia di Milano nell'epoca di Carlo V.* Turin: Einaudi, 1961.
Chakrabarty, Dipesh. "The Time of History and the Times of Gods." In *The Politics of Culture in the Shadow of Capital,* ed. Lisa Lowe and David Lloyd. Durham: Duke University Press, 1997.
Chartier, Roger. *The Order of Books: Readers, Authors, and Libraries in Europe between the Fourteenth and Eighteenth Centuries.* Stanford: Stanford University Press, 1994.
Chiantera-Stutte, Patricia. *Res nostra agitur: Il pensiero di Delio Cantimori, 1928–1937.* Bari: Palomar, 2005.
Chojnacki, Stanley. "'The Most Serious Duty': Motherhood, Gender, and Patrician Culture in Renaissance Venice." In *Refiguring Women: Perspectives on Gender and the Italian Renaissance,* ed. Marilyn Migiel and Juliana Schiesari (Ithaca: Cornell University Press, 1991), 133–54.
Ciampini, Raffaele. *Vita di Niccolò Tommaseo.* Florence: G. C. Sansoni, 1945.
Ciliberto, Michele. "Cantimori e gli eretici: Filosofia, storiografia e politica tra gli anni venti e gli anni trenta." In *Storia e storiografia: Studi su Delio Cantimori.* Atti del convegno tenuto a Russi (Ravenna) il 7–8 ottobre 1978, ed.

Bruno V. Bandini, 152–93. Rome: Editori Riuniti, 1979.
———. *Intellettuali e fascismo: Saggio su Delio Cantimori*. Bari: De Donato, 1977.
Ciureanu, Petre. *Hortense Allart e Anna Woodcock con lettere inedite*. Genoa: Tolozzi, 1961.
———. *Saggi e ricerche su scrittori francesi*. Genoa: Italica, 1955.
Cochrane, Eric, and John Tedeschi. "Delio Cantimori: Historian." *Journal of Modern History* 39, no. 4 (1967): 438–45.
Comenius, Johann Amos. *The Orbis pictus*. Trans. Charles Hoole. Detroit: Singing Tree Press, 1968.
Conti Odorisio, Ginevra. *Donna e società nel Seicento: Lucrezia Marinelli e Arcangela Tarabotti*. Rome: Bulzoni, 1979.
———. *Famiglia e Stato nella "République" di Jean Bodin*. Turin: G. Giappichelli, 1993.
———. *Storia dell'idea femminista in Italia*. Turin: ERI, 1980.
Cortelazzo, Manlio, and Paolo Zolli. *Dizionario etimologico della lingua italiana*. Bologna: Zanichelli, 1988.
Cox, Virginia. "The Single Self: Feminist Thought and the Marriage Market in Early Modern Venice." *Renaissance Quarterly* 48 (1995): 513–81.
———. *Women's Writing in Italy, 1400–1650*. Baltimore: Johns Hopkins University Press, 2008.
Craveri, Benedetta. *Madame Du Deffand and Her World*. Boston: D. R. Godine, 1994.
Craveri, Piero. "Delio Cantimori." In *Dizionario biografico degli italiani*. Rome: Istituto della Enciclopedia Italiana, 1960–. www.treccani.it/Portale/elements/categoriesItems.jsp?pathFile=/sites/default/BancaDati/Enciclopedia_online/C/BIOGRAFIE_-_EDICOLA_C_113455.xml.
Creamer, Paul. "Woman-Hating in Marie de France's Bisclavret." *Romanic Review* 93, no. 3 (2002): 259–74.
Damien, Robert. *Bibliothèque et état: Naissance d'une raison politique dans la France du XVIIe siècle*. Paris: Presses universitaires de France, 1995.
Datta, Satya Brata. *Women and Men in Early Modern Venice: Reassessing History*. Aldershot: Ashgate, 2003.
Davis, Natalie Zemon. "Rabelais among the Censors (1940s, 1540s)." *Representations* 32 (1990): 1–32.
———. *Women on the Margins: Three Seventeenth-Century Lives*. Cambridge, MA: Harvard University Press, 1995.
Decreus, Juliette. *Henry Bulwer-Lytton et Hortense Allart, d'apres des documents inédits*. Paris: M. J. Minard, 1961.
Defert, Daniel. "The Collection of the World: Accounts of Voyages from the Sixteenth to the Eighteenth Centuries." *Dialectical Anthropology* 7, no. 1 (1982): 11–20.
de Lauretis, Teresa. *Alice Doesn't: Feminism, Semiotics, Cinema*. Bloomington: Indiana University Press, 1984.
D'Elia, Nicola. *Delio Cantimori e la cultura politica tedesca: 1927–1940*. Rome: Viella, 2007.
Díaz del Castillo, Bernal. *The Discovery and Conquest of Mexico, 1517–1521*.

Ed. and introd. Irving Leonard. Trans. A. P. Maudslay. New York: Farrar, Straus and Giroux, 1979.

———. *Historia verdadera de la conquista de la Nueva España*. Ed. Joaquín Ramírez Cabañas. 2 vols. Mexico City: Editorial Porrúa, 1960.

Di Mauro, Alberto, and Alessandro Gregorio Capponi. *Bibliografia delle stampe popolari profane dal fondo Capponi della Biblioteca Vaticana*. Florence: Olschki, 1981.

Eisenstein, Elizabeth L. *The Printing Press as an Agent of Change*. Cambridge: Cambridge University Press, 1985.

Elliott, John Huxtable. *The Old World and the New, 1492–1650*. Cambridge: Cambridge University Press, 1992.

Emerton, Ephraim. *Humanism and Tyranny: Studies in the Italian Trecento*. Cambridge, MA: Harvard University Press, 1925.

Enciclopedia universale Garzanti. Milan: Garzanti, 1995.

Ferguson, Kathy E. "Work, Text, and Act in Discourses of Organization." *Women and Politics* 7, no. 2 (1987): 1–21.

Ferrai, Luigi Alberto. *Lorenzino de' Medici e la società cortigiana del Cinquecento*. Milan: U. Hoepli, 1891.

Ferri, Pietro Leopoldo. *Biblioteca femminile italiana*. Padua: Crescini, 1842.

Findlen, Paula. "The Museum: Its Classical Etymology and Renaissance Genealogy." *Journal of the History of Collections* 1, no. 1 (1989): 59–78.

———. *Possessing Nature: Museums, Collecting, and Scientific Culture in Early Modern Italy*. Berkeley: University of California Press, 1994.

Fraisse, Geneviève. *Reason's Muse: Sexual Difference and the Birth of Democracy*. Chicago: University of Chicago Press, 1994.

Franklin, Alfred. *Histoire de la Bibliothèque Mazarine depuis sa fondation jusqu'à nos jours*. Paris: A. Aubry, 1860.

Fumaroli, Marc. "La république des lettres." *Diogène* 143 (1988): 131–50.

Gamucci, Bernardo. *Le antichità della citta di Roma*. Vinegia: Giovanni Farisco, 1580.

Garin, Eugenio. *Intellettuali italiani del XX secolo*. Rome: Editori Riuniti, 1974.

Gerbi, Antonello. *Nature in the New World: From Christopher Columbus to Gonzalo Fernández de Oviedo*. Trans. Jeremy Moyle. Pittsburgh: University of Pittsburgh Press, 1985.

Ghibellini da Prato, Lorenzo. *Il lamento che fa in fra se Lorenzino de' Medici che amazzò l'iIllustrissimo Signor Alessandro de Medici Duca primo di Fiorenza*. Florence: Giovanni Baleni, 1584.

Giard, Luce, and Christian Jacob, eds. *Des Alexandries I: Du livre au texte*. Paris: Bibliothèque Nationale de France, 2001.

Gili, Jean A. "Film storico e film in costume." In *Cinema sotto il fascismo*, ed. Riccardo Redi. Venice: Marsilio, 1979.

Gilly, Adolfo, Subcomandante Marcos, and Carlo Ginzburg. *Discusión sobre la historia*. Mexico City: Taurus, 1995.

Ginzburg, Carlo. *The Cheese and the Worms: The Cosmos of a Sixteenth-Century Miller*. Trans. John and Anne Tedeschi. New York: Penguin Books, 1982.

———. "Clues: Roots of an Evidential Paradigm." In *Clues, Myths, and the*

Historical Method, trans. John and Anne Tedeschi. Baltimore: Johns Hopkins University Press, 1989. Originally published as "Spie: Radici di un paradigma indiziario," in *Crisi della ragione,* ed. Aldo Giorgio Gargani (Turin: Einaudi, 1979), and then as "Morelli, Freud and Sherlock Holmes: Clues and Scientific Method," *History Workshop Journal* 9 (1980): 5–36.

Giovio, Paolo. *Historiarum sui temporis.* Florence: Lorenzo Torrentino, 1550–52.

———. *Le iscrittioni poste sotto le vere imagini de gli huomini famosi le quali a Como nel Museo del Giovio si veggiono.* Trans. Hippolito Orio Ferrarese. Florence: Lorenzo Torrentino, 1552.

———. *Istorie del suo tempo.* Trans. Lodovico Domenichi. Venetia: Giovan Maria Bonelli, 1560.

Goldsmid, Edmund. *Un-natural History, or Myths of Ancient Science.* Edinburgh, 1886. http://web.archive.org/web/20051221164921/www.herper.com/ebooks/library/biofort/AncientMyths.pdf.

Goody, Jack, and Ian Watt. "The Consequences of Literacy." In *Literacy in Traditional Societies,* ed. Jack Goody. New York: Cambridge University Press, 1968.

Gordon, Avery. *Ghostly Matters: Haunting and the Sociological Imagination.* Minneapolis: University of Minnesota Press, 1996.

Gori, Gianfranco. *Patria diva: La storia d'Italia nei film del ventennio.* Florence: La Casa Usher, 1988.

Gramsci, Antonio. *Quaderni del carcere.* Ed. Valentino Gerratana. Turin: Einaudi, 1975.

Greene, Roland Arthur. "Petrarchism among the Discourses of Imperialism." In *America in European Consciousness, 1493–1750,* ed. Karen Kupperman. Chapel Hill: University of North Carolina Press, 1995.

———. *Unrequited Conquests: Love and Empire in the Colonial Americas.* Chicago: University of Chicago Press, 1999.

Groebner, Valentin, and Pamela Selwyn. "Losing Face, Saving Face: Noses and Honour in the Late Medieval Town." *History Workshop Journal* 40 (1995): 1–15.

Hampton, Timothy. *Fictions of Embassy: Literature and Diplomacy in Early Modern Europe.* Ithaca: Cornell University Press, 2009.

———. "'Turkish Dogs': Rabelais, Erasmus, and the Rhetoric of Alterity." *Representations* 41 (1993): 58–82.

Hansen, Helynne Hollstein. *Hortense Allart: The Woman and the Novelist.* Lanham, MD: University Press of America, 1998.

Heller, Wendy Beth. *Emblems of Eloquence: Opera and Women's Voices in Seventeenth-Century Venice.* Berkeley: University of California Press, 2003. http://site.ebrary.com/lib/ucsd/docDetail.action?docID=10058567.

Hendricks, Margo, and Patricia A. Parker. *Women, "Race," and Writing in the Early Modern Period.* London: Routledge, 1994.

Herodotus. *Herodoto Alicarnaseo Historico delle guerre de Greci et de Persi.* Trans. Mattheo Maria Boiardo. Venetia, 1533.

Hunt, Lynn Avery. *The Family Romance of the French Revolution.* Berkeley: University of California Press, 1992.

Hutson, Lorna. *Feminism and Renaissance Studies.* Oxford: Oxford University Press, 1999.

———. *The Usurer's Daughter: Male Friendship and Fictions of Women in Sixteenth-Century England.* London: Routledge, 1994.

Ilardi, Vincenzo. "The Assassination of Galeazzo Maria Sforza and the Reaction of Italian Diplomacy." In *Violence and Civil Disorder in Italian Cities,* ed. Lauro Martines. Berkeley: University of California Press, 1972.

Ileto, Reynaldo C. "Outlines of a Non-linear Emplotment of Philippine History," in *Reflections on Development in Southeast Asia,* ed. Lim Teck Ghee. Singapore: ASEAN Economic Research Unit, Institute of Southeast Asian Studies, 1988. Reprinted in *The Politics of Culture in the Shadow of Capital,* ed. Lisa Lowe and David Lloyd, 98–131 (Durham: Duke University Press, 1997).

Infelise, Mario. "Libri e politica nella Venezia di Arcangela Tarabotti." *Annali di storia moderna e contemporanea* 8 (2002): 31–45.

Jed, Stephanie. "Arcangela Tarabotti and Gabriel Naudé: Libraries, Taxonomies, and *Ragion di Stato.*" In *Arcangela Tarabotti: A Literary Nun in Baroque Venice,* ed. Elissa B. Weaver, 129–40. Ravenna: Longo, 2006.

———. "Making History Straight: Collecting and Recording in Sixteenth-Century Italy." *Bucknell Review* 35, no. 2 (1992): 104–20.

———. "Proof and Transnational Rhetorics: Opening Up the Conversation," *History and Theory* 40, no. 3 (2001): 372–84.

———. "Relations of Prose: Knights Errant in the Archives of Early Modern Italy." In *The Project of Prose in the Early Modern West,* ed. Elizabeth Fowler and Roland Greene. Cambridge: Cambridge University Press, 1997.

———. "Reorganizing Knowledge: A Feminist Scholar's Everyday Relation to the Florentine Past." In *Renaissance Culture and the Everyday,* ed. Patricia Fumerton and Simon Hunt. Philadelphia: University of Pennsylvania Press, 1999.

———. "Sapere conservato e conservatori del sapere: Relazioni transnazionali nella ricerca storica." *Storia e problemi contemporanei* 28 (2001): 215–27.

———. "The Scene of Tyranny: Violence and the Humanistic Tradition." In *The Violence of Representation,* ed. Nancy Armstrong and Leonard Tennenhouse. London: Routledge, 1989.

———. "Social Spaces of History: Gender, Erudition, and the Italian Nation." In *Writing Relations: American Scholars in Italian Archives,* ed. Deanna Shemek and Michael Wyatt, 165–90. Florence: Olschki, 2008.

———. "The Tenth Muse: Gender, Rationality and the Marketing of Knowledge." In *Women, "Race," and Writing in the Early Modern Period,* ed. Margo Hendricks and Patricia Parker. London: Routledge, 1994. Reprinted in Lorna Hutson, ed., *Feminism and Renaissance Studies* (London: Oxford University Press, 1999).

Jones, Ann Rosalind. *The Currency of Eros: Women's Love Lyric in Europe, 1540–1620.* Bloomington: Indiana University Press, 1990.

Jones, Ann Rosalind, and Peter Stallybrass. *Renaissance Clothing and the Materials of Memory.* Cambridge Studies in Renaissance Literature and Culture. Cambridge: Cambridge University Press, 2000.

Joplin, Patricia Klindienst. "The Voice of the Shuttle Is Ours." *Stanford Literature Review* 1 (1984): 25–53.
Juana Inés de la Cruz. *A Sor Juana Anthology*. Trans. Alan S. Trueblood. Cambridge, MA: Harvard University Press, 1988.
Jung, Carl Gustav. *Symbols of Transformation*. Trans. R. F. C. Hull. Princeton: Princeton University Press, 1967.
Justinus, Marcus Junianus. *Nelle Historie di Trogo Pompeio. nouamente in lingua toscana. tradotto: [et] con somma diligentia [et] cura stampato*. Venetia: Nicolo Zopino e Vicentio, 1524.
Juvenal. *Saturae*. With commentaries by Domizio Calderino and Giorgio Valla. Venetia: Theodorus de Ragazonibus, 1491.
Kastan, David Scott. *Shakespeare and the Book*. Cambridge: Cambridge University Press, 2001.
Kierkegaard, Soren. *Fear and Trembling and The Sickness unto Death*, trans. and introd. Walter Lowrie. New York: Doubleday Anchor Books, 1954.
Kristeller, Paul Oskar. *Renaissance Thought: The Classic, Scholastic, and Humanist Strains*. New York: Harper and Row, 1961.
Kupperman, Karen Ordahl. *America in European Consciousness, 1493–1750*. Chapel Hill: University of North Carolina Press, 1995.
LaCapra, Dominick, and Steven L. Kaplan, eds. *Modern European Intellectual History: Reappraisals and New Perspectives*. Ithaca: Cornell University Press, 1982.
Landy, Marcia. *Fascism in Film: The Italian Commercial Cinema, 1931–43*. Princeton: Princeton University Press, 1986.
Leonard, Irving. *Books of the Brave: Being an Account of Books and Men in the Spanish Conquest and Settlement of the Sixteenth-Century New World*. Introd. Rolena Adorno. 1949. Reprint, Berkeley: University of California Press, 1992.
Levins Morales, Aurora. *Medicine Stories: History, Culture, and the Politics of Integrity*. Cambridge, MA: South End Press, 1998.
Libreria delle donne di Milano. *Non credere di avere dei diritti: La generazione della libertà femminile nell'idea e nelle vicende di un gruppo di donne*. Turin: Rosenberg e Sellier, 1987. Translated by Teresa de Lauretis as *Sexual Difference: A Theory of Social-Symbolic Practice* (Bloomington: Indiana University Press, 1990).
Lisio, Giuseppe, ed. *Orazioni scelte del secolo XVI*. Florence: Sansoni, 1897.
Livy. *Le Deche di T. Livio Padovano delle Historie Romane*. Trans. Iacopo Nardi. Venetia: Nella stamperia degli heredi di Luc'Antonio Giunti Fiorentino, 1547.
Lonzi, Carla. "Sputiamo su Hegel" [1970]. In *Sputiamo su Hegel: La donna clitoridea e la donna vaginale*. Milan: Rivolta Femminile, 1977. Excerpted in translation in Paola Bono and Sandra Kemp, *Italian Feminist Thought: A Reader*, 40–59 (Oxford: Blackwell, 1991).
Lorenzino de' Medici. *Apologia e lettere*. Ed. Francesco Erspamer. Rome: Salerno, 1991.
———. *Aridosia-Apologia, rime e lettere*. Ed. Federico Ravello. Turin: UTET, 1921.

———. *Scritti e documenti per la prima volta raccolti.* Ed. Carlo Téoli. Milan: G. Daelli e comp., 1862.

Macchia, Guglielmo. "Il segretario di Gino Capponi: Alessandro Carraresi (1819–1902)." *Nuova rivista storica* 40, no. 2 (1956): 298–315.

Machiavelli, Niccolò. *Discorsi sopra la prima Deca di Tito Livio.* Ed. Mario Bonfantini. Milan: Ricciardi, 1963.

———. *Discorsi sopra la prima Deca di Tito Livio.* Ed. Sergio Bertelli. Milan: Feltrinelli, 1981.

Mangoni, Luisa. *L'interventismo della cultura: Intellettuali e riviste del fascismo.* Bari: Laterza, 1977.

Manzoni, Alessandro, and Gino Capponi. *Saggio di vocabolario italiano secondo l'uso a Firenze compilato in collaborazione a Varramista nel 1856.* Ed. Guglielmo Macchia. Florence: Le Monnier, 1957.

Marin, Louis. "Pour une théorie baroque de l'action politique." Introduction to *Considérations politiques sur les coups d'état*, by Gabriel Naudé. Paris: Ed. de Paris, 1989.

Marinella, Lucrezia. *La nobiltà et l'eccellenza delle donne co' diffetti et mancamenti de gli huomini.* Venetia: Gio Battista Ciotti, 1601.

Marlatt, Daphne. *Ana Historic.* 2nd ed. Concord, Ontario: House of Anansi Press, 1997.

Martines, Lauro. *The Social World of the Florentine Humanists, 1390–1460.* London: Routledge and Kegan Paul, 1963.

Martini, Feruccio. *Lorenzino de' Medici e il tirannicidio nel Rinascimento.* Florence: G. B. Giachetti, 1882.

McGann, Jerome J. *The Textual Condition.* Princeton Studies in Culture/Power/History. Princeton: Princeton University Press, 1991.

McGrath, Elizabeth. "Journal of the Warburg and Courtauld Institutes: A Short History." n.d. http://warburg.sas.ac.uk/journal/historyjwci.htm.

Merrim, Stephanie. *Early Modern Women's Writing and Sor Juana Inés de la Cruz.* Nashville: Vanderbilt University Press, 1999.

———, ed. *Feminist Perspectives on Sor Juana Inés de la Cruz.* Detroit: Wayne State University Press, 1991.

Miccoli, Giovanni. *Delio Cantimori: La ricerca di una nuova critica storiografica.* Turin: Einaudi, 1970.

Mohanty, Chandra Talpade. *Feminism without Borders: Decolonizing Theory, Practicing Solidarity.* Durham: Duke University Press, 2003. http://site.ebrary.com/lib/dukelibraries/Doc?id=10198322.

———. "Under Western Eyes: Feminist Scholarship and Colonial Discourses." In *Third World Women and the Politics of Feminism,* ed. Chandra Talpade Mohanty, Ann Russo, and Lourdes Torres, 51–80. Bloomington: Indiana University Press, 1991.

Molza, Francesco Maria. "Orazione contro Lorenzino de' Medici." In Lorenzino de' Medici, *Scritti e documenti per la prima volta raccolti*, ed. Carlo Téoli, 135–49. Milan: G. Daelli e comp., 1862.

Moranti, Maria, and Luigi Moranti. *Il trasferimento dei "Codices urbinates" alla Biblioteca vaticana: Cronistoria, documenti e inventario.* Urbino: Accademia Raffaello, 1981.

Morbio, Carlo, ed. *Codice Visconteo-Sforzesco, ossia Raccolta di leggi, decreti e lettere famigliari dei duchi di Milano*. Milan: Società Tipografica de' Classici Italiani, 1846.

Mozzoni, Anna Maria. *La donna e i suoi rapporti sociali*. Milan: Tipografia Sociale, 1864.

———. *La liberazione della donna*. Ed. Franca Pieroni Bortolotti. Milan: G. Mazzotta, 1975.

———. *Un passo avanti nella cultura femminile: Tesi e progetto*. Milan: Tipografia Internazionale, 1866.

Muir, Edward. *The Culture Wars of the Late Renaissance: Skeptics, Libertines, and Opera*. Cambridge, MA: Harvard University Press, 2007.

Muoni, Damiano. *Archivi di stato in Milano: Prefetti o direttori, 1488–1874*. Milan: C. Molinari, 1874.

Mussolini, Benito. "Fascismo." *Enciclopedia italiana di scienze, lettere ed arti*. Milan: Istituto Giovanni Treccani, 1932.

Nardi, Jacopo. *Istorie della città di Firenze di Iacopo Nardi*. Ed. Agenore Gelli. Florence: Le Monnier, 1858.

———. "Orazione." In *Orazioni scelte del secolo XVI*, ed. Giuseppe Lisio. Florence: Sansoni, 1997.

Naudé, Gabriel. *Advice on Establishing a Library*. Ed. Archer Taylor. Trans. W. H. Alexander, J. S. Gildersleeve, H. A. Small, and T. Webb Jr. Berkeley: University of California Press, 1950.

———. *Advis à Nos Seigneurs du Parlement, sur la vente de la Bibliothèque de M. le Cardinal Mazarin*. In *Recherches sur les bibliothèques anciennes et modernes, jusqu'à la fondation de la Bibliothèque Mazarine, et sur les causes qui ont favorisé l'accroissement successif du nombre des livres*. Ed. Petit-Radel and Louis Charles François. Paris: Rey et Gravier, 1819.

———. *Advis pour dresser une bibliothèque, présenté à Monseigeur le Président de Mesme*. 1627. Reprint, Paris: J. Liseux, 1876.

———. *Avvertenze per la costituzione di una biblioteca*. Ed. Vittoria Lacchini. Bologna: Editrice CLUEB, 1992.

———. *Bibliografia politica*. Ed. Domenico Bosco. Rome: Bulzoni, 1997.

———. *Considérations politiques sur les coups d'état*. Introd. Louis Marin. Paris: Ed. de Paris, 1989.

———. *News from France; or, A description of the library of Cardinal Mazarin, preceded by the surrender of the library*. Trans. Victoria Richmond and John Cotton Dana. Chicago: A. C. McClurg, 1907.

Naudé, Gabriel, and Jules Mazarin. *Considérations politiques sur la Fronde: La correspondance entre Gabriel Naudé et le cardinal Mazarin*. Ed. Kathryn Willis Wolfe and Phillip J. Wolfe. Paris: Papers on French Seventeenth Century Literature, 1991.

Nerli, Filippo de'. *Commentari dei fatti civili occorsi dentro la città di Firenze dall' anno 1215 al 1537*. Trieste: Colombo Coen, 1859.

Non credere di avere dei diritti: La generazione della libertà femminile nell'idea e nelle vicende di un gruppo di donne. Turin: Rosenberg e Sellier, 1987. Translated by Teresa de Lauretis as *Sexual Difference: A Theory of Social-Symbolic Practice* (Bloomington: Indiana University Press, 1990).

Nulli, Siro Attilio. *L'emulo di Bruto: Lorenzino de' Medici*. Milan: Athena, 1933.
Onians, Richard Broxton. *The Origins of European Thought*. New York: Arno Press, 1973.
Oviedo, Gonzalo Fernández de. *Historia general y natural de las Indias*. Ed. Juan Pérez de Tudela Bueso. Madrid: Atlas, 1959.
Panicali, Anna. "L'intellettuale fascista." In *Cinema sotto il fascismo*, ed. Riccardo Redi. Venice: Marsilio, 1979.
———. *Le riviste del periodo fascista: Un saggio introduttivo*. Messina: G. D'Anna, 1978.
Parker, Patricia A. "Rhetorics of Property: Exploration, Inventory, Blazon." In *Literary Fat Ladies: Rhetoric, Gender, Property*. London: Methuen, 1987.
Pateman, Carole. *The Sexual Contract*. Stanford: Stanford University Press, 1988.
Patin, Guy. *Lettres de Gui Patin, 1630–1672*. Paris: Champion, 1907.
Paz, Octavio. Foreword to *Quetzalcóatl and Guadalupe: The Formation of Mexican National Consciousness, 1531–1813*, by Jacques Lafaye. Chicago: University of Chicago Press, 1976.
Perac, Stefano du. *I vestigi dell'antichità di Roma raccolti et ritratti in perspettiva*. Rome: Carlo Losi, 1773.
Petrucci, Armando. "L'illusione della storia autentica: Le testimonianze documentarie." In *L'insegnamento della storia e i materiali del lavoro storico*. Messina: Società degli storici italiani, 1984. Translated by Charles Radding as "The Illusion of Authentic History: Documentary Evidence," in *Writers and Readers in Medieval Italy. Studies in the History of Written Culture*, ed. Charles Radding (New Haven: Yale University Press, 1995).
———. "Pouvoir de l'écriture, pouvoir sur l'écriture dans la renaissance italienne." *Annales ESC* 4 (1988): 823–47.
———. "La scrittura del testo." In *Letteratura italiana*, ed. Alberto Asor Rosa, vol. 4, *L'interpretazione*, 285–308. Turin: Einaudi, 1985.
———. *Writing the Dead: Death and Writing Strategies in the Western Tradition*. Stanford: Stanford University Press, 1998.
Piccolomini, Manfredi. *The Brutus Revival: Parricide and Tyrannicide during the Renaissance*. Carbondale: Southern Illinois University Press, 1991.
Pieri, Mario. *Vita scritta da lui medesimo*. Florence: Le Monnier, 1850.
Pintard, René. *Le libertinage érudit dans la première moitié du 17e siècle*. Paris: Boivin, 1943.
Plutarch. *Vite di Plutarco cheroneo de gli huomini illustri greci et romani*. Trans. Lodovico Domenichi et al. Venice: Appresso Felice Valgrisio, 1582.
Poliziano, Angelo. *Della congiura dei pazzi: Coniurationis commentarium*. Ed. Alessandro Perosa. Padua: Antenore, 1958.
Povolo, Claudio. *Il romanziere e l'archivista: Da un processo veneziano del '600 all'anonimo manoscritto dei Promessi sposi*. Venice: Istituto Veneto di Scienze, Lettere ed Arti, 1993.
Punzi, Rosaria. "Fonti documentarie per una rilettura delle vicende post-antiche dell'arco di Costantino." In *Arco di Costantino tra archeologia e archeometria*, ed. Patrizio Pensabene e Clementina Panella. Rome: "L'Erma" di Bretschneider, 2001.

Rabasa, José María. "Fantasy, Errancy and Symbolism in New World Motifs: An Essay on Sixteenth Century Spanish Historiography." PhD diss., University of California, Santa Cruz, 1985.
Rambures, Jean-Louis de. *Comment travaillent les écrivains: Entretiens avec Roland Barthes et al.* Paris: Flammarion, 1978.
Ramusio, Giovanni Battista. *Navigazioni e viaggi.* Ed. Marica Milanesi. 6 vols. Turin: Einaudi, 1978–85.
Raponi, Nicola. "Per la storia dell'Archivio di Stato di Milano: Erudizione e cultura nell' 'Annuario' del Fumi (1909–1919)." *Rassegna degli Archivi di stato* 31, no. 2 (1971): 313–34.
Ray, Meredith K. "'A Gloria Del Sesso Feminile': Epistolary Constructions of Gender in Early Modern Italian Letter Collections." PhD diss., University of Chicago, 2002.
——— . "Letters from the Cloister: Defending the Literary Self in Arcangela Tarabotti's *Lettere familiari e di complimento.*" *Italica: Bulletin of the American Association of Teachers of Italian* 81 (Spring 2004): 24–43.
——— . *Writing Gender in Women's Letter Collections of the Italian Renaissance.* Toronto: University of Toronto Press, 2009.
Redi, Riccardo, ed. *Cinema sotto il fascismo.* Venice: Marsilio, 1979.
"Registi, storia e film." *Cinema,* o.s., 5, no. 86 (January 25, 1940): 48–49.
Rice, James V. *Gabriel Naudé, 1600–1653.* John Hopkins Studies in Romance Literatures and Languages 35. Baltimore: Johns Hopkins University Press, 1939.
Rich, Adrienne. "Anne Bradstreet and Her Poetry." In Anne Bradstreet, *The Works of Anne Bradstreet,* ed. Jeannine Hensley. Cambridge, MA: Harvard University Press, 2005 (thirteenth printing).
——— . "Notes toward a Politics of Location." In *Blood, Bread, and Poetry: Selected Prose, 1979–1985.* New York: Norton, 1995.
Ricoeur, Paul. *The Rule of Metaphor.* Toronto: University of Toronto Press, 1977.
Ridolfi, Roberto. *Lorenzino, sfinge medicea.* Florence: SP 44, 1983.
Robbia, Luca della. "Narrazione del caso di Pietro Paolo Boscoli e di Agostino Capponi (1513)." Ed. F. Polidori. *Archivio storico italiano,* 1st ser., 1 (1842): 275–309.
Rosa, Mario. "I depositi del sapere: Biblioteche, accademie, archivi." In *La memoria del sapere: Forme di conservazione e strutture organizzative dall'antichità a oggi,* ed. Pietro Rossi. Bari: Laterza, 1988.
Rosini, Giovanni. *Luisa Strozzi: Storia del secolo XVI.* Pisa: Niccolò Capurro, 1833.
Rossi, Filippo de'. *Ritratto di Roma antica.* Rome: F. Moneta, 1645.
Rostagno, Lucia. *Mi faccio turco: Esperienze ed immagini dell'islam nell'Italia moderna.* Rome: Istituto per l'Oriente C. A. Nallino, 1983.
Rouse, Richard. "Latin Paleography and Manuscript Studies in North America." In *Un secolo di paleografia e diplomatica (1887–1986),* ed. Armando Petrucci and Alessandro Pratesi. Rome: Gela, 1988.
Ruggiero, Guido. *The Boundaries of Eros: Sex, Crime, and Sexuality in Renais-*

sance Venice. New York: Oxford University Press, 1985.
Ruscelli, Girolamo, ed. *Lettere di principi le quali si scrivono o da principi, o a principi, o ragionano di principi.* 3 vols. Venetia: Giordano Ziletti, 1570–77.
Sainte-Beuve, Charles Augustin. *Portraits littéraires.* Ed. Gérald Antoine. Paris: R. Laffont, 1993.
Salutati, Coluccio. *Il trattato "De tyranno" e lettere scelte.* Ed. Francesco Ercole. Bologna: Zanichelli, 1942.
Santoro, Caterina, ed. *Stampe popolari della Biblioteca Trivulziana.* Milan: Castello Sforzesco, 1964.
Savonarola, Girolamo. "Trattato circa el reggimento e governo della città di Firenze." In *Prediche sopra Aggeo con il Trattato circa el reggimento e governo della città di Firenze.* Ed. Luigi Firpo. Rome: Angelo Belardetti, 1965.
Scarry, Elaine. *The Body in Pain: The Making and Unmaking of the World.* New York: Oxford University Press, 1985.
Scott, Joan Wallach. "The Evidence of Experience." *Critical Inquiry* 17, no. 4 (1991): 773–97.
———. *Only Paradoxes to Offer: French Feminists and the Rights of Man.* Cambridge, MA: Harvard University Press, 1996.
Segarizzi, Arnaldo. *Bibliografia delle stampe popolari italiane.* Bergamo: Istituto Italiano di Arti Grafiche, 1913.
Segni, Bernardo. *Storie fiorentine.* Milan: Società Tipografica de' Classici Italiani, 1805.
Seneca, Lucius Annaeus. *Moral essays.* Trans. John W. Basore. London: W. Heinemann, 1958.
Serrai, Alfredo. *Dai "loci communes" alla bibliometria.* Rome: Bulzoni, 1984.
Servius. *Servii grammatici qui feruntur in Vergilii Bucolica et Georgica commentarii.* Ed. Georgius Thilo. Hildesheim: Georg Olms, 1961.
Sestan, Ernesto. *La Firenze di Vieusseux e di Capponi.* Ed. Giovanni Spadolini. Florence: Leo S. Olschki, 1986.
Shakespeare, William. *The Tragedy of Julius Caesar.* Ed. Barbara A. Mowat and Paul Werstine. New York: Washington Square Press, 1992.
———. *The Tragedy of Richard II.* Ed. Louis B. Wright and Virginia A. Lamar. New York: Simon and Schuster, 1962.
Shell, Marc. *The Economy of Literature.* Baltimore: Johns Hopkins University Press, 1978.
Silverblatt, Irene. "Interpreting Women in States: New Feminist Ethnohistories." In *Gender at the Crossroads of Knowledge: Feminist Anthropology in the Postmodern Era,* ed. Micaela di Leonardo, 140–74. Berkeley: University of California Press, 1991.
Simoncelli, Paolo. *Cantimori e il libro mai edito: il movimento nazionalsocialista dal 1919 al 1933.* Florence: Le Lettere, 2008.
Smarr, Janet Levarie. *Joining the Conversation: Dialogues by Renaissance Women.* Ann Arbor: University of Michigan Press, 2005.
Smith, Bonnie G. *The Gender of History: Men, Women, and Historical Practice.* Cambridge, MA: Harvard University Press, 1998.
Smith, Dorothy E. *The Conceptual Practices of Power: A Feminist Sociology of Knowledge.* Boston: Northeastern University Press, 1991.

———. *The Everyday World as Problematic: A Feminist Sociology.* Boston: Northeastern University Press, 1989.
———. *Texts, Facts and Femininity: Exploring the Relations of Ruling.* London: Routledge, 1993.
Solaroli, Libero. "La Terza Cines indossa la camicia nera." *Cinema nuovo* 2, no. 8 (April 1, 1953): 213–14.
Sperling, Jutta Gisela. *Convents and the Body Politic in late Renaissance Venice.* Women in Culture and Society. Chicago: University of Chicago Press, 1999.
Spivak, Gayatri. "Scattered Speculations on the Question of Cultural Studies." In *Outside in the Teaching Machine.* New York: Routledge, 1993.
Suetonius. *Le vite de dodici cesari di Gaio Suetonio.* Trans. Paolo del Rosso. Venice: Hieronymo Calepino, 1550.
Tabarrini, Marco. *Gino Capponi, i suoi tempi, i suoi studi, i suoi amici: Memorie raccolte da Marco Tabarrini.* Florence: G. Barbèra, 1879.
———. *Vite e ricordi d'italiani illustri del secolo XIX.* Florence: Barbèra, 1884.
Tacitus. *Gli annali de' fatti e guerre de' Romani.* Trans. Giorgio Dati. Venice: Ad instantia de' Giunti di Firenze, 1563.
Tarabotti, Arcangela. *Antisatira.* In Francesco Buoninsegni and Arcangela Tarabotti, *Satira e antisatira,* ed. Elissa B. Weaver. Rome: Salerno, 1998.
———. *Che le donne siano della spezie degli uomini.* Ed. Letizia Panizza. London: Institute of Romance Studies, 1994.
———. *L'"Inferno monacale" di Arcangela Tarabotti.* Ed. Francesca Medioli. Turin: Rosenberg e Sellier, 1990.
———. *Lettere familiari e di complimento.* Venice: Guerigli, 1650.
———. *Lettere familiari e di complimento.* Ed. Meredith Kennedy Ray and Lynn Lara Westwater. Turin: Rosenberg e Sellier, 2005.
———. *Paternal Tyranny.* Ed. and trans. Letizia Panizza. Chicago: University of Chicago Press, 2004.
———. *La semplicità ingannata.* Leiden: Gio. Sambix, 1654.
———. *La semplicità ingannata.* Critical ed. Ed. Simona Bortot. Padua: Il Poligrafo, 2007.
Taricone, Fiorenza, and Susanna Bucci. *La condizione della donna nel XVII e XVIII secolo.* Rome: Carucci, 1983.
Thucydides. *Gli otto libri di Thvcydide Atheniese delle guerre fatte . . .* Trans. Francesco di Soldo Strozzi. Venetia: Baldassar de Costantini, 1545.
Tommaseo, Niccolò. *Diario intimo.* Ed. Raffaele Ciampini. Turin: Einaudi, 1946.
Tommaseo, Niccolò, and Gino Capponi. *Carteggio inedito dal 1833 al 1874.* Ed. Isidoro Del Lungo, and Paolo Prunas. Bologna: N. Zanichelli, 1911–32.
Trenker, Luis. "Le mie idee sul film." *Cinema,* no. 25 (1937): 10.
Uffenbeck, Lorin A. "The Life and Writings of Hortense Allart (1801–79)." PhD diss., University of Wisconsin–Madison, 1957.
Valerius Maximus. *Dei detti et fatti memorabili.* Trans. Giorgio Dati. Rome: Antonio Blado d'Asola, 1539.
Valesio, Paolo. "The Virtues of Traducement: A Sketch of a Theory of Translation." *Semiotica* 18, no. 1 (1976): 1–96.
Varchi, Benedetto. *Storia fiorentina.* 5 vols. Milan: Società Tipografica de' Classici Italiani, 1804.

Vasari, Giorgio. *Le vite de' più eccellenti pittori scultori ed architettori.* Florence: Sansoni, 1878.
Walton, Whitney. *Eve's Proud Descendants: Four Women Writers and Republican Politics in Nineteenth-Century France.* Stanford: Stanford University Press, 2000.
Waquet, Françoise. "Qu'est-ce que la république des lettres? Essai de sémantique historique." *Bibliothèque de l'école des Chartes* 147 (1989): 473–502.
Weaver, Elissa B. "Arcangela Tarabotti." In *Italian Women Writers: A Bio-bibliographical Sourcebook,* ed. Rinaldina Russell. Westport, CT: Greenwood Press, 1994.
———, ed. *Arcangela Tarabotti: A Literary Nun in Baroque Venice.* Ravenna: Longo, 2006.
Westwater, Lynn Lara. "The Disquieting Voice: Women's Writing and Antifeminism in Seventeenth Century Venice." PhD diss., University of Chicago, 2003.
Wheeler, G. W. *The Earliest Catalogues of the Bodleian Library.* Oxford: Oxford University Press, 1928.
White, Hayden. *The Content of the Form: Narrative Discourse and Historical Representation.* Baltimore: Johns Hopkins University Press, 1987.
———. "Method and Ideology in Intellectual History: The Case of Henry Adams." In *Modern European Intellectual History: Reappraisals and New Perspectives,* ed. Dominick LaCapra and Steven L. Kaplan. Ithaca: Cornell University Press, 1982. Reprinted as "The Context in the Text: Method and Ideology in Intellectual History," in Hayden White, *The Content of the Form: Narrative Discourse and Historical Representation* (Baltimore: Johns Hopkins University Press, 1987).
———. "The Politics of Historical Interpretation: Discipline and De-sublimation," *Critical Inquiry* 9, no. 1 (1982): 113–37.
———. *Tropics of Discourse: Essays in Cultural Criticism.* Baltimore: Johns Hopkins University Press, 1978.
Woolf, Virginia. *A Room of One's Own.* London: Hogarth Press, 1929. http://ebooks.adelaide.edu.au/w/woolf/virginia/w91r/.
Zanette, Emilio. *Suor Arcangela monaca del Seicento veneziano.* Venice: Istituto per la Collaborazione Culturale, 1960.

Index

Agoult, Marie d', 172, 249n32
Albertini, Rudolf von, 45, 194, 215n79
Allart, Hortense, 7–8, 14–17, 140,
    142–56, 158–85, 194, 197–98, 201,
    203nn21, 24, 204nn30–31, 230n171,
    240n86, 248–60nn
Althusser, Louis, 26, 206, 221n109
Alvar, Manuel, 222n121
Alvarez-Ossorio Alvariño, Antonio,
    221n119
Ammirato, Scipione, 3, 213n62, 215n77
Anderson, Benedict, 144
Andreini, Isabella, 96, 98
Ariosto, Ludovico, 59, 152, 250n54
Aristotle, 3, 4, 12, 51, 67, 68, 217n98,
    227n151, 229n157
Ascoli, Albert, 247n1

Baldoni, Eride, 205n4
Balsamo, Luigi, 233n2, 234nn8, 11
Bardi, Alessandro, 226n143
Baron, Hans, 30
Barone, Giulia, 259n193
Barthes, Roland, 103, 105–6, 233n3,
    239nn59–60
Bartolus of Sassoferrato, 213–14n64
Beccaria, Gian Luigi, 221n119
Benjamin, Walter, 86, 202n13, 207n9,
    234n5
Biga, Emilia, 97, 116, 237n41, 238n51
Boccaccio, Giovanni, 1, 96, 98, 216n84

Boccalini, Traiano, 91–98, 100, 109, 199,
    235–36nn16–19, 237n35
Bodin, Jean, 116, 119, 242n101
Bodley, Thomas, 87–89, 234n8
Bois, Yve-Alain, 103, 239n59
Bonaini, Francesco, 142, 148, 157
Boose, Lynda, 118, 241n98
Borromeo, Federico, 87–89
Bortolotti, Franca Pieroni, 103, 239n67,
    258n73, 260n3
Bortolotti, Maria Pia, 25, 205n3
Bortot, Simona, 91, 97, 109, 113, 116,
    120, 203n18, 236n22, 237n41,
    245n146
Bosco, Domenico, 234–35nn10–12
Boscoli, Pier Paolo, 30, 33–34, 40, 44–45,
    193–94, 208n15, 210nn29, 32, 38,
    211n40, 215n78
Bottasso, Enzo, 87, 203n15, 234nn8–9
Bradstreet, Anne, 108–9, 130–31, 239n70,
    245nn142–43
Branch, Watson, 222–23
Brignone, Guido, 30, 31, 35–36, 38–39
Bromfield, Joyce G., 205n4
Brose, Margaret, 247n12
Brucioli, Antonio, 51, 217n99, 227n151
Brunetta, Gian Piero, 209n17
Brunnsåker, Sture, 66, 227n150
Brutus, Lucius Junius and Marcus, 25–27,
    33–34, 42, 44, 68, 72, 74–75, 137, 143,
    183–84, 187, 191, 194, 206n6, 207n9,

277

278 | Index

Brutus, Lucius Junius and Marcus (*continued*)
  214n64, 225n139, 227nn154–55, 230–31n171; "the new Brutus," 26, 137, 183–84, 230n171
Bucci, Susanna, 91, 96, 109, 235–36nn19–20, 237n38, 238nn43, 45
Bullard, Melissa Meriam, 226nn143, 145–46
Bulwer-Lytton, Henry, 156, 177, 248n13, 255n140, 257n159
Buoninsegni, Francesco, 103, 106, 123–24, 126–28, 238n51, 244n134

Caesar, Julius, 25, 43, 44, 56, 67, 68, 74–75, 137, 183, 191, 194, 212n62, 214n64, 215nn75–76, 225n139, 227nn154–55, 231nn171, 175
Calderino, Domizio, 64, 225n140
Campana, Augusto, 221n109
Canepa, Nancy L., 97, 116, 238n52
Canestrini, Giuseppe, 141, 142, 148, 157, 247n8
Canfora, Luciano, 4, 201n2
Canonici Fachini, Ginevra, 96, 237n33, 238n44
Cantimori, Delio, 30–34, 39–40, 136, 208n15, 209nn18–19, 21–22, 24, 210nn27–29, 32–40, 211nn56–59
Capei, Pietro, 143–44, 150–51, 162, 163, 170, 178, 182, 203n24, 249nn24, 31, 253n107, 254n115, 258–59nn180–81
Capponi, Alessandro Gregorio, 223n134
Capponi, Gino, 7–8, 14–17, 19, 141, 143–71, 174–85, 194, 197–98, 201, 203nn22–24, 204nn25–26, 30, 205n33, 215n80, 230n169, 247–60nn
Caracciolo, Marino, 9, 25, 27, 42, 48, 49, 54, 55–56, 67, 69–70, 71, 192, 214–15n70, 217n94
Carraresi, Alessandro, 14, 149, 152–53, 178, 250n41, 259n182
Cassius, 17, 44, 194, 207n9, 215n75, 224–25nn138–39, 231n171
catalog, 5, 11, 46, 87–90, 96–102, 130–31, 133, 203n15, 234nn8, 11, 235nn13, 19, 237n33, 245n145
Cato, 127–28, 244n134
Cattaneo, Carlo, 103, 189
Cavriani, Filippo, 52, 218n103
Cellini, Benvenuto, 65, 225–26n142, 231n171
Ceres (and Persephone), 64–66, 224–25nn137–39

Certeau, Michel de, 103–4, 108
Chabod, Federico, 217nn93–95
Chakrabarty, Dipesh, 232–33n11
Charles V, 9, 10, 25, 28, 29, 42, 44, 48, 50, 54–59, 65, 102, 168, 192, 195, 216n92, 221n117, 223n134
Chartier, Roger, 13, 85–86, 87, 97, 103, 203nn15, 19, 233–34nn2–4, 238n47, 239n56, 243n117
Chojnacki, Stanley, 116, 241n97
Ciampini, Raffaele, 249n30, 252n85
Ciano, Galeazzo, 35–36
Cicero, 107, 143, 227n157, 257–58n160
Ciliberto, Michele, 31, 209nn18–19, 21–22, 24, 210n37
Ciureanu, Petre, 201, 204n30, 247n13, 249n31, 251n69, 252nn86–87, 95, 257n159, 260n210–11
Colonna, Vittoria, 1, 91–92, 96, 98, 199
Comenius, Johann Amos, 103, 104–5, 239n57, 240n83
Conihout, Isabelle de, 245–46n147
Conti Odorisio, Ginevra, 103, 116, 238n51, 242n101
Cox, Virginia, 91, 97, 116, 119, 236n19, 238n52, 241n97
Craveri, Benedetta, 233n1
Creamer, Paul, 236n22
Cruz, Juana Inés de la, 129, 245nn136, 138

Damien, Robert, 113, 234n10, 240n85, 242n101
Datta, Satya Brata, 109, 119, 240n74
daughters, 12–13, 48, 64–65, 66, 70, 85, 93, 110, 114–21, 123–24, 131, 133–35, 153, 159–60, 171, 172, 179, 196–97, 199, 213n62, 216n92, 224n137, 228n157, 240n77, 242nn100–101, 103, 243n104, 246n148, 247n4, 251n58, 260n210
Davis, Natalie Zemon, 8, 202n11, 208n16
Decreus, Juliette, 248n13
Defert, Daniel, 223n129
de Lauretis, Teresa, 221n110, 233n1
Díaz del Castillo, Bernal, 58, 221–22nn120–22
Di Mauro, Alberto, 223n134

Elliott, John Huxtable, 203n15, 216n88, 217n95, 222n123, 223nn126, 131
El Saadawi, Nawal, 247n5
Erasmus, 47, 216nn90–91
Erspamer, Francesco, 205n4

Farinola, Marianna, 153, 171, 251n62
Fauveau, Félicie de, 171, 253n98
Ferguson, Kathy E., 233n3
Ferrai, Luigi Alberto, 205n4
Ferri, Pietro Leopoldo, 96, 237n33
Findlen, Paula, 94, 203n15, 207n12, 236n25
Fonte, Moderata, 96, 98
Fraisse, Geneviève, 227n157, 251n55
Franklin, Alfred, 134–35, 246n148
Frenk, Margit, 224nn136–37
Fumaroli, Marc, 216nn83–84, 251n78

Gagliani, Dianella, 208n16, 211n47
Gambara, Veronica, 91–92, 96, 98, 199
Gar, Tommaso, 140, 141, 157
Gassendi, Pierre, 113–14, 196
Gentile, Giovanni, 31, 33, 210n37
Gerbi, Antonello, 223nn130, 132
Ghibellini da Prato, Lorenzo, 63–64, 223n135
Giard, Luce, 233n2
Gili, Jean, 35, 211n41
Gilly, Adolfo, 10, 79–83, 232nn1–2, 6
Ginzburg, Carlo (and Menocchio), 10, 31, 79–83, 220n106, 232nn1–10
Giovanni Antonio detto "il sarto," 23–25, 27–29, 78, 192–93, 205nn1–2, 206n9, 208n13
Giovio, Paolo, 3, 206n9, 216n84, 219–20n106, 230n171
Giunti, Tommaso, 63, 102
Goody, Jack, 202n12
Gordon, Avery, 202n10, 246n1
Gori, Gianfranco, 211n45
Gramsci, Antonio, 40, 201n1, 206n7, 208n13
Greene, Roland Arthur, 208n14, 222n123
Groebner, Valentin, 236n22
Guicciardini, Francesco, 148

Hampton, Timothy, 208n14, 223–24n136
hand, handwriting, handling, and transcription, 1, 3, 4, 5, 10, 12, 17, 20, 23, 24, 25–29, 37, 45–46, 51, 52, 56, 57, 62, 69, 73–78, 79, 97, 104, 105, 108–12, 113, 115, 117, 138, 151, 161, 168, 170, 171, 172, 175, 179, 183, 191–93, 197, 199, 204n27, 206n9, 214n64, 231n175, 240n77, 243n104
Hansen, Helynne Hollstein, 248n13
Harmodius, Aristogiton, Hipparchus, 4, 25, 66–67, 68, 137, 187, 218n106, 227n150

Heller, Wendy Beth, 91, 236n21, 239n69
Henneberg, Krystyna Von, 247n1
Henry Earl of Monmouth, 97, 235nn16, 19, 237n35
Herodotus, 3, 52, 53, 217n97
Hunt, Lynn Avery, 233n1
Hutson, Lorna, 97, 116, 118–19, 237n34, 242nn99, 102, 243n104

Ilardi, Vincenzo, 212n61
Ileto, Reynaldo, 202–3n13
Infelise, Mario, 243n115
inventory, 8, 9–10, 30, 49, 77, 88, 97, 131, 138, 190

Jacob, Christian, 233n2
Janus Bey, 55–58
Jones, Ann Rosalind, 109, 239nn71, 73
Joplin, Patricia Klindienst, 109, 116, 240n76, 242nn101, 103, 245nn137, 139
Justinus, 67, 227n151
Juvenal, 64, 225n139–40

Kastan, David Scott, 233–34n3
Kristeller, Paul Oskar, 30, 221n109

Lacchini, Vittoria, 234n110
La Croix du Maine, François de, 103–4, 239n56
Landriano, Alessandro, 71, 72, 214n69, 215n73, 229n165
Landy, Marcia, 209n17, 211n51
Larsen, Susan, 260n215
Leonard, Irving, 222n120
lexicon, 8, 16–17, 138, 144, 145, 190, 205n33
Libri, Guglielmo, 143, 168
Livy, 3, 51, 75, 217n100, 226n149, 230n171, 231n176
Lonzi, Carla, 233n1
Lope de Soria, 55–57, 69, 221nn112–13, 118, 229n159
Lucretia, 25, 66, 68, 75, 137, 187, 227n156, 255n140

Macchia, Guglielmo, 250n41, 251n57, 253n99
Machiavelli, Niccolò, 3, 12, 31, 36, 64, 66, 68, 124, 161, 172–73, 175, 210n30, 211n47, 212nn60, 62, 218nn101, 106, 224–25n139, 226n149, 227nn156–57, 231n176, 256n157
Mangoni, Luisa, 209nn20–21

Manzoni, Alessandro, 253n99
Marin, Louis, 124–25, 218n104, 234n10, 243–44nn119–26
Marinella, Lucrezia, 96, 98, 108, 239n74
Marino, John, 221n119
Marlatt, Daphne, 76, 109, 207–8n12, 232n183, 240n77
Martines, Lauro, 212n61, 221n109
Martini, Ferruccio, 205n4
Mazarin, Giulio, 84, 89, 90, 91, 95–6, 112–14, 116, 120–21, 125, 134–35, 196, 234n10, 241n87, 256n157
Mazarine Library, 8, 11–13, 20, 85–87, 89–91, 95–6, 113–15, 117–19, 125–26, 129, 131–34, 196–97, 240n86, 241n87, 245–46nn147–54, 256n157
McClure, Kirstie, 206n8
McGann, Jerome J., 234n3
Medici, Alessandro de', 2, 7, 9, 23–26, 28, 36, 42–43, 48–49, 54, 63, 65–68, 70–73, 137, 179, 183, 187, 193, 206n9, 213n62, 215n70, 216n92, 223nn134–35, 225n142, 226n147, 228–29n157, 230nn169, 171
Medici, Cosimo de', 4, 28, 49, 221n117
Medici, Lorenzino de', 2–3, 7–12, 17, 23–30, 35–36, 40, 45–46, 48–50, 52–55, 60, 63–64, 68–69, 71–73, 75–76, 78, 83, 85, 102, 136–38, 183, 187, 192–94, 205nn1, 4, 206nn6, 9, 207n10, 209n19, 213n62, 216n92, 218–20n106, 221n117, 223nn134–35, 225–26nn142, 147, 228–29n157, 230–31nn171, 179, 246n3
Medioli, Francesca, 116, 235n16, 238n51
Miccoli, Giovanni, 209n18
Milanese State Archive 9, 17, 23–25, 27, 49, 205n3, 217n95; Cancelleria dello stato di Milano 9, 10, 23–25, 29, 46, 49–50, 55–57, 67–68, 70, 73, 193, 201, 205n3, 214–15nn65–73, 217nn93–94, 221nn111–16, 229nn158–60, 162–65, 230nn170–71
Milanesi, Marica, 223n127
Mohanty, Chandra Talpade, 86, 234n5
Molini, Giuseppe, 168, 170, 253n98
Molza, Francesco Maria, 52, 218–19n106
Montano, Cola, 41–43
Morales, Aurora Levins, 76, 78, 232n182
Moranti, Maria and Luigi, 5–6, 202nn5–8
Mozzoni, Anna Maria, 96, 101–2, 103, 106–8, 188–89, 238n50, 258n173, 260nn1–2, 5–6
Muir, Edward, 120, 243n115
Mussolini, Benito, 31, 36, 38, 211n48

Nardelli, Franca, 1, 2, 201n1
Nardi, Iacopo, 3, 175, 206n9, 213n62, 217n100, 226n149, 228n157, 231n171
nation, nation-building, state formation, ragion di stato, 3, 7, 8, 9, 12–13, 15–17, 29, 32, 40, 48, 85, 86, 89, 91, 95, 100, 102, 103, 108, 117–18, 123, 126, 131–33, 140–46, 156–58, 160, 165–67, 183–85, 188–89, 205n33, 208n15, 230n169, 237n33, 241n96
Naudé, Gabriel, 7–8, 11–12, 52, 84–85, 86–91, 95–96, 99–100, 112–26, 131–35, 172, 196–97, 203n14, 218n104, 234–35nn10–12, 238nn47–49, 51, 241nn87, 90–92, 242n101, 243nn104–114, 117–18, 122, 244n125, 246n148, 256n157
Nerli, Filippo de', 3, 206n9, 216n92, 230–31n171
Nero, 117, 125, 179, 212–13n62, 224n138, 241n95, 244n125
Newman, Jane, 208n16
Niccolini, Giovan Battista, 150, 157, 169, 194
Nulli, Siro Attilio, 205n4, 217n92, 226n147

Olgiati, Girolamo, 33–34, 41, 211n40, 212n60
Onians, Richard Broxton, 224n137, 229n157
Oviedo, Gonzalo Fernández de, 59–63, 102, 195, 222n123, 223nn124, 130

Panicali, Anna, 209nn20, 25
Panizza, Letizia, 91, 103, 109, 113, 116, 120, 238n51, 239n64, 240n78, 245n146
Parker, Patricia, 97, 237–38n42, 245n145
Pateman, Carole, 233n1
Patin, Guy, 112–14, 196, 240n86
Paz, Octavio, 244–45n136
Pearce, Roy Harvey, 246n1
Periander and Thrasybulus, 50–54, 64, 217n99
Petrucci, Armando, 1, 2, 16, 144, 201n1, 204nn27–28, 207n11, 216n87, 259n193; relations of writing 6, 7, 10, 28, 104, 142, 143, 163, 185, 201n1, 204n27
Piccolomini, Alfonso, 54, 221n111
Piccolomini, Manfredi, 206n4
Pieri, Mario, 140, 143, 155, 164, 169, 248nn14, 22, 251n69, 259n194
Pintard, René, 123

Plutarch, 44, 74, 96, 98, 191, 194, 215nn74, 76, 224n138, 231nn171, 174, 177
Polidori, F. L., 140, 208n15, 215n78, 250n41, 259nn188, 194
Poliziano, Angelo, 207n9
Povolo, Claudio, 222n121

Rabasa, José María, 222n121
Ramusio, Giovanni Battista, 60–63, 195, 223nn127, 132–33
Ray, Meredith, 87, 94, 120, 235n14, 237n30
Redi, Riccardo, 209n17
relations with books, 8, 172; relations of power 2, 100, 133, 172, 203n18; relations of research 6, 8, 13, 30, 53, 139, 205n32; relations of ruling 29, 60, 106; scholarly relations 3, 6, 11, 15, 106; social relations 1, 7, 10, 16, 45, 46, 56, 61, 78, 95, 120, 126, 130, 139, 142, 171, 189, 201n1, 237n33–34, 242n103
republic of letters, 10, 29, 30, 33–35, 41–42, 44–48, 50, 53–54, 60, 63, 78, 109, 119, 211n40, 216n90
republican thought, politics, etc., 7, 8, 12, 13, 17, 28, 33, 42, 46, 48, 50, 64, 66, 75, 83, 85–87, 96, 118, 126, 131, 134–35, 143, 172, 179, 184, 187, 238n52
Rice, James V., 234n10
Rich, Adrienne, 130, 202n9, 245nn142–44
Ricoeur, Paul, 213n63
Ridolfi, Roberto, 206n4
Rizzo, Silvia, 17
Robbia, Luca della, 33, 44, 193, 208n15, 210n31, 215n78
Rosa, Mario, 5–6, 49, 202nn4–5, 203n15, 217n96
Rosini, Giovanni, 230n169
Rostagno, Lucia, 224n136
Rouse, Richard H., 77–78, 232nn184–86
Ruggiero, Guido, 236n22

Sainte-Beuve, Charles Augustin, 112, 173, 182, 240n86, 252n86, 254n122, 255n138, 256n157, 257n160, 259n190, 260n204
Salutati, Coluccio, 68, 213–14n64, 225n140, 227n155
Salvemini, Gaetano, 30, 210n37
Salveti, Maddalena, 96, 98
Salviati, Giovanni (Cardinal), 43–44, 67, 214–15nn70–72, 227n153
Sanctio, Bernardo, 42, 72, 214n65, 230nn170–71

Sand, George, 158, 172, 205n4, 252n86, 255n140
Santoro, Caterina, 223n134
Sarocchi, Margherita, 96, 98
Savonarola, Girolamo, 52, 218n102, 224n137, 228n157
Scarry, Elaine, 116, 241n94
Scoronconcolo (Michele Tavolaccino), 26, 137
Scott, Joan Wallach, 8, 202n11, 233n1
Segarizzi, Arnaldo, 223n134
Segni, Bernardo, 175, 206n9, 226n142, 229n166, 230–31n171, 246n3
Selwyn, Pamela, 236n22
Seneca, 112–13, 240n85
Serrai, Alfredo, 233n2, 245n145
Sestan, Ernesto, 14, 140–41, 149, 157, 165, 166, 184–85, 203n23, 204nn25, 29, 247nn1–11, 248n14, 249nn35–37, 250nn38–39, 49, 251nn79–82, 252nn83–84, 253n102, 254nn126, 128, 255n133, 260n219
Sforza, Galeazzo Maria, 33, 41, 212n61, 213n62, 218n106, 227n157
Shakespeare, William, 17, 44, 53, 86, 194, 214n64, 215nn75–76, 220n107, 231n171
Shell, Marc, 65, 225n141
Silverblatt, Irene, 13, 86, 94, 124, 202–3nn13, 16–17, 20, 205n34, 207n9, 234nn5–7, 235n15, 237nn27–29, 31, 244n127, 129, 132, 245nn139–41
Smarr, Janet Levarie, 116, 242n103
Smith, Bonnie G., 248nn13, 21, 252n97, 254nn109, 114, 255n147, 256n155, 257n159, 258n161
Smith, Dorothy E., 208n12, 223n125
Spadolini, Giovanni, 165, 254n126
Sperling, Jutta Gisela, 116, 118, 241n97
Spirito, Ugo, 33, 40, 210n27, 211n58
Spivak, Gayatri, 232n11
Stallybrass, Peter, 109, 239n73
Stimpson, Catharine, 251n55
Strozzi, Filippo, 48, 65–66, 69, 70–71, 137, 226nn143–46, 227n153, 230nn169, 171
Strozzi, Luisa, 66, 70–71, 230n169
Subcomandante Marcos (nom de guerre), 10, 79–83, 232nn1–4, 6, 8, 10
Suetonius, 3, 68, 74, 191, 192, 212n62, 214n64, 227nn154–55, 231n175

Tabarrini, Marco, 204n26, 250nn38, 49, 253nn99–100, 103
Tacitus, 3, 52, 124, 212n62, 218n103, 224n138, 230n171

Tarabotti, Arcangela, 7, 8, 10, 11–13, 20, 84–87, 90–98, 100–103, 106–13, 115–24, 126, 128–35, 179, 196–97, 199, 203nn14, 18, 235nn14, 16, 236nn21–24, 237nn30, 32, 40–41, 238nn51–52, 239nn63–66, 74, 240nn75–82, 241nn88–89, 93, 95–96, 242nn101, 103, 243nn115–16, 244nn128, 130–31, 133–35, 245n146, 246nn147, 151, 259n192

Tarquinius, Sextus and Tarquinius Superbus, 25, 51–52, 66, 75, 137, 143, 218n106, 220n107, 227n156

Terracina, Laura, 91–92, 96, 98, 199

Thucydides, 3, 4, 66, 219n106, 227n150

Tommaseo, Niccolò, 140, 144, 147, 149, 151–52, 153, 155, 157, 158, 160, 162, 180, 184, 194, 197–98, 201, 248nn16, 19–20, 249n30, 250nn40, 50–54, 251nn64–64, 70, 81, 252nn85–89, 95–96, 253nn105–6, 254n120, 260nn210, 217

Tonkovich, Nicole, 239n72

Trenker, Luis, 30, 31, 35, 37–38, 211n49–50

Uffenbeck, Lorin A., 248n13, 254n122, 256n157

Valesio, Paolo, 231n181

Varchi, Benedetto, 3, 161, 206n9, 213n62, 219n106, 226n147, 228n157, 229n161, 230–31nn168, 171

Vasari, Giorgio, 216n84, 218n106

Vespasiano de' Bisticci, 3, 4, 216n84

Vieusseux, Gian Pietro (and the Gabinetto Vieusseux), 17, 140–45, 148–49, 151, 158, 184–85, 194, 197, 247n1, 248n19, 250nn39–40, 49, 52, 252n87

Walton, Whitney, 172, 247–48n13, 249n32, 255n140, 256nn153–53, 156–57, 257n159, 258n170

Waquet, Françoise, 215–16nn81–82, 86–91

Watt, Ian, 202n12

Weaver, Elissa, 103, 124, 238n51, 244n134, 245n146

Westwater, Lynn Lara, 87, 94, 120, 235n14

Wheeler, G. W., 87, 203n15, 234n8

White, Hayden, 87, 202n13, 207n12, 220n108, 221n109, 226n148, 235n13

Woolf, Virginia, 7, 236n26, 237n34

Zanette, Emilio, 116, 238n51, 242n103

TEXT
10/13 Sabon Open Type

DISPLAY
Sabon Open Type

COMPOSITOR
Field Editorial

TEXT PRINTER AND BINDER
Odyssey Publications